D1605812

The Dynamics of Entrepreneurship

The Dynamics of Entrepreneurship

Evidence from the Global
Entrepreneurship Monitor Data

Edited by
Maria Minniti

OXFORD
UNIVERSITY PRESS

OXFORD
UNIVERSITY PRESS

Great Clarendon Street, Oxford OX2 6DP

Oxford University Press is a department of the University of Oxford.
It furthers the University's objective of excellence in research, scholarship,
and education by publishing worldwide in

Oxford New York

Auckland Cape Town Dar es Salaam Hong Kong Karachi
Kuala Lumpur Madrid Melbourne Mexico City Nairobi
New Delhi Shanghai Taipei Toronto

With offices in

Argentina Austria Brazil Chile Czech Republic France Greece
Guatemala Hungary Italy Japan Poland Portugal Singapore
South Korea Switzerland Thailand Turkey Ukraine Vietnam

Oxford is a registered trade mark of Oxford University Press
in the UK and in certain other countries

Published in the United States
by Oxford University Press Inc., New York

British Library Cataloguing in Publication Data
Data available

Library of Congress Cataloging in Publication Data
Data available

Typeset by SPI Publisher Services, Pondicherry, India
Printed in Great Britain
on acid-free paper by
MPG Books Group, Bodmin and King's Lynn

ISBN 978–0–19–958086–6

1 3 5 7 9 10 8 6 4 2

Acknowledgments

Many people have contributed to this Volume in a variety of ways. I thank the twenty-six authors from eleven countries who provided excellent contributions for the Volume. Many thanks go to the anonymous reviewers who read the chapters and provided helpful comments and suggestions. Many thanks go also to the Global Entrepreneurship Research Association (GERA), Global Entrepreneurship Monitor's (GEM) founding and sponsoring institutions, the GEM coordination team, and the more than ninety-five GEM national and regional teams and their sponsors. Since GEM's inception in 1999, hundreds of researchers in over eighty countries have contributed, over the years, to collecting, harmonizing, and documenting the data used in this Volume. Their hard work and dedication make GEM possible. Roger Koppl provided excellent comments and advice. Emma Lambert at Oxford University Press provided competent and patient assistance. Jeanne Milazzo at the Cox School of Business of Southern Methodist University provided invaluable technical support. Finally, I am enormously grateful to the Cox School of Business at Southern Methodist University and, in particular, to Dr. Bobby B. Lyle, whose generosity and vision support and sustain my passion for entrepreneurship research.

Table of Contents

Contents

List of Figures

List of Figures

List of Tables

List of Contributors

Zoltan J. Acs is University Professor at the School of Public Policy and Director of the Center for Entrepreneurship and Public Policy of George Mason University. He is also a Research Scholar at the Max Planck Institute for Economics in Jena, Germany, and Scholar-in-Residence at the Kauffman Foundation. He is co-editor and founder of the *Small Business Economics Journal,* a leading entrepreneurship and small business publication in the world. Dr. Acs is a leading advocate of the importance of entrepreneurship for economic development. He received the *2001 International Award for Entrepreneurship and Small Business Research,* on behalf of The Swedish National Board for Industrial and Technical Development. His most recent publication is the *Handbook of Entrepreneurship Research*, 2nd edition, with David B. Audretsch, eds., Springer Publishers (2010).

I. Elaine Allen is the Research Director of the Arthur M. Blank Center for Entrepreneurship and an Associate Professor of Statistics and Entrepreneurship at Babson College where she teaches advanced statistics and analytics courses. She is also Co-Director of the Babson Survey Research Group (BSRG). She is a statistician on several large survey projects including the Global Entrepreneurship Monitor and the Sloan Survey on online education. She has published widely in statistical, clinical, and managed care journals on statistical issues in meta-analysis, data mining, survey research methods, clinical and biological research methodology, and statistical computing. Allen has been conducting research on the impact of technology on higher education since 2002. Prior to joining Babson, she founded and held executive positions in the healthcare and biotechnology industry, including at Centocor, ARIAD, and MetaWorks, Inc. She was Co-Director of the Evidence-based Practice Center at MetaWorks, funded through the Agency for Healthcare Quality. She serves on several National Institutes of Health research panels on best practices in statistics and on evidence and effectiveness-based research. Dr. Allen is a Fellow of the American Statistical Association.

José Ernesto Amorós is Professor and Director of the Global Entrepreneurship Research Center at Universidad del Desarrollo in Santiago, Chile. Dr. Amorós is the coordinator and chief researcher of the GEM Chilean Team, as well as a member of the GEM Board and the GEM Research Committee. He holds a PhD. in Management Sciences from ESADE Business School and was a World Bank-CONICYT Postdoctoral Research Fellow at the Universidad Adolfo Ibáñez, Chile. He also holds a Bachelor's Degree in Business Administration and MSc in Marketing from Monterrey's Institute of

Technology, Mexico. Dr. Amorós is a member of the Ibero-American Academy of Management and has lectured in several Latin-American and Spanish universities. His research interests are in entrepreneurship, competitiveness and regional development, high-growth new businesses, entrepreneurship and gender, and corporate entrepreneurship.

David Audretsch is a Distinguished Professor and Ameritech Chair of Economic Development at Indiana University, where he also serves as Director of the Institute for Development Strategies. He also is an Honorary Professor of Industrial Economics and Entrepreneurship at the WHU-Otto Beisheim School of Management in Germany. In addition, he serves as a Visiting Professor at the King Saud University in Saudi Arabia and as a Research Professor at Durham University, as External Director of Research at the Kiel Institute for the World Economics, Honorary Professor at the Friedrich Schiller University of Jena in Germany, and is a Research Fellow of the Centre for Economic Policy Research in London. Dr. Audretsch's research has focused on the links between entrepreneurship, government policy, innovation, economic development, and global competitiveness and has been published in over one hundred scholarly articles in leading academic journals. His books include *Entrepreneurship and Economic Growth*, with Oxford University Press in 2006, and *The Entrepreneurial Society*, also with Oxford University Press in 2007. He is co-founder and co-editor of *Small Business Economics Journal*. He was awarded the 2001 Global Award for Entrepreneurship Research by the Swedish Foundation for Small Business Research. In 2008, he received an honorary doctorate degree from the University of Augsburg. Dr Audretsch is also a member of the Advisory Board to a number of international research and policy institutes, including the Zentrum fuer Europaeisch Wirtschaftsforschung (ZEW, Centre for Economic Research), Mannheim, the Deutsches Institut fuer Wirtschaftsforschung (German Institute for Economic Analysis), the Basque Institute for Competitiveness, the Deutsche Telekom Foundation, and the Swedish Entrepreneurship Forum.

Erkko Autio is the QinetiQ-EPSRC Chair in Technology Transfer and Entrepreneurship at the Business School of Imperial College London. He was a founding coordination team member of the Global Entrepreneurship Monitor and served in GEM's global coordination team from 1997 to 2007. He continues to serve on GEM's research committee. His research focuses on new venture internationalization, high-growth entrepreneurship, and technology venturing, and he has published in the leading entrepreneurship journals as well as in the *Academy of Management Journal*, *Academy of Management Review*, *Strategic Management Journal*, *Journal of International Business Studies*, *Journal of Management Studies and Research Policy*. Dr. Autio contributes regularly to doctoral consortia at the Babson College Entrepreneurship Research Conference as well as in various European PhD consortia. His PhD students have received numerous PhD awards, including the AoM's Heizer and NFIB awards. He has held permanent and visiting positions in Lausanne, Helsinki, London, Geneva, and Bangkok.

Niels Bosma holds a PhD in entrepreneurship and economic geography and is a postdoctoral researcher at Utrecht University's department of economic geography.

His main research interests lie in the fields of entrepreneurship, entry and exit, and regional economic development. After obtaining his MSc degree in econometrics in 1998 from the University of Groningen, he completed a research trainee program at Erasmus University in Rotterdam. Dr. Bosma is Research Director with the Global Entrepreneurship Research Association (the umbrella organization hosting the Global Entrepreneurship Monitor) and is affiliated to EIM Business and Policy research group, where he worked during 2000–2004.

William Bygrave is Professor Emeritus and a Trustee at Babson College. He was a co-founder of GEM in 1997. He is co-editor/author of *The Portable MBA in Entrepreneurship* (4th edition, 2009), *Entrepreneurship* (2nd edition, 2010), *The Venture Capital Handbook* (1999), *Venture capital at the Crossroads* (1993), *The Portable MBA in Entrepreneurship Case Studies*; and co-editor of *Realizing Enterprise Value*. Dr. Bygrave was lead editor of *Frontiers of Entrepreneurship Research* for six years, was an editor of *Entrepreneurship Theory and Practice*, and served on the review boards of the three leading entrepreneurship journals. William Bygrave holds a MA and a DPhil (Physics) from Oxford University, an MBA from Northeastern University, a DBA (Strategy and Entrepreneurship) from Boston University, and honorary doctorates from the University of Ghent and from Glasgow Caledonian University. Dr. Bygrave served as Frederic C. Hamilton Professor for Free Enterprise at Babson College, and as Visiting Professor at the London Business School and INSEAD European Institute of Business Administration. He was Director of the Arthur M. Blank Center for Entrepreneurial Studies at Babson College (1993–1999).

Oscar Cristi is Professor and a Research Fellow at the Business Research Center of the Universidad del Desarrollo in Santiago, Chile. Dr. Cristi is an academic lecturer with teaching experience in natural resources economics, applied econometrics, and microeconomics at the top five Chilean Universities. He holds a PhD in Agricultural and Resource Economics from University of Maryland College Park, USA. He has a MS in International Economics and a Bachelor's Degree in Economics from Universidad de Chile. Dr. Cristi's research interests are in resource economics, water economics, and entrepreneurship dynamics. He is also founder partner and consultant of ESTIMA, a consulting company on econometrics with applications to advertising and technological efficiency.

Saul Estrin is a Professor of Management and Head of the Department of Management at the London School of Economics. His areas of research include labor and industrial economics, transition economics, and economic development. He is best known for his work on privatization, competition, and foreign direct investment. He was formerly Adecco Professor of Business and Society at London Business School where he was also the Research Director of the Centre for New and Emerging Markets. He was also formerly Director of the CIS Middle Europe Centre at London Business School. Dr. Estrin has published more than one hundred scholarly articles and books. His books include the widely cited *Privatisation in Central and Eastern Europe*; *Foreign Direct Investment into Transition Economies*; and recently, *Investment Strategies in Emerging Markets*. His papers have appeared in scholarly journals including *Quarterly*

Journal of Economics, *European Economic Review*, *Journal of Public Economics*, *Journal of Industrial Economics*, and *Journal of Comparative Economics*. Dr. Estrin also writes for policy journals such as *Economic Policy* and *Business Strategy Review*, of which he was editor for some years. Saul Estrin has considerable practitioner experience. He is currently on the Board of Barings Emerging Markets and Foursquare Ltd, as well as a member of the Academic Panel of the postal regulator, Postcomm. He has been a consultant to the World Bank, European Union, OECD, DfID, and NERA. He has taught executive programs for a large number of major companies including BA, BT, Lloyds TSB, Marks and Spencer, Vauxhall, Powergen, Deutsche Bank, ING Barings, Swedbank, and ABN-AMRO Bank. Dr. Estrin has been a visiting Professor at Stanford University, Michigan Business School, Cornell University, and the European University Institute. He is a Fellow of the Centre for Economic Policy Research, IZA and William Davidson Institute.

Mark Hart is Professor of Small Business and Entrepreneurship in the Economics and Strategy Group, Aston Business School, Aston University, United Kingdom. Over the last 30 years Professor Hart has worked and published extensively in the general area of entrepreneurship, enterprise, and small business development. He jointly manages the Global Entrepreneurship Monitor (GEM) project in the UK, advises a number of UK and Irish Government Departments (including BIS, UKTI, HMT, and HMRC) on enterprise issues, and has undertaken a number of national evaluations of business support products and services (e.g., Business Link, Regional Selective Assistance, and SFIE). Professor Hart is currently leading a team of researchers in the UK analyzing longitudinal firm-level data for the UK (1997–2009) and has undertaken an investigation of the nature and impact of high-growth firms in the UK (http://www. nesta.org.uk/publications/reports/assets/features/measuring_business_growth). He is also a Board member of PRIME—the Prince's Initiative for Mature Enterprise (www. primeinitiative.org.uk) as well as the Regional Studies Association (www.regional-studies-assoc.ac.uk). Professor Hart is a member of the Editorial Board of the *International Small Business Journal, International Journal of Entrepreneurial Behaviour and Research*, and the *International Journal of Gender and Entrepreneurship*.

Chantal Hartog is a policy researcher at the Strategic Research department of EIM Business and Policy Research in Zoetermeer, the Netherlands, since November 2007. She holds a Bachelor's Degree in Econometrics and Management Science (2007), and a Master's Degree in Quantitative Marketing and Econometrics (2008), both from Erasmus University in Rotterdam. Her Master Thesis dealt with the two-way relationship between entrepreneurship and economic performance, for which a Vector Error Correction Model (VECM) with co-integration was estimated. Ms. Hartog specializes in quantitative research, as well as processing and analyzing large data sets. She is involved in the annual updates of EIM's COMPENDIA data set which includes harmonized business ownership rates for all OECD countries. In addition, Ms. Hartog is a member of the Dutch GEM team, where she is one of the authors of the annual country report for the Netherlands. Her current work includes researching the effect of business regulations on entrepreneurship, and issues in the area of social entrepreneurship. Ms. Hartog's other research interests include ambitious entrepreneurship, fast-growing firms, entry and exit, solo self-employment, and entrepreneurial finance. Her paper on the determinants of business angel prevalence was recently published in *Venture Capital*.

Kent Jones is Professor of Economics at Babson College, where he has taught since 1982. He has also been a visiting professor at the University of Innsbruck and at Brandeis University. Dr. Jones specializes in trade policy and institutional issues, particularly those focusing on the World Trade Organization. He has served as a consultant to the National Science Foundation and the International Labor Office and as a research associate at the US International Trade Commission, and was senior economist for trade policy at the US Department of State. Dr. Jones is the author of numerous articles, including 'Global Institutions, National Regulations, and Entrepreneurship' (with Jonathan Levie) in the 2008 *Global Entrepreneurship Monitor Executive Report*. He has also published four books: *Politics vs. Economics in World Steel Trade, Export Restraint and the New Protectionism, Who's Afraid of the WTO?* and most recently, *The Doha Blues: Institutional Crisis and Reform in the WTO*.

Philipp Koellinger is assistant professor in economics and entrepreneurship at Erasmus University in Rotterdam. His current research interests are in the fields of entrepreneurship behavioral economics and genetics. Dr. Koellinger's research has won several prizes including the EARIE 2009 Young Economists Essay Award. His work has been published in numerous journals including *Journal of Economic Perspectives, Review of Economics and Statistics, Small Business Economics Journal, Journal of Economic Psychology, Economics Letters, Research Policy, Kyklos*, and the *European Journal of Epidemiology*. He is associate editor of *Small Business Economics: An Entrepreneurship Journal*, research fellow at Tinbergen Institute, member of the Erasmus Research Institute for Management, research affiliate at the German Institute for Economic Research (DIW Berlin), and researcher at EIM. Before joining Erasmus University Rotterdam in 2006, he received his PhD in economics and management science from Humboldt-University (Berlin) and worked as researcher at DIW Berlin. He was tenured at Erasmus University Rotterdam in 2009.

Nan S. Langowitz is Professor of Management and Entrepreneurship at Babson College. She served as Founding Director of Babson's Center for Women's Leadership, the first comprehensive center dedicated to advancing women in business and entrepreneurship at a leading school of management. Her research is focused on the entrepreneurial leadership of women as well as the challenges and opportunities organizations and managers face developing and leveraging talent. In the classroom, Professor Langowitz teaches about leadership, professional development, and managing diversity through courses in Babson's MBA program as well as at Babson Executive Education. She was awarded the Dean's Teaching Award for the Graduate Program in 2009. Dr. Langowitz is the author of numerous scholarly journal articles, research monographs, and cases and has been quoted in leading media outlets. She has over twenty years of experience in executive development design and delivery, having worked as a consultant, researcher, and educator with organizations ranging from complex global corporations to new start-up ventures. She has also served on corporate and non-profit boards. Professor Langowitz earned her doctorate at Harvard Business School and holds an MBA from New York University and a BA from Cornell University.

Jonathan Levie is a Reader in the Hunter Centre for Entrepreneurship at the University of Strathclyde, Glasgow, Scotland, where he was Director from 2000 to 2005. He has held research and teaching posts at the London Business School, Babson College, INSEAD, and University College, Cork, Ireland. He was visiting faculty at IMD International, Lausanne, in 2005, and is a visiting member of the teaching faculty of Audencia School of Management, Nantes, France. He holds a PhD from London Business School and a BSc and MSc from the National University of Ireland. Dr. Levie has been researching and teaching entrepreneurship for over 25 years and has managed both new and growing firms. His current research interests include entrepreneurship and institutions, entrepreneurial management and performance, and strategic value creation and exit. He has published in *Entrepreneurship Theory & Practice, Small Business Economics, Venture Capital, Family Business Review, Journal of Economic Issues*, and *Frontiers of Entrepreneurship Research*, among others. Dr. Levie is an elected board member of the Global Entrepreneurship Research Association, the organization that runs Global Entrepreneurship Monitor (GEM) and he leads the GEM UK team with Professor Mark Hart. He is a member of the Academic Advisory Board of the Institute for Innovation and Information Productivity, San Francisco, CA. He was a founder director of Cumbrae Community Development Company, a social enterprise which recently raised £5 million in public money to regenerate the Scottish island community which has been his home for the past ten years. Dr. Levie is also a principal of Enable Ventures Inc., an entrepreneurial coaching company based in the United States that provides entrepreneurship training to a wide range of clients, including the National Collegiate Inventors and Innovators Alliance and the University of Kentucky Agricultural Extension Service.

Tomasz Marek Mickiewicz is a Professor of Comparative Economics at University College London. He holds the habilitation degree from Marie Curie University, and a PhD and MA from the Catholic University of Lublin, Poland. His former employers include University of California at Davis and the City of Lublin, where he served as the deputy mayor responsible for economic policy and privatization in the first democratically elected local government in Poland in 1990–1991. He now also serves on the board of trustees of the Centre for Research into Post-Communist Economies (London), on the editorial board of the journal *Post-Communist Economies*, on the steering committee of the UK-wide 'Managing Economic Transition' research network, and is also an affiliate of the CASE Institute in Warsaw. Dr. Mickiewicz's research is focused on the role of institutions, institutional change and reforms as factors affecting entrepreneurship and entrepreneurial entry, performance, and socio-economic outcomes. His current publications (2007–2009) include papers in *The Lancet, Journal of Business Venturing, Europe Asia Studies, Economics of Transition*, and *Emerging Markets Finance and Trade*. His new book, *Economics of Institutional Change* (Palgrave Macmillan) is forthcoming in September 2010. His current funded research projects focus on the financing of new ventures and entrepreneurs and on the role of institutions as determinants of FDI. He is also working on the link between entrepreneurship and philanthropy.

Maria Minniti is Professor and Bobby B. Lyle Chair of Entrepreneurship at the Cox School of Business at Southern Methodist University. Prior to SMU, Minniti was Professor of Economics and Professor of Entrepreneurship at Babson College. She has been also a visiting professor at the London Business School, Humboldt-University, Copenhagen Business School, and the Max Planck Institute in Jena, Germany. She has published numerous articles on entrepreneurship, economic growth, and complexity theory, as well as book chapters and research monographs. Her articles have appeared in several peer reviewed journals including *Economics Letters*, the *Journal of Economic Behavior and Organization*, the *Journal of Business Venturing*, the *Journal of Economic Psychology*, *Entrepreneurship Theory and Practice*, the *Small Business Economics Journal*, and *Comparative Economics Studies*. Dr. Minniti is field editor of economics for the *Journal of Business Venturing*, and associate editor for *Small Business Economics Journal* and the *International Small Business Journal*. She is a member of the Global Entrepreneurship Monitor (GEM) project, the world's largest study of entrepreneurial dynamics, and a Council Member of the Entrepreneurial Lab at the University of Bergamo and Kilometro Rosso Science Park in Italy. In 2009, Minniti received an Award for Outstanding Teaching in the MBA Program at the Cox School of Business at Southern Methodist University. Dr. Minniti holds a PhD in Economics from New York University, a MS in Economics from Auburn University, and a BS in Political Science from the University of Rome, Italy. She is currently working on a volume on the relationship between poverty, institutions, and entrepreneurship.

Ivory Robinson Phinisee is Research Associate at the Lawrence N. Field Center for Entrepreneurship–Zicklin School of Business at Baruch College, The City University of New York, in New York City. He is a PhD student in Economics at the Graduate School of the City University of New York while working at Baruch College. Mr. Phinisee earned a Master's Degree in Statistics from Rutgers University in New Brunswick, New Jersey and a Master's Degree in Economics from Roosevelt University in Chicago, Illinois, his home town. Prior to joining Baruch College in 2005, Mr. Phinisee was an Adjunct Professor at Kean University in Union, New Jersey, where he taught Introductory Microeconomics and Health Economics. Ivory Phinisee worked in management at AT&T for over 18 years until his early retirement. He held several positions at AT&T including Manager in the Analysis and Forecasting Department for over 10 years.

Edward G. Rogoff is the Lawrence N. Field Professor of Entrepreneurship in the Department of Management of the Zicklin School of Business at Baruch College, The City University of New York. He is also Chair of the Department of Management. He also teaches at the Columbia Business School and received a BA, MBA, MA, and PhD from Columbia University where he wrote his thesis under the supervision of Nobel Laureate William Vickrey. Dr. Rogoff has served as the Academic Director of the Lawrence N. Field Center for Entrepreneurship at Baruch College, and conducts research in entrepreneurship, particularly relative to minority and later-life issues.

Dr. Rogoff has been named the 2010 Outstanding Entrepreneurship Educator of the Year by the United States Association of Small Business and Entrepreneurship. He is the author of *Bankable Business Plans* and co-author of *The Entrepreneurial Conversation*. His most recent book is *The Second Chance Revolution: Working for Yourself after 50*, co-authored with David Carroll. He has published in such journals as *The Journal of Business and Entrepreneurship*, *The Journal of Developmental Entrepreneurship*, *Family Business Review*, and *Journal of Small Business Management*. Dr. Rogoff was a 2003 Guest Co-Editor of the *Journal of Business Venturing*, and a 2007 Guest Co-Editor of the *Journal of Developmental Entrepreneurship*. He has written articles for the *New York Times*, *Forbes*, and *Newsday*, as well as having been a guest on CNN. He has trained and worked with hundreds of entrepreneurs in many industries.

Christian Schade is Professor and Director of the Institute for Entrepreneurial Studies and Innovation Management at Humboldt-Universität zu Berlin. In addition to being a visiting faculty of ESMT, he is a Research Professor at the German Institute for Economic Research (DIW Berlin) and a Research Fellow at Wharton's Risk Management and Decision Processes Center. Dr. Schade's research contributes to improving our understanding of entrepreneurial decision making and is based on experimental economics and economic psychology.

Erik Stam is Associate Professor at the Utrecht School of Economics, Utrecht University. He is also affiliated with the Scientific Council for Government Policy (The Hague) and EIM Business & Policy Research. He received his MSc in Economics and Geography as well as his PhD from Utrecht University. After earning his PhD, Dr. Stam spent two years as a postdoctoral researcher at Erasmus University Rotterdam and three years as an AIM research fellow at the University of Cambridge. His research focuses on entrepreneurship, innovation and the relationships with economic growth at the micro and macro levels. He has published five books (including *Micro-Foundations for Innovation Policy*) and over fifty book chapters and articles in journals such as *Economic Geography*, *Industrial and Corporate Change*, *Journal of Evolutionary Economics*, *Regional Studies*, and *Small Business Economics Journal*. In 2007 he was awarded the Herbert Simon Prize of the European Association for Evolutionary Political Economy. He is currently associate editor of *Small Business Economics Journal*. Next to his academic work he is often consulted by local, regional, national, and supra-national policy makers on innovation and entrepreneurship policy.

Rolf Sternberg is an Economic Geographer at the Leibniz Universität in Hannover, Germany. He has studied economic geography and received his first degree (1984), as well as his PhD (1987) and his Habilitation (1994), from the University of Hannover. Between 1995 and 1996 he worked as a Professor for regional geography at the Department of Geography, Technical University of Munich (Bavaria, Germany). Between 1996 and 2005 he was a full Professor (Chair) of Economic and Social Geography at the University of Cologne, Faculty of Economics and Social Science. In 2005 he moved to the Leibniz Universität Hannover, Germany, to become Head of the Institute of Economic and Cultural Geography. His main research interests are in the field of spatial consequences of policy activities (e.g., technology policy instruments like innovation centers/science parks), in the area of impacts of networks between innovative actors (firms, research institutions, politicians) on regional development, new firm formation process and effects, and in the field of regional-sectoral clusters and their economic impacts. In addition to six books, he has published about 180 articles in highly ranked journals including *Research Policy*, *Regional Studies*, *Economic Geography*, *European Planning Studies*, and *Small Business Economics Journal* (see also www.wigeo. uni-hannover.de). He is the leader, since 1998, of the German team of the Global Entrepreneurship Monitor (GEM).

Roy Thurik is Professor of Economics and Entrepreneurship at Erasmus University Rotterdam and at the Free University in Amsterdam. He is Scientific Advisor at EIM Business and Policy Research (A Panteia company) in Zoetermeer, the Netherlands. He is also a Research Fellow at the Tinbergen Institute for Economic Sciences and the Erasmus Research Institute for Management. His research has been widely published in leading academic journals, including *Journal of Business Venturing*, *Small Business Economics Journal*, *Journal of Small Business Management*, *Entrepreneurship Theory and Practice*, *Review of Industrial Organisation*, *Scottish Journal of Political Economy*, *Kyklos*, *International Journal of Industrial Organization*, *Industrial and Corporate Change*, *Technological Forecasting and Social Change*, *Journal of Evolutionary Economics*, *Economics Letters*, *Southern Economic Journal*, *Journal of Economic Behavior and Organization*, *Applied Economics*, *De Economist*, *Journal of Institutional and Theoretical Economics*, *Weltwirtschaftliches Archiv*, *Japan and the World Economy*, *European Journal of Operations Research*, *International Journal of Research in Marketing*, *European Economic Review*. Dr. Thurik is (co)-editor of the books *Innovation, Industry Evolution and Employment* with Cambridge Press (1999), *Entrepreneurship: Determinants and Policy in a European-US Comparison* with Kluwer Press (2002), *The Handbook of Entrepreneurship and Economic Growth* with Elgar (2006), *The Handbook of Entrepreneurship Policies* with Elgar (2007), *Business Regulation and Public Policy: the Costs and Benefits of Compliance* with Springer (2008), and *Entrepreneurship and Culture* with Springer (2010). He is associate editor of *Small Business Economics Journal*. He is on the editorial board of *Service Industries Journal*, *Entrepreneurship: Theory and Practice*, *Journal of Marketing Channels*, *International Review of Retail, Distribution and Consumer Research*, *International Review of Entrepreneurship*, *Journal of Small Business and Enterprise Development*, *Journal of Small Business Management*, *International Entrepreneurship and Management Journal*, *Journal of Business Venturing*, *Foundations and Trends in Entrepreneurship*, and *Entrepreneurship Research Journal*. Dr. Thurik consults with many firms and (international) institutions.

André van Stel is a senior researcher at EIM Business and Policy Research in Zoetermeer, the Netherlands. He holds a PhD in Economics and a Master's Degree in Econometrics, both from Erasmus University Rotterdam. Dr. van Stel's main research interests are on the determinants and consequences of entrepreneurship and in topics of industrial organization. His book, *Empirical Analysis of Entrepreneurship and Economic Growth*, was published by Springer Science in 2006. In addition, Dr. van Stel has published in numerous journals including *Kyklos*, *Journal of Business Venturing*, *Regional Studies*, and *Small Business Economics Journal*. He is a member of the Dutch team of the Global Entrepreneurship Monitor (GEM) project.

Megan McDonald Way is an Assistant Professor at Babson College. She received her doctorate in economics from Boston College in 2009. Her dissertation examined intergenerational transfers and, in particular, how demographic changes in marriage affect the way money gets passed between generations. Other research interests include immigration/migration, remittances, and international business networks. Prior to graduate school, Dr. Way spent 8 years as a marketing professional in the software industry in entrepreneurial organizations. Her work experience includes growing an internet start-up company from the founding stages to maturity, forming international channels partnerships, and coordinating national and international product marketing strategies. She also spent two years teaching in an MBA program in Cordoba, Spain.

Ramona Kay Zachary is the Peter S. Jonas Distinguished Professor of Entrepreneurship in the Department of Management of the Zicklin School of Business at Baruch College, City University of New York, in New York City. Currently, she is serving as the Academic Director of the Lawrence N. Field Programs in Entrepreneurship at Baruch College. From January 1 through July 31, 2000, Dr. Zachary served as the inaugural Jonas Visiting Professor of Entrepreneurship at Baruch College. Just prior to arriving at Baruch College, Dr. Heck was Professor and the J. Thomas Clark Fellow and Professor of Entrepreneurship and Personal Enterprise at Cornell University, Ithaca, New York. She led the Family Business Research Institute involving a multidisciplinary group of faculty, and positioned it on Cornell University campus as a major institute within the Bronfenbrenner Life Course Center, with a formal organizational link to the Entrepreneurship and Personal Enterprise program. Dr. Zachary teaches and conducts research on family businesses, the owning family's internal social and economic dynamics, the effects of family on the business viability over time, the economic impact of family businesses on communities, minority business ownership, gender issues within family firms, as well as on entrepreneurship issues and research. She has published numerous articles on family business, home-based businesses, family labor force, family management and decision making theory, and public and private policies related to businesses and families. She has also edited two books entitled, *Home-Based Employment and Family Life* and *The Entrepreneurial Family*. Most recently, Dr. Zachary is serving as a co-editor of the new *Entrepreneurship Research Journal* with The Berkeley Electronic Press. She received her PhD from Purdue University and is associated with several professional organizations including the International Family Enterprise Research Academy where she is a Board member.

Introduction

Maria Minniti

Why are some individuals more entrepreneurial than others? What types of institutional environments are more conducive to entrepreneurship? Does entrepreneurship contribute to the growth of a nation? Answering these questions is particularly important at a time when governments all over the world are looking to entrepreneurship as a way to increase employment and the competitiveness of their countries.

The chapters in this Volume address these questions and cover topics such as entrepreneurial motivation, gender and migration, entrepreneurial financing, urban entrepreneurship, growth-oriented entrepreneurship, economic growth, and regional entrepreneurship policies. An important feature of this Volume is that, although independent and self-contained, each chapter is based on data from the Global Entrepreneurship Monitor (GEM) project, in some cases complemented by additional data. The GEM project collects detailed and comparable data on representative population samples in more than 80 countries. No other existing book provides such a coherent global view of entrepreneurship and its implications.

Other studies use a hodge-podge of data from different sources to study entrepreneurship. The data used to support the different parts of a given argument are not always consistent with one another or easily compared. The scientific validity of such empirical findings is limited as the various pieces of evidence do not belong to the same puzzle. Therefore, the coherence of a universal approach is lost and important aspects of the entrepreneurial process may be overlooked or undervalued. This Volume, on the other hand, tests all theoretical arguments against the same empirical data, all the pieces fit into the same puzzle and a coherent and unitary picture of entrepreneurial activity, from its causes and motivations to its macroeconomic impact and implications, emerges.

Entrepreneurship is a complex phenomenon and can be found in a variety of settings and situations. No single measurement, no matter how precise, can capture the entrepreneurial landscape of a country. Someone who is just starting a venture and trying to make it in a very competitive market is an entrepreneur even in spite of not having high-growth aspirations. On the other hand, a person may be an established business owner who has been in business for quite a number of years and still be innovative, competitive, and growth minded. This person is also an entrepreneur. Following Kirzner's (1973, 1997) approach, the contributions in this Volume are consistent with the view that entrepreneurship is an aspect of human action in which all individual-based acts of arbitrage are, to various degrees, expressions of entrepreneurial attitudes. This view provides an umbrella under which a wide variety of entrepreneurial characteristics, such as motivations, innovativeness, high-growth aspirations, and the relationship between entrepreneurial activity and aggregate outcomes can be systematically and rigorously studied (Koppl and Minniti 2010).

Since its inception in 1999, the GEM project has taken a holistic approach to the study of entrepreneurship and provided a comprehensive (though by no means exhaustive) set of measurements aimed at describing several aspects of the entrepreneurial make-up of a country. It takes several years for a data set of GEM's size and scope to settle and get established. Now in its thirteenth annual cycle, the GEM data set is internationally recognized as an invaluable source of information for entrepreneurship scholars, students, and policymakers. Several peer reviewed articles based on GEM data are in progress or have been published in major academic journals such as *Economics Letters, Journal of Business Venturing, Entrepreneurship Theory and Practice, Journal of Economic Psychology, Journal of Evolutionary Economics, Small Business Economics Journal, European Journal of Development Research, Regional Studies,* and *Entrepreneurship and Regional Development,* among others.

The data collected by the GEM project focus on measuring differences in the level of entrepreneurial activity between countries, on the main factors determining the levels of entrepreneurial activity, and on the relationship between entrepreneurship and aggregate economic activity. GEM data cover the life-cycle of the entrepreneurial process and looks at individuals at the point when they commit resources to starting a business (nascent entrepreneurs); when they own and manage a new business that has paid salaries for more than three months but less than 42 months (new business owners); and when they own and manage an established business that has been in operation for more than 42 months (established business owners). GEM data provide also information on business owners' motivation and document whether people start new businesses due to opportunity recognition or because of the lack of better job alternatives. Importantly, GEM data also provide information about survey respondents who are not entrepreneurs, thereby providing a very valuable control group.

There exists wide consensus that growth expectations and innovativeness are fundamental aspects of the entrepreneurial process. Schumpeter (1934) focuses on innovation and the role of entrepreneurship as an act of creative destruction that, by introducing new products and processes, increases productivity and promotes economic growth. Hart (2003) stresses that, for policy purposes, entrepreneurship should be viewed primarily as an expression of novelty and dynamism. Within this context, GEM data provide measures of product novelty, competitor differentiation, use of technology, social entrepreneurship intent, and growth and aspirations of businesses by looking at their employment and expansion plans.

Finally, the quantity and quality of entrepreneurial activity taking place in a country is a function of the entrepreneurial capacity of that country. Assessing such capacity requires assessing the characteristics of a country's most important resource, namely the human capital of its people. GEM data include socioeconomic characteristics of the individuals surveyed, as well as measures of their subjective perceptions and expectations about the entrepreneurial environment. In addition to population surveys, the GEM project also collects data through detailed semi-open interviews. These data, however, are not used in this Volume. All chapters in this Volume are based on GEM data obtained through adult population surveys of representative samples of population. In several chapters, GEM data are complemented with data from the Organization for Economic Cooperation and Development (OECD), the World Bank, the International Monetary Fund (IMF), the Heritage Foundation, and the United Nations, among others.

More information about the GEM data, the collection process, and their statistical properties is provided in the Data Appendix. In addition, more information about the GEM project in general, as well as the data files and contact information, can be found on the GEM website at www.gemconsortium.org.

The Volume consists of 12 chapters and a brief conclusion. Each chapter is self-contained and deals with a different area of inquiry. Still, all chapters are connected as they take readers from the individual to the aggregate level in a logical sequence from which a coherent picture of entrepreneurial activity emerges. The 12 chapters in the Volume may be divided roughly into three parts. Chapters 1 through 4 focus on entrepreneurial activity at the individual level and describe some relevant components of the entrepreneur's decision process. Chapters 5 through 8 focus on contextual factors that influence the entrepreneurial activity of individuals. Finally, Chapters 9 through 12 focus on the country level implications of entrepreneurial activity and the relationship between entrepreneurship and economic growth.

Several variables correlate systematically, and universally, to an individual's decision to start a new business (among others, see Blanchflower 2004). Arenius and Minniti (2005) grouped individual-level factors associated to entrepreneurial decisions into economic and demographic factors, perceptual factors, and contextual factors. In the first part of the book, Chapters 1 through 4 focus on some of these factors and provide original evidence on the process and characteristics of entrepreneurial activity at the individual level.

Chapter 1, entitled "Excess entry and entrepreneurial decisions: the role of overconfidence," describes how heuristics and biases, such as overconfidence, can influence decision making and why they may be particularly relevant for entrepreneurial decisions. Koellinger, Minniti, and Schade build on recent literature on entry decisions (Koellinger et al. 2007) and argue that, although intuitively appealing, the issue of excess entry and its relationship to overconfidence are far from settled. They demonstrate the difficulty of capturing overconfidence unambiguously and provide some evidence that its impact on entry decisions may, in fact, be negligible. They also discuss the idea that, if at all present, overconfidence may be a desirable factor in some settings, both for individuals and at the aggregate level.

Chapter 2, "Understanding the gender gap in entrepreneurship: a multi-country examination," addresses the issue of gender differences in entrepreneurial behavior and their causes. Allen and Langowitz examine the landscape of female early-stage entrepreneurship across thirty-nine countries. They complement existing literature by confirming the existence of a gender gap in entrepreneurship at the global level (Minniti 2009) and by showing evidence that the relationship between economic development, measured by per capita gross domestic product (GDP), and female entrepreneurial activity follows a U-shaped pattern. They also find some preliminary evidence that institutional support aimed specifically at fostering gender parity influences both the proportion and rate of women's entrepreneurship.

Chapter 3, "Defining and identifying family entrepreneurship: a new view of entrepreneurs," investigates entrepreneurial activity in the context of the family and the related issues of wealth and succession. Using data from twenty-eight countries participating in the GEM project in 2008, Zachary, Rogoff, and Phinisee argue that it is virtually impossible to investigate entrepreneurial behavior while abstracting from the family context from which such a behavior emerges. Their exploratory study reveals that the family plays a very significant role in entrepreneurial activities, and that the family dimension of entrepreneurial behavior is a universal phenomenon with worldwide implications.

Chapter 4, "Investor altruism: financial returns from informal investments in businesses owned by relatives, friends, and strangers," discusses issues related to start-ups and informal financing. Using data from fifty-four countries, Bygrave and Bosma find evidence that the expected returns on investments by family, friends, and angel investors in start-up activity are characterized by altruism. Their results also show that as the personal relationship becomes more distant, the influence of altruism decreases and agency concerns increase up to a threshold level where they dominate the transaction. Interestingly, they also find that entrepreneurs expect higher returns from investments in their own businesses than in those of others.

The contributions in the second part of this Volume (Chapters 5–8) analyze alternative entrepreneurial contexts and the way in which they motivate individuals to act entrepreneurially or discourage them from doing so. Entrepreneurial behavior, of course, does not take place in a vacuum. Rather, it is embedded in a variety of social contexts where institutions provide the formal and informal rules governing human behavior (Baumol 1990). In other words, Chapters 5 through 8 focus on how the type and quantity of entrepreneurship in a community are determined endogenously by the context in which individuals live and by their position and aspirations in society.

Chapter 5, "The contribution of migrants and ethnic minorities to entrepreneurship in the United Kingdom," studies the behavior of minorities and immigrant groups with respect to starting new businesses. Levie and Hart compare the entrepreneurial attitudes, activity, and aspiration of a large representative sample of over 38,000 individuals in the United Kingdom. Their results show that white life-long residents tend to have less favorable attitudes to entrepreneurship than other ethnic/migrant categories. Interestingly, they also find blacks to exhibit a higher entrepreneurial propensity but that this does not translate into significantly higher levels of actual business ownership. This confirms results by Koellinger and Minniti (2006) for black Americans.

Chapter 6, "Entrepreneurship in world cities," studies the role played by entrepreneurial activity in urban areas and its distinguishing characteristics. Acs, Bosma, and Sternberg investigate recent discussions in the economic geography literature and argue that entrepreneurs are of key importance in translating creativity into economic output. Using entrepreneurship indices based on GEM data for thirty-five world cities, they show that entrepreneurial attitudes are higher in the vast majority of world cities than in their respective countries. Albeit exploratory, their results document empirically the existence of a potential entrepreneurial advantage of world cities hypothesized in the literature (Florida et al. 2008).

Chapter 7, "Interregional disparities, entrepreneurship, and EU regional policy," focuses on how entrepreneurial activity influences regions and the related implications for policy. Sternberg sheds an empirical light on the relationship between entrepreneurial activities and entrepreneurial perceptions, and the economic performance of regions in Spain, Great Britain, and Germany. The selected regions lag behind the EU average in terms of GDP per capita and/or rates of unemployment and are, therefore, eligible for European Union (EU) support. Sternberg shows that while EU regional policies have some impact on entrepreneurial activities and attitudes, other factors such as gender and perceptions have a stronger impact.

Chapter 8, "Entrepreneurship in transition economies: the role of institutions and generational change," provides comparative evidence on the characteristics of entrepreneurial activity in alternative economic systems. Estrin and Mickiewicz show that transition economies have lower rates of entrepreneurship than most developed and developing market economies, and that this difference is even more marked in countries of the former Soviet Union than those of Central and Eastern Europe. Complementing existing literature (Boettke and Coyne 2007), the authors suggest that this is due to the lack of appropriate informal institutions and social attitudes, in particular trust, and that the slow pace of the transformation is due to longer communist rules in the former Soviet Union than elsewhere which, in turn, resulted in a generational lack of institutional memory.

Chapters 7 and 8 bridge organically local and country-wide contexts and set the stage for the third part of the book. Chapters 9 through 12 explore how and when entrepreneurial activity influences living standards at the aggregate level. In other words, the third part of the Volume presents contributions analyzing the relationship between entrepreneurial activity and economic growth but also, how entrepreneurship, in turn, acts as an important factor of economic change. Although the relationship between entrepreneurship and economic growth is now taken for granted, there is still much we do not know about its nature and two-way causality.

Chapter 9, "Poverty and entrepreneurship in developing countries," tests the role that productive entrepreneurial activity plays in the battle against poverty. Much existing research argues that there is a positive relationship between entrepreneurial activity and economic growth in richer nations, and that only high-growth entrepreneurs have a tangible effect on aggregate economic activity (Audretsch 2007; Audretsch, Keilbach, and Lehmann 2006). Amorós and Cristi complement these works by providing evidence that both total and necessity-motivated early-stage entrepreneurship have a positive effect on countries' poverty reduction trends. Specifically, their results suggest that higher levels of poverty and income inequality are associated with higher levels of entrepreneurial activity.

Although even necessity-motivated entrepreneurship has an economy-wide impact (as Chapter 9 shows), there is no doubt that, on average, high-growth entrepreneurs are the ones who produce more visible economic changes. Chapters 10 and 11 both focus on these entrepreneurs.

Chapter 10, "Ambitious entrepreneurship, high-growth firms, and macro-economic growth," studies the relationship between the activity of growth-oriented entrepreneurs and economic growth. Stam, Hartog, van Stel, and Thurik examine the delayed impact of entrepreneurs who expect or have realized high growth rates in a sample of high- and low-income countries for the period 2002–2005. They show that these entrepreneurs contribute significantly to macroeconomic growth in all countries. However, they also show that once the share of growth-oriented entrepreneurs is controlled for, the effect of entrepreneurship on economic growth disappears in high-income countries but not in low-income ones. This is consistent with recent theoretical developments (Minniti and Lévesque 2010) and with results in Chapter 9. Interestingly, the authors find also asymmetries in the effects that new and established growth-oriented entrepreneurs have on growth with the latter being significantly less important.

Chapter 11, "High-aspiration entrepreneurship," focuses also on the characteristics of growth-oriented entrepreneurs but, in contrast to Chapter 10, Autio analyzes the prevalence of high-aspiration entrepreneurs at the country and individual levels focusing on the impact of institutional framework conditions. His analysis of institutional influences shows that while the effect of higher opportunity costs of entrepreneurship is unclear, the difficulty of firing is negatively and significantly associated to the prevalence of early-stage, growth-oriented entrepreneurship. Interestingly, Autio's results suggest that this association applies to the behavior of individuals who have already entered into entrepreneurship but does not seem to prevent new entry.

Chapter 12, "Entrepreneurship and the decision to export," discusses the role and opportunities available to entrepreneurial firms through trade. Jones and Way investigate what motivates entrepreneurs, particularly early-stage entrepreneurs, to export. This study looks at cross-country, cross-industry data focusing on firm stage and the innovativeness of products and technology to determine how these characteristics correlate with export participation. Within the context of the entrepreneur's specific economic and business environment, products embodying new technologies and innovativeness, along with reduced competition, are shown to contribute to increased export participation. The authors also find that nascent and early-stage entrepreneurs report a higher rate of export participation than established entrepreneurs. While the data is inconclusive as to why this pattern exists, it shows that while early-stage entrepreneurs may decide to enter export markets, some of them choose to exit export markets when domestic markets mature or, in an alternative, that riskier early-stage exporters may fail.

Finally, in the Conclusion, Audretsch discusses briefly the growing international debate on entrepreneurship policy and highlights the policy implications emerging from the contributions in the Volume. In his comments, Audretsch points out that after decades of neglect, entrepreneurship and small businesses are now at the forefront of the policy debate on growth and employment. In fact, only in the past couple of decades have academics and policymakers focused on the role that entrepreneurship plays in generating sustainable economic growth. Within this context, Audretsch's plea is that, in the future, and thanks to the availability of more empirical evidence such as that produced by GEM data, scholarly work on entrepreneurship may inform and guide policymakers to make choices that will allow entrepreneurship to flourish.

Overall, the Volume provides a comprehensive and consistent picture of entrepreneurship from its microeconomic foundations, where an individual decides to start a business, to its aggregate effects, where the unintended consequences of many individual decisions contribute to create a country's economic landscape. Along the way, the Volume highlights the importance of institutions, the rules of the game determining how individuals behave. As Baumol (1990) indicates, the institutional environment of a society determines the relative payoffs attached to various opportunities. As such, the institutional environment directs entrepreneurial activity toward those activities with the highest payoff.

Finally, far from exhausting the topics in each chapter, the goal of the Volume is not only to provide answers, but also to inspire new questions. Scholars of entrepreneurial studies may lack a disciplinary core, but they share a vision of entrepreneurship. Entrepreneurship is a dynamic process of change, in which some individuals undertake innovative actions in a variety of institutional settings, and face a variety of opportunities and challenges. Understanding entrepreneurship has major implications for the way we understand economic change and progress or the lack thereof. Entrepreneurship matters. It matters for individuals, it matters for communities, and it matters for countries as well. Contributing to understanding this important phenomenon is a privilege scholars cannot pass.

References

Arenius, P. and Minniti, M. (2005), "Perceptual Variables and Nascent Entrepreneurship." *Small Business Economics Journal* 24(3): 233–47.

Audretsch, D. (2007), "Entrepreneurship Capital and Economic Growth." *Oxford Review of Economic Policy* (23)1: 63–78.

Audretsch, D., Keilbach, M., and Lehmann, E. (2006), *Entrepreneurship and Economic Growth*. Oxford: Oxford University Press.

Baumol, W. J. (1990), "Entrepreneurship: Productive, Unproductive, and Destructive." *Journal of Political Economy* 98: 893–921.

Blanchflower, D. G. (2004), "Self-Employment: More May Not Be Better." *Swedish Economic Policy Review* 11: 15–74.

Boettke, P. and Coyne, C. (2007), Entrepreneurial Behavior and Institutions. In M. Minniti (ed.), *Entrepreneurship: The Engine of Growth – Volume 1* – Perspective Series. Westport, CA: Praeger Publisher – Greenwood Publishing Group.

Florida, R., Mellander, C., and Stolarick, K. (2008), "Inside the Black Box of Regional Development – Human Capital, the Creative Class and Tolerance." *Journal of Economic Geography* 8: 615–50.

Hart, M. (2003), Entrepreneurship Policy: What It Is and Where It Came From. In M. Hart (ed.), *The Emergence of Entrepreneurship Policy: Governance, Start–ups and Growth in the US Knowledge Economy*. Cambridge, UK: Cambridge University Press, pp. 3–19.

Kirzner, I. M. (1997), "Entrepreneurial Discovery and the Competitive Market Process: An Austrian Approach." *Journal of Economic Literature*, 35: 60–85.

Kirzner, I. M. (1973), *Competition and Entrepreneurship*. Chicago: The University of Chicago Press.

Koellinger, P., Minniti, M., and Schade, C. (2007), "I Think I Can, I Think I Can . . . : A Study of Entrepreneurial Behavior." *Journal of Economic Psychology* 28: 502–27.

Koellinger, P. and Minniti, M. (2006), "Not for Lack of Trying: American Entrepreneurship in Black and White." *Small Business Economics Journal* 27(1): 59–79.

Koppl, R. and Minniti, M. (2010), Market Processes and Entrepreneurial Studies. In Z. Acs and D. Audretsch (eds.), *Handbook of Entrepreneurship Research* (2nd edn). Kluwer Press International, UK. Forthcoming.

Minniti, M. (2009), "Gender Issues in Entrepreneurship." *Foundations and Trends in Entrepreneurship*: Vol. 5: Nos. 7–8, pp. 497–621.

Minniti, M. and Lévesque, M. (2010), "Entrepreneurial Types and Economic Growth." *Journal of Business Venturing* 25: 305–14.

Schumpeter, J. A. (1934), *The Theory of Economic Development*. Cambridge, MA: Harvard University Press.

1

Excess Entry and Entrepreneurial Decisions: The Role of Overconfidence

Philipp Koellinger, Maria Minniti, and Christian Schade

1.1 Introduction

Traditionally, interpersonal variations in entrepreneurial activity have been explained on the basis of socio-demographics and objectively measurable factors (Evans and Jovanovic 1989; Legros and Newman 1996; Lévesque and Minniti 2006; Laussel and LeBreton 1995; Lazear 2004), as well as on the existence of different preferences among individuals (Kihlstrom and Laffont 1979). More recently, however, researchers have found that entrepreneurs may exhibit different cognitive processes that result in different perceptions and interpretations of themselves and their environment (Busenitz and Barney 1997; Camerer and Lovallo 1999; Koellinger et al. 2007; Burmeister and Schade 2007). It has also been suggested that the behavior of entrepreneurs may rely significantly on perceptions and rules of thumb, and that their decisions may be more biased than those of other individuals at least in some respects (Schade and Koellinger 2007). This relatively recent stream of research is grounded in behavioral economics and cognitive psychology.

Because of the uncertainty that typically surrounds entrepreneurial activity, and because of the idiosyncrasies characterizing many entrepreneurial decisions, it can be expected that probability judgments are especially difficult. Furthermore, it can be expected that heuristics and biases contribute significantly to explain many entrepreneurial decisions, such as the choice of business activities that an entrepreneur engages in, the choice of the business' location, and the selection of staff and business partners. The use of simplifying heuristics and biases may lead to sub-optimal outcomes, such as excess entry into markets and low average survival chances for young businesses (Camerer and Lovallo 1999). On the other side, it can be argued that the use of simplifying heuristics is desirable, or even necessary for entrepreneurial decisions in situations of particular complexity (Busenitz and Barney 1997; Stevenson and Gumpert 1985; Hambrick and Crozier 1985). Some entrepreneurship scholars propose a compromise between these two positions and advocate the appropriateness of certain heuristics in some cases, but the inappropriateness of the same heuristics in other situations (Lévesque and Schade 2005).

In their early seminal work, Kahneman and Tversky (1974) demonstrated that the reason for the use of heuristics by individuals and their susceptibility to biases is straightforward: individuals are boundedly rational in the sense of being intentionally rational but having only limited capacity to be so (Simon 1957). Heuristics can then be described as informal tools and short-cuts the human brain uses to quickly identify and interpret patterns in its environment and in order to select a course of action. In general, abstracting from asymmetric information, individual preferences are the economic explanation of behavioral differences between individuals in a given situation. Heuristics, instead, influence the perception and processing of information and the (intuitive) optimization process used by individuals in selecting the preferred course of action (Lévesque and Schade 2005). Thus, behavior reflects more than preferences, it also reflects biases due to the use of heuristics.

Schade and Koellinger (2007) divide biases into three distinct groups: reference dependent behaviors; biases in probability perceptions; and biases in self-perceptions. Under reference dependent behavior they include all situations in which behavior is influenced by a specific predetermined anchor, or reference point, that influences subsequent behavior. A rational decision maker should not react to these kinds of past "experiences" or at least not very strongly. Examples of such biases are escalation of commitment, anchoring and adjustment, reference dependence, and status quo bias. Under the heading biases in probability perceptions they include heuristics used to judge the probability of potential events that typically lead to deviations from an objective processing of information about probabilities. Examples of such biases are availability and representativeness. Last, in biases in self-perceptions they include biases indicating the tendency of individuals to judge their own behavior and abilities more favorably than they objectively should. Examples of such biases are self-serving bias, illusion of control, and overconfidence.

In this chapter, we focus on overconfidence. The reason for our choice rests on the fact that overconfidence is one of the most pervasive biases in human behavior, as well as on the fact that it has often been linked to individuals' entrepreneurial choices. In particular, overconfidence has been offered as an explanation for the high failure rates of business start-ups (among others see Cooper et al. 1988; Koellinger et al. 2007). However, although intuitively appealing, the issue of excess entry, below-average returns to entrepreneurship, and their relationship with overconfidence are far from settled (Roessler and Koellinger 2010). Thus, we ask the following questions: (1) Is overconfidence (as a bias) a significant explanation for high entry and high failure rates? and (2) Could there be something beneficial about being overconfident in entrepreneurial decisions?

To address these questions, we use Global Entrepreneurship Monitor (GEM) data to provide new empirical evidence on overconfidence and argue that the latter is (1) not easy to observe unambiguously outside the experimental laboratory and (2) may not necessarily be a judgmental fallacy in need of correcting. After reviewing recent empirical results that have claimed to show overconfidence, as well as presenting new results from our GEM sample, we discuss some potential implications of overconfidence that may counterbalance or even outweigh its negative effects at both the individual and society level. We believe this discussion to be very important for any attempt to make normative statements about the decision-making process of entrepreneurs, and also for our understanding of entrepreneurial behavior in general, and of effective entrepreneurial decision-making in particular.

We test our argument using a balanced cross-country panel of individuals' entrepreneurial perceptions and activity aggregate at the country level for the period 2001–6 for 17 countries. Data are obtained from the adult population surveys of the GEM project. In the rest of the chapter, Section 1.2 discusses the theoretical background of our argument. Section 1.3 describes the data and presents some descriptive statistics. Section 1.4 describes our methods and presents our results. Section 1.5 discusses our results and their implications.

1.2 Theoretical background

Scholars in behavioral decision-making, economic psychology, and behavioral economics agree that people, as well as animals, use simple heuristics to deal with the complexities of the world, and that those heuristics, as well as (resulting) perceptions, have a large impact on the decisions people (or animals) make. Albeit useful in many cases, the paradigm of a "homo economicus" operating under perfect information is clearly an oversimplification and a new orthodoxy of decision-making is emerging even among mainstream economists (Colander et al. 2004).

Traditionally, many aspects of entrepreneurship and its implications have been studied taking the lens of neoclassical economics (for a review see Minniti and Lévesque 2008). This literature has focused on entrepreneurship and employment choice (Lazear 2004; Parker and Robson 2004; Michelacci 2003), personal characteristics (Djankov et al. 2006), immigration (Fairlie and

Meyer 2003), networks and social capital (Minniti 2005), innovation and knowledge creation (Audretsch and Keilbach 2004; Hellmann 2007), financial decisions (Hurst and Lusardi 2004; Paulson, Townsend, and Karaivanov 2006), economic growth (Acs, Audretsch, Braunerhjelm, and Carlsson 2004) and, finally, the role of governments (van Stel and Storey 2004; Gilbert, Audretsch and McDougall 2004).

The last two decades, however, have seen the emergence of new fields of economic analysis. Economists are moving somewhat from homo economicus to homo sapiens (Koppl 2006; Thaler 2000) and the distance between economics and other social and management sciences is declining. Interestingly, all new fields of economic inquiry share some common basic principles, namely the importance they attribute to bounded rationality, rule following, institutions, cognition, and evolution (Koppl 2006). Of course, once the assumption of bounded rationality is introduced, it is almost impossible to ignore the importance of cognition and the linkage between economic (and entrepreneurial) behavior and cognitive psychology. In most decision theoretic approaches, decision alternatives are assumed to exist exogenously. As a result, the task of the decision maker is to choose the best course of action among the available alternatives and given one's preferences and knowledge about outcomes and their likelihood. Sarasvathy (2001) argues that this traditional decision-making framework might only be applicable to a small subset of entrepreneurial decisions and that many "large world" decisions—a term coined by Simon to oppose the many theories and experiments dealing with "small worlds," that is, with artificial environments—might be better captured by a concept she calls "effectuation" where the decision maker is seen as somebody who starts with a certain set of skills and tools, and tries to a get as far as he or she can.

But once the idea of a fully rational homo economicus is abandoned, how do heuristics and biases contribute to decision-making? There seem to be two different ways of looking at the consequences of using simple heuristics. Scholars in the "heuristics and biases" tradition have a tendency to look at heuristics as being simplifying rules of thumb that economize on time and mental capacity but that, unfortunately, tend to lead to more or less severe deviations from optimal behavior (see, e.g., Kahneman, Knetsch, and Thaler 1991). Scholars in the "adaptive toolbox" tradition, on the other hand, argue that simple heuristics might often outperform more complex judgment and decision procedures in terms of their predictive ability, even if enough time and mental capacity to apply more complex procedures should be available (Gigerenzer and Brighton 2009). The reason behind the argument for "'biased minds' making better inferences" is that models that are too complex tend to be too flexible and are thus impaired by the large impact of small sample errors (Gigerenzer and Brighton 2009). A similar phenomenon is addressed by the statistics' literature when talking about "overfitting" (Gigerenzer and Brighton 2009).

Of course, how successful entrepreneurs might be when applying simple heuristics is a very specific and complicated question since how well or badly a heuristic might work is largely determined by its ecological rationality, in other words by the environment in which is it applied (Gigerenzer et al. 1999; Dudey and Todd 2001). Also, while entrepreneurs have been shown to be biased (perhaps more biased than other individuals) in various situations (e.g., Busenitz and Barney 1997; for an overview, see Schade and Burmeister 2009), there is evidence that they might be less biased in other scenarios (Burmeister and Schade 2007). Unfortunately, most of these behaviors have been evaluated only in quite simple experimental environments, thus, the evidence can be considered only suggestive and more research testing how well entrepreneurs perform in more complex decision situations relative to others is still needed. In this chapter, we approach our investigation on overconfidence by taking a balanced view of the role and implications of heuristic decisions by considering both the "adaptive toolbox" and the "heuristics and biases" perspectives.

There are different ways to perceive oneself or the outside world too optimistically. In fact, overconfidence may take one of three different forms. First, the term may describe the overestimation of one's own performance and ability relatively to others. Indeed, the majority of people consider their abilities, for instance their driving abilities, as being above the average (Svenson 1981; Kruger 1999). A number of studies have shown that most people are overconfident about their own relative abilities and unreasonably optimistic about their future (Weinstein 1980; Taylor and Brown 1988). It is also well known that the vast majority of people claim to be "above average" on almost any positive trait, although of course, only half can actually be above average (Svenson 1981). Thus, this concept is closely related to self-efficacy. That is, the belief in one's own ability to perform a given task (Bandura 1997).

Second, in the (original) definition within the psychology literature, overconfidence is often defined as a person's disproportionate confidence in the accuracy of his or her own forecasts (Oskamp 1965). Third, individuals often overestimate their own abilities relative to what their actual skills may be from an objective point of view (Huck and Oechssler 2000). In general, overconfidence is greatest for difficult tasks, for forecasts with low predictability, and for undertakings lacking fast, clear feedback (Fischhoff et al. 1977; Lichtenstein et al. 1982; Yates 1990; Griffin and Tversky 1992). In addition to these three aspects, a phenomenon closely related to overconfidence is overoptimistic behavior. Taylor and Brown (1988) and Weinstein (1980), for example, have shown that people tend to evaluate their future in an overoptimistic light. As will become clearer later, our data are closest to the third type of overconfidence, namely the fact that individuals tend to perceive their skills as being higher than they really are.

Schade and Koellinger (2007) discuss in detail how several types of heuristics and biases affect entrepreneurs and whether such effects are stronger or weaker than those on the general population. Koellinger et al. (2007) discuss, in detail, the relationship between overconfidence and entrepreneurial behavior. Overconfidence encourages people to exploit opportunities and to enter markets, and there is robust empirical evidence showing entrepreneurial decisions to be related to overconfidence. Cooper et al. (1988), for example, report that one-third of the new business founders they surveyed were certain of their success and 81 percent believed their chances of success to be at least 70 percent. Respondents also estimated their chances of survival to be much higher than those of other comparable companies. Yet, at the time of Cooper et al.'s study, 66 percent of all newly founded businesses were failing.

Along similar lines, Camerer and Lovallo (1999) conducted an incentive compatible market entry experiment and found that subjects overestimate their chances of success. More surprisingly, they also found that overconfidence in success is even higher when subjects know that their success will depend on their skills. According to Mahajan (1992) not even experience helps against overconfidence. In a study with marketing managers, those with the broadest job experience exhibited the largest degree of overconfidence. Aldrich (1999) found that entrepreneurs often overstate their own skills and abilities, and Bhide (2000) found evidence that entrepreneurs exploit opportunities despite a lack of competitive advantage. Given the complexity of factors that influence the possible success or failure of a new business, the lack of fast and clear feedback, and the high uncertainty of the outcome, it is not surprising that potential entrepreneurs should tend to be overconfident. Perhaps overconfidence may also contribute to the high level of self-efficacy found among entrepreneurs (Robinson et al. 1991; Zietsma 1999).

In general, in the context of entrepreneurship, overconfidence is most frequently mentioned as an explanation for excess entry, below-average returns, and high failure rates of entrepreneurs (Koellinger et al. 2007). The standard story is that entrepreneurs tend to overestimate their (relative) abilities and, as a result, their likelihood of success. This encourages them to enter markets when they should not, and many fail as a result of having to compete with too many others and/or with other entrepreneurs with better skills. This interpretation of excessive entry, however, has recently been challenged in a simulation study under non-strategic conditions by Hogarth and Karelaia (2009). In addition, in a model of the labor market with endogenous organizations, Roessler and Koellinger (2010) have shown that entrepreneurial incomes can be lower than wages under conditions of perfect information and rationality: if individuals are different from each other in their abilities, complementarities between people can arise that will be maximized in efficient organizations. In equilibrium, people who generate more value managing themselves than being managed by someone else will choose to be entrepreneurs. According to this view, entrepreneurs are relatively unmanageable and they do not have access to better paid jobs in other organizations, even though their entrepreneurial talent might generate a lot of well-paid jobs for others and they might earn high incomes themselves. The reason for below-average returns to entrepreneurship can be a population with a high share of relatively unmanageable people because high rates of self-employment raise average wages and depress average entrepreneurial incomes. Overall, given the evidence in the literature, two important unanswered questions emerge: (1) Is overconfidence (as a bias) a significant explanation for high entry and high failure rates? and (2) Could there be something beneficial about being overconfident in entrepreneurial decisions?

Although a definitive answer is beyond the scope of this article, we provide a first investigation of these questions by providing some new empirical evidence and revisiting an important topic in the economic, psychological, and entrepreneurship literatures with respect to overconfidence (see e.g. Camerer and Lovallo 1999; Oskamp 1965; Bernardo and Welch 2001).

1.3 Data and descriptive statistics

Data used in our analysis were collected for the population surveys of the GEM project between 2001 and 2006. GEM is an ongoing large scale project designed to collect data on the causes and implications of entrepreneurial behavior across countries. From 2001 to 2006, seventeen countries participated in the study every year. They are Argentina, Australia, Belgium, Brazil, Denmark, Finland, Germany, Ireland, Italy, Japan, the Netherlands, Norway, Singapore, Spain, Sweden, the United Kingdom, and the United States. Each year, a new randomly-drawn representative sample of population was surveyed in each country. The main purpose of the surveys was to identify individuals who, at the time of the survey, owned and managed a business or were in the process of starting one. If either or both of these criteria applied, respondents were asked follow-up questions that allowed the construction of a profile for them and their businesses. Details about data collection procedures and measures of reliability are reported in Reynolds et al. (2005).

Surveyed individuals were classified as nascent entrepreneurs (*nascent*) if they were engaged in start-up activities during the 12 months preceding the survey, were full or part owners of the new business, and the business had paid wages to the owners or others for a period not exceeding 3 months. Individuals were classified as new entrepreneurs (*newentr*) if they were managing and owning a business that had paid wages for the 3–42 months preceding the survey. Individuals were classified as established entrepreneurs (*establ*) if, at the time of the survey, they owned all or part of a business they helped manage, and that had paid wages or profits for longer than 42 months. Finally, individuals were classified as non-entrepreneurs if they were not involved in any business.

All survey participants were asked whether they believed they had the knowledge, skill, and experience required to start a business (*suskill*), and whether they thought that good opportunities for starting a business could be found in the area where they lived in the six months following the survey (*opport*). The variables *suskill* and *opport* allow for subjective and possibly biased interpretations and for judgment errors, and are used to capture potentially overconfident behaviors. Respondents were also asked whether fear of failure (*fearfail*) would prevent them from starting a business. This variable is a proxy for loss aversion and may reflect differences in preferences.

The data allow us to construct a balanced cross-country panel of entrepreneurial perceptions and activity at the aggregate level (N = 102) over the 2001–6 period. Ideally, to test for differences in perceived skills as a possible result of overconfidence, we would want individual-level panel data tracking entrepreneurs' confidence and performance over time. Unfortunately, this is not possible with GEM data. However, we are able to produce indirect evidence using country level prevalence rates for nascent entrepreneurial activity and average survival chances approximated by the ratio of established to nascent entrepreneurs (Koellinger et al. 2007). Since this information is available for seventeen countries over six years, we constructed a balanced cross-country panel. The panel contains the prevalence of *suskill, opport, fearfail, nascent, establ* and *establ/nascent* across countries and years. We then used the panel to test whether countries with high levels of *suskill* have lower estimated survival chances (*establ/nascent*), thereby suggesting some evidence for country-specific overconfidence.

Although the ratio of nascent to established entrepreneurs is not a perfect measure of entrepreneurial success, it is a valid proxy for average survival chances across countries under two assumptions. First, the prevalence of start-up activity and the survival chances of new business do not change much over time. While this is clearly a strong assumption, the problem is alleviated by the panel structure of our data which provides measurements for six consecutive years. Second, exit from entrepreneurship to non-entrepreneurship is primarily involuntary, that is, it represents failure.

Unfortunately, one more potentially problematic issue must be considered when interpreting our empirical results as evidence of overconfidence. As Koellinger et al. (2010) show, *suskill* is a potentially *endogenous* variable since it is clearly directly influenced by the decision of becoming an entrepreneur in itself (perhaps because of *ex post* cognitive dissonance; Festinger 1957) rather than being a driver of this decision exclusively. The issue of endogeneity is important because it implies that the higher failure rates of entrepreneurs in countries with large confidence levels may be, at least in part, a direct (and plausible) effect of higher entry than of overconfidence as will be discussed in more detail below.

Table 1.1 shows the average prevalence of sufficient skill perceptions (*suskill*), beliefs in the existence of good business opportunities (*opport*) and fear of failure (*fearfail*) across seventeen countries from 2001–6. Argentina, Australia, the United States, and Canada rank highly in entrepreneurial skill perceptions, while Belgium, Italy, and Singapore rank lowest among the seventeen countries included. Confidence in entrepreneurial skills is positively correlated with opportunity perceptions at the country level (correlation coefficient 0.53, significant at >99%) and weakly with fear of failure (correlation coefficient 0.18, significant at >90%).[1]

Table 1.2 shows the average prevalence rates of nascent (*nascent*) and established entrepreneurs (*establ*) across countries, and the ratio of established to nascent entrepreneurs (*establ/nascent*). Argentina, Australia, the United States, and Canada appear again at the top of the ranking with the highest average shares of nascent entrepreneurs. Belgium is again among the lowest ranked

Table 1.1. Perceptual variables as percentage of adult population across 17 countries, 2001–6

Country	Suskill	Opport	Fearfail
Argentina	0.64	0.47	0.37
Australia	0.61	0.47	0.34
United States	0.59	0.35	0.21
Canada	0.57	0.39	0.26
Brazil	0.56	0.43	0.38
Ireland	0.52	0.43	0.37
United Kingdom	0.50	0.33	0.34
Spain	0.47	0.39	0.43
Sweden	0.45	0.44	0.33
Norway	0.45	0.48	0.26
Germany	0.44	0.22	0.44
Netherlands	0.42	0.43	0.27
Denmark	0.41	0.54	0.32
Finland	0.41	0.49	0.35
Belgium	0.39	0.26	0.30
Italy	0.38	0.31	0.35
Singapore	0.31	0.18	0.37

---

[1] Individual level correlations between *suskill* and *fearfail* confirm the aggregate results in most countries.

Table 1.2. Entrepreneurial activity as percentage of adult population and transition rates across 17 countries, 2001–6

Country	Nascent	Establ	Establ/Nascent
Argentina	0.09	0.09	0.94
Australia	0.08	0.13	1.62
United States	0.08	0.06	0.84
Canada	0.06	0.05	0.92
Brazil	0.05	0.09	1.66
Ireland	0.05	0.07	1.39
Norway	0.04	0.08	1.94
Germany	0.04	0.06	1.50
Singapore	0.03	0.04	1.30
Denmark	0.03	0.05	1.81
Finland	0.03	0.09	3.14
Spain	0.03	0.07	2.54
Italy	0.03	0.05	1.69
United Kingdom	0.03	0.05	1.77
Netherlands	0.03	0.06	2.11
Belgium	0.02	0.04	1.64
Sweden	0.02	0.06	3.27

countries in this measure. This is in line with Koellinger et al. (2007) who report that *suskill* is highly correlated with nascent entrepreneurial activity.

Simple bivariate correlations reveal that countries with current and past high levels of nascent entrepreneurship also have significantly higher prevalence rates of established entrepreneurship (coefficients vary from 0.50 to 0.57). However, current and past high levels of nascent entrepreneurship are also significantly and negatively correlated with our roughly approximated average survival chances (*establ/nascent* coefficients vary from −0.35 to −0.49). In other words, the more people start, the more are selected out. This descriptive evidence suggests that countries with high levels of sufficient skill perceptions tend to have more start-ups, but also more failures than countries with lower absolute levels of sufficient skill perceptions.

1.4 Empirical analysis

To establish whether the descriptive statistics presented above suggest the presence of country-specific overconfidence, we estimate various regressions of *suskill*, *opport*, and *fearfail* on the ratio of established to nascent entrepreneurs (*establ/nascent*). We specify models with time lags for the perceptual variables ranging from *t* to *t-3*. Including time lags in the regressions is important because nascent entrepreneurs who survived in the market place will turn into established entrepreneurs 39–42 months after they started their venture. Hence, by comparing the cohorts of nascent entrepreneurs in *t-3* with the established entrepreneurs in t, we obtain a proxy of the average survival chances of this cohort of nascent entrepreneurs, while shorter time lags may confound different survival chances of different cohorts.

An important question is also if the negative correlation between sufficient skill perceptions and approximated survival chances is robust or if, instead, it reflects unobserved country-specific differences that have nothing to do with overconfidence but that nonetheless correlate positively with *suskill* and negatively with *establ/nascent*. For example, one possible reason could be country specific policies that encourage temporary self-employment among relatively low-skilled or unemployed persons. In this case, the negative correlation between *suskill* and *establ/nascent* would not necessarily indicate overconfidence. Instead, it would be the spurious result of unobserved institutional differences between countries. The standard way of testing for this alternative explanation is to use panel econometric methods. In technical terms, we want to know if the error term in a regression equation of *suskill* on *establ/nascent* is independent from *suskill*. Furthermore, we want to know how the effect of *suskill* on *establ/nascent* changes if we allow the error term to be correlated with *suskill*. Econometrically, this boils down to a comparison between a random effects and a fixed effects model. The random effects model assumes that the country-specific error term is independent from *suskill*, while the fixed effects model allows the country-specific error term to be correlated to *suskill*. The specification test suggested by Hausman (1978) enables us to decide which of the two models is correct. As a benchmark solution, we also estimated standard ordinary least squares (OLS) models that rely on the most restrictive assumptions, that is, the error term is independent of *suskill* and the country under investigation. Results are reported in Table 1.3. Country-specific effects were highly significant in all models. In other words, OLS is clearly rejected and Hausman tests have to be carried out to decide if either random or fixed effects are appropriate.

The estimated benchmark OLS coefficients on *suskill* are all strongly negative and significant. Also, all random effects coefficients are strongly negative, although country-specific effects are significant and reduce the effect of *suskill*

Table 1.3. Balanced cross-country panel regressions on ratios of nascent entrepreneurs to established business owners (approximated survival rates), 2001–6

	OLS		Random effects		Fixed effects		Hausman test		N
	B	$P>|t|$	β	$P>|t|$	β	$P>|t|$	Chi^2	$P>Chi^2$	
Suskill	−6.11	0.00	−2.96	0.07	**1.24**	**0.57**	9.04	0.03	102
suskill (t−1)	−5.74	0.00	−3.32	0.06	**0.22**	**0.93**	5.74	0.13	85
suskill (t−2)	−5.09	0.00	**−3.57**	**0.05**	−0.03	0.99	2.78	0.43	68
suskill (t−3)	−5.54	0.00	**−5.05**	**0.02**	−1.98	0.62	1.02	0.80	51

Note: Regressions additionally included *opport*, *fearfail*, and a constant. Bold numbers indicate models preferred by Hausman test.

somewhat. These results suggest the presence of some overconfidence among nascent entrepreneurs: Countries with high levels of confidence have high levels of entrepreneurial activity, but also significantly lower average survival chances for every nascent entrepreneur. Note that this analysis does not completely rule out the endogeneity issue surrounding the *suskill* variable as mentioned earlier. If *suskill* is partially a result rather than a cause of entrepreneurial activity, part of the negative effect of this variable on the analyzed ratios might be due to a direct effect of higher nascent entrepreneurial activity on lower chances of survival.

Finally, and partially consistent with the latter interpretation, the estimated coefficients on *suskill* in the fixed effects models are never significant. This could suggest that differences in sufficient skill perceptions as well as survival rates are driven by country-specific characteristics that are not observed in our data. Alternatively, it could be that within-country variations in GEM data are primarily random and the result of sampling issues (Reynolds 2009), which would also result in insignificant coefficients in the fixed effects estimation. Note, however, that the fixed effects specification is preferable to random effects only in two out of four cases according to the Hausman tests (in one of the two cases the Hausman test is only weakly significant). In the two remaining cases, the random effects model is supported. We indicated the regressions underlying our respective interpretation using bold coefficients and p-values. Hence, we use the random effects specification for the time lags of *t-2* and *t-3*, whereas we use the fixed effects specification for *t* and *t-1* lags.

We first look at the short lags. Here, as already mentioned, the coefficient for *suskill* is not significant. One possible reason is that variations in entrepreneurial activity and perceptions reported in GEM data within countries over time are entirely noise and do not reflect actual changes in survival and perceptions over time. Alternatively, the insignificant coefficients in the fixed effects regression could suggest that the negative correlation between *suskill* and survival in the OLS and random effects models can be explained by country-specific characteristics that are unobserved in our data and that correlate both with survival and *suskill*. For example, low switching cost between self-employment and regular employment in some countries (with a more flexible labor market) could influence the perception of what skills are perceived as "sufficient" to start a business (individuals would appear to be more self-confident in the GEM data) and account for high entry and (at least partially voluntary) exit rates. In other words, different institutions and cultures across countries could influence the aspiration levels of individuals regarding what they consider to be a "success" in starting a business and what skills they perceive to be sufficient to achieve this success.

Interestingly, the evidence for overconfidence in the GEM data is more straightforward for longer time lags, which is the more appropriate measure for the average survival chances of each cohort of nascent entrepreneurs per country, as discussed above. The estimated results for longer time lags suggest that more confidence in the past leads to higher failure rates in the future. This result is independent of alternative constructs that might interact with the variables in focus (i.e., the Hausman test supports the random effects specification for *t-2* and *t-3*).

If entrepreneurs are on average correct in the assessment of their own skill (self-perception), and if true skills are positively related to survival, our results should show a positive correlation between *suskill* and survival chances. Instead, our results show that the higher the entrepreneurial confidence of a country, the higher its failure rate is in the long run. Hence, the empirical evidence suggests the presence of some degree of overconfidence among nascent entrepreneurs that cannot be entirely explained by unobserved country-specific characteristics. Note that the above argument with respect to different aspiration levels being driven by the same country-specific effects than the survival rate does not apply for the random effects regression since there is no significant correlation between unobserved variables and variables in the regression equation. Unfortunately, however, the endogeneity issue with respect to *suskill* (Koellinger et al. 2010) can still not be ruled out completely. If *suskill* is partially the *effect* of entry and high entry leads to higher failure, the overconfidence interpretation is still somewhat inconclusive. To resolve the remaining uncertainty about the interpretation of these results, detailed individual-level panel data would be required, measuring objective and perceived skills, reasons for exit from self-employment, income, and other measures of personal success. Such data, unfortunately, is not available.

1.5 Discussion and implications

We began our investigation asking the questions, (1) Is overconfidence (as a bias) a significant explanation for high entry and high failure rates? and (2) Could there be something beneficial about being overconfident in entrepreneurial decisions? We can now discuss possible answers in light of our results.

Addressing Question 1, our results can be interpreted as indirect evidence for country-specific relative overconfidence. However, the fact that sufficient skill perceptions might be the result rather than a cause of nascent entrepreneurial activity, as well as the different structure of labor markets in different countries, make this indirect evidence somewhat inconclusive. Also, while in the general population high confidence is associated with more market entry (see also Koellinger et al. 2007), such a positive correlation would not be surprising in models of entrepreneurship in which minimum threshold skill levels are assumed necessary across countries for survival in the market. This would hold even if the sufficient skill perception were not partially endogenous. High confidence leads to large entry rates, large failure rates, and, most likely, few forgone chances. Low confidence levels, instead, lead to small entry rates, small failure rates, and many foregone chances (Hogarth and Karelaia 2009).

Expanding the point above further, is excess entry really the result of systematic *ex ante* overconfidence or does it just stem from uncertainty about one's own skills that eventually lead to *ex post* overconfidence in the entrepreneurial population? Excessive entry may result from a skewed distribution of utility (low probabilities of very high utility) together with uncertainty about one's own skills, or from positive effects of self-employment on future chances in the labor market (e.g., if previously self-employed individuals were to have better chances to find regular employment than individuals who were unemployed or who worked in low status wage jobs). Only if the expected utility of becoming an entrepreneur were to be lower than the best available alternative we could infer the presence of overconfidence *as a bias*. Along this line, Hamilton (2000) found that the *monetary payoffs* from self-employment are below those from dependent jobs for the majority of entrepreneurs in the US, even when only successful entrepreneurs are considered. Thus, at least for the US, expected earnings are surprisingly low, and fewer people should opt for self-employment if they had access to better paid jobs. However, as Roessler and Koellinger (2010) argue, this might not be the case even under conditions of perfect information and rationality. Low average returns to self-employment compared to high average wages in the US might simply result from a large share of relatively unmanageable individuals and a highly efficient entrepreneurial sector that creates well paid jobs for many. Hence, the return structure found by Hamilton might not be a "paradox" but the result of an efficient allocation of individuals and jobs.

In addition, non-monetary benefits of entrepreneurial activity are also important and may account for (even rational) people's acceptance of lower monetary returns (Croson and Minniti 2010). Indeed, it is well known that entrepreneurs' utility *is not* solely based on (expected) monetary payoffs but on non-monetary components as well (e.g., autonomy and flexibility). In the GEM data, the US has one of the highest rates of entrepreneurial confidence and exit, which suggests overconfidence as a likely explanation unless exit does not really represent failure in the US.

Some experimental evidence suggests that – despite some interesting differences in reaction patterns – enterpreneurs may not differ from other individuals with respect to their tendency toward overconfidence. In a study on simultaneous market entry by Schade and Boewe (2010) entrepreneurs do not enter significantly more often than a group of students. In such a controlled setting with strictly induced monetary preferences, there should be no alternative interpretation than to conclude that entrepreneurs exhibit overconfidence as a bias. However, since the study by Schade and Boewe test a situation in which the own abilities of the players (and their self-estimation) play no role, this may not be interpreted as a conclusive test of overconfidence.

We now turn to our second question about whether overconfidence might be beneficial for entrepreneurs. At the individual level, overconfidence can be a motivating factor for new entrepreneurs. It may help them survive the difficulties encountered at the inception of the business and in crisis situations by giving them the confidence to deal with adversities (Markman, Balkin, and Baron 2002; Gist and Mitchell 1992). The effort and steps necessary to starting may help them to acquire the skills and the experience that they actually need. While entrepreneurs are trying things out, they can learn and actually achieve the skills that they (erroneously) believed they already had at the beginning. The underlying concept here is self-efficacy, in other words, individuals' belief in their ability to effectively succeed in specific situations (Bandura 1997; Wood and Bandura 1989; Chen et al. 2001). Also, Busenitz and Barney (1997) argue that the use of biases and heuristics can be an effective and efficient guide for decisions with high environmental uncertainty and complexity, such as starting a business. For example, overconfidence may be beneficial in implementing a specific decision and persuading others to be enthusiastic about it as well.

One additional argument is related to mental health: "[C]onsiderable research evidence suggests that overly positive self-evaluations, exaggerated perceptions of control or mastery, and unrealistic optimism are characteristic of normal human thought. Moreover, these illusions appear to promote other criteria of mental health, including the ability to care about others, the ability to be happy or contented, and the ability to engage in productive and creative work" (Taylor and Brown 1988: S. 193).

Benefits from overconfidence are possible at the aggregate and societal level as well. Mathematical simulations have shown that a certain number of overconfident individuals is good for societies since such individuals test new opportunities and, even in the event of failure, produce information by executing ideas others will not have to test out (Bernardo and Welch 2001). An additional potential benefit of overconfident entrepreneurs at the aggregate level could be related to the contestable markets hypothesis (Baumol 1982). The latter suggests that the threat of market entry makes incumbent firms more efficient, leading to lower prices, higher output, and ultimately improving social welfare. As Baumol 1982 points out, the credible threat of entry is enough to produce the beneficial effects of competition. Countries with many nascent entrepreneurs trying to enter existing markets may benefit from higher efficiency by incumbent firms. Indeed, sustained entry, with its implications for business churning, is at the core of the competitive process characterizing economies with a long history of growth and productivity increases (Baumol 2002).

Finally, overconfidence may counterbalance other biases. In other words, in some cases, exhibiting two biases might be better than exhibiting only one: For example, many individuals—including entrepreneurs—suffer from a status quo bias (Burmeister and Schade 2007). Status quo bias is defined as the tendency to select a previously chosen alternative disproportionately often. Instead of considering all available information in the decision-making process, people tend to rely on what they have chosen before, on what represents the current state, or even what someone else has chosen for them and consequently is the status quo. Porter and McIntyre (1984) found evidence that status quo bias may result in aversion to innovation, a distinguishing feature of entrepreneurship. Roca et al. (2005) found evidence in an experimental study that status quo bias might even reduce individuals' aversion to ambiguity when the ambiguous option is the status quo. Status quo bias makes people less likely to start a business, while overconfidence increases the chances to do so.

To summarize, although our results show the presence of some entrepreneurial overconfidence as a cause of excess entry, our evidence as to its importance is still inconclusive. Our discussion suggests the difficulty of capturing overconfidence unambiguously even in laboratory experiments, and suggests that some aspects of entrepreneurial behavior often explained using overconfidence are instead possible even when individuals are perfectly rational and no bias is present. Thus, the role played by overconfidence and its implications for entrepreneurship should be handled with care. Overall, entrepreneurial decisions are linked to some overconfidence. However, it is very difficult to say how much overconfidence really matters. Furthermore, our discussion provides arguments supporting the idea that overconfidence may not be always bad and, in fact, be a desirable factor in some settings, both for individuals and at the aggregate level. In other words, sometimes, when it does exist, this bias may not represent "over" but just the "right" amount of confidence.

Acknowledgments

Many thanks go to an anonymous reviewer for helpful comments. Although GEM data were used in this study, their interpretation and use are the sole responsibility of the authors. All errors are ours.

References

Acs, Z. J., Audretsch, D. B., Braunerhjelm, P., and Carlsson, B. (2004), The missing link: The knowledge filter and entrepreneurship in endogenous growth. CEPR Discussion paper No. 4783, Center for Economic Policy Research, London.

Aldrich, H. (1999), *Organizations Evolving*. London, UK: Sage.

Audretsch, D. B. and Keilbach, M. (2004), Entrepreneurship and regional growth: An evolutionary interpretation. *Journal of Evolutionary Economics* 14(5): 605–16.

Bandura, A. (1997), *Self-efficacy: The exercise of control*. New York, NY: Freeman.

Baumol, W. J. (2002), *The Free-Market Innovation Machine: Analyzing the Growth Miracle of Capitalism*. Princeton, NJ: Princeton University Press.

Baumol, W. J. (1982), Contestable markets: an uprising in the theory of industry structure. *American Economic Review* 72(1): 1–15.

Bernardo, A. E. and Welch, I. (2001), On the evolution of overconfidence and entrepreneurs. *Journal of Economics and Management Strategy* 10: 301–30.

Bhide, A. (2000), *The Origin and Evolution of New Businesses*. New York, US: Oxford University Press.

Burmeister, K. and Schade, C. (2007), Are entrepreneurs' decisions more biased? An experimental investigation of the susceptibility to status quo bias. *Journal of Business Venturing* 22: 340–62.

Busenitz, L. W. and Barney, J. B. (1997), Differences between entrepreneurs and managers in large organizations: Biases and heuristics in strategic decision-making. *Journal of Business Venturing* 12: 9–30.

Camerer, C. F. and Lovallo, D. (1999), Overconfidence and excess entry: An experimental approach. *American Economic Review* 89: 306–18.

Chen, G., Gully, S. M., and Eden, D. (2001), Validation of a new general self-efficacy scale. *Organizational Research Methods* 4(1): 62–83.

Colander, D., Holt, R. P. F., and Rosser, J. B. Jr, (2004), The changing face of mainstream economics. *Review of Political Economy* 16(4): 485–99.

Cooper, A., Woo, C. Y., and Dunkelberg, W. (1988), "Entrepreneurs' perceived chances of success," *Journal of Business Venturing* 3: 97–108.

Croson, D. and Minniti, M. (2010), Slipping the Surly Bonds. Mimeo.

Djankov, S., Qian, Y., Roland, G., and Zhuravskaya, E. (2006), Who Are China's Entrepreneurs? *American Economic Review* 96(2): 348–52.

Dudey, T. and Todd, P. (2001), Making Good Decisions with Minimal Information: Simultaneous and Sequential Choice. *Journal of Bioeconomics* 3(2): 195–215.

Evans, D. and Jovanovic, B. (1989), An estimated model of entrepreneurial choice under liquidity constraints. *Journal of Political Economy* 97: 808–27.

Fairlie, R. W. and Meyer, B. D. (2003), The effect of immigration on native self-employment. *Journal of Labor Economics* 21(3): 619–50.

Festinger, L. (1957), *A Theory of Cognitive Dissonance*. Stanford, CA: Stanford University Press.

Fischhoff, B., Slovic, P., and Lichtenstein, S. (1977), "Knowing with certainty: The appropriateness of extreme confidence," *Journal of Experimental Psychology* III: 552–64.

Gigerenzer, G. and Brighton, H. (2009), Homo heuristicus: Why biased minds make better inferences. *Topics in Cognitive Science* 1: 107–43.

Gigerenzer, G., Todd, P. M., and ABC Research Group (1999), *Simple Heuristics that Make Us Smart*. New York, NY: Oxford University Press.

Gilbert, B. A., Audretsch, D. B., and McDougall, P. P. (2004), The emergence of entrepreneurship policy. *Small Business Economics* 22(3/4): 313–23.

Gist, M. E. and Mitchell, T. R. (1992), Self-efficacy: A theoretical analysis of its determinants and malleability. *Academy of Management Review* 17(2): 183–211.

Griffin, D. and Tversky, A. (1992), "The weighing of evidence and the determinants of confidence," *Cognitive Psychology* XXIV: 411–35.

Hambrick, D. C. and Crozier, L. (1985), Stumblers and stars in the management of rapid growth. *Journal of Business Venturing* 1(1): 31–45.

Hamilton, B. H. (2000), Does entrepreneurship pay? An empirical analysis of the returns to self-employment. *Journal of Political Economy* 108: 604–31.

Hausman, J. A. (1978), Specification tests in econometrics. *Econometrica* 46: 1251–71.

Hellmann, T. (2007), When do employees become entrepreneurs? *Management Science* 53(6): 919–33.

Hogarth, R. M. and Karelaia, N. (2009), Excess entry: Confidence and fallible judgment. *Working paper*.

Huck, S. and Oechssler, J. (2000), Information cascades in the laboratory: Do they occur for the right reasons? *Journal of Economic Psychology* 21: 661–71.

Hurst, E. and Lusardi, A. (2004), Liquidity constraints, household wealth, and entrepreneurship. *Journal of Political Economy* 112(2): 319–47.

Kahneman, D., Knetsch, J. L., and Thaler, R. H. (1991), Anomalies: The endowment effect, loss aversion, and status quo bias. *The Journal of Economic Perspectives* 5: 193–206.

Kahneman, D. and Tversky, A. (1974), Judgment under uncertainty: Heuristics and biases. *Science* 185: 1124–31.

Kihlstrom, R. and Laffont, J. (1979), A general equilibrium entrepreneurial theory of firm formation based on risk aversion. *Journal of Political Economy* 87: 719–40.

Koellinger, P., Minniti, M., and Schade, C. (2010), Gender differences in entrepreneurial propensity. Mimeo.

Koellinger, P., Minniti, M., and Schade, C. (2007). "I think I can, I think I can: Overconfidence and entrepreneurial behaviour." *Journal of Economic Psychology* 28: 502–27.

Koppl, R. (2006), Austrian economics at the cutting edge. *Review of Austrian Economics* 19: 231–41.

Kruger, J. (1999), Lake Wobegon be gone! The "below-average effect" and the egocentric nature of comparative ability judgments. *Journal of Personality and Social Psychology*, 77: 221–32.

Laussel, D. and LeBreton, M. (1995), A general equilibrium theory of firm formation based on individual unobservable skills. *European Economic Review* 39: 1303–19.

Lazear, E. P. (2004), Balanced skills and entrepreneurship. *American Economic Review* 94: 208–11.

Legros, P. and Newman, A. (1996), Wealth Effects, Distribution and the Theory of Organization. *Journal of Economic Theory* 70: 312–41.

Lévesque, M. and Minniti, M. (2006), The effect of aging on entrepreneurial behaviour. *Journal of Business Venturing* 21: 177–94.

Lévesque, M. and Schade, C. (2005), Intuitive optimizing: Experimental findings on time allocation decisions with newly formed ventures. *Journal of Business Venturing* 20(3): 313–42.

Lichtenstein, S., Fischhoff, B., and Phillips, L. D. (1982), "Calibration of probabilities: The state of the art in 1980," in D. Kahneman, P. Slovic, and A. Tversky (eds.) *Judgment Under Uncertainty: Heuristics and Biases* (Cambridge, UK: Cambridge University Press).

Mahajan, J. (1992), "The Overconfidence Effect in Marketing Management Decisions," *Journal of Marketing Research* 39: 329–42.

Markman, G. D., Balkin, D. B., and Baron R. A. (2002), Inventors and new venture formation: The effects of general self-efficacy and regretful thinking. *Entrepreneurship Theory & Practice* 27(2): 149–65.

Michelacci, C. (2003), Low returns in R&D due to the lack of entrepreneurial skills. *The Economic Journal* 113: 207–25.

Minniti, M. (2005), Entrepreneurship and network externalities. *Journal of Economic Behavior and Organization* 57(1): 1–27.

Minniti, M. and Lévesque, M. (2008), Recent Developments in the Economics of Entrepreneurship. *Journal of Business Venturing* 23(6): 603–12.

Oskamp, S. (1965), Overconfidence in Case-Study Judgements. *The Journal of Consulting Psychology* 29: 261–5.

Parker, S. C. and Robson, M. T. (2004), Explaining international variations in self-employment: Evidence from a panel of OECD countries. *Southern Economic Journal* 71(2): 287–301.

Paulson, A. L., Townsend, R. M., and Karaivanov, A. (2006), Distinguishing limited liability from moral hazard in a model of entrepreneurship. *Journal of Political Economy* 114(1): 100–44.

Porter, M. and McIntyre, S. (1984), What is, must be best: a research note on conservative or deferential responses to antenatal care provision. *Social Science & Medicine* 19: 1197–200.

Reynolds, P. D. (2009), Screening item effects in estimating the prevalence of nascent entrepreneurs. *Small Business Economics* 33(2): 151–63.

Reynolds, P. D., Bosma, N. S., Autio, E., Hunt, S., De Bono, N., Servais, I., Lopez-Garcia, P., and Chin, N. (2005), Global Entrepreneurship Monitor: Data collection design and implementation 1998–2003. *Small Business Economics* 24: 205–31.

Robinson, P., Stimpson, D., Heufner, J., and Hunt, H. (1991), "An attitude approach to the prediction of entrepreneurship," *Entrepreneurship Theory and Practice* 15(4): 13–31.

Roca, M., Hogarth, R. and Maule, J. A. (2005), Ambiguity seeking as a result of the status quo bias. Department of Economics and Business, Universitat Pompeu Fabra, Economics Working Paper 882.

Roessler, C. and Koellinger, P. (2010), A law of labor demand and the return to entrepreneurship. Working Paper.

Sarasvathy, S. D. (2001), Causation and Effectuation: Toward a theoretical shift from economic inevitability to entrepreneurial contingency. *Academy of Management Review* 26(2): 243–88.

Schade, C. and Boewe, S. (2010), Strategic Decisions in a Realistic Context: Gender is More Important than Being an Entrepreneur, Mimeo.

Schade, C. and Burmeister, K. (2009), Experiments on entrepreneurial decision making: A different lens through which to look at entrepreneurship. *Foundations and Trends in Entrepreneurship* 5(2): 81–134.

Schade, C. and Koellinger, P. (2007), Heuristics, biases, and the behavior of entrepreneurs, in M. Minniti et al. (eds.) *Entrepreneurship; The Engin of Growth*. Westport, Connecticut London, USA: Praeger, Vol. 1, S. 41–63.

Simon, H. A. (1957), *Administrative Behaviour*. New York, US: Macmillan.

Stevenson, H. H. and Gumpert, D. E. (1985), The heart of entrepreneurship. *Harvard Business Review* 63(2): 85–94.

Svenson, O. (1981), Are we all less risky and more skillful than our fellow drivers? *Acta Psychologica* 47: 143–8.

Taylor, S. E. and Brown, J. D. (1988), Illusion and well-being: A social psychological perspective on mental health. *Psychological Bulletin* 103: 193–210.

Thaler, R. (2000), From Homo Economicus to Homo Sapiens. *Journal of Economic Perspectives* 14(1): 133–41.

van Stel, A. J. and Storey, D. J. (2004), The Link between Firm Births and Job Creation: Is there a Upas Tree Effect? *Regional Studies* 38(8): 893–917.

Weinstein, N. D. (1980). Unrealistic Optimism About Future Life Events. *Journal of Personality and Social Psychology* 39(5): 806–20.

Wood, R. and Bandura, A. (1989), Impact of conceptions of ability on self-regulatory mechanisms and complex decision making. *Journal of Personality and Social Psychology* 56: 407–15.

Yates, F. J. (1990), *Judgment and Decision Making*. Englewood Cliffs, US: Prentice Hal.

Zietsma, C. (1999), "Opportunity knocks – or does it hide? An examination of the role of opportunity recognition in entrepreneurship," in P. Reynolds, W. Bygrave, S. Manigart, C. Mason, G. Meyer, H. Sapienza, and K. Shaver (eds.) *Frontiers in Entrepreneurship Research*, (Babson Park, US: Babson College), 242–56.

2

Understanding the Gender Gap in Entrepreneurship: A Multicountry Examination

I. Elaine Allen and Nan S. Langowitz

2.1 Introduction

Recent cross-country studies of entrepreneurial behavior have shown that early stage entrepreneurship varies significantly across countries and by gender (Bosma et al. 2009). A number of studies have also provided compelling evidence of a gender gap in entrepreneurship at the global level (Minniti, Arenius, and Langowitz 2005; Verheul, Van Stel, and Thurik 2006). But how can differences in entrepreneurial activity between women and men living in the same country and for any given level of economic development be explained? The answer to this question is multilayered and complex, and cross-country comparisons must necessarily take into account the issue of embedded contextual differences.

Studies aimed at understanding the drivers of entrepreneurial choice have been framed in terms of supply and demand (Verheul et al. 2002; Verheul, Van Stel, and Thurik 2006; Audretsch 2007; Audretsch, Grilo, and Thurik 2007). In these studies, the wealth of a country creates demand for entrepreneurial activity, whereas demographic characteristics, culture, and institutional norms create the supply of entrepreneurs. Empirically, these studies have shown the existence of a U-shaped relationship between per capita gross domestic product (GDP) and the rate of entrepreneurship. The U shape implies that the percentage of population involved in start-up activities declines as per capita GDP increases up to a threshold level beyond which the number of people involved in new businesses grows again (Carree et al. 2002; Wennekers et al. 2005; Bosma et al. 2009). Complementing this evidence on the importance of GDP, Mueller and Thomas (2001) have shown that culture is an important determinant of entrepreneurial potential, and Busenitz, Gomez, and Spencer (2000) have suggested that the institutional profile of a country is an important variable influencing the ease of the entrepreneurial process. But do these arguments and findings hold equally for men and women? Studies focusing on gender have suggested that the institutional context plays a significant role in the emergence of observed differences in entrepreneurial behavior between men and women (Mueller 2004; Baughn, Chua, and Neupert 2006; Grilo and Irigoyen 2006; Verheul, Van Stel, and Thurik 2006). Up-to-date, however, the evidence base focusing on gender suffered from lack of data and, as a result, existing studies tend to have a narrow geographical breadth and limited explanatory power.

The goal of this chapter is to begin filling this gap in the literature and to complement extant literature in three ways. First, we investigate whether the observed U-shaped relationship between per capita GDP and entrepreneurial activity in general holds even when only women are considered. Second, we investigate whether institutional factors, by affecting men and women in different ways, also play a role in the emergence of a systematic gap between the entrepreneurial decisions of men and women. Third, we investigate whether institutional support specifically aimed at fostering gender parity influences the proportion of women in entrepreneurship. Although studies examining the entrepreneurial gender gap and the role of institutions in general already exist, because of the size and scope of our sample, and because of our focus on institutions aimed at gender parity, this chapter adds unique breadth to these important research questions.

Our study is conducted using data on early stage entrepreneurial activity across thirty-nine countries in two time periods, 2003 to 2005 and 2006 to 2008. Data are from the Global Entrepreneurship Monitor (GEM) project. In each country, and for each year of analysis, a minimum of 2,000 individuals were surveyed yielding a very large sample. In addition, we use data from the United Nations and the Heritage Foundation. Descriptive statistics and standard econometric techniques are used to develop our argument.

Albeit exploratory, our results provide some initial but important cross-country evidence on several phenomena: First, we confirm the existence of a global gender gap in entrepreneurship and show that while the U-shaped relationship between per capita GDP and entrepreneurial activity holds for both women and men, its quantitative characteristics and intensity vary across genders. Second, we document the explanatory power of institutional support, and particularly its normative dimension for understanding the gender gap in entrepreneurship and the constraints faced by women entrepreneurs. Last, we provide some exploratory evidence of how institutional support specifically aimed at fostering gender parity may influence the proportion and rate of women's entrepreneurship.

2.2 Theoretical background

Recent research has shown the existence of a U-shaped relationship between the level of a country's economic development as measured by GDP and its rate of entrepreneurial activity (Carree et al. 2002; Wennekers et al. 2005; Bosma et al. 2009). This can be understood by considering the opportunity created by the economic environment. In low per capita income countries, the supply of entrepreneurship may be high as entrepreneurship represents an alternative to a labor market in which jobs are scarce. As per capita income increases, often through the entrepreneurial activity which was triggered by lower levels of wealth, new markets and firms are formed, investment in technology and greater scale occurs and traditional jobs become more widely available. As the number of new firms, traditional employment, and concomitant economic growth climb, an eventual decline in the supply of entrepreneurship results as individuals find stable work in larger companies. Finally, as wealth becomes widespread, entrepreneurship again rises as individuals experience the freedom to make career choices and have discretionary resources to foster new ventures. These phenomena, when taken together across a range of countries, explain the U-shaped curve relationship. *Ceteris paribus*, we would expect to see country context have an equal draw upon women and men. Our first research question, then, examines whether, in fact, the U-shaped relationship holds for both women and men or whether, instead, gender differences exist.

   If increased wealth clearly creates a demand for new markets (and therefore entrepreneurship), it is reasonable to consider the ways in which the supply of women and men as entrepreneurs may vary for reasons other than labor market constraints. The socio-demographic variables of income level, employment, age, and education have received considerable attention in past research for their potential influence on the supply of early stage entrepreneurs in a country context. New venture creation necessarily requires resources and research clearly points to a positive correlation between entrepreneurial activities and individuals' incomes (Evans and Jovanovic 1989; Smallbone and Welter 2001) since the availability of income increases an individual's discretionary ability to invest in a business start-up. While financial resources are a constraint for both men and women, women tend to be over represented in lower income brackets and may face stronger challenges in their aspirations to become entrepreneurs (Carter, Williams, and Reynolds 1997; Carter and Rosa 1998; Langowitz, Sharpe, and Godwyn

2006; Verheul and Thurik 2001). Employment status is an obvious means by which income levels might be increased and a strong positive relationship exists between employment and early stage entrepreneurship, regardless of gender (Minniti, Arenius, and Langowitz 2005). Business start-up most typically occurs in early adult years (Blanchflower 2004) and the relationship between age and the likelihood of creating a new venture follows an inverted U-shaped curve for both men and women (Lévesque and Minniti 2006; Bosma et al. 2009) with the highest prevalence of early stage entrepreneurs in the 25–34 age group. Finally, while educational background may influence the business sector focus of an entrepreneur's new venture (Reynolds et al. 2001) there is little evidence to suggest a clear causal relationship between education and entrepreneurship (Blanchflower 2004).

In addition to socio-demographic variables, and although their boundaries overlap, institutional and cultural factors influence the supply of entrepreneurship (Bruton, Fried, and Manigart 2005). Given that entrepreneurship is a choice made by individuals, it is essential to consider the nature of political and economic institutions' influence on individuals (Harper 1998), and the impact of institutional structure on the quantity and type of entrepreneurial activity (Baumol 1990). The institutional view argues that the normative context influences choices and what is considered acceptable or appropriate (North 1990; Scott 1995). Busenitz, Gomez, and Spencer (2000), for example, distinguish between regulatory, cognitive, and normative dimensions in their work on how institutional profiles may influence entrepreneurial activity in a country. Along similar lines, Verheul et al. (2002) discuss how government may influence the rate of entrepreneurship through institutional policies impacting technology development, business licensing, availability of capital, labor market regulation, and fiscal policy, among others. Indeed a recent cross-country comparison has shown that the level of entrepreneurship is related to institutional context variables such as financial capital, regulatory environment, and educational support (Bowen and De Clercq 2008). Thus, where there is greater economic freedom in the institutional context of a country, productive entrepreneurship is likely to be more prevalent. But, whether women and men have equal ability to take advantage of economic freedom is often subject to cultural and social norms. Societal norms may influence individual behavior through the values and attitudes considered to be socially acceptable (Ross and Nisbett 1991). Several studies have found a relationship between new venture creation and indicators of culture (Shane 1993; Davidsson 1995; Davidsson and Wiklund 1997; Thomas and Mueller 2001). Evidence suggests that culture seems to make a difference in entrepreneurial attitudes and choices (Reynolds, Storey, and Westhead 1994; McGrath, MacMillan, and Scheinberg 1992; McGrath et al. 1992b). Social admiration of entrepreneurship is considered to be a normative institutional factor (Scott 1995; Busenitz,

Gomez, and Spencer 2000) and recent findings suggest that it is positively related with entrepreneurial activity (Baughn, Chua, and Neupert 2006). Our second research question examines how institutional support may influence differences in the proportion and rate of women's entrepreneurship compared to men.

Pushing this line of inquiry further, it has been noted that institutional and cultural influences on the supply of early stage entrepreneurship likely take on an additional dimension when gender is taken into account (Lorber 1994; Ridgeway and Correll 2000). That is, not only are a country's institutions and normative social values and attitudes shaping the supply of entrepreneurs in general, but they may particularly have a role to play in determining those career pursuits which are considered acceptable for men and women, including business start-up (Emrich, Denmark, and Den Hartog 2004). In any particular country context, individuals must make their choices within the understood expectations and attitudes of the gender construct (Alvesson and Billing 1997). Evidence of these effects with regard to entrepreneurial pursuit has been found with respect to gender and family roles (Achtenhagen and Welter 2003; Welter et al. 2003), situational and cultural barriers (Brush 1997); gender stereotyping (Fagenson and Marcus 1991; Baron, Markman, and Hirza 2001; Bird and Brush 2002; Langowitz and Morgan 2003), and motivations and perceptions (Jianakoplos and Bernasek 1998; Arenius and Minniti 2005; Langowitz and Minniti 2007). Given the power of social cues regarding gender and appropriate roles and attitudes for women versus men, it might be expected that women's entrepreneurial activity may be different from that of their male counterparts. Normative gender inequality influences the level of women's entrepreneurial activity and may be predictive of the proportion of female entrepreneurship (Baughn, Chua, and Neupert 2006). Thus, we might expect that where there is greater gender disparity in a country, the level and proportion of women entrepreneurs will be lower, regardless of the regulatory and institutional support for entrepreneurial activity in general. Within this context, our final research question considers how institutional support specifically aimed at fostering gender parity may influence the proportion and rate of women's entrepreneurship.

2.3 Variables and techniques

2.3.1 *Data and measures*

To address gender differences in entrepreneurship we use individual level data from the Global Entrepreneurship Monitor (GEM) project. Starting in 1999, GEM surveyed at least 2,000 individuals in each participating country with the aim of measuring global entrepreneurial activity (Bosma et al. 2009).

A longitudinal database of individual country data on the rate of entrepreneurship and individual motivations and knowledge was created combining surveys from 2001–8. This dataset, the GEM Adult Population Survey (APS), provides the primary basis for this chapter. Data were weighted using country specific weights to ensure they are representative of the population in each country and comparable across countries.[1] Given the countries included in the GEM project, two country groups were identified. The groups were obtained using the definitions of the GEM project based on per capita GDP: low/middle income countries have modest per capita GDP (mean of US $11,000 in 2008) and faster GDP growth (6% in 2008) and high income countries have higher per capita GDP (mean of US$35,000 in 2008) and lower GDP growth (3% in 2008).[2]

Additional measures and indices at the country level were also included in the analyses and gathered at two points, 2005 and 2008. These include GDP per capita in each country (measured in purchasing power parity (PPP) with US dollars), the Heritage Foundation's Index of Economic Freedom (IEF), the United Nations indices of gender empowerment (GEMPWR) and gender development (GDI), and a composite measure to assess normative support for entrepreneurship developed from GEM data.

The Heritage Foundation calculates an annual IEF aimed at measuring individuals' ability to control their own labor activity and property (Miller and Holmes 2009). Ten "freedoms" are included in the index, they are business freedom, trade freedom, fiscal freedom, government size, monetary freedom, investment freedom, financial freedom, property rights, freedom from corruption, and labor freedom.

Each year the United Nations Development Programme calculates and publishes a set of measures of economic and human development (Watkins 2005; Watkins 2008). Included in our analyses are the Gender Empowerment Index (GEMPWR) and the Gender Development Index (GDI). Both indexes are based on data collected by the United Nations and are processed to enable cross-country comparisons (see http://hdr.undp.org/en/statistics/indices/gdi_gem/ for details). The GEMPWR measures female political participation and decision-making, economic participation, and command over resources. It captures the status of women's standing in a country's political and

---

[1] Details on weights and weighing methods can be found in the statistical appendices to the GEM data at www.gemconsortium.org

[2] The rationale and methods used to divide countries into groups can be found in Minniti et al. (2005). Countries included in the study are Argentina, Australia, Austria, Belgium, Brazil, Canada, Chile, China, Croatia, Denmark, Ecuador, Finland, France, Germany, Greece, Hong Kong, Hungary, Iceland, Ireland, Israel, Italy, Japan, Jamaica, Latvia, Mexico, the Netherlands, Norway, Peru, Portugal, Singapore, Slovenia, South Africa, Spain, Sweden, Switzerland, Thailand, Venezuela, United Kingdom, and United States.

economic realms. This index has four indicators: female members of the legislature, female participation in selected positions in the public and private sectors, female participation in academic and technical work, and estimated income. The range of this index is from 0 to 1 with a greater number representing higher gender equality. The GDI is a gender-based subset of the Human Development Index (HDI) which focuses on life expectancy, and on the educational and per capita income characteristics of a country (see http:// hdr.undp.org/en/statistics/indices/hdi/ for details). The GDI tracks the same capabilities captured by the HDI but notes inequality in achievement between women and men. Thus, the GDI "discounts" the HDI for gender disparity. The range of this index is from 0 to 1 with a lower number representing greater disparity.

We used the ratio of Gender Development Index to Human Development Index (GDI/HDI) as one indicator of gender disparity in a country and the GEMPWR as another. The lower the ratio GDI/HDI, the greater is the disparity among men and women in a country. The GEMPWR is a more direct measure of gender inequality in a country and the lower the level of GEMPWR, the lower the equality between genders. Thus, countries with high normative support for gender equity would have high levels of GDI/HDI and high levels of GEMPWR.

Finally, a composite measure of social attitudes toward entrepreneurship was created to assess the normative institutional support for entrepreneurship. Borrowing from Baughn, Chua, and Neupert (2006), the GEM APS questions regarding social attitudes toward entrepreneurship were used to create a composite scale with a coefficient alpha of 0.87 for the 2003–5 time period, and 0.80 for the 2006–8 time period, and 0.895 over both time periods. The composite measure was created for each country for each set of years (2003–5) and (2006–8). Three yes/no questions were used: (1) Starting a new business is considered as a good career choice, (2) Persons growing a successful new business receive high status, and (3) There is lots of media coverage for new businesses. The proportion of individuals responding "yes" for each country was calculated and the three questions were combined as a single normative institutional support factor in the models. In the presentation of our results this composite measure of social attitudes is labeled "combined normative support."

2.3.2 Statistic and econometric methods

Descriptive statistics and correlations between indices and entrepreneurial activity are examined to identify strong gender-related relationships and any strong collinearity between the continuous variables and indices. These analyses are done overall and by country GDP groups using GEM survey data.

Categorical relationships are examined using chi-squared cross-tabulations. Analysis of variance (ANOVA) is used to compare indices and ratios over country income groups and gender. For these analyses of variance models, GEM data are aggregated by country by year.

The coefficients of quadratic models of the gender differences in the U-shaped relationship of total early-stage entrepreneurial activity (TEA) to GDP were tested using t tests.

Two hierarchical linear models were fit to the combined individual level GEM data and the country-level indices data to examine relationships between economic and gender-related indices, GDP, and normative institutional factors and the ratio of female to male entrepreneurship and the rate of female entrepreneurship over both time periods. These hierarchical models use the individual level GEM survey data as the lowest level of the hierarchy and then country level data are incorporated into the next levels of the hierarchical model. The correlation between the indices, including GDP per capita, is presented in Table 2.1. All of the indices are significantly correlated but not at such a high level as to cause multicollinearity problems in a linear model. In both models, GDP was entered in the first stage of the model, the GEMPWR and the normative factor were added in the second stage of the model, and the ratio of the GDI to the HDI and the IEF were entered in the final stage of the model. The results for the 2003–5 time period were so similar to the 2006–8 time period that only results from the later models are shown.[3]

2.4 Analysis of the data

2.4.1 *Comparative entrepreneurial characteristics*

Table 2.2 summarizes the countries and indices used in this chapter. There were thirty-nine countries with sufficient data from the GEM APS in both time periods, 2003–5 and 2006–8. These countries include twenty-six countries classified as high income by GDP and thirteen countries classified as low/middle income by GEM.

Figure 2.1 (2003–5) and Figure 2.2 (2006–8) show TEA by gender for each country displayed from highest TEA to lowest. From these figures it is easy to see that female entrepreneurship lags behind that of males, who have higher TEA than females in all countries and at all time periods. Further, in general, low/middle income countries exhibit higher levels of entrepreneurship for both genders. That is, the gender entrepreneurship gap is lower in low/middle income countries. Exceptions to this include Latvia, Croatia, and Hungary, all

---

[3] Results for the period 2003–5 are available from the authors upon request.

Table 2.1. Correlation matrix

	GDP 2008	TEA Female 2003–5	TEA Male 2003–5	TEA Ratio F/M 2003–5	TEA Female 2006–8	TEA Male 2006–8	TEA Ratio F/M 2006–8	HDI 2005	GDI 2005	HDI 2008	GDI 2008	GDI/HDI Ratio 2005	GDI/HDI Ratio 2008	GEMPWR 2005	GEMPWR 2008	Combined Institutional Norms	Good Job 2008	High Status 2008	Media Attention 2008	IEF 2005	IEF 2008
GDP 2005	.965**	−.626**	−.542*	−.704**	−.673**	−.638**	−.577**	.912**	.893**	.931**	.870**	−.360*	−.058	.829**	.774**	−.415*	−.596**	−.098	−.157	.662**	.723**
GDP 2008		−.586**	−.496**	−.714**	−.645**	−.602**	−.579**	.887**	.887**	.917**	.856**	−.377**	−.062	.820**	.764**	−.395*	−.558**	−.134	−.134	.685**	.734**
TEA Female 2003–5			.973**	.674**	.952**	.912**	.694**	−.620**	−.584**	−.580**	−.534**	.087	.086	−.418*	−.472**	.595**	.592**	.296	.380*	−.353*	−.393*
TEA Male 2003–5				.552**	.917**	.902**	.652**	−.536**	−.491**	−.493**	−.428**	.022	.148	−.338*	−.402*	.636**	.598**	.306	.446**	−.311	−.348*
TEA Ratio F/M 2003–5					.701**	.667**	.621**	−.720**	−.700**	−.714**	−.755**	.192	−.318	−.552**	−.569**	.345*	.408**	.256	.107	−.340*	−.406*
TEA Female 2006–8						.952**	.782**	−.675**	−.651**	−.646**	−.608**	.119	.085	−.481**	−.541**	.664**	.641**	.300	.460**	−.351*	−.401*
TEA Male 2006–8							.609**	−.625**	−.601**	−.595**	−.565**	.104	.035	−.470**	−.521**	.728**	.687**	.349*	.508**	−.332*	−.393*
TEA Ratio F/M 2006–8								−.615**	−.593**	−.597**	−.557**	−.025	.078	−.464**	−.520**	.364*	.335*	.101	.306	−.266	−.301
HDI 2005									.999**	.992**	.976**	−.152	−.061	.753**	.810**	−.454**	−.559**	−.102	−.263	.538**	.612**
GDI 2005										.992**	.977**	−.100	−.048	.767**	.821**	−.439**	−.519**	−.076	−.291	.505**	.583**
HDI 2008											.984**	−.152	−.058	.745**	.812**	−.442**	−.526**	−.082	−.284	.515**	.590**
GDI 2008												−.128	.121	.739**	.804**	−.400*	−.482**	−.052	−.272	.491**	.567**
GDI/HDI Ratio 2005													.136	−.053	−.047	.135	.329*	.092	−.104	−.405*	−.402*
GDI/HDI Ratio 2008														−.009	−.050	.148	.086	.125	.122	−.027	−.030
GEMPWR 2005															.966**	−.214	−.353*	.005	−.064	.484**	.552**
GEMPWR 2008																−.283	−.386*	−.031	−.147	.508**	.575**
Combined Normative Support																	.746**	.624**	.797**	−.174	−.249
Good Job 2008																		.242	.310	−.385*	−.444**
High Status 2008																			.339*	.015	−.020
Media Attention 2008																				.029	−.036
IEF 2005																					.977**

* $p < 0.05$; ** $p < 0.01$; *** $p < 0.001$

Table 2.2. Summary of entrepreneurship rates by gender, economic, and human development indices 2003–5 and 2006–8

Country Name	GEM Country Group	TEA Female 2003–5	TEA Male 2003–5	TEA Female 2006–8	TEA Male 2006–8	GEM-PWR 2005	GEM-PWR 2008	GDI/HDI 2005	GDI/I-DI 2008	IEF 2005	IEF 2008
Australia	High Income	7.540	12.490	7.853	11.697	0.866	0.847	0.9979	0.9979	79.0	82.2
Austria	High Income	3.640	6.830	1.881	3.040	0.748	0.788	0.9852	0.9769	68.8	71.4
Belgium	High Income	2.030	4.980	1.572	4.182	0.841	0.85	0.9937	0.9905	69.0	71.7
Canada	High Income	4.660	10.950	5.955	7.755	0.829	0.82	0.9948	0.9907	75.8	80.2
Denmark	High Income	2.950	7.390	3.375	6.752	0.887	0.875	0.9947	0.9937	75.3	79.2
Finland	High Income	2.530	4.740	4.468	8.309	0.892	0.887	0.9947	0.9948	71.0	74.6
France	High Income	2.240	5.000	2.025	4.715	0.78	0.718	0.9979	0.9969	60.5	64.7
Germany	High Income	2.650	5.740	3.033	4.865	0.852	0.831	0.9957	0.9968	68.1	70.6
Greece	High Income	3.420	9.210	5.256	10.387	0.691	0.622	0.9957	0.9926	59.0	60.6
Hong Kong	High Income	1.630	4.200	4.915	12.298			0.9883	0.9926	89.5	89.7
Iceland	High Income	6.940	14.280	6.178	14.873	0.881	0.862	0.9938	0.9948	76.6	75.8
Ireland	High Income	3.990	10.970	4.668	10.696	0.727	0.699	0.9802	0.9333	80.8	82.5
Israel	High Income	3.870	7.260	3.249	6.830	0.662	0.66	0.9946		62.6	66.3
Italy	High Income	2.480	4.870	2.784	5.599	0.734	0.693	0.9947	0.9937	64.9	62.6
Japan	High Income	1.000	2.750	2.772	3.659	0.575	0.557	0.9885	0.9874	67.3	73.0
Netherlands	High Income	1.980	5.370	2.828	5.731	0.872	0.859	0.9979	0.9927	72.9	77.4
Norway	High Income	3.070	9.680	3.923	8.820	0.915	0.91	0.9886	0.9897	64.5	68.6
Portugal	High Income	3.900	3.820	5.963	11.688	0.741	0.692	0.9978	0.992	62.4	63.9
Singapore	High Income	3.930	8.170	3.221	6.230	0.782	0.761		0.9793	88.6	87.3
Slovenia	High Income	1.920	4.900	2.962	7.461	0.625	0.611	0.9967	0.9967	59.6	60.2
South Africa	High Income	3.980	5.010	4.801	6.962			0.9896	0.5896	62.9	63.4

Spain	High Income	3.420	7.190	5.640	8.680	0.825	0.794	0.9947	0.9958	67.0	69.1
Sweden	High Income	1.810	4.520	1.913	4.377	0.925	0.906	0.999	1	69.8	70.8
Switzerland	High Income	4.430	7.490	4.967	7.586	0.829	0.66	0.9906	0.9906	79.3	79.5
United Kingdom	High Income	3.080	7.530	3.158	6.887	0.786	0.783	0.9979	0.9989	79.2	79.4
United States	High Income	7.090	13.050	6.807	10.351	0.769	0.762	0.9853	0.9863	79.9	81.0
Argentina	Low/Middle Income	8.260	16.220	9.406	13.748	0.692	0.728	0.9954	0.9953	51.7	54.2
Brazil	Low/Middle Income	11.400	14.150	11.115	13.174	0.498	0.49	0.9975	0.9963	61.7	56.2
Chile	Low/Middle Income	11.370	15.580	8.805	13.958	0.521	0.519	0.9908	0.9897	77.8	78.6
China	Low/Middle Income	11.020	14.070	13.515	18.724	0.526	0.534	0.9987	0.9974	53.7	53.1
Croatia	Low/Middle Income	1.410	5.400	3.678	8.348	0.622	0.612	0.9976	0.9965	51.9	54.1
Ecuador	Low/Middle Income	23.690	29.690	15.877	18.498	0.605	0.6			52.9	55.2
Hungary	Low/Middle Income	2.790	3.230	4.531	8.347	0.586	0.569	0.9977	0.9977	63.5	67.6
Jamaica	Low/Middle Income	13.760	17.050	15.680	17.785	0.526		0.9946	0.9948	67.0	65.7
Latvia	Low/Middle Income	4.630	7.970	2.924	8.751	0.644	0.619	0.9977	0.9988	66.3	68.3
Mexico	Low/Middle Income	4.290	7.080	7.847	9.679	0.603	0.589	0.9891	0.9917	65.2	66.2
Peru	Low/Middle Income	38.770	40.510	29.857	30.911	0.627	0.636	0.9948	0.9949	61.3	63.8
Thailand	Low/Middle Income	19.280	22.060	21.587	21.918	0.506	0.472	0.9974	0.9987	62.5	62.3
Venezuela	Low/Middle Income	22.630	26.250	15.854	22.620	0.577	0.542	0.9937	0.9891	45.2	44.7

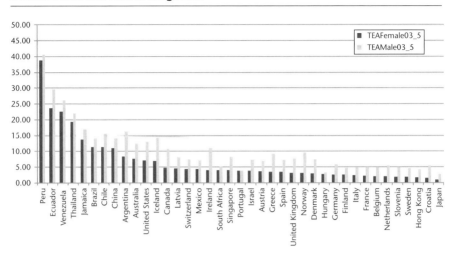

Figure 2.1 Early-stage entrepreneurial activity (TEA) by country and gender (2003–5)

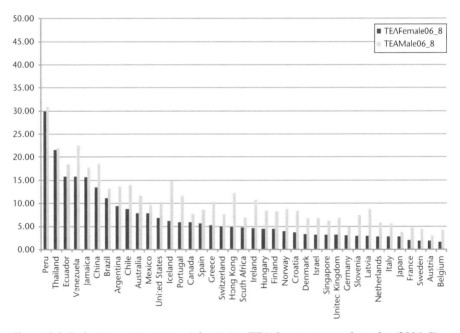

Figure 2.2 Early-stage entrepreneurial activity (TEA) by country and gender (2006–8)

transition economies in Eastern Europe. These countries resemble more closely their high income neighboring countries than low/middle income countries in Asia or Latin America.

Figure 2.3 shows that the expected U-shaped curve emerges when per capita GDP is plotted against the rate of early stage entrepreneurship (TEA) for men and women (2006–8). This was the case for both time periods and the

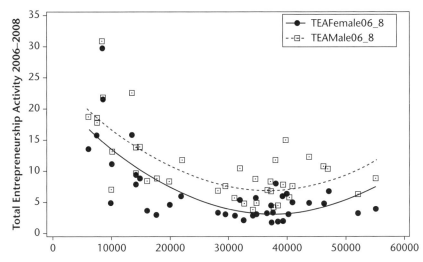

Figure 2.3 Early-stage entrepreneurial activity (TEA) by gender (2006–8) by country per capita GDP level (2006 US$)

differences between the coefficients of the fitted curves were statistically significant ($p = 0.041$). In other words, as expected, the rate of early-stage entrepreneurship in a country is related to its level of per capita income. Specifically, early-stage entrepreneurship is higher in contexts where per capita income is low and tapers off as per capita income rises, only to increase again as levels of per capita income above a critical threshold level are considered. Further, we find that when only women are considered, the curve shifts downward to reflect lower prevalence rates for women than men but, still, it retains its shape. This suggests that, overall, the relationship between female entrepreneurship and average per capita GDP is similar to that of men albeit, at low levels of income the two curves become closer to reflect a narrowing of the gender gap due to women's more than proportional presence among necessity entrepreneurs. As might be expected, the U-shaped pattern also holds with respect to the ratio of female to male entrepreneurship in relation to per capita GDP.

Summaries of the TEA and ratio of female/male TEA by GDP income groups are given in Figures 2.4 and 2.5. TEA rates are significantly different between GDP income groups and between genders ($p < 0.001$ for both) but there was no significant difference between the two time periods. Also, there was no significant interaction between gender and GDP income group using ANOVA. Figure 2.5 shows the ratio of female/male TEA by time period and GDP income group. There is a significant difference between country groups at each time

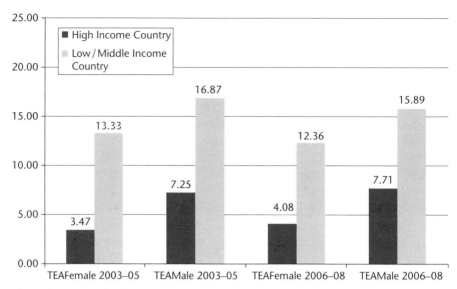

Figure 2.4 Rates of early stage entrepreneurial activity in high and low/middle income countries by gender (2003–5 and 2006–8)

Results of ANOVA comparing gender, country income group, and year group:
$p < 0.001$ comparing gender; $p < 0.001$ comparing country group; $p =$ NS comparing year group

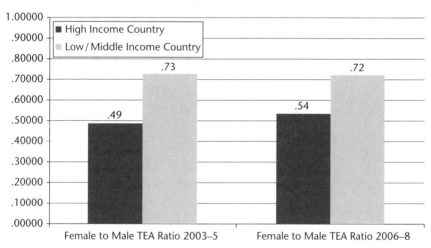

Figure 2.5 Ratio of female to male early stage entrepreneurship (TEA) for 2003–5 and 2006–8

Results of ANOVA comparing country income group and year group:
$p < 0.001$ comparing country group; $p =$ NS comparing year group

period with low/middle income countries showing more parity between genders (0.73 and 0.72 for each time period) than high income countries (0.49 and 0.54 for each time period). It should be noted that the slightly higher parity in the 2006–8 time period is due to the fact that female TEA increased slightly whereas male TEA decreased slightly.

To sum up, our descriptive statistics suggest a U-shaped relationship between per capita income and the rate of business start-up in a country that is consistent across genders but characterized by more pronounced rates among men. Also, while there is a persistent gender entrepreneurship gap across all the countries studied, the context of developing economies has the effect of narrowing that gap as the comparatively stronger impact of poverty on women has the effect of increasing their participation in entrepreneurship relative to men.

Given the gender entrepreneurship gap, we next consider the institutional support factors that may influence the rate and level of women's entrepreneurship. In particular, we want to consider how normative support for gender parity in a country may influence the supply of women entrepreneurs. Understanding that economic development will be a significant predictor of the participation of female entrepreneurs (Baughn, Chua, and Neupert 2006), we use a model to control for per capita GDP and to test the influence of the various dimensions of a country's institutional support on women's entrepreneurial propensity.

2.4.2 Institutional support for entrepreneurship

Institutional support in a country is hypothesized to have an impact on the rate of early stage entrepreneurship through regulatory and normative effects. We use the IEF as an indicator of regulatory institutional support for entrepreneurship. As a measure of normative institutional support, instead, we use a composite measure of social attitudes toward entrepreneurship. This variable was constructed using GEM survey data as described earlier. Both the IEF and the composite measure of social attitudes toward entrepreneurship are presented in Table 2.1 and show positive correlations with the rate of entrepreneurship. Consistently with existing literature, this suggests that a country's rate of early-stage entrepreneurship will be positively associated to regulatory and normative institutional support for entrepreneurial activity that promotes personal and economic freedoms. We next turn to gender specific indicators of institutional support and investigate the impact of these indicators with respect to the rate and proportion of women entrepreneurs across all countries in our sample.

Gender differences in accepted active participation in various social and economic realms are a function of social norms. Thus, normative support for gender parity may be expected to influence not only women's entrepreneurship rates but also the proportion of a country's entrepreneurs who are women. Looking at Table 2.2, we see no significant correlation between the GDI/HDI ratio and TEA rates for women (or men) in either time period. The GEMPWR, however, shows significant negative correlations. This suggests that as gender equity rises, entrepreneurial activity rates fall, regardless of gender. Because GEMPWR is highly and positively correlated to per capita GDP, it may be that these correlations are simply masking an income effect. Indeed the United Nations notes that it is impossible for a low-income country to have a high GEMPWR score and vice versa (see http://hdr.undp.org/en/ statistics/indices/gdi_gem/). It is important, then, to control for income in assessing the impact of institutional support for gender equity on women's early stage entrepreneurship.

Two hierarchical linear models were fit to the GEM data and the country-level indices data for each time period to examine relationships between GDP, institutional support factors, the ratio of female to male entrepreneurship, and the rate of female early stage entrepreneurship over both time periods. Again due to their similarity, only the results for the 2006–8 time period models are shown. In subsequent stages of the model we controlled for country income, for regulatory and normative institutional support, and last for gender specific institutional support. That is, GDP was entered in the first stage of the model, the IEF and the composite measure of social attitudes (called "combined normative support") factors were added in the second stage of the model, and the GEMPWR and the GDI/HDI ratio were entered in the final stage of the model. The results are shown in Table 2.3. Using this hierarchical method allows for the examination of the incremental effect of the indices after controlling for the country's GDP. The models fit very well with adjusted R-squares of 0.633 and 0.567, for the proportion and rate of women's early stage entrepreneurship, respectively.

In both models, per capita GDP has a negative coefficient, suggesting an inverse relationship between GDP per capita and the rate and proportion of women's early stage entrepreneurship. This is consistent with existing literature. The intuition is that poverty is associated to a stronger supply of women entrepreneurs. Recalling the U-shaped relationship between per capita GDP and both overall TEA rates, as well as the ratio of female to male TEA, it is not surprising to see a negative coefficient for per capita GDP in these models. Since per capita GDP is highly significant at the $p < 0.001$ level, it is also not a surprise that it exhibits greater heterogeneity across countries than do some of the other factors.

The most significant factor in both models is the composite social attitudes factor indicating normative institutional support for entrepreneurship. The composite factor has a highly significant relationship ($p < 0.001$) with both the

Table 2.3. Hierarchical models

2.3a. Hierarchical model predicting the ratio of female to male early stage entrepreneurship

	Model 1	Model 2	Model 3
GDP 2008	−.714***	−.650*	−.860*
IEF		.268*	.257*
Combined norm. support		.078***	.118***
GEMPWR			−.027*
GDI/HDI			−.374***
	Model Diagnostics		
F-statistic	38.555	16.571	14.097
R-square	.510	.534	.501
Adjusted R-square	.497	.501	.633

2.3b. Hierarchical model predicting the percentage of early stage female entrepreneurship

	Model 1	Model 2	Model 3
GDP 2008	−.645***	−.385*	−.472*
IEF		.114**	0.113
Combined norm. support		.497***	.489***
GEMPWR			−.090*
GDI/HDI			−.016
	Model Diagnostics		
F-statistic	26.369	19.034	10.964
R-square	.416	.620	.624
Adjusted R-square	.400	.587	.567

* $p < 0.05$;
** $p < 0.01$;
*** $p < 0.001$

proportion and rate of women's entrepreneurship. As shown in Table 2.1 (where it is labeled "combined normative support"), the composite social attitudes factor is significantly and negatively correlated to per capita GDP, reinforcing our intuition that low income economies may place a premium on the notion of being a "self-made" person since more people are forced to create their own employment outside of the established labor market. Further, in both models, regulatory and economic freedom has a positive and significant relationship to the ratio of female to male early stage entrepreneurship and to the rate of women's early stage entrepreneurship. This suggests that regulatory support is important in understanding the gender gap in entrepreneurship.

In the final stage of the models, we examine how normative support for gender parity may influence the gender entrepreneurship gap. Both the rate and proportion of women's early stage entrepreneurship are associated significantly to the two indicators of normative gender support. The indicator of gender disparity (GDI/HDI) shows a negative and highly significant relationship with respect to the share of women's entrepreneurship, but loses significance as a predictor of the prevalence of women's entrepreneurship. Looking

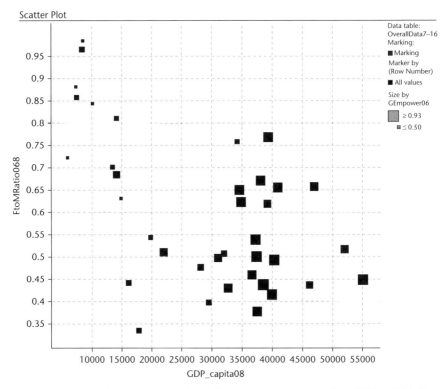

Scatter Plot

Data table:
OverallData7–16
Marking:
■ Marking
Marker by
(Row Number)
■ All values
Size by
GEmpower06
▨ ≥ 0.93
▪ ≤ 0.50

Figure 2.6 Ratio of female to male early stage entrepreneurship (TEA) 2006–8 vs US$GDP 2008 by GEMPWR 2008* (size)

*data unavailable for South Africa and Hong Kong

Minimum GEMPWR = 0.506 for Thailand; Maximum GEMPWR = 0.925 for Sweden

next at GEMPWR, we see a significant and negative relationship with respect to both the proportion and rate of women's early stage entrepreneurship. Given the significant correlation between GEMPWR and GDP per capita, this is not surprising. Specifically, for each country, Figure 2.6 depicts the ratio of female to male early stage entrepreneurship (TEA) against per capita GDP, with the value of GEMPWR represented by the size of the symbol. Values close to one indicate a small gender gap in entrepreneurship (regardless of the actual rate). Low/middle income countries are clustered in the upper left part of the figure showing they have the highest TEA ratios but also the lowest GEMPWR values. A very rough U-shaped relationship could also be hypothesized.

Figure 2.7, instead, depicts TEA rates for men and women against per capita GDP, with the value of the GEMPWR again represented by the size of the symbol. Not surprisingly, high income countries have higher GEMPWR and lower TEA. Moreover, GEMPWR is somewhat relevant for both male and

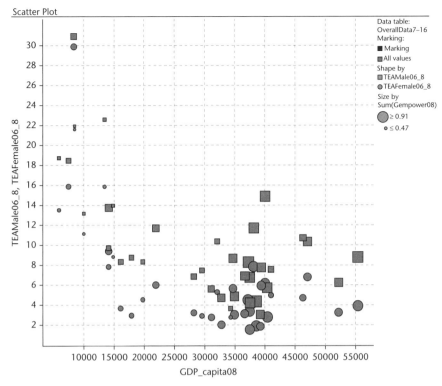

Figure 2.7 Total early stage entrepreneurship (TEA) by gender 2006–8 (shape) vs GDP per capita 2006 by GEMPWR (size)*

*data unavailable for South Africa and Hong Kong
Minimum GEMPWR = 0.49 for Brazil; Maximum GEMPWR = 0.93 for Sweden

female early stage entrepreneurship. Thus, despite the negative signs GEMPWR and GDI/HDI have in the models, our results suggest that gender parity does have a positive influence even after controlling for income effects.

Overall, our analysis confirms the existence of a persistent gender gap in early stage entrepreneurship and of a somewhat U-shaped relationship between per capita GDP and both the relative (female to male TEA ratio) and absolute (TEA rate) proportions of women in early stage entrepreneurship. Regulatory and normative institutional dimensions supporting entrepreneurial activity appear to play a significant role with respect to the gender gap in entrepreneurship, with social attitudes, in particular, showing a strong association with the proportion and rate of women's entrepreneurship in a country. Less clear, but nonetheless significant, is the role of gender empowerment and gender parity as normative institutional dimensions. Gender empowerment seems to follow a U-shaped relationship to both the proportion and rate of women's entrepreneurship, similar to that of per capita GDP. Gender parity, as measured in our model, instead, appears to have a significant negative influence on the proportion of women's early stage entrepreneurship but not on their prevalence rate.

2.5 Discussion and limitations

Only recently have studies begun to focus on understanding gender and entrepreneurship at the macro level. Using data from thirty-nine countries we extend that line of research.

First, our analysis confirms the existence of a persistent gender gap in entrepreneurship for all countries in our sample and provides some exploratory evidence on women's participation in early stage entrepreneurship. We confirm the existence of a U-shaped relationship between a country's rate of early stage entrepreneurship and per capita GDP and add that while the U-shaped relationship holds for both women and men, it holds with higher levels of involvement for men than women in all countries in our sample. This U-shaped relationship can be explained in terms of the supply of early stage entrepreneurs created by low levels of income which give way to alternative employment choices as income rises and wealth spreads in the economy. A similar relationship emerges with respect to the gender gap in entrepreneurship. In fact, the gap is lower in countries with lower per capita GDP where poverty reduces the opportunity costs of self-employment and increases the supply of women entrepreneurs relative to that of men. However, as income rises and women find access to more employment opportunities, the gender gap increases until a critical threshold level of per capita GDP, beyond which highly educated and experienced women return to entrepreneurship by choice rather than necessity.

Second, our analysis finds evidence that institutional support is significantly associated to the existence of a gender gap in entrepreneurship. The IEF provides one way to assess the relative control an individual has over his or her own labor and property, and is an indicator of the regulatory support for entrepreneurship. Albeit exploratory, our results suggest that the gender gap in entrepreneurship narrows in those countries where economic freedom prevails and individual control is greatest. Social support for business start-up is another significant factor. We use a composite index of social attitudes to assess attitudes toward entrepreneurship as a career choice, whether business success receives media attention and whether those who grow successful businesses receive high status. We find that positive normative attitudes toward entrepreneurship are positively associated to the proportion and rate of women's entrepreneurship. This is observed in low and middle income countries. Perhaps in these countries becoming a self-made man or woman is not only more acceptable, it is also a necessity. In fact, we know that women are over-represented among necessity entrepreneurs, especially in low/middle income countries (Minniti, Arenius, and Langowitz 2005). Unfortunately, our data do not allow us to establish a causal relationship between these variables. While it has been argued that institutional support may be less relevant in countries where individuals are pushed into entrepreneurship by need (Baughn, Chua, and Neupert 2006), we wonder whether institutional support in the form of normative positive attitudes towards entrepreneurship is the result of economic necessity. In fact, the positive attitude in favor of entrepreneurship is clearly an endogenous variable and our results may have more to do with survival than with wealth creation.

Finally, we investigate the more nuanced relationship between the gender gap in entrepreneurship and support for gender empowerment. In the poorest contexts, necessity creates a comparatively high supply of female entrepreneurs which declines as per capita income rises. However, our results also show that a positive upturn does occur beyond a critical threshold level of GDP. We hypothesize that women may be empowered to make choices. We suggest that the effect of normative support for gender parity that enables women to exercise individual control and participate more equally in the social and economic realms has the effect of enabling wider career choices for women, both entrepreneurial and traditional, in high income contexts where economic choices are possible. By contrast, it may be that in low income contexts, poverty trumps all. If we are correct in our hypotheses, gender empowerment will be associated with female entrepreneurial activity. The direction of such association, however, is not yet clear. Our results are clearly exploratory and more work is needed in this important area.

There are of course limitations to our analysis. GEM data are probably the largest set of data on entrepreneurial dynamics. However, the number of developing countries included in our sample is still relatively small. Further, the indices used in this chapter each have their own limitations. The IEF, for example, is a composite index of ten dimensions of freedom, each with its own sub-factors. The ten dimensions are given equal weight in the composite index. This, however, may not be the appropriate weighting distribution to represent institutional support for entrepreneurship. Similarly, while the United Nations Development Programme (UNDP) has worked hard to create strong measures of gender empowerment and equity, each of the indices has particular flaws. The GEMPWR uses estimated earned income to measure economic participation and, as a result, a poor country can never achieve a high value for the GEMPWR, nor can a high income country ever exhibit a very low one. This may inherently overweight the role of poverty in our findings while suppressing the effect of other factors in the index which support gender empowerment. In an alternative, the GDI/HDI is the preferred method espoused by the UNDP for gauging gender inequality. However, it has a known tendency to reflect only small differences which may explain its diminished effect observed in our models.

Despite these limitations, and the exploratory nature of our results, because of the broad scope of our data, this chapter has uncovered several starting points for future research. It has also shed a new light on the relationship between income and early stage entrepreneurial activity. Poverty has the effect of masking gender equity, as it narrows the gender gap in entrepreneurship in low-income countries where normative support for gender parity tends to be lower. In general, our intuition is that a focus on economic development through greater normative support for entrepreneurship will benefit both women and men, as well as reduce the gender gap in entrepreneurship. In fact, as countries transition to higher levels of income, our analysis suggests that they may expect normative support for gender equity to be associated, among other things, to higher rates of female entrepreneurship.

Acknowledgments

The authors wish to thank the Center for Women's Leadership at Babson College and the Babson College Faculty Research Fund for their financial support of this work. Many thanks go to an anonymous reviewer for helpful comments. Although GEM data were used in this study, their interpretation and use are the sole responsibility of the authors. All errors are ours.

References

Achtenhagen, L. and Welter, F. (2003), Female Entrepreneurship in Germany: Context, Development and its Reflection in German Media, in J. Butler (ed.), *New Perspectives on Women Entrepreneurs* (pp. 77–100), Greenwich, CT: Information Age Publishing.

Alvesson, M. and Billing, Y. D. (1997), *Understanding Gender and Organizations,* Thousand Oaks, CA: Sage.

Arenius, P. and Minniti, M. (2005), Perceptual Variables and Nascent Entrepreneurship, *Small Business Economics,* 24: 233–47.

Audretsch, D. B. (2007), Entrepreneurship: A Survey of the Literature for Public Policy, *International Journal of Entrepreneurship Education,* 5: 3–72.

Audretsch, D. B., Grilo, I., and Thurik, A. R. (2007), *The Handbook of Entrepreneurship Policy,* New York: Springer.

Baron, R., Markman, G., and Hirza, A. (2001), Perceptions of Women and Men as Entrepreneurs: Evidence for Differential Effects of Attributional Augmenting, *Journal of Applied Psychology,* 86(5): 923–9.

Baughn, C. C., Chua, B., and Neupert, K. (2006), The Normative Context for Women's Participation in Entrepreneurship: A Multicountry Study. *Entrepreneurship Theory and Practice*, 30(5): 687–708.

Baumol, W. J. (1990), Entrepreneurship: Productive, Unproductive, and Destructive, *Journal of Political Economy*, 98: 893–921.

Bird, B. and Brush, C. (2002), A Gendered Perspective on Organizational Creation, *Entrepreneurship Theory and Practice*, 26(3): 41–66.

Blanchflower, D. G. (2004), *Self-Employment: More May Not Be Better,* NBER Working Paper No.10286, Cambridge, MA: National Bureau of Economic Research.

Bosma, N., Acs, Z. J., Autio, E., Coduras, A., and Levie, J. (2009), *Global Entrepreneurship Monitor: 2008 Executive Report,* available at *http://www.gemconsortium.org.*

Bowen, H. P. and De Clercq, D. (2008), Institutional Context and the Allocation of Entrepreneurial Effort, *Journal of International Business Studies,* 39: 747–67.

Brush, C. (1997), Women-owned Businesses: Obstacles and Opportunities, *Journal of Developmental Entrepreneurship*, 2(1): 1–24.

Bruton, G. D., Fried, V. H., and Manigart, S. (2005), Institutional Influences on the Worldwide Expansion of Venture Capital, *Entrepreneurship Theory and Practice*, 29(6): 737–60.

Busenitz, L. W., Gomez, C., and Spencer, J. (2000), Country Institutional Profiles: Unlocking Entrepreneurial Phenomena, *Academy of Management Journal*, 43(5): 994–1003.

Carree, M. A. and Thurik, A.R. (2006), *Entrepreneurship and Economic Growth,* Cheltenham, UK: Edward Elgar Publishing Limited.

Carree, M. A., Van Stel, A., Thurik, A. R., and Wennekers, A. R. M. (2002), "Economic Development and Business Ownership," *Small Business Economics*, 19(3): 271–90.

Carter, N. M. and Rosa, P. (1998), The Financing of Male and Female Owned Business, *Entrepreneurship and Regional Development,* 10(3): 225–41.

Carter, N. M., Williams, M., and Reynolds, P. D. (1997), Discontinuance Among New Firms in Retail: The Influence of Initial Resources, Strategy and Gender, *Journal of Business Venturing,* 12(2): 125–45.

Davidsson, P. (1995), Culture, Structure and Regional Levels of Entrepreneurship, *Entrepreneurship and Regional Development,* 7: 41–62.

Davidsson, P. and Wiklund, J. (1997), Values, Beliefs and Regional Variations in New Firm Formation Rates, *Journal of Economic Psychology,* 18: 179–99.

Emrich, C., Denmark, F., and Den Hartog, D. (2004), Cross-cultural differences in gender egalitarianism, in R. House, P. Hanges, P. Dorfman, M. Javidan, and V. Gupta (eds.), *Culture, Leadership, and Organizations: The GLOBE Study of 62 Societies* (pp. 343–94). Thousand Oaks, CA: Sage Publications.

Evans, D. and Jovanovic, B. (1989), An Estimated Model of Entrepreneurial Choice Under Liquidity Constraints, *Journal of Political Economy,* 97: 808–27.

Fagenson, E. and Marcus, E. (1991), Perceptions of the Sex-role Stereotypic Characteristics of Entrepreneurs: Women's Evaluations, *Entrepreneurship Theory and Practice,* 15(4): 33–47.

Grilo, I. and Irigoyen, J. (2006), Entrepreneurship in the EU: To Wish and Not to Be, *Small Business Economics,* 26(4): 305–18.

Harper, D. (1998), Institutional Conditions for Entrepreneurship, *Advances in Austrian Economics,* 5: 241–75.

Jianakoplos, N. A. and Bernasek, A. (1998), Are Women More Risk Averse? *Economic Inquiry,* 36(4): 620–30.

Langowitz, N. S. and Minniti, M. (2007), The Entrepreneurial Propensity of Women, *Entrepreneurship Theory and Practice,* 31(3): 341–64.

Langowitz, N. S. and Morgan, C. (2003), Women entrepreneurs: Breaking Through the Glass Barrier, in J. Butler (ed.), *New Perspectives on Women Entrepreneurs* (pp. 101–19), Greenwich, CT: Information Age Publishing.

Langowitz, N. S., Sharpe, N., and Godwyn, M. (2006), Women's Business Centers in the United States: Effective Entrepreneurship Training and Policy Implementation, *Journal of Small Business and Entrepreneurship,* 19(2): 167–82.

Lévesque, M. and Minniti, M. (2006), The Effect of Aging on Entrepreneurial Behavior, *Journal of Business Venturing,* 21(2): 177–94.

Lorber, J. (1994), *Paradoxes of Gender,* New Haven, CT: Yale University Press.

McGrath, R. G., MacMillan, I. C., and Scheinberg, S. (1992), Elitists, Risk-Takers and Rugged Individualists? An Exploratory Analysis of Cultural Differences Between Entrepreneurs and Non-Entrepreneurs, *Journal of Business Venturing,* 7(2): 115–36.

McGrath, R. G., MacMillan, I. C., Yang, E. A., and Tsai, W. (1992b), Does Culture Endure, or is it Malleable? Issues for Entrepreneurial Economic Development, *Journal of Business Venturing,* 7(2): 441–58.

Miller, T. and Holmes, K. (2009), *Index of Economic Freedom,* Washington, D.C.: The Heritage Foundation; Appendix, 441–452, available at http://www.heritage.org/Index/PDF/Index09_Methodology.pdf

Minniti, M., Arenius, P., and Langowitz, N. (2005), *Global Entrepreneurship Monitor 2004 Report on Women and Entrepreneurship.* Babson Park, MA: Center for Women's Leadership at Babson College.

Mueller, S. L. (2004), Gender Gaps in Potential for Entrepreneurship Across Countries and Cultures, *Journal of Developmental Entrepreneurship,* 9(3): 199–220.

Mueller, S. L. and Thomas, A. S. (2001), Culture and Entrepreneurial Potential: A Nine Country Study of Locus of Control and Innovativeness, *Journal of Business Venturing,* 16(1): 51–75.

North, D. C. (1990), *Institutions, Institutional Change and Economic Performance,* Cambridge, UK: Cambridge University Press.

Reynolds, P. D., Camp, S. M., Bygrave, W. D., Autio, E., and Hay, M. (2001), *Global Entrepreneurship Monitor: 2001 Executive Report,* available at *http://www.gemconsortium. org.*

Reynolds, P. D., Storey, D. J., and Westhead, P. (1994), Cross-National Comparisons of the Variation in New Firm Formation Rates, *Regional Studies,* 28(4): 443–56.

Ridgeway, C. L. and Correll, S. J. (2000), Limiting inequality through interaction: The end(s) of gender, *Contemporary Sociology,* 29: 110–20.

Ross, L. and Nisbett, R. E. (1991), *The Person and the Situation: Perspectives of Social Psychology,* New York: McGraw-Hill.

Scott, W. R. (1995), *Institutions and Organizations,* Thousand Oaks, CA: Sage.

Shane, S. (1993), Cultural Influences on National Rates of Innovation, *Journal of Business Venturing,* 8: 59–73.

Smallbone, D. and Welter, F. (2001), The Distinctiveness of Entrepreneurship in Transition Economies, *Small Business Economics,* 16(4): 249–62.

Thomas, A. S. and Mueller, S. L. (2001), A Case for Comparative Entrepreneurship: Assessing the Relevance of Culture, *Journal of International Business Studies,* 31(2): 287–301.

Verheul, I. and Thurik, A. R. (2001), Start-Up Capital: Does Gender Matter? *Small Business Economics,* 16: 329–45.

Verheul, I., Van Stel, A., and Thurik, A. R. (2006), Explaining Female and Male Entrepreneurship at the Country Level, *Entrepreneurship and Regional Development,* 18(2): 151–83.

Verheul, I., Wennekers, A. R. M., Audretsch, D. B., and Thurik, A.R. (2002), An Eclectic Theory of Entrepreneurship, in D.B. Audretsch, A. R. Thurik, I. Verheul, and A. R. M. Wennekers (eds.), *Entrepreneurship: Determinants and Policy in a European-US Comparison,* Boston/Dordecht: Kluwer Academic Publishers.

Watkins, K. (2005), *Human Development Report 2005,* New York: United Nations Development Programme.

Watkins, K. (2008), *Human Development Report 2007/08,* New York: United Nations Development Programme.

Welter, F., Smallbone, D., Aculai, E., Isakova, N., and Schakirova, N. (2003), Female Entrepreneurship in post-Soviet Countries, in J. Butler (ed.), *New Perspectives on Women Entrepreneurs* (pp. 243–69). Greenwich, CT: Information Age Publishing.

Wennekers, S., Van Stel, A., Thurik, A. R., and Reynolds, P. (2005), Nascent Entrepreneurship and the Level of Economic Development, *Small Business Economics,* 24(3): 293–309.

3

Defining and Identifying Family Entrepreneurship: A New View of Entrepreneurs

Ramona K. Zachary, Edward G. Rogoff, and Ivory Phinisee

3.1 Introduction

Family business is as old as civilization itself. Yet, family entrepreneurship as a field of academic study is relatively new. Only very recently scholars have begun to posit an expanded understanding of entrepreneurship (Rogoff and Heck 2003), and a few have begun to show that, worldwide, the family firm is the most prevalent business structure (Heck and Trent 1999; International Family Enterprise Research Academy (IFERA) 2003; Morck and Yeung 2004). In fact, although studying the entrepreneur is important, it represents only part of the entrepreneurial phenomenon and a new approach based on the concept of family entrepreneurship may be the most accurate description of most businesses throughout the world (Danes et al. 2008; Heck et al. 2006; Rogoff and Heck 2003; Stafford et al. 1999).

The term family entrepreneurship has many meanings and applications; however, in the very least, it is used to describe the *role of family in entrepreneurial activities* of all types (Heck et al. 2008). This chapter focuses on the importance of the family context from which entrepreneurial behaviors emerge, and its overriding purpose is to define and identify family entrepreneurship worldwide. As a result, we focus on the prevalence or occurrence of family entrepreneurship itself. The emphasis of the chapter will be descriptive in nature in an attempt to fully explore the dimensions of this important phenomenon across countries for the first time.

The importance, role, and definitions relative to families and entrepreneurship will be explored and critiqued. Previous research models and findings will be examined and compared to their relative emphasis on the family system. Finally, using data from twenty-eight countries that participated in the Global Entrepreneurship Monitor (GEM) project in 2008, the population of entrepreneurs in the sample will be analyzed by stratifying them into two groups: family entrepreneurs and non-family entrepreneurs. Differences in levels of entrepreneurship activity, household income, age, education, and gender will be examined. Further, business motivations and industry sectors will be investigated. The chapter will reveal the role of family in entrepreneurial activities, the family dimension of entrepreneurial behavior worldwide, and conclude with recommendations and suggestions for future research.

3.2 Conceptual frameworks and definitions

The importance, role, and conceptualization of family entrepreneurship are critical to our understanding of how entrepreneurial activity not only emerges but sustains itself via its interactions with environmental contexts both near and far. Conceptually, after years of studies centered on the entrepreneur as an individual, scholars have begun re-examining the entrepreneur through a wider lens. What has been revealed is that focusing only on the entrepreneur provides an incomplete picture of the entrepreneurial phenomenon, and scholars can no longer ignore a broader and more comprehensive view of entrepreneurial activity namely, the role played by family entrepreneurship (Danes et al. 2008).

3.2.1 *The evolution of family entrepreneurship as a field of study*

Since the beginning of the human experience, families have been the ubiquitous social unit. Beyond the biological necessity of reproducing and maintaining our societies, families are the most important sources of human capital, social capital, financial capital, and physical capital. Indeed, throughout history, families have been central to the vital processes that create and operate businesses. Worldwide, from ancient to modern times, and from agricultural and cottage industries to multinational corporations, family ownership is pervasive (IFERA 2003). Morck and Yeung (2004), for example, note that in some countries, like Mexico, family firms make up about 100% of all firms, in others, like Sweden, they represent about 50% of all firms, and in yet others, such as the United States and the United Kingdom, family firms are a minority. The reasons why family entrepreneurship has long been ignored stem from the fact that most business research has historically been industry based in its samples and methodologies, leaving a long legacy of segmented and disjointed studies which are most often industry or market specific.

Only a few notable exceptions existed for many years. However, although they gave some early recognition to businesses who involved family members, these early exceptions were predominantly business consultants or otherwise people observing the nature of business in general. Donnelley (1964) was likely the first to define, though quite narrowly, a family business. His definition included one or more of the following conditions: (1) existence of family relationships as a key factor in succession; (2) presence of family member on board of directors; (3) reflection of family values in business; (4) actions of family member reflected on reputation of business; (5) presence of relatives involved and who felt obligated to hold stock for more than financial reasons; (6) relationship between family members' positions in the business and their standing in the family; and (7) entering the firm being part of family members' career decisions. Donnelley's definition reflected early consulting observations of family businesses but was burdensome in meaning, empirically complicated to implement, and was not utilized in subsequent research studies.

About ten years later, Hershon (1976) suggested that, in the US, half of the gross national product (GNP) was produced by family firms and that these firms employed half of the workforce. However, neither of these initial acknowledgments of family entrepreneurship looked beyond the business setting. Similarly, Lansberg (1988), Brockhaus (1994), Dyer and Handler (1994), and Hoy and Verser (1994), who followed them, prioritized the business aspects of the family business, but did not explore the owning family. Their models were very simplistic, unbalanced toward the business, and limited in their depictions of the owning family. Equally myopic, early researchers in family studies rarely recognized the presence of business ownership within the families studied. Finally, classical family systems theory (Bowen 1985) developed from clinical work with actual families, but did not include any specific recognition that owning and operating a business might alter family life.

Twenty years after Donnelley's work, and from the perspective of family sociology, the qualitative research on family businesses by Rosenblatt et al. (1985) explored both the family system and the business system, and included the overlap between these systems, tensions, role carryovers, compensation, management of the business, working with relatives, and succession and inheritance. By 1993, Cramton identified the missing perspective in most business research of family firms and forged a new path by bringing both family and business perspectives together to explore the uniqueness of a family firm and the vital role that families play in the creation, operation, growth, maturity, and succession of most businesses. Unfortunately, since then, still little attention has been paid to how family dynamics affect the fundamental entrepreneurial process, particularly in business research (notable exceptions are Aldrich and Cliff 2003; Rogoff and Heck 2003).

These pioneers' early recognition of the role of family in entrepreneurship led family economists and family studies researchers to attempt the simultaneous and comprehensive study of both the family and the business (Sharma 2004). Among others, Heck (1998a; 1998b) discussed the phenomenon of an entrepreneurial family and suggested the notion that both the family and the business were equal contributors to the family firm. In the late 1990s, along lines similar to Cramton's (1993), the Family Business Research Group (FBRG) began developing its conceptualizations of the first nationally representative sample of US family businesses. The project used a household sampling frame and developed the 1997 National Family Business Survey (1997 NFBS) (Stafford et al. 1999; Winter et al. 1998). This conceptualization yielded the Sustainable Family Business Theory (SFBT), which was hailed as innovative because of its ability to delineate both functional families and profitable businesses (Trent and Astrachan 1999). Using a household sampling perspective was deemed as "[possibly] one of the biggest methodological breakthroughs since the founding of the family business field" (Astrachan and Kurtz 1998, p. v). Finally, researchers had available a model and high quality data to begin studying of the role of family in entrepreneurship.

3.2.2 Conceptual frameworks of the family firm

A number of conceptualizations and theories are applicable to the notion of "*family entrepreneurship.*" These include, in descending chronological order: (a) the Sustainable Family Business Theory Model (SFBT Model) (Danes et al. 2008; Heck et al. 2006; Stafford et al. 1999); (b) the Bulleye model of an open-system approach (Pieper and Klein 2007); (c) the Family Embeddedness Perspective (FEP) (Aldrich and Cliff 2003); (d) the Family Influence, F-PEC Scale (Astrachan, Klein, and Smyrnios 2002); (e) the Theory of Agency and Altruism in Family Firms (TAA) (Schulze, Lubatkin, and Dino 2003); (f) the Resource-Based Framework (Habbershon and Williams 1999); and (g) the Unified Systems Perspective of Family Firm Performance (USP) (Habbershon, Williams, and MacMillan 2003).

Among these frameworks, discipline based frameworks such as TAA attracted significant attention because of their ability to allow a specific representation of economic concepts and theories. Unfortunately they also are less comprehensive in scope (Schulze, Lubatkin, and Dino 2003). Greenwood (2003), for example, argued that economics as a singular framework may not be sufficient. Also, the Bulleye model of an open-system approach (Pieper and Klein 2007), the F-PEC scale (Astrachan, Klein, and Smyrnios 2002), and the notion of familiness (Habbershon, Williams, and MacMillan 2003; Habbershon and Williams 1999) have only succeeded in modeling firm level concepts and associated measures. Thus, these frameworks fall short in identifying or recognizing that the family system in and of itself, is separate from, yet inextricably intertwined with the business system. Simply put, these models are examining family constructs as manifested within the business only, and do not address the family system as a whole.

Other frameworks have sought to integrate a multi-perspective along with greater detail, namely, the FEP (Aldrich and Cliff 2003) and SFBT (Danes et al. 2008; Heck et al. 2006; Stafford et al. 1999), for example, seek to illustrate the relationships between the family system and the business system. Among the frameworks considered above, only the latter two have specified the family system in relation to the business entity, though they each conceptualize these systems and their relationship to each other differently.

In general, the increasing number of research frameworks allows researchers varied approaches based on the scope and depth of the research questions and foci under study. At the same time, researchers must acknowledge the advantages and disadvantages of the framework choice. Research that recognizes both the family system and the business system will offer the most comprehensive examination and are the most likely to increase our future understandings of the family firm and family entrepreneurship (Danes et al. 2008; Dimov 2007; Jennings and McDougald 2007; Heck et al. 2006; Rogoff and Heck 2003). This chapter aims at providing the most comprehensive examination compatible with the available data.

3.3 The role of family in entrepreneurship

From Donnelley (1964) to today's family business definitions (e.g., Pearson, Carr, and Shaw 2008), family entrepreneurship remains in limited use. Most definitions seem to include notions of family ownership, family involvement, family control, and/or the intention to transfer the family firm (Heck and Trent 1999). Some definitions are very limited by the need to have two generations involved in the business while others are very inclusive of any business owned by one or more family members. Litz (1995) identified family businesses conceptually based on ownership, management, and intention to transfer. He developed a classification of nine business types and identified four of the nine types as family businesses or potential family businesses. Along similar lines, Handler (1992) identified four ways in which theorists usually define family business: degree of ownership and/or management by family members, degree of family involvement, potential for generational transfer, or multiple criteria. Although these conceptual works developed new definitions of family business, their definitions were not applied in empirical studies.

The notion of "familiness" has sometimes been employed in the literature. Habbershon and Williams (1999) and others that followed have attempted to identify the influence of the family on and in the business by delineating ways in which the family's factors were present within the business. Family's presence in the business is simply the manifestation of the internal dynamics of the family in and of itself. Pearson, Carr, and Shaw (2008) explored this familiness notion further, but these researchers still only recognize the family presence in the business and do not recognize the presence, importance, and the role the family itself relative to the business or entrepreneurial activity.

Winter et al. (1998) defined family business as a business that is owned and managed by one or more family members. These same researchers used the concept of a *family household* which was defined as a group of people related by blood, marriage, or adoption, who share a common dwelling unit and participated in the ownership of a business. For the nationally representative 1997/2000/2007 National Family Business Panels (NFBP), a minimum of a one-year work intensity requirement for the owner-manager was also imposed. Specifically, the owner had to have worked at least 6 hours per week year round or a minimum of 312 hours a year in the business (Heck and Trent 1999).

Of course, the owning family brings together and creates the resources and conditions from which entrepreneurial behavior emerges and is sustained over time. The family, with its own dynamics, is an important and fundamental milieu for combining and creating behaviors described in the literature as entrepreneurial behavior and experience (Danes et al. 2008; Rogoff and Heck 2003; Stafford et al. 1999). Rogoff and Heck (2003) note that "the growing body of research points to the fundamental guiding principle that the combustion of entrepreneurship cannot ignite and grow without the mobilization of family forces" (p. 560). Olson et al. (2003) have empirically shown that both business outcomes and family outcomes are simultaneously determined by factors from and within *both* systems. But what is exactly the role of family in entrepreneurship? The SFBT introduced in the previous section posits a dynamic, behaviorally-based, multidimensional family theory of the firm that accommodates both business and family complexities, and provides a useful framework for the analysis of key concepts related to family entrepreneurship (Danes et al. 2008).

First, families and businesses provide *resources* to the entrepreneurial endeavors of family members in the form of social capital, human capital, and assets including both financial and physical capital (Danes et al. 2008). Social capital includes the interrelations between and among family members. For example, trust is a specific aspect crucial to entrepreneurial activity. Family entrepreneurship has an advantage over non-family entrepreneurship due to the enhanced possibility of trust among family members. Human capital includes the human attributes of the individuals in the family such as personal time and energy, as well as emotional support. The concepts of financial and physical capital include money, credit and financial investments of all kinds, as well as land, real estate, and equipment (Danes et al. 2008).

But families and businesses also have *constraints* that limit entrepreneurship. These constraints may be social, cultural, legal, economic, and technical. Socio-cultural constraints center on the norms and mores of the community and the social sanctions imposed by the violation of these norms. Legal constraints are the laws and regulations imposed by political entities. Economic constraints are limitations imposed by finite resources. Technical constraints are the laws of biology, chemistry, and physics that processes must abide by (Danes et al. 2008).

The effects of resources and constraints generated by the family and the business are mediated by *family structure* as well as *business structure*. Family structure includes the roles and rules of the family system. In family firms, owning families may need additional family structure, for example, a family council to handle or manage a variety of family matters. Such family structures help to reveal which member leads and how, and how to manage and allocate family resources and adjust constraints (Danes et al. 2008). Business structure includes ownership and governance (Danes et al. 2008).

Along side with constraints, families and businesses encompass *disruptions*. Normative disruptions are those, for example, that may occur when major family events occur such as birth or death and holidays or ceremonies. Non-normative disruptions, instead, are those that are not foreseeable or highly unusual. An example would be a natural disaster that forces temporary or permanent closure of the business (Danes et al. 2008).

Families and businesses also provide *processes*. Processes within families and family owned businesses are a form of social capital and operate during times of stability and take place within each system. These processes can be thought of as routine, or standard operating procedures. Processes during times of change occur in the overlap of the family and the business (Danes et al. 2008).

Finally, families and businesses evaluate *achievements* in multidimensional ways where subjective indicators such as family and business harmony, satisfaction in the family and in the business, and the achievements of goals in both systems are as important as financial success (Stafford et al. 1999). And the family firm interacts with its surrounding community as well as the community affecting both the family and business systems (Danes et al. 2008). Both short-term family business viability and long-term family business sustainability are evolved over time via the SFBT and its delineations (Danes et al. 2008).

Overall, it is with the breath of scope highlighted by the SFBT that we now turn to examining the data.

3.4 Data and methodology

We use data from the Adult Population Survey (APS) of the GEM project. GEM data provide a unique opportunity to study and compare family entrepreneurship worldwide. More information about GEM and its methodology is summarized in Phinisee et al. (2008). Since its conception in 1999, GEM has grown to include sixty-four countries. GEM's surveys ask a representative sample of at least 2,000 adults in each country about their attitudes to and their involvement in, entrepreneurship.

GEM data currently include only a limited number of family-related variables, however, the data do include a variable measuring the amount of money invested by the owner of the business. We use this variable to divide the sample into businesses which are financially supported by family members or other relatives (family entrepreneurship or FE) and those which are not (non-family entrepreneurship or NFE). This variable is, of course, a crude measure of family entrepreneurship. It no doubt underestimates the extent of family involvement in the business because families contribute in many other significant ways, such as family labor, use of the family's physical capital such as cars, in-home offices as well as the cadre of less tangible assets such as division of labor between the family and the business, emotional support, trust, family spirit, recognition and reputation of the family name in the market, etc. (Kepner 1983; Heck and Trent 1999; Winter et al. 2004).

The evolution of family business definitions was previously discussed in Section 3.2. The operationalization we use in this chapter relates to the "family investment" in the business and is directly linked to measures of family ownership and involvement in the creation and operation of the business as conceptualized by other researchers (Heck and Trent 1999; Winter et al. 1998).

GEM data include information on the amount of money invested by the business owner in the start-up and the total amount of money required to start the business. In this chapter, businesses with 50% or more of start-up money invested by the business owner are classified as family businesses, whereas businesses with less than 50% of start-up money invested by the business owner are classified as non-family businesses. The rationale for using the percentage of start-up money invested by the business owner as a determinant for whether the business is classified as a family or non-family business is that the more the owner invests of his own assets the higher the probability that the business is a family business. Once divided into those financially supported by their families (FE) and those who are not (NFE), businesses from the twenty-eight countries that participated in the GEM survey were examined and their business profile characteristics compared. Comparisons were also conducted with respect to their age in operation, whether they were early-stage entrepreneurial activity (less than forty-two months in operation) or established entrepreneurs (more then forty-two months in operation). House-hold income, age, gender, and education attainment of the business owner were also examined by countries. Finally, family entrepreneurs and non-family entrepreneurs were also compared with respect to business motivations and industry sectors.

The Pearson chi-square test or the Fisher exact test were used to determine whether statistically significant differences between family entrepreneur (FE) and non-family entrepreneur (NFE) exist. The percentage of high income entrepreneurs, mean age, gender, motivation (opportunity and necessity) were categories included in the tests. The Pearson chi-square test and the Fisher exact test allow for tests of the independence of two categorical variables.

The chi-square test becomes inaccurate when fewer than fifty observations are available or when a two by two correlation is analyzed such as, for example, gender by FE versus NFE. The Yate's correction for continuity was therefore applied. In an alternative to the chi-square, the Fisher exact test can be used. The Fisher exact test produces a more accurate significance test for categorical variables and small sample sizes. For continuous variables such as age, the t test was used to test differences in means between FEs and NFEs by country.

Unfortunately, further explanatory modeling was impossible for two reasons. First, the data among the twenty-eight countries used in this research contained missing observations in ten out of the twenty-eight countries for several of the variables examined descriptively. Second, and more importantly, GEM data provide only a very limited set of variables related to entrepreneurship. Previous research by Olson et al. (2003) conceptualized and empirically tested the effects of families on business performance and vice versa. In doing so, family factors such as the number of children, generation, family management, family type, family tensions, and the number of family employees were shown to directly affect the levels of gross business revenues and perceived business success. Neglecting to include these dimensions of family dynamics may lead to very biased results (Gufarati 2003; Johnston and DiNardo 1997).

Overall, the main goal of this chapter is to provide a first exploratory investigation of family entrepreneurship across countries using the GEM data, keeping in mind that our results are severely limited by the available data and much more work needs to be conducted.

3.5 Results and discussion

GEM data allow a new examination of family entrepreneurship across a large sample of countries. Such research is vital to the acknowledgment and understanding that entrepreneurship is neither started nor continued by entrepreneurs alone. Although data constraints force us to restrict this chapter to an exploratory analysis, our cross-country exploration, the first of this scope, is critical to understanding patterns of family entrepreneurship worldwide.

3.5.1 *Family entrepreneurial activity by type and country*

Throughout history and around the world, family and business have been virtually inseparable. In many cultures, family names are derived from their business names, such as Taylor for a tailor, Smith for a blacksmith, and Farmer for farming. In other cases, the family name is translated directly into businesses such as the Campbell family and Campbell Soup or Ford family and the Ford Motor Company. Yet in others, it is the cultural norm that children follow into the family business, such as in India. This overwhelming connection of family to business is seen in data from the twenty-eight countries within the 2008 GEM data.

There is no doubt that our measure of personal/family investment as a surrogate for the definition of family entrepreneurship is crude. Nonetheless, in the GEM distribution of the percentages of start-up investments by all business owners, the mode and the median exceed 50% in all countries combined. This is consistent with Puryear et al. (2008) who used data from the 2003 and 2005 National Minority Business Owner Surveys to investigate the percentage of business owners' start-up investments in family businesses. Their results show that between 78% and 85% of the family business owners owned 91–100% of the businesses, and reflects the high investment by the family business owners in start-up costs.

Table 3.1 shows that the overall rate of family enterprises for early-stage ventures is 6.9%, while the percentage of non-family businesses is 4.2%. Even though some of the differences in Table 3.1 are large between family and non-family prevalence rates, most of the differences by country are not statistically significant due to small sample sizes. In judging the relative prevalence of family entrepreneurship within both samples of total early stage entrepreneurial activity and established enterprises, it is important to keep in mind that, overall, the rates of family entrepreneurship is more than half the totals in all the twenty-eight countries.

Table 3.1 also shows that the total early-stage entrepreneurial activity prevalence rates and the established business prevalence rates are split into family (FE) and non-family business (NFE) prevalence rates based on the definitions of family and non-family businesses stated previously. Since only a small percentage of respondents reported the amount of money invested in start-up costs, the sample sizes used to project the countries' distributions are small. Nonetheless, some patterns emerge. For example, six Latin American

Table 3.1. Early-stage entrepreneurial activity (family vs non-family), 2008

COUNTRY	Early-Stage Entrepreneurs Activity (%)			Established Entrepreneurs Activity (%)		
	Total TEA%	FE*	NFE**	Total Estab%	FE*	NFE**
Argentina	16.5	12.0	4.5	13.5	9.0	4.5
Belgium	2.9	1.7	1.2	2.6	0.0	2.6
Bolivia	29.8	19.9	9.9	19.1	13.1	6.0
Bosnia and Herzegovina	9.0	6.2	2.8	8.7	8.7	0.0
Brazil	12.0	7.7	4.3	14.6	9.7	4.9
Chile	14.1	8.5	5.6	6.8	3.3	3.5
Colombia	24.5	13.3	11.2	14.1	5.1†	9.0†
Croatia	7.6	4.9	2.7	4.8	0.0	4.8
Denmark	4.4	3.9	0.5	4.4	1.5	2.9
Dominican Republic	20.4	12.9†	7.5†	8.2	6.8	1.4
Ecuador	17.2	12.2	5.0	11.9	8.7	3.2
Germany	3.8	1.6	2.2	4.0	2.5	1.5
Greece	9.9	5.7	4.2	12.6	7.0	5.6
Hungary	6.6	3.6	3.0	5.3	3.5	1.8
Iceland	10.1	3.7	6.4	7.1	3.0	4.1
Korea Republic	10.0	6.4	3.6	12.8	8.4†	4.4†
Latvia	6.5	5.4††	1.1††	3.0	1.0	2.0
Mexico	13.1	9.2	3.9	4.9	2.5	2.5
Netherlands	5.2	3.9	1.3	7.2	7.2	0.0
Norway	8.7	4.0	4.7	7.7	3.4	4.3
Peru	25.6	14.0†	11.6†	8.3	8.3†	0.1†
Russia	3.5	2.7	0.8	1.1	0.7	0.4
Serbia	7.6	5.1†	2.5†	9.3	4.0	5.3
Slovenia	6.4	4.6	1.8	5.6	1.9†	3.7†
South Africa	7.8	5.0	2.8	2.3	1.2	1.2
United Kingdom	5.9	3.7†	2.2†	6.0	4.2	1.8
United States	10.8	6.6††	4.2††	8.3	6.6	1.7
Uruguay	11.9	4.6††	7.3††	7.9	2.6	5.3
Overall Average	11.1	6.9	4.2	7.8	4.8	3.2

* FE: family entrepreneur
** NFE: non-family entrepreneur
† Statistically significant at 95% C.I. for FE vs NFE
†† Statistically significant at 99% C.I. for FE vs NFE

Source: Global Entrepreneurship Monitor (GEM) APS Country Files for 18–64 year old population

countries, Argentina, Bolivia, Colombia, Dominican Republic, Ecuador, and Peru, exhibit the highest percentages of early-stage family entrepreneurship, all in excess of 12%. Of those, Argentina, Bolivia, Ecuador, and Peru also rank among the top seven countries in rates of established family entrepreneurship. Also, Peru, the Dominican Republic, and Uruguay are three of the seven countries exhibiting significant differences between FE and NFE in early-stage entrepreneurial activity, and Colombia and Peru are two of the four countries exhibiting significant differences between established FE and NFE. These findings suggest that family entrepreneurship in Latin America is relatively more prevalent than in other countries and cultures. Some scholars have examined the cultural dimensions of Latin American and other ethnic groups to illustrate the link between culture orientations and their respective entrepreneurial experiences (Danes et al. 2008). The collective orientations of Latin American cultures may be related to these higher and significantly different levels of family entrepreneurship, particularly in the early stage.

3.5.2 Family entrepreneurial activity by household income, age, gender, and educational attainment

Tables 3.2 and 3.3 show household demographic information investigated based on the categorizations of FE and NFE for early-stage and established entrepreneurship respectively. The tables contain the following demographic variables: (1) the percentage of business responders that are in the upper one-third of the total countries estimated household incomes; (2) the mean age of the business responders; (3) the hypothetical distribution of the countries' early-stage and established business prevalence activity by gender; and (4) the distribution of the responders' education levels.

Table 3.2 shows that for early-stage family entrepreneurship some key differences among FE and NFE exist with regard to income, age, gender, and education. Non-family enterprises have higher income, higher mean age, and greater post-secondary education. With regard to gender, both the male and female samples have a higher rate of family funding (7.7% and 6.0% respectively) than non-family funding (5.6% and 2.9% respectively), but the difference between family and non-family funding is significantly wider for female entrepreneurs.

Table 3.3 shows the breakout of the samples for established businesses and shows, similar to early-stage ventures, income, age, and prevalence among females. On the other hand, the males and education attainment shows opposite patterns compared to early-stage ventures. In established businesses, males were likely to be in non-family enterprise compared to family enterprise. Also in established business those with high school level education are more likely to be in non-family enterprises while those with post-secondary education are more likely to be family enterprises. This may suggest that males fair better with businesses which are not family businesses. And those with more education choose family-run enterprises as compared to non-family enterprises.

3.5.3 Family entrepreneurial activity by opportunities/motivations and sectors

Table 3.4 addresses early-stage entrepreneurial activity by motivation and industry sectors. Motivation is categorized as either opportunity oriented or necessity focused. Family enterprises are equally motivated by opportunity

COUNTRY	% in High Income		Mean Age		Male Entrepreneurial Activity (%)		Female Entrepreneurial Activity (%)		Some Secondary and Secondary Degree Entrepreneurial Activity (%)		Post-Secondary Degree and Graduate Entrepreneurial (%)	
	FE*	NFE**	FE*	NFE**	FE*	NFE**	FE*	NFE**	FE*	NFE**	FE*	NFE**
Argentina	NA	NA	31.0†	34.8†	12.4	4.8	11.7	4.2	NA	NA	NA	NA
Belgium	33.3	80.0	38.0	31.5	3.4	0.6	1.0	0.6	55.6	50.0	44.4	50.0
Bolivia	30.4	39.7	36.1†	30.0†	22.1	9.7	17.3	10.6	54.6	49.2	45.4	50.8
Bosnia and Herzegovina	39.1	36.4	37.7	37.5	7.2	3.8	5.0	2.0	85.2	66.7	14.8	33.3
Brazil	13.3	44.4	32.4	27.9	7.8	5.2	7.3	3.7	75.0	55.6	25.0	44.4
Chile	52.5	61.5	36.0	38.8	8.4	6.5	7.3	3.9	48.4	29.3	51.6	70.7
Colombia	38.6	34.7	35.8	35.0	15.4	14.8	11.8	7.3	100.0	100.0	0.0	0.0
Croatia	61.9	42.9	28.6	35.3	7.6	3.2	2.2	2.2	88.0	85.7	12.0	14.3
Denmark	40.0	100.0	40.4	42.0	4.5	0.8	2.7	0.0	25.0	0.0	75.0	100.0
Dominican Republic	28.1†	34.9†	31.5	31.8	15.3†	9.7†	10.3	5.2	67.4	53.3	32.6	46.7
Ecuador	48.4	66.7	35.4†	30.1†	11.8	6.7	12.8	3.1	71.2	59.3	28.8	40.7
Germany	31.3	46.4	44.3†	31.8†	1.3	2.8	2.3	1.1	6.2	52.2	93.8	47.8
Greece	59.1	53.3	33.8	34.1	5.4	6.7	5.5	2.1	40.9	37.5	59.1	62.5
Hungary	75.0	20.0	34.6	44.5	2.7	5.3	3.7	1.5	14.3	16.7	85.7	83.3
Iceland	50.0	52.9	35.1	36.3	4.4	8.4	3.4	3.8	55.0	43.2	45.0	56.8
Korea Republic	53.8	57.1	37.6	38.7	8.1†	6.7†	2.6	2.4	18.5	22.7	81.5	77.3
Latvia	55.3	66.7	31.0	31.2	5.9††	3.6††	3.5††	0.2††	18.0	20.0	82.0	80.0
Mexico	31.3†	23.7†	34.9	40.4	10.1	4.3	8.9	3.0	41.8	38.5	58.2	61.5
Netherlands	71.4	100.0	29.8†	43.3†	4.7	2.3	NA	NA	83.3	83.3	16.7	16.7
Norway	52.2	50.0	35.7	34.2	4.4	7.7	3.1	2.1	53.6	56.4	46.4	43.6
Peru	49.2	40.0	36.8	31.1	14.1	13.4	16.2	7.4	38.2	35.5	61.8	64.5
Russia	42.9	50.0	27.5†	45.8†	3.6	0.9	1.8	0.7	35.3	0.0	64.7	100.0
Serbia	28.1	25.0	35.2	34.7	6.5††	3.5††	2.8	2.5	70.6	66.7	29.4	33.3
Slovenia	55.2	56.3	32.9	34.7	5.1	3.6	3.5	0.5	45.8	45.5	54.2	54.5
South Africa	44.4	37.0	32.4	32.4	7.0†	2.6†	3.3	2.6	74.1	81.5	25.9	18.5
United Kingdom	29.1	50.0	38.6	32.5	5.2†	2.9†	1.9	1.9	47.5	57.5	52.5	42.5
United States	32.1	39.3	38.1	37.4	6.8	5.9	5.7†	3.2†	34.1	25.4	65.9	74.6
Uruguay	45.7	40.0	35.9	35.7	5.0	10.3	4.2	4.4	54.1	60.3	45.9	39.7
Overall Average	44.1	50.0	34.9	35.7	7.7	5.6	6.0	2.9	51.9	47.9	48.1	52.2

* FE: family entrepreneur ** NFE: non-family entrepreneur
NA: No data or insufficient data
† Statistically significant at 95% C.I. for FE vs NFE †† Statistically significant at 99% C.I. for FE vs NFE

Source: Global Entrepreneurship Monitor (GEM) APS Country Files for 18–64 year old population

Table 3.3. Family and non-family established entrepreneurial activity by income, age, gender, and education (18–64 year old population), 2008

COUNTRY	% in High Income		Mean Age		Male Entrepreneurial Activity (%)		Female Entrepreneurial Activity (%)		Some Secondary and Secondary Degree Entrepreneurial Activity (%)		Post-Secondary Degree and Graduate Entrepreneurial (%)	
	FE*	NFE**	FE*	NFE**	FE*	NFE**	FE*	NFE**	FE*	NFE**	FE*	NFE**
Argentina	NA	NA	36.2	34.0	12.8	5.1	9.2	0.0	NA	NA	NA	NA
Belgium	NA	100.0	NA	33.3	0.0	3.9	0.0	1.3	NA	NA	NA	NA
Bolivia	54.5†	16.7†	41.7	35.9	12.7	5.9	12.5	6.9	62.5	72.7	37.5	27.3
Bosnia and Herzegovina	66.7	NA	38.3	NA	10.9	NA	6.5	NA	57.1	NA	42.9	NA
Brazil	50.0	100.0	28.0†	55.0†	11.9	5.9	NA	NA	NA	NA	NA	NA
Chile	66.7	61.5	37.8	39.8	3.6	5.3	2.7	1.8	25.0	53.8	75.0	46.2
Colombia	36.4	40.0	40.1	36.7	7.8	10.5	0.0	10.0	0.0	NA	100.0	NA
Croatia	0.0	100.0	0.0	42.5	0.0	6.0	NA	NA	NA	NA	NA	NA
Denmark	0.0	50.0	43.0†	22.0†	1.5	2.9	NA	NA	NA	NA	NA	NA
Dominican Republic	76.9	50.0	44.6†	30.0†	8.5	1.6	3.8	2.5	20.0	50.0	80.0	50.0
Ecuador	75.0	66.7	38.9	37.3	9.2	6.9	5.8	1.9	62.5	33.3	37.5	66.7
Germany	50.0	100.0	43.4†	26.7†	2.8	2.8	1.9	0.6	0.0	0.0	100.0	100.0
Greece	60.0	100.0	42.6	39.0	5.9	11.7	7.7	0.0	80.0	75.0	20.0	25.0
Hungary	NA	0.0	NA	41.0	0.0	7.4	NA	NA	NA	NA	NA	NA
Iceland	66.7	100.0	35.0	37.3	1.9	7.7	4.7	0.0	67.0	0.0	33.0	100.0
Korea Republic	33.3	41.7	48.5	51.2	4.8	14.3	3.3	3.3	67.0	50.0	33.0	50.0
Latvia	50.0	100.0	32.0†	37.7†	2.2	2.2	NA	NA	33.3	33.3	66.7	66.7
Mexico	12.5	0.0	43.7	41.6	3.7	1.9	2.9	1.5	NA	NA	NA	NA
Netherlands	0.0	0.0	33.0	39.0	0.0	9.1	5.2	0.0	NA	NA	NA	NA
Norway	42.9	44.4	41.4	48.4	3.1	7.7	3.0	1.5	57.1	63.6	42.9	36.4
Peru	56.5†	33.3†	38.6	43.0	9.7	0.9	5.9	0.0	NA	NA	NA	NA
Russia	NA	NA	NA	NA	1.0	0.0	NA	NA	NA	NA	NA	NA
Serbia	25.0	41.7	37.7†	47.3†	2.9	9.4	5.2	0.9	60.0	64.3	40.0	35.7
Slovenia	33.3	80.0	41.8	48.6	2.6	5.2	3.3	0.0	NA	NA	NA	NA
South Africa	33.3	33.3	43.7	39.5	1.5	1.5	0.8	0.8	40.0	67.0	60.0	33.0
United Kingdom	33.3	80.0	39.9	44.8	3.6	5.0	2.4	1.0	25.0	33.3	75.0	66.7
United States	36.4	61.5	45.0	48.4	5.5	4.8	4.6†	1.8†	25.0	0.0	75.0	100.0
Uruguay	100.0	77.8	37.8	44.7	4.2	5.9	3.9	1.9	27.3	45.5	72.7	54.5
Overall Average	44.1	59.1	38.1	40.2	4.8	5.4	4.3	1.8	41.7	42.8	58.3	57.2

* FE: family entrepreneur   ** non-FE: non-family entrepreneur
NA: No data or insufficient data
† Statistically significant at 95% C.I. for FE vs NFE   †† Statistically significant at 99 C.I. for FE vs NFE

old population), 2008

COUNTRY	Early Stage Opportunity Entrepreneurship		Early Stage Necessity Entrepreneurship		Early Stage Extractive Sectors		Early Stage Transforming Sectors		Early Stage Business Sectors		Early Stage Consumer Sectors	
	FE*	NFE**	FE*	NFE**	FE*	NFE**	FE*	NFE**	FE*	NFE**	FE*	NFE**
Argentina	2.2	1.1	4.4	2.0	0.0	0.0	24.5	31.6	20.4	26.3	55.1	42.1
Belgium	0.4	0.5	0.3	0.0	0.0	20.0	33.3	0.0	22.2	20.0	44.4	60.0
Bolivia	5.4	3.8	5.8	2.8	8.5	15.8	23.1	8.8	10.3	15.8	58.1	59.6
Bosnia and Herzegovina	0.8	0.6	2.5	1.3	11.5	7.7	19.2	38.5	0.0	7.7	69.2	46.2
Brazil	0.6	0.7	3.3	0.7	6.2	0.0	18.8	33.3	12.5	22.2	62.5	44.4
Chile	2.8	2.8	2.3	1.3	3.4	0.0	32.8	47.4	15.5	10.5	48.3	42.1
Colombia	3.3	3.8	5.4	4.8	10.0	7.7	24.4	33.3	14.4	25.6	51.1	33.3
Croatia	1.0	0.7	1.3	0.9	12.0	0.0	24.0	50.0	8.0	7.1	56.0	42.9
Denmark	0.3	0.0	0.2	0.0	NA	NA	NA	NA	NA	NA	NA	NA
Dominican Republic††	3.3	2.9	4.1	2.1	5.3	0.0	14.7	34.1	14.7	25.0	65.3	40.9
Ecuador	3.2	1.9	3.2	1.7	5.5	8.0	12.7	12.0	9.1	20.0	72.7	60.0
Germany	0.6	1.5	0.5	0.5	10.0	3.6	5.0	17.9	5.0	20.0	80.0	60.7
Greece	1.0	1.1	2.1	1.0	0.0	0.0	14.3	33.3	19.0	20.0	66.7	46.7
Hungary	0.2	0.3	1.0	1.0	16.7	0.0	16.7	40.0	33.3	40.0	33.3	20.0
Iceland	1.0	2.8	0.3	0.3	14.3	2.9	28.6	23.5	28.6	38.2	28.6	35.3
Korea Republic	1.1	1.5	2.7	1.3	8.0	0.0	16.0	31.8	24.0	27.3	52.0	40.9
Latvia	1.9†	1.2†	1.0††	0.3††	4.2	5.3	43.8	47.4	25.0	26.3	27.1	21.1
Mexico	4.6	2.4	1.0	0.8	2.1	0.0	11.7	16.7	16.0	11.1	70.2	72.2
Netherlands	0.5	0.5	0.5	0.0	0.0	16.7	61.5	50.0	0.0	16.7	38.5	16.7
Norway††	1.2	3.0	0.6†	0.1†	8.0	6.2	12.0	31.2	16.0	40.6	64.0	21.9
Peru†	5.3	5.2	4.4	3.6	5.8	11.1	20.7	33.3	6.6	8.9	66.9	46.7
Russia	0.6	0.4	0.7	0.0	6.2	0.0	56.2	60.0	12.5	0.0	25.0	40.0
Serbia	1.4	1.1	1.6	0.9	3.0	20.0	24.2	40.0	30.3	15.0	42.4	25.0
Slovenia	2.5	1.8	0.8	0.0	0.0	0.0	40.0	31.6	33.3	47.4	26.7	21.0
South Africa	2.4	1.7	0.9	0.7	3.9	0.0	21.6	14.8	13.7	14.8	60.8	70.4
United Kingdom	2.7	2.5	0.5	0.3	NA	NA	NA	NA	NA	NA	NA	NA
United States	4.4	4.6	0.9†	0.4†	1.1	7.8	25.0	15.6	39.8	35.9	34.1	40.6
Uruguay	2.2	1.1	4.4††	2.0††	0.0	0.0	24.5	31.6	20.4	26.3	55.1	42.1
Overall Average	2.0	1.8	2.0	1.1	5.6	5.1	25.0	31.1	17.3	21.8	52.1	42.0

* FE: family entrepreneur   ** NFE: non-family entrepreneur

NA: No data or insufficient data

† Statistically significant at 95% C.I. for FE vs NFE   †† Statistically significant at 99% C.I. for FE vs NFE

Source: Global Entrepreneurship Monitor (GEM) APS Country Files for 18–64 year old population

and necessity and more motivated by both family and non-family enterprises. Again, these findings indicate the ubiquitous nature of family entrepreneurship, particularly from its financial support as emphasized by the definition used in this research. The investments by families into their early-stage entrepreneurial activities are pivotal whether pursuing opportunities or motivated by necessity. In addition, a number of scholars have begun to examine both "family angels" (Erikson, Sorheim, and Reitan 2003) and in particular the interactions between families and their businesses with regard to their finances (Haynes et al. 1999). In both cases, family investors view family businesses differently than non-family investors and manage their financing differently. Further, Lyagoubi (2008) has examined the effect of family shareholder preferences influencing the firms' financing. Steier (2003) conceptualizes the family-finance ventures as systematically different from other financing situations. He suggests that the parameters of family-financed ventures often operate on trust and the strength of the family relationships and kinship ties as well as other nonmarket rationalities.

With regard to sectors, extractive and consumer sectors show higher prevalence of family enterprises while transforming and business sectors show higher prevalence among the non-family sample. The extractive sectors may be tied to other family assets such as land and related minerals rights. Also, consumer sectors may be more likely to be retail and service related businesses which have traditionally been more likely family business (Puryear et al. 2008; Winter et al. 1998).

3.6 Conclusions and recommendations for future research

The data presented in this paper show the prevalence of family entrepreneurship and its preponderance worldwide. This preponderance reaches across borders, cultures, business characteristics and motivations, and industrial sectors. Certainly the measures used in this analysis are crude surrogates for more specific and quantifiable measures, but the evidence is, nonetheless, clear. In the twenty-eight countries that provided data for this analysis, early-stage entrepreneurship and established entrepreneurship show prevalence rates of family businesses to be about 50% higher than non-family businesses. As one may expect, given constraints in formal labor markets, women's participation rates in family enterprise are even higher in many countries. Among high income individuals, non-family enterprise is a more common form of business, future research may shed light on the family origins of businesses that today do not meet the definitions of family enterprises.

Similarly to entrepreneurship research in general, GEM data do not directly focus on the issues of family business. This is a shortcoming of the GEM data and could be corrected by adding questions about family involvement such as contributions of financial and human capital, motivations for starting a venture that relate to family issues, and ownership and management characteristics. Other surveys that focus more on family business issues have benefited from interviewing spouses and other family members to learn more about their involvement in the business and specifically how the business and family interact (Winter et al. 1998). The geographical scope of GEM would render its data of particular value for answering questions about family entrepreneurship and its characteristics across countries.

There is still so much we do not know. Because of its widespread presence, it is particularly important that questions related to family entrepreneurship be addressed. Future research should provide answers to questions that address economic and social policies and parameters such as: (a) how much of the labor force is comprised of family members working in family enterprises; (b) what is the volume of monetary and non-monetary transfers between families and their businesses; (c) how does management differ in substance and style between family and non-family businesses; and (d) what are succession plans and exit strategies for family enterprises? The resulting knowledge could inform governmental and private business policies around the world. Indeed, researchers could begin to create a new comprehensive business model for entrepreneurs that would encompass the realities of their businesses and owning-families and that could be utilized across borders and within country-specific settings.

Acknowledgments

Many thanks go to an anonymous reviewer for helpful comments. Although GEM data were used in this study, their interpretation and use are the sole responsibility of the authors. All errors are ours.

References

Aldrich, H. E. and Cliff, J. E. (2003), The Pervasive Effects of Family on Entrepreneurship: Toward a Family Embeddedness Perspective. *Journal of Business Venturing*, 18(5): 573–96.

Astrachan, J. H., Klein, S. B., and Smyrnios, K. X. (2002), The F-PEC Scale of Family Influence: A Proposal for Solving the Family Business Definition Problem. *Family Business Review*, 15(1): 45–58.

Astrachan, J. H. and Kurtz, A. M. (1998), Editors' Notes. *Family Business Review*, 11: v–vi.

Bowen, M. (1985), *Family Therapy in Clinical Practice*. New York: Jason Aaronson.

Brockhaus, R. H. (1994), Entrepreneurship and Family Business: Comparisons, Critique, and Lessons. *Entrepreneurship Theory and Practice*, 19(1): 25–38.

Cramton, C. D. (1993), Is Rugged Individualism the Whole Story? Public and Private Accounts of a Firm's Founding. *Family Business Review*, 6(3): 233–61.

Danes, S. M., Lee, J., Stafford, K., and Heck, R. K. Z. (2008), The Effects of Ethnicity, Families and Culture on Entrepreneurial Experience: An Extension of Sustainable Family Business Theory. *Journal of Developmental Entrepreneurship*, 13(3): 229–68.

Dimov, D. (2007), Beyond the Single-Person, Single-Insight Attribution in Understanding Entrepreneurial Opportunities. *Entrepreneurship, Theory, and Practice*, 31(5): 713–31.

Donnelley, R. G. (1964), The Family Business. *Harvard Business Review*, 42: 93–105.

Dyer, W. G. and Handler, W. (1994), Entrepreneurship and Family Business: Exploring the Connections. *Entrepreneurship Theory and Practice*, 19(1): 71–83.

Erikson, T., Sorheim, R., and Reitan, B. (2003), Family Angels v.s. Other Informal Investors. *Family Business Review*, 16(3): 163–71.

Greenwood, R. (2003), Commentary on: "Toward a Theory of Agency and Altruism in Family Firms." *Journal of Business Venturing*, 18(4): 491–4.

Gufarati, D. N. (2003) *Basic Econometrics*. New York: McGraw–Hill Irwin.

Habbershon, T. G. and Williams, M. L. (1999), A Resources-Based Framework for Assessing the Strategic Advantages of Family Firms. *Family Business Review*, 12: 1–25.

Habbershon, T. G., Williams, M. L., and MacMillan, I. C. (2003), A Unified Systems Perspective of Family Firm Performance. *Journal of Business Venturing*, 18(4): 451–65.

Handler, W. (1992), The Succession Experience of the Next Generation. *Family Business Review*, 5(3): 283–307.

Haynes, G. W., Walker, R., Rowe, B. S., and Hong, G. S. (1999), The Intermingling of Business and Family Finances in Family-Owned Businesses. *Family Business Review*, 12 (3): 225–39.

Heck, R. K. Z. (ed.). (1998a), *The Entrepreneurial Family*. Needham, MA: Family Business Resources Publishing.

Heck, R. K. Z. (1998b), The Entrepreneurial Family: Refocusing on the Family in Business. In R. K. Z. Heck, *The entrepreneurial family* (pp. 1–7). Needham, MA: Family Business Resources Publishing.

Heck, R. K. Z., Danes, S. M., Fitzgerald, M. A., Haynes, G. W., Jasper, C. R., Schrank, H. L., Stafford, K., and Winter, M. (2006), The Family's Dynamic Role within Family Business Entrepreneurship. In P. Z. Poutziouris, K. X. Smyrnios, and S. B. Klein (eds.) (pp. 80–105). *Handbook of Research on Family Business*. Cheltenham, UK: Edward Elgar Publishers.

Heck, R. K. Z., Hoy, F., Poutziouris, P. Z., and Steier, L. P. (2008), Emerging Paths of Family Entrepreneurship Research. *Journal of Small Business Management*, 46(3): 317–30.

Heck, R. K. Z. and Trent, E. S. (1999), The Prevalence of Family Business from a Household Sample. *Family Business Review*, 12(3): 209–24.

Hershon, S. A. (1976), *The Problem of Management Succession in Family Businesses*. Unpublished doctoral dissertation, Business Administration, Harvard University.

Hoy, F. and Verser T. G. (1994), Emerging Business, Emerging Field: Entrepreneurship and the Family Firm. *Entrepreneurship Theory and Practice*, 19(1): 9–24.

International Family Enterprise Research Academy (IFERA) (2003), Family Businesses Dominate. *Family Business Review*, 16(4): 235–40.

Jennings, J. E. and McDougald, M. S. (2007), Work-Family Interface Experiences and Coping Strategies: Implications for Entrepreneurship Research and Practice. *Academy of Management Review*, 33(3): 747–60.

Johnston, J. and DiNardo, J. (1997), *Econometric Methods* (4th edn). New York: McGraw Hill.

Kepner, E. (1983), The Family and the Firm: A Coevolutionary Perspective. *Organizational Dynamics*, 12(1): 57–70.

Lansberg, I. (1988), The Succession Conspiracy. *Family Business Review*, 1(2): 119–43.

Litz, R. A. (1995), The Family Business: Toward Definitional Clarity. *Family Business Review*, 8(2): 71–81.

Lyagoubi, M. (2008), Family Firms and Financial Behavior: How Family Shareholder Preferences Influence Firms' Financing. In P. Z. Poutziouris, K. X. Smyrnios, and S. Klein (eds.), *Handbook of Research on Family Business* (Chapter 1, pp. 11–24). Edward Elgar Publishing in association with International Family Enterprise Research Academy (IFERA), Cheltenham, UK.

Morck, R. and Yeung, B. (2004), Family Control and the Rent-seeking Society. *Entrepreneurship Theory and Practice*, 28(4): 391–409.

Olson, P. D., Zuiker, V. S., Danes, S. M., Stafford, K., Heck, R. K. Z., and Duncan, K. A. (2003), Impact of Family and Business on Family Business Sustainability. *Journal of Business Venturing*, 18(5): 639–66.

Pearson, A. W., Carr, J. C., and Shaw, J. C. (2008), Toward a Theory of Familiness: A Social Capital Perspective. *Entrepreneuship Theory and Practice*, 32(6): 949–69.

Phinisee, I., Allen, I. E., Rogoff, E., Onochie, J., and Dean, M. (2008), *The Global Entrepreneurship Monitor: National Entrepreneurial Assessment for the United States of America, 2006–2007 Executive Report*. Babson College and Baruch College: The Authur M. Blank Center for Entrepreneurship and The Lawrence N. Field Programs in Entrepreneurship.

Pieper, T. and Klein, S. B. (2007), "The Bulleye: A Systems Approach to Modeling Family Firms," *Family Business Review*, 20(4): 301–19.

Puryear, A., Rogoff, E., Lee, M.-S., Heck, R. K. Z., Grossman, E. B., Haynes, G. W., and Onochie, J. (2008), Sampling Minority Business Owners and their Families: The Understudied Entrepreneurial Experience. *Journal of Small Business Management*, 46(3): 422–55.

Rogoff, E. G. and Heck, R. K. Z. (2003), Evolving Research in Entrepreneurship and Family Business: Recognizing Family as the Oxygen that Feeds the Fire of Entrepreneurship. *Journal of Business Venturing*, 18(5): 559–66.

Rosenblatt, P. C., de Mik, L., Anderson, R. M., and Johnson, P. A. (1985), *The Family in Business: Understanding and Dealing with the Challenges Entrepreneurial Families Face*. San Francisco: Jossey-Bass Publishers.

Schulze, W. S., Lubatkin, M. H., and Dino, R. N. (2003), Toward a Theory of Agency and Altruism in Family Firms. *Journal of Business Venturing*, 18(4): 473–90.

Sharma, P. (2004), An Overview of the Field of Family Business Studies: Current Status and Directions for the Future. *Family Business Review*, 17(1): 1–36.

Stafford, K., Duncan, K. A., Danes, S. M., and Winter, M. (1999), A Research Model of Sustainable Family Businesses. *Family Business Review*, 12(3): 197–208.

Steier, L. (2003), Variants of Agency Contracts in Family-Financed Ventures as a Continuum of Familial Altruistic and Market Rationalities. *Journal of Business Venturing*, 18 (5): 597–618.

Trent, E. S. (guest ed.), and Astrachan, J. H. (ed.) (1999), Editors' Notes: Family Businesses from the Household perspective. *Family Business Review*, 12: v–vi.

Winter, M., Fitzgerald, M. A., Heck, R. K. Z., Haynes, G. W., and Danes, S. M. (1998), Revisiting the Study of Family Businesses: Methodological Challenges, Dilemmas, and Alternative Approaches. *Family Business Review*, 11(3): 239–52.

Winter, M., Danes, S. M., Koh, S., Fredericks, K., and Paul, J. J. (2004), Tracking Family Businesses and their Owners Over Time: Panel Attrition, Manager Departure, and Business Demise. *Journal of Business Venturing*, 19: 535–59.

4

Investor Altruism: Financial Returns from Informal Investments in Businesses Owned by Relatives, Friends, and Strangers

William D. Bygrave and Niels Bosma

4.1 Introduction

Informal investment from the 3Fs (family, friends, and foolhardy strangers including business angels) is the lifeblood of entrepreneurial ventures. In the USA, for example, informal investors provide more than US$100 billion to millions of new and infant businesses every year. In contrast venture capitalists supply around a billion dollars to a few hundred seed-stage businesses (NVCA 2009). In 2006, for example, US$25.9 billion of classic venture capital was invested in 2,910 companies at all stages from seed to expansion (NVCA 2007) compared with US$106 billion of informal investment in 3.5 million companies.[1] Put another way: Less than one in a thousand companies received classic venture capital in the USA in 2006. We estimated that only 1 in 10,000 seed-stage companies received venture capital. But despite the importance of informal investing, only one segment, business angels, has been extensively studied. The bulk of informal investments and at least two-thirds of the total amount invested have hardly been studied at all. This chapter focuses on one very important aspect of informal investing: the financial returns expected by the 3Fs.

The systematic study of informal investments in early-stage companies can be traced to the work of William Wetzel at the beginning of the 1980s, when

---

[1] Classic venture capital comprises investments in seed, early, start-up, and expansion stage companies.

he wrote on informal risk capital in New England (Wetzel 1981). A year or so later, Wetzel's study was replicated in California by Tynes and Krasner (1983), and, towards the end of the 1980s, Mason and Harrison began to study informal investments in the United Kingdom. As Wetzel and his associates had pioneered informal investor research in the USA, Harrison and Mason (1988) led the way to the study of informal investments in the United Kingdom.

Based on the ground-breaking studies of Wetzel and his associates in the USA and Harrison and Mason in the UK, van Osnabrugge (1999) wrote that "the BA [business angel] market in UK and the USA is the largest single source of risk financing for entrepreneurial firms, exceeding the institutional VC [venture capital] industry (Mason and Harrison 1996). In fact, estimates in the UK and the US suggest that BAs fund an annual amount of two to five times more money to entrepreneurial firms than the VC industry (Wetzel 1987; Freear et al. 1996; Mason and Harrison 1993)...it is 'guesstimated' that BAs fund between 30–40 times the number of entrepreneurial firms financed by the formal VC industry (Wetzel and Freear 1994)."

Most of the research on informal investments has focused on business angels who invest comparatively large sums of money in entrepreneurial ventures with the potential to become substantial companies. It is probable that studies of investments by business angels miss not only—as expected— micro-companies that are destined to stay tiny, but also many—perhaps most—companies that grow to become superstars. For instance, according to an analysis of the Inc. 500 "America's fastest-growing private companies" in 2000, 16 percent started with less than US$1,000, 42 percent with US$10,000 or less, and 58 percent with US$20,000 or less.[2] We believe it is very unlikely that companies starting with US$20,000 or less received seed money from business angels. Granted, when both seed and post-start-up rounds of investment are combined, 12 percent of the 500 companies received financing from business angels. But looked at another way, 88 percent of "America's [500] fastest-growing private companies" never received financing from business angels. In contrast, 33 percent of the same 500 companies raised start-up capital "by tapping assets of family and friends (*Inc.* 2000)."

Previous studies of the returns on informal investment dealt exclusively with business angels. In an alternative, in this chapter we include all men and women who personally invested in a business start-up that was not their own, excluding stocks and mutual funds. Informal investments in our study range from tiny amounts put into micro-ventures to huge sums invested in high-potential ventures. Our research gives a comprehensive picture of the returns

---

[2] All information in this paragraph comes from analyzing America's Inc. 500 in 2000.

expected by informal investors because it comprises all sizes of informal investments in all types of companies, of which business angel investments are just one—albeit very important—subset. To our knowledge, this chapter, albeit exploratory, is the first to investigate systematically the returns on all informal investing across countries. To explain our empirical findings, we develop a theoretical framework which combines agency and altruism theory.

4.2 Literature review

Entrepreneurs are the engines that drive new companies, and financing is the fuel that propels them. Informal investment is crucial to the global economy. It is fair to claim that if there were no informal investment (including investment by entrepreneurs themselves in their own companies), there would be no new companies, because essentially every company begins life with informal investment whereas almost no new company has classic venture capital on hand when it is newly born. Figure 4.1 provides a model of the role informal investors play for entrepreneurial activity.

In the model, entrepreneurs are motivated by what they perceive to be opportunities to start a new business, and believe that they have the necessary

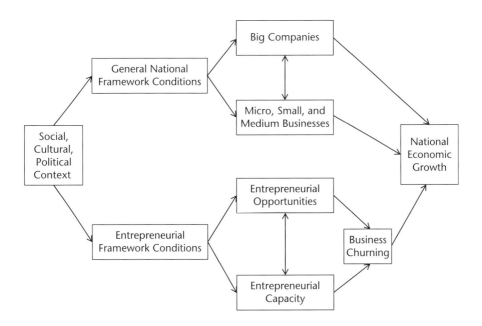

GEM (Global Entrepreneurship Monitor) Conceptual Model

Figure 4.1 GEM model for informal investment

knowledge, skills, and experience to develop those businesses. The principal source of external financial support to launch many of those new businesses is informal investors.

Of course, what sources of financing are available depends on where a start-up sits on the entrepreneurship spectrum. At one end of that spectrum is a lone, self-employed person in an impoverished region for whom eking out a subsistence living from a micro-business is better than no work at all. At the other end is a team of high-tech superstars in a technology metropolis with a high-potential opportunity that they believe will change the way in which we work, live, and play. In the middle are start-up ventures founded on opportunities that are more limited than high-potential ones but have the prospect of developing into viable companies that will eventually provide a comfortable living for the entrepreneur and, in some cases, full-time employees. At the bottom end of the spectrum, micro-entrepreneurs pushed into self-employment to survive have no choice other than self-financing. In the middle, entrepreneurs pulled into a start-up by an opportunity with ordinary potential usually get financing from informal investors—the 3Fs. At the top end, superstars with extraordinary opportunities launch their businesses with financing from professional venture capital, strategic partners, and the 3Fs.[3]

There is only scanty information on informal investment in the academic literature, largely because, as Wiltbank and Sarasvathy (2002) point out, reliable data on informal investors such as business angels is very hard to come by. The importance of informal investing to entrepreneurship is illustrated in Figure 4.2, which is based on annual investments from informal to venture capital to initial public offerings (IPOs) in entrepreneurial companies in the USA averaged over the period 2004–8.

Figure 4.2 shows that informal investors and entrepreneurs themselves are far and away the most important sources of money for fledgling ventures. But while there is an abundance of cross-sectional and longitudinal information on financial returns on formal venture capital at all levels—individual deals, portfolios, stages, and aggregates—and vast amounts of information on IPOs, there is almost no information on informal investors other than business angels. Academic research has all but ignored informal investors and self-funding by entrepreneurs, and the amount of academic research into financing of new ventures has been inversely proportional to its relevance to entrepreneurs.[4]

---

[3] For example, Google was funded initially by its founders, Sergey Brin and Larry Page; then it received funding from a business angel and family and friends; next, when it was more than 2 years old it raised venture capital.

[4] For instance, the annual Babson College Entrepreneurship Research Conferences (BCERC) is one of the oldest and largest international conferences focusing on entrepreneurship research. At ten annual BCERC combined (from 1998–2007), there were 221 papers on venture capital and IPOs, 43 on business angels, but only 7 on informal investors, and none whatsoever on financing by the founders themselves.

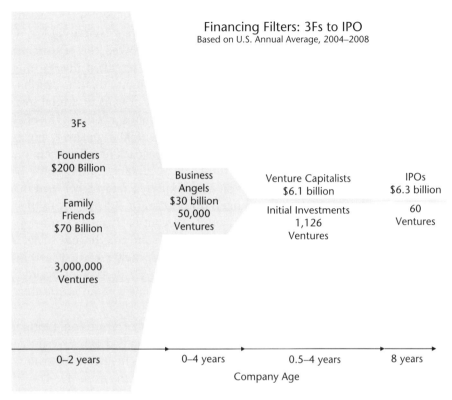

Figure 4.2 Financing filters: Start-up to IPO

Business angels are an important subset of informal investors. According to The Center for Venture Research at the University of New Hampshire (UNH), a conservative estimate suggests that between 300,000 and 350,000 angels invest approximately US$30 billion every year in close to 50,000 ventures in the USA (Sohl 2003). However, as Sohl (2003) noted, research on actual angel investment origination and conclusion is acutely missing from the current knowledge base. Indeed, there is almost no systematic information on actual returns on angel investments at the deal level, which in turn means that there are no reliable data on returns at the portfolio level or the national aggregate level. Sohl (2003) reports that angel returns hover in the 20% and 40% range, that angel investors expect an average annual return of 26% at the time they invest, and that they believe that about one-third of their investments are likely to result in a substantial capital loss.

Lumme, Mason, and Suomi (1996) examined the performance of investments from which business angels in Finland had exited and found that 20 percent of the exits produced a significant internal rate of return (IRR) in excess of 20 percent; 13 percent had a modest return (IRR<20%); 13 percent broke even; 16 percent were partial losses; and 38 percent were total losses. Along similar lines, Mason and Harrison (1999) analyzed the returns on informal venture capital investment using data on 128 exited investments from a survey of 127 business angels in the UK. They found that the distribution of returns was highly skewed, with 34 percent of exits at a total loss, 13 percent at a partial loss or break-even, and 23 percent showing an IRR of at least 50 percent. Finally, according to Wainwright (2005), business angels expect an IRR of 15 percent to 25 percent with a payback time between five and seven years. A Massachusetts Institute of Technology (MIT) study of twenty-two business angels found that they expected returns between 3:1 and 10:1, but that actual returns ranged from losses on 32 percent of their investments to returns exceeding 10:1 on 23 percent of them (Venture Support Systems Project 2002). The same MIT study found that business angels were evenly split between IPOs and acquisitions as their preferred method of exit; and none preferred a buyback. In practice, 27 percent of business angel investments were exited with an IPO, 35 percent with an acquisition, 5 percent with a buyback, and 32 percent were losses.

In 2005, Wiltbank provided the most extensive study of returns on informal investments up to that date (Wiltbank 2005). He studied the investment activities of 121 angel investors self-reporting on 1,038 investments totaling US$218 million invested.[5] Wiltbank examined the returns from the 414 (of the 1,038 ventures) that had been exited. He found that the angels lost money on 61.5 percent of their investments; earned an IRR between 0 percent and 24 percent on 8 percent; 25 percent–49 percent on 7 percent; 50 percent–99 percent on 3.5 percent; and 100 percent or more on 20 percent.

Wiltbank's results, however, are somewhat puzzling. In general, we would expect business angels to expect lower returns than venture capitalists because, unlike venture capitalists, they have only minimum operating costs and they do not have to pay carried interest on any capital gains. Venture capitalists charge as much as 3 percent per year on the money they manage, and deduct an additional 20 percent—sometimes more—from the capital gains they pass on to their investors. Hence, to produce a return of 25 percent for their investors, venture capitalists need to get a return of 35 percent or more from their investment portfolio. It is, therefore, surprising that self-reported returns of business angels are somewhat higher than the returns of professional venture capitalists (Wiltbank 2005, especially Figure 2).

---

[5] Approximately 75 percent of the angels were members of 12 angel investor groups in nine US states and 25 percent were reached through a survey of 150 members of an online investment network, NVST. In all, 600 angels were contacted and 121 usable replies were received.

A possible explanation is that Wiltbank's results are affected by a strong self-selection bias. Indeed, his response rate was only 23 percent, and 11 percent of these responses were incomplete. Also, it is likely that his results were biased upward. In fact, in his study, business angel returns were only calculated from deals that had been exited (39.9 percent of the total), whereas returns to venture capitalists were calculated from overall returns on all venture capital investments—both exited and un-exited. Just like venture capitalists, business angels have in their un-exited portfolios "living dead" and "walking wounded," which they may have been unwilling to mark down and reluctant to write off. If Wiltbank had included the investments that had not yet been exited (61.1 percent), it is likely business angel returns would have been lower and more in line with venture capital returns.

Supporting the intuition that, everything else being the same, informal investors would accept lower returns, Bygrave and Hunt (2007) studied 3,613 informal investments in thirty-five countries tracked by the Global Entrepreneurship Monitor (GEM) project in 2004 and 2005. They reported that, on average, 25 percent of informal investors expected IRRs of −3 percent or less; 50 percent expected just to get their money back with no additional return; and 25 percent expected an IRR of 42 percent or more. The lowest expected returns were for close family members and the highest returns were expected by strangers and entrepreneurs. Women expected lower returns than men. And non-entrepreneurs expected lower returns than entrepreneurs. Bygrave and Hunt (2007) proposed that altruism might explain some of the differences in the returns expected by different groups.

While scholars, especially in recent years, have written about altruism in family businesses (e.g., Gomez-Mejia, Nuñez-Nickel, and Gutierrez 2002; Greenwood 2003; Schulze, Lubatkin, and Dino 2003; Sharma 2004), there is almost no scholarly literature linking informal investment with altruism, and what little there is sheds very little light on the topic. Sullivan (1994) provides some evidence that most business angels in the US would be willing to forego *some* financial return to invest in businesses that were seen as socially beneficial. Along similar lines, Wetzel (1981) found that some US business angels are simply willing to support new entrepreneurs (Wetzel 1981). On the other hand, Mason (2006) stated that while some US angels express altruistic motives, evidence of altruistic motives is much weaker in other countries. Yet, Lumme et al. (1996) found some evidence that unsuccessful angel investors in Finland were motivated to a greater extent by altruism than successful angels were.

In general, altruism has been neglected in economics, and in entrepreneurial financing specifically, for a long time. Simon (1993) stated, "Economic theory has treated economic gain as the primary human motive. An empirically grounded theory would assign comparable weight to other motives, including altruism and the organizational identifications associated with it." Simon called for economics based upon social life. It would be an economics reasoned a posteriori from many "painfully gathered facts." And it would have the merit of describing the world in which we actually live. And altruism would play a major role in it. In this chapter we draw on existing empirical work—scanty as it may be—to build an argument and derive hypotheses in which altruism plays a major role, and that we test with a large set of data gathered through the GEM project in fifty-four nations.

4.3 Agency and altruism theory

Traditionally, agency theory has been used to explain how the conflicting interests of humans involved within a firm seldom lead to value maximization and, instead, lead to arrangements that keep in check potential conflict of interest among those involved with the firm (Jensen and Meckling 1976). In other words, agency theory argues that because humans are self-interested, they will have conflicts of interest over some issues whenever they interact, and that incentives can be put in place to reduce or control conflicts of interest, thereby minimizing losses and sharing the gains among the self-interested parties.

Self-interest, however, does not exclude altruism, which is concern for the well-being of others; nor does altruism make a person a perfect agent who always does the bidding of the principal (Jensen 1994). We combine agency and altruism theory to explain the behavior of informal investors—encompassing relatives, friends, neighbors, work colleagues, and strangers (business angels)—who put money into entrepreneurial ventures. The overarching proposition is that as the relationship between an investor and an entrepreneur becomes more distant, the influence of altruism decreases and agency concerns increase to the point where they dominate, as in the case of formal investments by professional venture capitalists.

Agency theory is especially useful in explaining why venture capitalists and informal investors use different approaches to limit agency risks in their investments, which is the potential risk of an entrepreneur's misuse of an investor's money (Van Osnabrugge 2000). Limited partnership is the most effective organizational form for managing venture capital because the interests of investors in venture capital funds are aligned with the interests of the venture capitalists who manage those funds; whose interests in turn are aligned with the interests of the entrepreneurs that run the companies in which the venture capitalists invest (e.g., Gompers 1995; Norton 1995; Gompers and Lerner 1996). Van Osnabrugge (2000) found that both venture capitalists and informal investors reduced agency risks, but that whereas venture capitalists relied on formal agreements set up before an investment was made (principal-agent approach), business angels tended to place more emphasis on monitoring after an investment was made (the incomplete contracts approach).

Venture capital firms spell out in a legal document running to several hundred pages the terms and conditions governing their investment in a portfolio company; in contrast, rather than relying on elaborate investment agreements many business angels watch over their investments by working closely with their entrepreneurs. Granted some informal investors, especially those who belong to formal business angel networks, are behaving more and more like venture capitalists, whose sole objective is to maximize financial returns; however, most informal investors do not belong to formal networks and they have reasons for investing in entrepreneurial businesses other than simply maximizing their financial returns. For instance, many business angels invest in entrepreneurs and their new ventures not only for a financial return but also for an altruistic return such as helping an entrepreneur to develop a fledgling venture idea into a viable business (for example, see Bygrave and Zacharakis 2007).

As mentioned in the previous section, altruism associated with informal investing in entrepreneurial companies has barely been considered in the scholarly literature. Bubna (2006) developed hypotheses about how relational distance affects various contractual arrangements such as guaranteed bank loans and tied assistance and gifts in financing new ventures. He provided arguments about how kinship altruism influences the likelihood that entrepreneurs can get access to bank loans. Unfortunately, however, there are almost no empirical studies of this topic. Bubna cites Avery et al. (1998), but the latter provides only skimpy evidence to support his hypotheses. Nonetheless, Bubna's reasoning is compelling and our chapter builds on some of his ideas.

We define altruism in informal investing as an investor's sacrifice of resources for the benefit of an entrepreneur. In the context of this chapter the resources are money invested in an entrepreneur's business, but they often comprise a person's time and energy. What causes a person to be altruistic? Reasons cited by Bubna include familiarity, personality traits, appearance, background, lifestyle, similarity of opinions, and meeting of minds. Influences such as those determine whether two people like each other and engage in altruistic behavior. If a person decides to invest in an entrepreneur whom he likes, the decision may not be determined solely by rational self-interest, instead altruism may moderate the expected financial return.

A search of the finance and economic literature for a theory that explains the return on informal investment when it is tempered by altruism yielded no results. There is, however, an extensive literature in biology that investigates the relationship between degrees of genetic relatedness and social behavior of animals that can be traced back to Hamilton's (1963) paper on the evolution of altruistic behavior. Some sociobiologically oriented researchers built on Hamilton's work and implied that an individual's altruistic behavior towards his kin is directly proportional to the coefficient of relationship (e.g., Trivers and Hare 1976). Kurland (1977) proposed that altruistic acts increase and selfish acts decrease as the degree of relatedness between individuals increases. Dawkins (1976) explained the direct connection between altruism and relatedness arguing that an individual should care for his brother as much as he cares for his own child and if his brother is his identical twin he should care twice as much for him as his own child. Weigel (1981) built on Altmann's (1979) suggestion that altruistic behavior is a curvilinear relationship and developed a mathematical model with a diminishing returns investment function to simulate how an altruist would distribute investment among a group of kin. He found that altruistic investment increased with genetic relatedness. The distribution of investment was a function of costs, benefits, and energy associated with a specific altruistic act. In early rounds of investment, the altruist favored close kin, but as the total investment increased, altruism was more evenly distributed among kin.

Overall, this literature leads us to the following propositions:

Proposition 1: The influence of altruism on an informal investment decreases with the distance of the relationship between an investor and an entrepreneur.
Proposition 2: In general, an investment decision that is based partly on altruism rather than purely on rational self-interest produces a lower return.

From Propositions 1 and 2 we derive the following hypothesis:

H1: The expected return on investment increases as the relational distance between an informal investor and a recipient of the investment increases; which means that the lowest return will be expected by close relatives and the highest return by strangers such as business angels.

Of course, there are other important factors that might have a bearing on an informal investor's expected return. Bygrave and Reynolds (2004) find them to include age, experience, financial sophistication, amount invested, and gender. Bygrave and Reynolds (2004), for example, found that entrepreneurs are four to five times more likely than non-entrepreneurs to be informal investors. Entrepreneurs themselves have experience in raising informal investment for their own companies so it seems reasonable to expect that they are more sophisticated than non-entrepreneurs when evaluating potential investments and are more likely to pick investments that will be successful. This leads to the following hypothesis:

H2: Entrepreneurs expect higher returns on their informal investments than non-entrepreneurs.

It also seems reasonable to expect that larger investments will be scrutinized more carefully than small ones; furthermore, decisions to invest larger amounts will be less swayed by altruism and influenced more by rational expectations. Hence we deduce the following:

H3: The larger the informal investment, the higher the expected return.

Proportionately fewer women than men are entrepreneurs who are also informal investors. Furthermore, women invest smaller amounts than men (Bygrave and Reynolds 2004). Thus, combining H2 and H3 and separating the expectations by gender produces the following:

H4: Male informal investors expect higher returns than female informal investors.

The age of informal investors may influence their expected returns. Older persons invest larger amounts than younger ones (Bygrave and Reynolds 2004); which implies that they would expect higher returns if H3 is correct. Also, some older informal investors, especially retirees and those approaching retirement, may be cautious and therefore more rational in their investment decisions. However, older persons have more income and higher net worth so they can afford to be more altruistic; which implies that they would expect lower returns. Also young informal investors may be overly optimistic about their expected returns than veterans; which implies that young informal investors would expect higher returns. As there is not compelling evidence that correlates expected returns with age, we propose a null hypothesis:

H5: The age of informal investors does not affect their expected returns.

Finally, entrepreneurs themselves invest in their own businesses. Bygrave (2004) found that approximately two-thirds of the initial capital for starting a venture comes from the founders themselves, which is consistent with the finding that 70 percent of the start-up capital of the Inc. 500 came from the founders themselves (*Inc.* 2003). When entrepreneurs invest in their own businesses it is purely out of self-interest, but when they invest in other entrepreneurs' businesses altruism is often involved; hence the following hypothesis:

H6: When entrepreneurs invest in their own businesses they expect higher returns than when they invest in other entrepreneurs' businesses.

4.4 Empirical analysis

We used data from the adult population surveys of the GEM project to test our hypotheses. GEM is an ongoing large scale effort to collect data on entrepreneurial activity across countries. Professional survey organizations administered an adult population questionnaire to households in fifty-four nations in 2007 and 2008. Those nations comprised more than 90 percent of the world's gross domestic product (GDP) and about two-thirds of its population. The survey questionnaire, which deals with various aspects of entrepreneurial activity in nascent and baby businesses, as well as more detailed information about GEM, can be obtained from the www.gemconsortium.org Web site.

We were interested in the responses of individuals who reported that they had, in the last three years preceding the survey, personally provided funds for a new business started by someone else (excluding any purchases of public stocks or mutual funds). Respondents were asked how much, in total, they had personally provided to those business start-ups. They were also asked what their relationship was to the person who received their last investment and what payback they expected on the money they had invested into that start-up. Individuals who reported to be entrepreneurs were asked how much money they needed to start their own ventures; how much money they themselves were providing; and what payback they expected.

We combined the GEM data sets for 2007 and 2008 which yielded a total of 5,497 valid replies from informal investors in fifty-four nations.[6] In the empirical analysis we display differences in the distribution of informal investment across the categories identified in the previous section and we use standard tests for comparisons of the means of the amounts of informal investment. To analyze the expected times return, we apply an ordinal regression using a logit link function. Even though the eight categories of expected times return distinguished in the survey have a scale dimension, respondents were restricted to select one of the eight categories. Therefore, we treat these data as ordinal and assume that the ordered categories are a function of an unmeasured latent variable.[7]

The relationship between the informal investor and the entrepreneur is shown in Table 4.1. Table 4.1 lists the percent of the number of informal

[6] Nations participating in GEM 2007–2008 were Angola, Argentina, Austria, Belgium, Bolivia, Bosnia and Herzegovina, Brazil, Chile, China, Colombia, Croatia, Denmark, Dominican Republic, Ecuador, Egypt, Finland, France, Germany, Greece, Hong Kong, Hungary, Iceland, India, Iran, Ireland, Israel, Italy, Jamaica, Japan, Kazakhstan, Latvia, Macedonia, Mexico, Netherlands, Norway, Peru, Portugal, Puerto Rico, Romania, Russia, Serbia, Slovenia, South Africa, South Korea, Spain, Sweden, Switzerland, Thailand, Turkey, United Arab Emirates, United Kingdom, United States, Uruguay, Venezuela.
[7] We have checked the robustness of our results by running an additional regression using ordinary least squares. The size and significance of the estimated coefficients remained unchanged.

investments in each category; for example in all fifty-four countries combined, 47.8 percent of investments were in businesses run by entrepreneurs who were close relatives (spouse, child, grandchild, brother, sister, parent, grandparent) and 9.6 percent were other relatives. The mean amount invested in each category is listed together with the median expected times return. It is very interesting that only 50 percent of informal investors who funded close relatives expected to get a positive return; or, put another way, 50 percent expected to lose part or all of their investment. In contrast, 50 percent of informal investors who funded strangers expected to get a return of at least twice their investment. In general, the expected times returns for all nations combined are in accord with what we predicted in our agency-altruism theory: the greater the distance of the relationship between the investor and the entrepreneur, the higher the expected return, with the exception of other relatives, who expect a higher return than friends/neighbors. However, when the countries are grouped as Organization for Economic Cooperation (OECD) and non-OECD, the times return in both groups is in accord with our theory. Informal investors in OECD countries invested more than three times as much as their counterparts in non-OECD countries.

The distributions of times returns expected by informal investors from their investments in other's businesses and by entrepreneurs from investments in their own businesses are shown in Figure 4.3. It is a simple demonstration of how altruism and self interest affect expected returns. As we hypothesized, informal investors, who are motivated to some extent by altruism, expect lower returns when investing in another's business than entrepreneurs, who are motivated by self interest not altruism, expect when investing in their own venture.

The percentile distribution of the amount invested by various categories of investors and recipients of informal investments (Table 4.2) shows that men invested larger amounts than women (US\$25,321 vs US\$16,824; $p<0.000$), entrepreneurs invested larger amounts than non-entrepreneurs (US\$32,746 vs US\$16,999; $p<0.000$) and persons in OECD countries invested larger amounts than persons in non-OECD countries (US\$34,004 vs US\$10,972; $p<0.000$). Table 4.2 also shows that the amount invested in close family members was considerably less than the amount invested in strangers (US\$20,946 vs US \$61,029; $p<0.000$).

Table 4.3 focuses on the group of informal investors who are also in the process of starting a business themselves. The amount that entrepreneurs invested in their own businesses (US\$35,486) was higher than the amount they invested in others' businesses (US\$29,196), but the difference was significant only at $p<0.073$. There appear to be much higher differences if we look at the expected times of return. The final two columns of Table 4.3 show that entrepreneurs expect considerably higher payoffs on their investments in

Table 4.1. Amount invested and expected return by informal investor–entrepreneur relationship

Relationship: Investor-Entrepreneur	All Countries			OECD Countries			non-OECD Countries		
	% Total Number	Mean Amount Invested US$	Median X return	% Total Number	Mean Amount Invested US$	Median X return	% Total Number	Mean Amount Invested US$	Median X return
Close family	47.8%	20,946	1 x	50.4%	31,903	1 x	45.6%	9,083	1.5 x
Other relative	9.6%	15,845	1.5 x	5.5%	22,455	1 x	13.2%	13,127	1.5 x
Friend, Neighbor	29.3%	17,530	1 x	28.7%	25,862	1 x	29.8%	10,101	1.5 x
Work colleague	8.4%	33,747	1.5 x	9.2%	51,536	1.5 x	7.7%	13,032	2 x
Stranger	4.9%	61,029	2 x	6.3%	79,310	2 x	3.7%	30,801	2 x
	100.0%	22,230	1 x	100.0%	34,004	1 x	100.0%	10,927	1.5 x

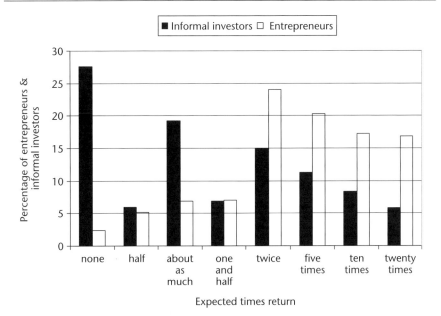

Figure 4.3 Times return expected by informal investors and self-funded entrepreneurs

their *own* businesses in comparison with their investments in *another's* business. The expected returns on investments in own businesses is roughly double that of investments in others' businesses, and the difference is significant at $p<0.001$.

The results of the ordinal logistic regression are shown in Table 4.4. The dependent variable consists of the categories of expected times return. Categorical independent variables entering the regression include gender, a binary variable indicating whether the informal investor lives in an OECD country or not, a variable reflecting the degree of household income (low-medium-high; these categories are country-specific), a binary variable indicating whether the informal investor is currently also an entrepreneur, and a variable indicating the informal investor's relationship to the recipient of the investment (close family, other relative, friend/neighbor, work colleague, stranger). Numeric independent variables are age of the informal investor and amount invested. The interpretation of the numeric independent variables is as follows: For each level of expected return, a positive estimate of the coefficient means that an increase in this variable, keeping the values of all other independent variables constant, increases the probability to "switch" to a higher level of expected return.

In ordinal regression the highest level of a categorical variable is the reference level and has a parameter value of zero. For example, the "stranger"

Table 4.2. Distribution of amount invested by type of investor and type of recipient

| | | Distribution of amount invested in $US | | | | | | | |
| | | Provider of Informal Investment | | | | | | Recipient of Informal Investment | |
		All	Male	Female	Entrepreneurs	Non-Entrepreneurs	OECD	Non-OECD	Close family	Stranger
Mean amount invested ($US)		22,230	25,321	16,824	32,746	16,999	34,004	10,972	20,946	61,029
Percentile of informal investors										
25 percentile		652	877	475	735	641	2,192	324	877	1,000
50 percentile		3,260	4,033	2,608	4,531	2,923	9,918	1,304	3,990	10,502
75 percentile		15,672	18,806	13,872	23,507	13,444	29,753	5,197	17,477	52,125
Comparison of means	F-statistic			30.408		101.121		249.779		120.062
	df			1		1		1		1
	p<			.000		.000		.000		.000
Measure of association	Eta-squared			0.004		0.014		0.035		0.032

Table 4.3. Comparison of amount invested and times of return expected on investments in own and another's business

	Distribution of amount invested in $US		Expected times of return	
	Own	Another's	Own	Another's
Mean amount invested ($US)	35,486	29,196		
Percentile of informal investors				
25 percentile	869	520	2 x	1 x
50 percentile	4,870	2,923	5 x	2 x
75 percentile	23,507	15,672	10 x	5 x
Paired sample t test t value	1.797		11.975[a)]	
df	786		680	
p<	0.073		0.000	

a) For this test the ordinal nature of the variable has been abandoned and the values of the expected times return have been used.

category of informal investor is the reference and has a parameter value of zero. The estimated parameter for "close family" is negative and significant; this indicates that investing in a new business by a close family member (rather than investing in a stranger's new business) reduces the probability of higher levels of expected return, keeping the value of other independent variables constant. The ordinal regression results confirm the significance of the eight distinguished categories in the dependent variable as a true ordinal scale. This can be seen by examining the estimated means and variances of the "thresholds" representing the intercepts attached to each category of the dependent variable. Some of the 95 percent confidence intervals attached to the estimated threshold values do not overlap. The largest gaps are observed between the step from expecting "half as much" to "about as much" (isolating the more altruistic informal investors at the lower end) and from "twice as much" to "five times" and "ten times" (isolating the extremely optimistic informal investors at the upper end).

The ordinal logistic regression shows that close family members expect lower times returns than strangers, which is the reference category ($p<0.000$), other relatives expect lower returns than strangers ($p<0.000$), and so do friends/neighbors ($p<0.000$); but there is no difference between the returns expected by work colleagues and strangers. Entrepreneurs expect higher returns than non-entrepreneurs ($p<0.000$); informal investors in non-OECD countries expect higher returns ($p<0.000$); men expect higher returns than women ($p<0.000$); the larger the amount invested the higher the expected return ($p<0.000$); and older investors expect lower returns ($p<0.001$).

Table 4.4. Ordinal logistic regression

Dependent variable: Times Return	Coefficient	Standard error	Wald	Significance
Thresholds				
–none	−1.573	0.134	137.888	0.000
–half	−1.289	0.133	93.255	0.000
–about as much	−0.416	0.133	9.836	0.000
–one and half	−0.114	0.132	0.740	0.390
–twice	0.589	0.133	19.661	0.000
–five times	1.311	0.135	95.039	0.000
–ten times	2.289	0.141	262.712	0.000
Non-OECD Country	0.500	0.050	99.583	0.000
Household Income				
–low	−0.328	0.063	27.112	0.000
–medium	−0.237	0.056	17.980	0.000
–high	reference			
Gender (male)	0.283	0.051	31.328	0.000
Age	−0.003	−0.001	11.692	0.001
Non-Entrepreneur	−0.479	0.052	84.188	0.000
Amount of Investment/ 1,000,000	1.634	0.377	18.758	0.000
Relationship to Investee				
–close family	−0.651	0.115	31.790	0.000
–other relative	−0.536	0.138	15.108	0.000
–work colleague	−0.169	0.139	1.475	0.225
–friend, neighbor	−0.518	0.119	18.999	0.000
–stranger	reference			
Cox and Snell R Square	0.069			
Nagelkerke R Square	0.071			
F	38.39			
n	5,430			
p	0.000			

In general, H1 is confirmed—expected times return increases with the relational distance between investors and recipients of the investments, with the exception of work colleagues. The lowest returns are expected when recipients are close family, second lowest returns when they are other relatives, and third lowest returns when they are friends/neighbors. There is no statistical difference between the returns expected by work colleagues and strangers; so it appears that work colleagues regard their investments in a way similar to strangers rather than in the manner of friends/neighbors. There are several possible explanations for this: first the survey question is ambiguous; it was intended to mean a colleague with whom a respondent worked while they were both employees, but it could be interpreted to mean a person with whom a respondent is now working in a new venture; in that case, a respondent might treat the investment as an entrepreneur does when investing in his own business, and therefore expect a higher return than an informal investor. Second, work colleagues invest almost twice as much as friends/neighbors, and the higher the amount invested the greater the expected return.

H2 is confirmed. Entrepreneurs expect higher returns than non-entrepreneurs.

H3 is confirmed. The larger the amount invested, the higher the expected return.

H4 is confirmed. Men expect higher returns than women.

H5 is a null hypotheses stating that the age of an informal investor does not affect expected returns. The null hypothesis is rejected: Expected returns decrease as informal investors get older. Possible explanations are that older investors are more experienced and wiser so they are more realistic than younger investors about expected returns.

Household income was used as a control variable. Interestingly, expected returns appear to increase with household income. This point deserves further investigation since a case could be made that investors with higher incomes could afford to be more altruistic and therefore expect lower returns. On the other hand, we know that households with higher incomes also invest larger amounts (Bygrave and Reynolds 2004), which implies higher expected returns. Also, the expected returns in OECD member countries were lower than in non-OECD countries. This is an interesting result and it could provide an interesting topic for future research.

The ordinal regression model that was used to test H1 through H5 was significant at the 0.000 level. Both the Nagelkerke and the Cox and Snell pseudo-R^2 are very small but it should be borne in mind that we were not building a model that explained the absolute values of times returns; rather we were simply testing for differences in times returns for a variety of factors and covariates.

Finally, H6 is confirmed. When entrepreneurs invest in their own businesses they expect higher returns than when they invest in other entrepreneurs' businesses (Table 4.3). This finding is not just a reflection of the higher amounts involved (H3), as the results in Table 4.3 indicate that for this group of entrepreneurs the amounts invested in their own business are only slightly higher than the amounts invested in others' businesses. As we suggested earlier, the difference is probably due to the fact that altruism is at work when entrepreneurs invest in others' businesses, whereas self-interest (with no altruism) is dominant when entrepreneurs invest in their own businesses.

4.5 Conclusion

This is the first extensive study of the returns expected by informal investors. With the exception of previous works based on GEM data, previous studies of informal investors have focused almost exclusively on business angels; and the scanty available data that exist for return on investment are for actual not expected returns. Nevertheless, we can compare some of our findings with those on business angels, because our category "stranger" includes them. The average investment of US\$79,310 in strangers' businesses in our OECD data is comparable with Sohl's (2003) estimate that a US business angel invests an average of US\$92,000 per venture; it is lower than Wiltbank's mean of US \$211,000 per venture but comparable to his median of US\$60,000. Returns on investments in strangers were expected to be zero or negative in approximately 50 percent of our cases compared with 61.5 percent of Wiltbank's (2005) and 47 percent of Mason and Harrison's (1999).

Overall, we think the expected returns on informal investments show that the decision to invest is partly motivated by altruism. The ratio of altruism to self-interest decreases as the relationship distance between an investor and an entrepreneur increases. We acknowledge that we are using the term investment in a broad sense to include not only an investment but also a loan and even a gift—the ultimate altruistic "investment." But we think our classification is justified because putting money into a fledgling business is very risky and the outcome is the same if the business fails: lenders and investors both lose money.

Our analysis indicates that the closer the relationship between an entrepreneur and an investor, the lower the expected return. Many informal investors were realistic when they put money into relatives' and friends' businesses because more than 50 percent expected to lose money or at best break even. It confirms a common piece of advice given to entrepreneurs who are seeking informal investments: make sure that investors, family and friends in particular, can afford to lose all their investment without having to change their lifestyle.

We believe that our findings have important implications for public policy. As we wrote earlier, informal investment is the lifeblood of entrepreneurship and it is crucial to the economy. There is a lot of altruism in informal investing. We think that public policy, especially income tax initiatives, could be tailored to encourage more informal investing. The US, for example, allows tax deductions for gifts to not-for-profit organizations; why not consider some kind of deduction for investments in new businesses at the time an investment is made. After all, when parents invest in a child's new venture they are helping to create at least one job; and their investment has an immediate economic impact.

Also, analyses presented in this chapter give glimpses of interactions between factors such as age, gender, household income, entrepreneur/non-entrepreneur, and amount invested. We intend to extend our research in the future by examining how interactions affect expected returns. It would be also interesting to investigate the effect of education on expected returns. Simon (1993) suggests that intelligent altruists are inclined to be less altruistic than unintelligent altruists.

To conclude, we believe that our research contributes to understanding the role of altruism in entrepreneurial investing. And heeding Simon's (1993) plea, we hope our data will be among "numerous gathered facts" that will one day play a small part in "an economics based upon the facts of . . . social life."

Acknowledgments

We thank all the GEM researchers, past and present, and their sponsors. Although GEM data were used in this study, their interpretation and use are the sole responsibility of the authors. Many thanks go also to an anonymous reviewer for helpful comments. All errors are ours.

References

Altmann, S. A. (1979), "Altruistic behavior: the fallacy of kin redeployment," *Animal Behavior*, 27: 958–9.

Avery, R., Bostic, R. W., and Samolyk, K. A. (1998), "The evolution of small business finance: The role of personal wealth," *Journal of Banking and Finance*, 22: 1019–61.

Bubna, A. (2006), "Relational distance and contracting—Family in credit markets," Working paper, Indian School of Business, Hyderabad. Amit_Bubna@isb.edu

Bygrave, W. D. (2004), *Global Entrepreneurship Monitor: 2004 Financing Report* (with Steve Hunt). www.gemconsortium.org

Bygrave, W. D. and Hunt, S. (2007), "For love or money? A study of financial returns on informal investments in businesses owned by relatives, friends, and strangers," in L. M. Gillin (ed.), *Regional Frontiers of Entrepreneurship Research 2007*. (Melbourne: Swinburne University) http://www.swinburne.edu.au/lib/ir/onlineconferences/agse2007/

Bygrave, W. D. and Reynolds, P. D. (2004), "Who finances startups in the USA? A comprehensive study of informal investors, 1999–2003," in S. A. Zahra et al. (eds.), *Frontiers of Entrepreneurship Research 2004*, pp. 37–47. (Wellesley, MA: Babson College).

Bygrave, W. D. and Zacharakis, A. L. (2007), *Entrepreneurship*. (New York: Wiley & Sons).

Dawkins, R. (1976), *The Selfish Gene*. (NY: Oxford University Press).

Freear, J., Sohl, J. E., and Wetzel, W. E., Jr (1996) "The informal venture capital market: Milestones passed and the road ahead," presented at The 4th State of the Art in Entrepreneurship Research Conference, May 9–11.

Global Entrepreneurship Monitor: National Assessment United States of America: Executive Reports, 1999 to 2005 can be downloaded from http://www.gemconsortium.org

Gomez-Mejia, L. R., Nuñez-Nickel, M., and Gutierrez, I. (2002), "The role of family ties in agency contracts," *Academy of Management Journal*, 44(1): 81–95.

Gompers, P. A. (1995), "Optimal investment, monitoring, and the staging of venture capital," *Journal of Finance*, 50(5): 1461–89.

Gompers, P. A. and Lerner, J. (1996), "The Use of Covenants: An Empirical Analysis of Venture Partnership Agreements," *Journal of Law and Economics,* 39(2): 463–98.

Greenwood, R. (2003), "Commentary on: Toward a theory of agency and altruism in family firms," *Journal of Business Venturing,* 18(4): 491–4.

Hamilton, W. (1963), "The evolution of altruistic behavior," *American Naturalist,* 97: 354–6.

Harrison, R. T. and Mason, C. M. (1988), "Risk finance, the equity gap and new venture Formation In the United Kingdom. The impact of the business expansion scheme," in B. A. Kirchhoff et al. (eds.), *Frontiers of Entrepreneurship Research 1988* (Wellesley, MA: Babson College).

Inc. (2000), "The Inc. 500: America's Fastest-Growing Private Companies," *Inc. magazine,* October 17, 2000, p. 65.

Inc. (2003), "The Inc. 500: America's Fastest-Growing Private Companies," *Inc. magazine,* Fall 2003, p. 89.

Jensen, M. C. (1994), "Self-interest, altruism, incentives, & agency theory," *Journal of Applied Corporate Finance,* VII:2.

Jensen, M. C. and Meckling, W. H. (1976), "Theory of the firm: Managerial behavior, agency costs, and ownership structure," *Journal of Financial Economics,* 3:4, 305–60.

Kurland, J. A. (1977), "Kin selection in the Japanese monkey." Contrib. Primatol, 12: 1–145.

Lumme, A., Mason, C., and Suomi, M. (1996), "The returns from informal venture capital investments: Some evidence from Finland," in P. D. Reynolds (ed.), *Frontiers of Entrepreneurship Research 1996,* pp. 344–58. (Wellesley, MA: Babson College).

Mason, C. M. and Harrison, R. T. (1993), "Strategies for expanding the informal venture capital market," *International Small Business Journal,* 11(4): 23–38.

Mason, C. M. and Harrison, R. T. (1996), "Informal venture capital: A study of the investment process, the post-investment experience and investment performance," *Entrepreneurship and Regional Development,* 8: 105–25.

Mason, C. M. and Harrison, R. T. (1999), "The rates of return from informal venture capital investment: Some UK evidence," in P. D. Reynolds et al. (ed.), *Frontiers of Entrepreneurship Research 1999.* (Wellesley, MA: Babson College).

Mason, C. M. (2006), "Informal sources of venture finance," in S. C. Parker (ed.), *The Life Cycle of Entrepreneurial Ventures,* pp. 259–99. (New York: Springer).

Norton, E. (1995), "Venture Capital as an Alternative Means to Allocate Capital: An Agency-Theoretic View," *Entrepreneurship: Theory and Practice,* 20(2): 19–29.

NVCA (2007), *National Venture Capital Association Yearbook, 2007.*

NVCA (2009), *National Venture Capital Association Yearbook, 2009.*

Schulze, W. S., Lubatkin, M. H., and Dino, R. N. (2003), Toward a theory of agency and altruism in family firms, *Journal of Business Venturing,* 18(4): 473–90.

Sharma, P. (2004), "An Overview of the Field of Family Business Studies: Current Status and Directions for the Future," Family Business Review, vol. XVII, no. 1.

Simon, H. A. (1993), "Altruism and Economics," *The American Economic Review,* Vol. 83, No. 2, Papers and Proceedings of the Hundred and Fifth Annual Meeting of the American Economic Association (May 1993), pp. 156–61.

Sohl, J. E. (2003), "The US Angel and Venture Capital Market: Recent Trends and Developments," *Journal of Private Equity,* 6(2): 7–17.

Sullivan, M. K. (1994), "Altruism and entrepreneurship," in W. D. Bygrave et al. (eds.), *Frontiers of Entrepreneurship Research,* in pp. 373–80 (Wellesley, MA: Babson College).

Trivers, R. L. and Hare, H. (1976), "Haplodploidy and evolution of social insects," *Science,* 191:249–63.

Tynes, E. B. and Krasner, O. J. (1983), "Informal risk capital in California," in J. A. Hornaday et al. (eds.), *Frontiers of Entrepreneurship Research 1983.* (Wellesley, MA: Babson College).

van Osnabrugge, M. (1999), "A comparison of business angel and venture capital investment procedures: An agency theory-based analysis," in P. D. Reynolds et al. (eds.), *Frontiers of Entrepreneurship Research 1999.* (Wellesley, MA: Babson College).

van Osnabrugge, M. (2000), "A comparison of business angel and venture capitalist investment procedures: an agency theory-based approach," *Venture Capital: An International Journal of Entrepreneurial Finance,* 2:2.

Venture Support Systems Project (2000), Angel Investors. Release 1.1. *MIT Entrepreneurship Center,* February 2002.

Wainwright, F. (2005), Note on Angel Investing. Tuck School of Business at Dartmouth: Center for Private Equity and Entrepreneurship. Case # 5 001.

Weigel, R. M. (1981), "The Distribution of Altruism Among Kin: A Mathematical Model," *American Naturalist,* 118(2): 191–201.

Wetzel, W. E. Jr (1981), "Informal risk capital in New England," in K. H. Vesper (ed.), *Frontiers of Entrepreneurship Research 1981.* (Wellesley, MA: Babson College).

Wetzel, W. E. Jr (1987), "The informal venture capital market: Aspects of scale and market efficiency," *Journal of Business Venturing,* 2: 299–313.

Wetzel, W. E. Jr and Freear, J. (1994), "Promoting informal venture capital in the United States: Reflections on the history of the Venture Capital Network," in R.T. Harrison and C. M. Mason (eds.), *Informal Venture Capital: Information, Networks and Public Policy.* (Hemel-Hemstead, UK: Woodhead-Faulkner).

Wiltbank, R. (2005), "Investment practices and outcomes of informal venture investors," *Venture Capital: An International Journal of Entrepreneurial Finance,* 7(4): 343–57.

Wiltbank, R. and Sarasvathy, S. (2002), "Selection and return in angel investment," in W. D. Bygrave et al. (eds.), *Frontiers of Entrepreneurship Research 2002,* p. 406. (Wellesley, MA: Babson College).

5

The Contribution of Migrants and Ethnic Minorities to Entrepreneurship in the United Kingdom

Jonathan Levie and Mark Hart

5.1 Introduction

We compare the entrepreneurial attitudes, activity, and aspiration of individuals in the United Kingdom (UK) who vary by ethnicity and place of birth. Immigration, and with it the growing presence of ethnic minorities in many regions of developed countries across the world, has become a significant political issue (Hanson 2009). With around twelve percent of its population composed of immigrants (House of Lords 2008), the UK occupies a middle position between the mainly immigrant nations such as the United States and Canada and more ethnically homogeneous nations in Scandinavia. The contribution of migrants and ethnic minorities to entrepreneurship is of interest to entrepreneurship scholars for a variety of reasons.

First, there is a need to understand why certain ethnic groups are more or less likely to engage in the entrepreneurial process (Volery 2007). Are these differences a function of ethnicity per se or, as Ram and Jones (2008) in the UK and Senik and Vernier (2008) and Fairlie and Robb (2008) in the US argue, the outcome of a complex interplay of social, economic, and institutional processes, known as "mixed embeddedness" (Kloosterman, Van der Leun, and Rath 1999)? Earlier work by Borooah and Hart (1999) in the UK provided an empirical investigation of one aspect of this notion by illustrating the relative importance of "ethnic disinclination" and "attribute disadvantage."

Second, there is a need to connect ethnicity and mobility to entrepreneurship (Levie and Smallbone 2006). Put simply, many ethnic minority entrepreneurs are also immigrants so it is important to separate the effects of migration or mobility from the direct effects of "ethnic culture." Specifically, which has the greater effect on the propensity to engage in new business activity: origin or ethnicity? Will people belonging to an ethnic minority group and who have lived all their life in the same place exhibit the same entrepreneurial tendencies as people in the same group who have recently arrived in that locality and were born outside the UK? The origin of the individual has been a neglected area of research on ethnic minority entrepreneurship (Williams, Balaz, and Ward 2004) but recent work by Levie (2007) has demonstrated the importance of the link between origin (life-long residents; in-migrants and immigrants), ethnicity, and new business activity both conceptually and empirically.

Third, ethnic minority groups who are under-represented in entrepreneurship have attracted a range of publicly funded initiatives in the UK designed to both increase their engagement with self-employment and address the more deep-rooted problem of social exclusion and disadvantage (Blackburn and Ram 2006). The rationale for these interventions is based on the evidence that ethnic minority businesses (EMBs) have been estimated to make a significant contribution to the UK economy (Mascarenhas-Keyes 2006; BERR 2008). The focus of the UK Government White Paper on Enterprise in 2008 was to address the barriers to entry for EMBs through initiatives on public procurement (e.g., CompeteFor in relation to the London Olympics in 2012), access to finance, and the provision of quality, accessible business support (BERR 2008).

Interestingly, while public policy in the UK concerns itself with encouraging and supporting EMBs it has been generally silent on the role of immigrant ethnic minority entrepreneurs (Levie 2007). Even less attention has been paid to the issue of inter-regional migration by ethnic minority individuals born in the UK and how that impacts upon entrepreneurship rates. In this chapter we draw on six years of Global Entrepreneurship Monitor (GEM) UK data (2003–8) to show how ethnicity and mobility affect entrepreneurial attitudes, activity, and aspiration. Most research on ethnic minority entrepreneurship in the UK has been conducted using small numbers of case studies or has relied on official data collected for Adult Population Surveys (APS) by the Office of National Statistics or from the decennial Census of Population in 2001 or 1991. Both these data types have weaknesses if used to estimate (or "gross up") rates of new business creation across ethnic groups. The problem lies with the inability to generalize from case studies and the narrow labor market focus in the official surveys, namely self-employment, as reported by the respondent.

In the next section, we survey the relevant literature on mobility, ethnicity, and entrepreneurship. Then, we provide a broad descriptive overview of the GEM UK dataset and how it was created. Using logistic regression analysis we then compare the contribution of different migrant groups and ethnic minorities to the different levels of engagement in entrepreneurship (defined here as business ownership/management). Five levels of engagement are recognized: no engagement, intention to start a business in the next three years but no activity, nascent entrepreneurship (someone who is actively trying to start a business that has not paid wages for longer than 3 months), new business ownership (someone owning and managing a business that has been paying wages for more than 3 months and up to 3½ years), and established business ownership. We conclude with implications for further research and for policy.

5.2 Previous studies on migration, ethnicity, and entrepreneurship

Considerable effort has been expended in research on ethnic minority entrepreneurship across the world in general (Dana and Morris 2007) and in the UK in particular, mainly on the assumption that entrepreneurial activity among ethnic minorities is different from entrepreneurship in the rest of the population and demands different forms of business support (Levie and Smallbone 2006; Smallbone, Bertotti, and Ekanem 2005). However, most of this work has been qualitative in nature, based on single cases or small numbers of interviews, often focusing on one or a limited number of ethnic groups; recent examples include Chaudry and Crick (2004; 2005), Nwankwo (2005), Ekwulugo (2006), Deakins et al. (2007) and Hussain, Scott, and Hannon (2008).

Twenty years ago, Aldrich and Waldinger (1990) made a plea for more multigroup comparative studies in ethnic entrepreneurship research and the GEM UK data provides a unique opportunity to address this plea. Studies that contain one hundred or more ethnic minority entrepreneurs are rare (for exceptions, see Smallbone et al. 2003; Jones, McEvoy, and Barrett 1994; Basu and Altinay 2002) and often focus on one or a limited number of ethnic minorities with no control groups (e.g. Altinay and Altinay 2008). Other studies have ethnic minority-owned businesses rather than individual entrepreneurs as the unit of analysis (e.g. Whitehead, Purdy, and Mascarenhas-Keyes 2006). Studies employing econometric methods are rarer still (see Borooah and Hart 1999 for one such example).

Investigating the large observed differences in self-employment rates between Indian and Black Caribbean males living in the UK, Borooah and Hart (1999) sought to isolate the relative contributions of ethnicity (an ethnic advantage or disadvantage) from an attribute advantage (e.g., education, housing tenure, or working partner). For example, it was argued that Indians are less assimilated than Black Caribbeans and see the UK less as a "home" but more as a "work-place." Related to this life-style characteristic of Indians is the notion of the extended family structure and the emphasis on pooled savings which means it is socially acceptable and economically feasible to become self-employed. However, these cultural norms within the Indian ethnic group in the UK are interwoven with a set of endowments that are positively associated with self-employment. This distinction is not too dissimilar to the analysis advanced more recently by Köllinger and Minniti (2006) when they highlight the contrast between the actual self-employment rate of Black Americans and their over-optimistic assessment of their likelihood to set up a business in the future. It also chimes with the study of work values of different first and second generation ethnic groups in France by Senik and Vernier (2008).

While "ethnic minority" and "migrant" may be convenient labels, they may mask important differences between different ethnic groups that affect entrepreneurship rates independently of ethnic status. In this study, we ask: how important are migrant status (or origin) and ethnicity as factors in the overall level of business start-up rates? It may be that other characteristics of ethnic minority and migrant groups, such as average age, gender-based stereotyping, education, employment status, and household income are more important variables than being a member of an ethnic minority or a migrant. For example, we know from the 2001 Census of Population that ethnic minority groups in the UK tend to be younger on average. So too do start-up entrepreneurs, on average. About half of immigrants come from groups classified in the UK as ethnic minorities. Could variation in origin, rather than ethnicity, better explain any differences in entrepreneurship rates between different ethnic groups? Or are both important?

Attempts to measure quantitative differences in entrepreneurial activity between the ethnic majority (White in the case of the UK) and different ethnic minority groups have been hampered by very small proportions of different ethnic minorities in the UK population, and by the need to combine immigrants with those born in the UK. To date, much reliance has been placed on self-employment survey data from the Labour Force Survey (recently renamed the Adult Population Survey), which may or may not be representative of either attempts to start new businesses or of the rate of new business creation (Clark and Drinkwater 2006; Ormerod 2007). There is also the issue of intergenerational change in entrepreneurial activity. It has been argued on the one hand that second and third generation immigrants might be more likely to enter the professions to gain social status, and on the other that continuing discrimination in the labor market might hinder this transition (Bachkaniwala, Wright, and Ram 2001). Such issues cannot be settled with small scale, multiple case methodologies.

Recently, several large scale quantitative studies that combined large samples from different annual cohorts have suggested that the independent effect of ethnicity on propensity to start a business is significant but very small, that origin (place of birth) may explain more of the variance, and that ethnicity and origin interact (Levie 2007; Levie et al. 2007a; 2007b). These studies were conducted using very broad ethnic groupings (e.g., White and non-White or White Mixed, Asian, Black, and Other) developed by the Office of National Statistics (2005). However, these categories lump together ethnic groups of very different heritage, such as Pakistanis and Chinese in the Asian category, for example, and Black Caribbean and Black African in the Black category.

In this chapter we pool six annual GEM UK surveys to reveal differences in entrepreneurial behavior between these very different ethnic groups and the effect of mobility, while controlling for other individual effects. We control for demographic differences such as gender, age, education, household income, and employment status. We include variables that signal awareness of and contact with entrepreneurship (knowing someone who has started a business in the past twelve months, having invested in someone else's new business in the last three years, and having shut a business in the past twelve months). We also incorporate three variables from the GEM survey which signal personal attitudes to entrepreneurship: self-perceived possession of start-up skills; fear of failure; and self-perception of good opportunities for start-up in the next six months. Finally, to control for the unique concentration of ethnic minorities and migrants in Inner London, we include a control variable for this sub-region of the UK.

5.3 Data: GEM UK sample characteristics

The methodology behind GEM adult population surveys has been comprehensively described elsewhere (Reynolds et al. 2005; Levie and Autio 2008). The GEM UK annual data consist of large samples of the working age (18–64) population and are stratified by twelve Government Office Regions. Different sample sizes are taken in each region each year, depending on funding. While regional samples can be analyzed by pooling, in order to simulate a national random sample, the annual samples from 2003 to 2008, some 148,000 cases in all, were pooled and random samples from each region were drawn in proportion to the region with the smallest sample, proportional to the UK population. Population data was generated by averaging the mid-year estimates for 2002 and 2007. The final sample of 38,635 cases was weighted by gender, age group, and ethnicity (white/non-white) to align it with population estimates.

People of different ethnic/migrant combinations have different demographic characteristics. Table 5.1 shows descriptive statistics for these groups, taken from the region-adjusted national sample. The table shows that migrants and/or ethnic minorities comprise around sixty percent of the working age population, but two-thirds are White regional in-migrants. Only six percent of the working age population are non-White immigrants.

Table 5.1. Descriptive statistics for different ethnic/migrant groups

	white life-long resident	white regional migrant	white immigrant	non-white life-long resident	non-white regional migrant	non-white immigrant	Total
% in sample	41.3	43.2	5.5	1.7	1.8	6.4	100.0
% male	50.0	48.9	49.6	47.1	46.6	54.1	49.6
Mean age	42.9	45.0	40.1	31.9	37.4	42.5	43.3
% graduates	18.3	39.1	53.1	29.5	48.2	45.5	31.6
% with HH income >=£50k	14.7	25.1	27.7	19.2	19.9	15.9	20.4
% students	2.1	1.7	4.2	11.2	5.4	5.1	2.5
% unemployed	4.7	3.8	4.4	7.3	7.1	8.0	4.6
% in London	6.7	10.3	31.9	31.7	35.7	41.6	12.8
% in Inner London	1.8	4.1	18.2	14.5	14.8	15.8	5.0

Source: GEM UK Adult Population Survey (2003–8)

This latter group tends to have more men than the other groups, while non-White life-long residents tend to be ten years younger on average than other groups. All ethnic and/or migrant groups tend to be better educated and they are more likely to be located in London. White life-long residents and non-White immigrants tend to be poorer than other groups, with White regional migrants and White immigrants the richest groups. In keeping with their younger age profile, non-White life-long residents are over four times more likely to be students than individuals from other groups. Finally, non-White individuals from all migrant groups are more likely to be unemployed.

In order to separate the effects of these demographic and locational differences on the propensity to engage in entrepreneurship from the effect of ethnic and origin differences, we employed binary logistic regression analysis. This technique is appropriate for studies in which the dependent variable is binary and reflects a propensity to be in one category versus another (Arenius and Minniti 2005; Levie 2007). A significant minority of individuals reported engagement at several levels from intention to established business owner/management. Since our interest was in identifying the effects of ethnicity and origin on increasing engagement in the entrepreneurial process, we categorized individuals according to their highest level of engagement. We chose to present separate logistic regressions for each category versus all other categories rather than conduct a multinomial logistic regression because of the relatively small numbers in some categories.

5.4 Descriptive statistics

Table 5.2 shows indicators of awareness of and attitudes to entrepreneurship in the UK, for different ethnic/migrant groups, comparing those who are not

Table 5.2. Awareness of and attitudes to entrepreneurship among different ethnic/migrant groups, by level of entrepreneurial activity (% answering yes)

	intention or activity	white life-long resident	white regional migrant	white immi-grant	non-white life-long resident	non-white regional migrant	non-white immigrant	Total
Know someone who started a business in last 2 years (yes versus no)	No	**18.1**	**21.6**	**29.1**	**28.6**	**29.4**	**20.8**	**20.7**
	Yes	**41.4**	**45.9**	**55.0**	**50.0**	**61.0**	**46.1**	**45.6**
Have knowledge, skills, experience to start a business (yes versus no)	No	**39.7**	**47.4**	**48.0**	**45.0**	**39.0**	**41.7**	**43.7**
	Yes	**83.4**	**87.0**	**87.4**	**70.7**	**84.6**	**80.3**	**84.8**
Good opportunities to start a business in my local area (yes versus no or don't know)	No	22.6	26.8	29.1	25.6	28.7	18.4	24.7
	Yes	**49.3**	**47.9**	**52.5**	**55.2**	**45.7**	**45.7**	**48.6**
Would not start a business for fear of failure (yes versus no)	No	**37.7**	**36.7**	**39.3**	**37.4**	**40.6**	**34.8**	**37.3**
	Yes	20.4	21.7	23.1	22.4	20.2	32.1	22.3

Note: Rows in bold show significant differences in percent saying yes across the six ethnic/migrant categories at the 5% level. Chi-square test results are available from the authors.

Source: GEM UK Adult Population Survey (2003–8)

currently running or trying to start their own business and have no intention of starting a business within the next three years with those who fit at least one of those descriptions. These results do not take into account the demographic differences between these groups shown in Table 5.1. Unsurprisingly, those who have no entrepreneurial inclination or behavior have less favorable attitudes and awareness. White life-long residents tend to have less awareness of and less favorable attitudes to entrepreneurship than other ethnic/migrant categories. Entrepreneurially-active non-White life-long residents stand out as having a lower skills perception than other groups. This may be because of their younger profile (see Table 5.1). White immigrants tend to have more favorable awareness and attitudes than other White groups, but non-White immigrants tend to have less favorable awareness and attitudes than other non-White groups. Again, this may reflect their different demographic characteristics.

Table 5.3 shows the distribution of entrepreneurial engagement, from no engagement through intention, nascent, and new entrepreneurial activity to established business owner/manager activity among working age (18–64) individuals in the UK. The least entrepreneurial group is White life-long residents. Intention rates are highest among non-White in-migrants and immigrants. However, early-stage activity rates (nascent and new entrepreneur rates)

Table 5.3. Distribution of engagement in entrepreneurial activity among the UK working age population by ethnicity and origin (%)

	white life-long resident	white regional migrant	white immigrant	non-white life-long resident	non-white regional migrant	non-white immigrant	Total
No	87.0	82.9	78.9	82.2	72.4	77.3	83.8
Intenders	2.9	4.1	7.9	9.9	11.9	12.8	4.6
nascent	2.0	2.7	3.8	3.7	6.5	4.2	2.6
New	2.2	3.4	3.7	2.4	6.2	2.5	2.9
established	5.9	6.9	5.7	1.8	3.0	3.3	6.0
Total	100.0	100.0	100.0	100.0	100.0	100.0	100.0

Source: GEM UK Adult Population Survey (2003–8)

appear to be higher among non-White in-migrants than among other groups, while established business ownership among White individuals of any origin is around double that of non-White groups of any origin.

Chi-square tests confirmed that the patterns of entrepreneurial activity are different across the three categories by origin, for both White and non-White samples (White: Chi-square = 243.241, df = 8, p = 0.000, N = 34,645; non-White: Chi-square = 43.654, df = 8, p = 0.000, N = 3,818). They are also different across the two categories of ethnicity by origin.

Table 5.4 shows the contribution made by these different groups to overall entrepreneurial activity among working age adults. Ethnic and migrant groups contribute more than their share of the population to overall activity, but their relative share declines from intention, where they make up almost three-quarters of the total, to established business ownership, where they make up less than sixty percent of all activity. While White regional in-migrants make up only forty-three percent of the working age population, they contribute half of all new and established business owner/managers. White and non-White immigrants have particularly high contributions to

Table 5.4. The contribution of different ethnic and migrant groups to entrepreneurial activity in the UK

	white life-long resident	white regional migrant	white immigrant	non-white life-long resident	non-white regional migrant	non-white immigrant	Total
No	42.9	42.8	5.2	1.7	1.6	5.9	100.0
Intenders	26.2	38.4	9.4	3.7	4.7	17.7	100.0
nascent	30.7	44.5	7.9	2.5	4.4	10.0	100.0
New	32.0	50.1	7.1	1.4	3.8	5.6	100.0
established	40.6	49.3	5.2	.5	.9	3.5	100.0
Total	41.3	43.2	5.5	1.7	1.8	6.4	100.0

Note: expressed as a percent of all individuals with that level of engagement in entrepreneurship

Source: GEM UK Adult Population Survey (2003–8)

intention, relative to their population. Immigrants make up only twelve percent of the working age population, yet contribute twenty-eight percent of intenders. It is possible that the reasons for this high intention rate differ between White and non-White individuals, given their different (non-ethnic) demographic characteristics, as shown in Table 5.1. For example, White immigrants are relatively wealthy, while non-White immigrants are more likely to be unemployed, even though they are relatively well-educated.

Table 5.5 shows the relative contribution of different ethnic and migrant groups to entrepreneurial activity in the UK. White life-long residents contribute around two-thirds of their population share to intention, around three-quarters to early-stage entrepreneurial activity, and a proportionate share to the established business owner/manager stock. White regional in-migrants have fewer intenders than one would predict, but more new and established business owner/managers. Non-White life-long residents and non-White immigrants have over twice as many intenders, 1.5 times as many nascent entrepreneurs, around ten to twenty percent fewer new business owner/managers and about half as many established business owner/managers as one would expect given their share of population. Non-White regional migrants make larger contributions, from 2 to 2.5 times their population share, to intention, nascent, and new entrepreneurial activity, but also have only half as many established business owner/managers.

At first sight, this pattern appears to be one of relatively high interest in entrepreneurial activity by non-White individuals from all migrant groups, but a low rate of conversion of intention and early-stage into established activity, in comparison with their White migrant counterparts. Partly, though, this is due to industry differences, as shown in Table 5.6. Migrants generally are less likely to enter extractive businesses, which tend to be based on land ownership in rural and remote regions. White in-migrants are less likely to enter transforming businesses (manufacturing and construction), but

Table 5.5. The relative contribution of different ethnic and migrant groups to entrepreneurial activity in the UK

	white life-long resident	white regional migrant	white immigrant	non-white life-long resident	non-white regional migrant	non-white immigrant
No	103.8	99.0	94.2	98.1	86.4	92.2
Intenders	63.3	88.8	170.4	213.5	258.1	277.1
nascent	74.2	103.1	142.6	141.3	244.5	157.3
New	77.3	116.0	128.3	82.4	212.7	87.0
established	98.2	114.1	94.8	29.8	50.2	54.2

Note: Relative contribution is expressed as the ratio of the rate for that group to the overall rate for the UK, for five levels of engagement in entrepreneurship

Source: GEM UK Adult Population Survey (2003–8)

Table 5.6. The contribution of different ethnic/migrant groups to the established business owner/manager stock, by industry type (%)

	white life-long resident	white regional migrant	white immigrant	non-white life-long resident	non-white regional migrant	non-white immigrant	Total
Extractive	59.0	38.2	1.7		1.1		100.0
Transforming	52.8	37.6	5.1	.5	.8	3.2	100.0
Business Services	26.2	63.5	6.2	.6	.5	3.0	100.0
Consumer Oriented	35.2	51.9	5.5	.6	1.4	5.3	100.0
Total	40.4	49.4	5.3	.5	.9	3.5	100.0

Source: GEM UK Adult Population Survey (2003–8)

dominate business services businesses. Non-White migrants are more likely to enter consumer-oriented type businesses, which may have lower barriers to entry but also have higher exit rates.

5.5 Independent effects of origin and ethnicity

To estimate whether migrant or ethnic status has an independent effect on engagement in different stages of the entrepreneurial process after controlling for other demographic and location effects, we conducted a binary logistic regression analysis. Table 5.7 shows five logistic regressions, one for each degree of entrepreneurial engagement. The results suggest that different characteristics affect the propensity of an individual to be in one category of engagement rather than any of the others. We focus specifically on migrant and ethnic status. The full model, including controls for gender, age, education, income, occupation, entrepreneurial awareness and attitudes, and the Inner London effect, and year of survey, are shown in Appendix 5.1. Ethnicity, for the purposes of the regressions, is broken down into the standard fifteen UK government ethnic groups.

All five logistic regression models were estimated including the same set of independent and control variables. They all had good model fit according to the Hosmer-Lemeshow test and all had a reasonable explanatory power (with Nagelkerke R-squares of around 0.2). All models predicted around seventy to eighty percent of both types of case ("positive" and "negative"), when the cut was adjusted to match the proportion of cases in the sample. The final sample size was 15,236 (attitude variables are only asked of half of non-entrepreneurially active individuals in the GEM UK survey, and the data was adjusted to account for this) and the sample was not weighted.

Table 5.7 and Appendix 5.1 display, for each independent variable category, the Wald statistic which gives an indication, to some extent, of the strength of

Table 5.7. Logistic regression of levels of engagement in entrepreneurship, showing results for migrant and ethnic categories

	No intention or activity versus others			Intention only versus others			Nascent entrepreneur versus others			New business owner/manager versus others			Established business owner/manager versus others		
	Wald	Sig.	Exp(B)	Wald	Sig.	Exp(B)	Wald	Sig.	Exp(B)	Wald	Sig.	Exp(B)	Wald	Sig.	Exp(B)
MIGRANT															
life-long residents (ref group)	10.476	.005		5.703	.058		4.418	.110		17.430	.000		.723	.697	
in-migrants	8.088	.004	.853	2.115	.146	1.148	4.035	.045	1.262	17.372	.000	1.617	.299	.585	.956
Immigrants	5.630	.018	.778	5.329	.021	1.411	1.772	.183	1.302	3.130	.077	1.455	.598	.440	.865
ETHNICITY															
White British (ref group)	50.742	.000		50.592	.000		32.542	.003		9.074	.826		7.157	.928	
White Irish	.032	.858	.970	1.066	.302	1.284	.830	.362	.710	.541	.462	1.252	.091	.763	.919
White other	.472	.492	.918	4.520	.033	1.454	.416	.519	.852	.001	.981	.994	.324	.569	.889
White and Black Caribbean	5.965	.015	.421	6.080	.014	2.920	3.347	.067	2.745	.202	.653	1.398	.430	.512	.508
White and Black African	1.987	.159	.540	6.004	.014	3.120	.121	.728	1.307	.238	.626	.597	.000	.998	.000
White and Asian	1.762	.184	.618	.759	.383	1.538	2.573	.109	2.448	.603	.437	1.637	.793	.373	.396
Mixed Other	4.392	.036	.543	2.602	.107	1.776	.007	.934	1.047	3.169	.075	2.326	.527	.468	.582
Indian	1.996	.158	.769	3.463	.063	1.589	.163	.687	1.150	.310	.578	1.213	.006	.936	1.027
Pakistani	2.466	.116	.672	.293	.588	1.206	3.559	.059	2.100	.181	.670	.769	.381	.537	1.368
Bangladeshi	.874	.350	.657	2.123	.145	2.074	.354	.552	.536	.012	.913	.890	.001	.973	1.037
Chinese	.799	.371	1.564	.005	.941	.955	.000	.997	.000	.061	.805	.774	.210	.646	.619
Asian Other	5.492	.019	.556	13.826	.000	2.886	.075	.785	1.146	.003	.954	1.032	1.078	.299	.518
Black Caribbean	15.084	.000	.442	9.452	.002	2.293	12.658	.000	3.021	2.054	.152	1.760	.550	.458	.700
Black African	21.897	.000	.361	29.081	.000	3.718	6.846	.009	2.356	1.478	.224	.469	3.300	.069	.156
Black Other	2.804	.094	.498	2.245	.134	2.172	3.815	.051	3.052	.052	.820	1.192	.000	.998	.000

Note: See Appendix 5.1 for full results including controls

Source: GEM UK Adult Population

the effect, the p value (values less than $p = 0.05$ indicate that the effect is statistically significant at the ninety-five percent level) and the exponent of the coefficient, which indicates the odds ratio, or the ratio of the odds of an individual having that level of entrepreneurial engagement versus any other level to the odds of a base case (of that independent variable) having that level of entrepreneurial engagement versus any other level. If the odds ratio is below 1, the direction of the effect is negative. For example, in Appendix 5.1, the first independent effect (gender) on the first level of engagement (no activity) suggests that the odds of males having no activity compared to any engagement are around two times lower than the odds of females having no activity versus any engagement. However, the odds of males intending to start a business versus any other level are around 1.3 times greater than the odds of a female intending to start a business versus any other level.

The following subsections highlight the main features of the regressions, focusing on ethnic and migrant effects. They refer to the "base case" individuals (the reference groups for each independent variable) described in Appendix 5.1.

5.5.1 No engagement in entrepreneurial activity

The odds of regional migrant or immigrant individuals having no current engagement in entrepreneurship versus at least some engagement are about 1.25 times lower than the odds of life-long residents of a region. The odds of White and Black Caribbean, Mixed Other, Asian Other, White and Black African having no current engagement in entrepreneurship versus any other level of engagement are about two times lower than the odds of White British individuals having no current engagement versus any other level of engagement in entrepreneurship. This suggests that mobility does increase one's propensity to engage in entrepreneurship, at least in some form, and that some but not all ethnic groups, particularly Black individuals, are more likely to engage in entrepreneurship at some level.

5.5.2 Intention to start within next three years

Migrant status does not appear to have an independent effect on intention to start versus other levels of engagement. However, the odds of a White Other (i.e. White, but not British or Irish) individual intending to start versus other levels of engagement are about 1.5 times higher than the odds of a White British individual intending to start. Individuals with Black ethnic heritage have even higher odds than White British: around three times for White and Black Caribbean and White and Black African individuals, around two times for Black Caribbean individuals and four times for Black African individuals.

Finally, the odds of Asian Other individuals intending to start versus other levels of engagement are around three times higher than the odds of White British individuals intending to start versus other levels of engagement. These patterns are generally consistent with the patterns from the previous category (no engagement).

5.5.3 *Nascent entrepreneurial activity (actively trying to start a business)*

Migrant status does not appear to have an independent effect on the odds of being a nascent entrepreneur versus other levels of engagement. The only ethnic groups to show independent effects were Black Caribbean, where the odds of being a nascent entrepreneur versus other levels of engagement were around triple the odds of a White British individual, and Black African, where the odds were around double the odds of a White British individual.

5.5.4 *New business owner/manager activity*

The odds of regional in-migrants being new business owner/managers versus other levels of engagement are around 1.6 times the odds of life-long residents. No significant independent ethnic effects are evident.

5.5.5 *Established business owner/manager activity*

No independent migrant or ethnic effects were evident at the $p = 0.05$ level of significance.

In the next section, we examine whether the aspirations of entrepreneurial individuals vary by migrant status and ethnicity.

5.6 Aspirations

One way of gauging the aspirations of entrepreneurs is to ask them their expectations of levels of employment in the future. GEM asks nascent and existing entrepreneurs how many people they expect to employ, other than the owners, in five years time. Table 5.8 charts the proportion of working age individuals who were engaged in nascent or new entrepreneurial activity and who expected to employ at least six or more, and at least twenty or more, employees by migrant and ethnic status. (The distribution of job expectation in the GEM UK sample shows significant step changes between five and six jobs and between nineteen and twenty jobs.) The table shows a significant increase in activity from White life-long residents to in-migrants to immigrants. This pattern is not repeated among non-Whites, however, with

Table 5.8. High-expectation early-stage entrepreneurial activity rates by migrant and ethnic status (% of working age population)

	life-long residents		in-migrants		immigrants	
	TEA 6 jobs or more	TEA 20 jobs or more	TEA 6 jobs or more	TEA 20 jobs or more	TEA 6 jobs or more	TEA 20 jobs or more
White	1.0	0.4	1.8	0.7	2.6	1.3
non White	1.6	1.1	3.7	1.9	2.8	0.9

Source: GEM UK Adult Population Survey (2003–8)

immigrants having middle to low levels of high-expectation entrepreneurial activity. Non-White life-long residents and in-migrants appear to have around twice the proportion of high-expectation early-stage entrepreneurial activity of Whites in these groups, with the proportion increasing with the level of expectation. Chi-square tests suggested that these differences were statistically significant. Non-White and White immigrants, however, appear to have similar levels of high expectation early-stage entrepreneurial activity.

Although the sample sizes were too small to test across more ethnic minority groups for life-long residents and in-migrants, there were no indications of substantial difference in the proportions of high-expectation entrepreneurial

Table 5.9. Logistic regression of high-expectation entrepreneurial activity

	Early-stage high-expectation entrepreneur		
	Wald	Sig.	Exp(B)
MIGRANT			
life-long residents (ref group)	20.834	.000	
in-migrants	**16.596**	**.000**	**1.947**
Immigrants	**13.794**	**.000**	**2.585**
ETHNICITY			
White British (ref group)	14.846	.389	
White Irish	.201	.654	.822
White Other	3.455	.063	.542
White and Black Caribbean	.005	.945	1.073
White and Black African	.025	.876	.847
White and Asian	6.130	.013	4.136
Mixed Other	.510	.475	1.515
Indian	.007	.933	.964
Pakistani	.238	.626	1.323
Bangladeshi	.577	.448	1.830
Chinese	.000	.997	.000
Asian Other	.635	.426	1.514
Black Caribbean	.269	.604	1.291
Black African	.582	.445	1.399
Black Other	.032	.858	.828

Note: See Appendix 5.2 for full results including controls

Source: GEM UK Adult Population Survey (2003–8)

activity (TEA 6 plus jobs) between Mixed, Asian, and Black individuals for these two migrant groups. However, for immigrants, the sample was large enough to permit analysis and a Chi-square test suggested that the proportions were not equal across the White (2.6 percent), Mixed (4.2 percent), Asian (1.9 percent) and Black (4.1 percent) groups.

A logistic regression was performed to predict the propensity to engage in high-expectation early-stage entrepreneurial activity at the six jobs or more level of expectation, using the same model as before, except that the reference group for income has been changed to better display the significant effects of this variable. The model displayed similar characteristics as the previous models in terms of model fit, variance explained, and prediction rates. Table 5.9 shows the results of that regression (test statistics for the full regression including all controls are shown in Appendix 5.2). It shows that the odds of a regional in-migrant being a high-expectation early-stage entrepreneur or not are double the odds of a life-long resident being a high-expectation early-stage entrepreneur or not. The odds of an immigrant are even higher at 2.6 times the odds of a life-long resident. However, ethnicity has no significant independent effect on aspiration, as measured in this way.

5.7 Conclusion

Using a very large sample representative of the regions of the UK, we found that White life-long residents had less favorable attitudes towards entrepreneurship than other groups. Controlling for gender, age, education, occupation, and household income, as well as awareness of and attitudes towards new business creation and ownership, we found significant differences in entrepreneurial intention and nascent entrepreneurial activity between the ethnic majority (White British) and some, mainly Black, ethnic groups. Those with Black ethnic backgrounds appear to have higher propensity to either intend or actively be trying to start new businesses, but this does not translate into significantly higher levels of actual business ownership. This result mirrors that of Köllinger and Minniti (2006) for the US.

Migrants are more likely to intend to start a business, and regional migrants are more likely to be running new businesses than life-long residents. This is in line with the earlier findings of Levie (2007) on a smaller set of GEM UK data. We found no effects of migrant or ethnic status on the propensity of individuals to be established business owner-managers.

Finally, we found that mobility influences one's propensity to be a high-expectation early-stage entrepreneur. Both UK-born regional in-migrants and immigrants are more likely to be high-expectation early-stage entrepreneurs than life-long residents. However, belonging to any of fifteen different ethnic minorities rather than White British appeared to have no effect on propensity to be a high-expectation early-stage entrepreneur.

The logistic regression results provide a formal affirmation of the views of Ram and Jones (2008) when they state that EMB activity emerges from the "mix" of social, economic, and institutional processes rather than any "innate cultural propensity for entrepreneurship" (pp. 367–8). The results also chime with recent results on ethnic minority and immigrant entrepreneurs in France (Senik and Vernier 2008). This is an important conclusion for policymakers as it points to ways in which they can achieve their objectives of encouraging start-up activity and business growth among the ethnic minority population.

The lack of importance of a direct "ethnic culture" effect permits those responsible for the design and delivery of business support programs and initiatives to be more confident about the likely effects as they seek to engage with the context within which the EMB operates. One important dimension of that context in an era of "super-diversity" (Vertovec 2007) of immigrant communities in the UK is the potential to connect to transnational social and economic networks that may deliver real benefits for the host economy in terms of trade and business opportunities.

An exception to this lack of an independent ethnic minority effect can be seen in the increased propensity of black ethnic minorities to intend to start a business and to actively try to start a business. The finding that this holds for both main black communities in the UK: Black Caribbean and Black African, is interesting. These communities are different not just in origin but in their assimilation history; the Black Caribbean community is relatively well-established while the Black African community is more recent. In our sample, Black Caribbean immigrants were around ten years older on average than Black African immigrants. Almost all Black Africans were immigrants, and around half of these had arrived in the region they currently resided in the last four years, while only half of Black Caribbeans were immigrants, of whom less than a third had recently arrived in the region they currently resided in.

The finding that for these Black groups, relatively high rates of intention and nascent activity do not translate into new business activity may reflect elevated levels of frustration with their current employment status, and perceived discrimination (Nwankwo 2005; Ekwulugo 2006; Clark and Drinkwater 2006) and echoes findings of perceived discrimination among African-Americans in the United States (Fairlie and Robb 2008; Köllinger and Minniti 2006). Alternatively, it may reflect genuinely elevated levels of interest in and perceived aptitude for entrepreneurship among Black ethnic minority individuals, something that has been shown in studies of young people in the UK (Athayde 2009) and the US (Walstad and Kourilsky 1998). Either way, these elevated levels do not feed through into activity.

It has been suggested that Black groups in the US have greater "failure" rates than Whites (Köllinger and Minniti 2006). In our sample, while two percent of White British in the UK had closed a business in the last twelve months that did not reopen, only 0.8 percent of Black Caribbeans had closed a business and 3.1 percent of Black Africans had done so. This does not suggest a connection between high closures and being Black. We could find no evidence in our data of Black Caribbean or Black African start-up entrepreneurs being more reluctant to seek external finance from financial institutions or government programs; in fact they were more likely to expect to get funding from these sources than their White British peers. We also found that Black Caribbeans and Black Africans were more likely to have received training in starting a business, both in school and after leaving school, than White British individuals.

The mismatch between intention, start-up activity, and established business activity among Black ethnic groups in the UK warrants further research, particularly as it spans two very different ethnic groups, with different endowments of human and social capital and business knowledge. While some studies hint at lack of professionalism among some Black entrepreneurs, a more constant theme in studies of Black entrepreneurs both in the UK and the US is discrimination among resource providers and ethnic majority customers. Discrimination breeds resentment. In many cases Black entrepreneurs have chosen the entrepreneurial path because of perceived discrimination at work. On entering an entrepreneurial career, they experience discrimination once again. If the UK is to make the most of its diverse workforce, deep-seated discrimination is something its government needs to continue to battle against.

Acknowledgments

Many thanks go to an anonymous reviewer for helpful comments. Although GEM data were used in this study, their interpretation and use are the sole responsibility of the authors. All errors are ours.

Appendix 5.1. Logistic regression of levels of engagement in entrepreneurship

	No intention or activity versus others			Intention only versus others			Nascent entrepreneur			New entrepreneur			Established business owner/ managers		
	Wald	Sig.	Exp(B)	Wald	Sig.	Exp(B)	Wald	Sig.	Exp(B)	Wald	Sig.	Exp(B)	Wald	Sig.	Exp(B)
Male	125.609	.000	.542	8.216	.004	1.288	16.663	.000	1.576	20.828	.000	1.668	60.959	.000	1.954
AGE 55–64 YRS (ref group)	5.864	.210		53.598	.000		5.380	.251		12.988	.011		135.437	.000	
18–24 YRS	.612	.434	1.104	43.842	.000	3.813	2.275	.131	1.467	2.068	.150	1.478	40.918	.000	.066
25–34 YRS	2.338	.126	1.142	31.958	.000	2.638	4.319	.038	1.459	9.743	.002	1.776	98.350	.000	.231
35–44 YRS	.131	.718	.972	28.332	.000	2.432	4.661	.031	1.442	9.467	.002	1.686	40.536	.000	.515
45–54 YRS	.001	.970	.997	11.135	.001	1.780	3.011	.083	1.350	2.667	.102	1.334	12.969	.000	.698
MIGRANT life-long residents (ref group)	10.476	.005		5.703	.058		4.418	.110		17.430	.000		.723	.697	
in-migrants	8.088	.004	.853	2.115	.146	1.148	4.035	.045	1.262	17.372	.000	1.617	.299	.585	.956
immigrants	5.630	.018	.778	5.329	.021	1.411	1.772	.183	1.302	3.130	.077	1.455	.598	.440	.865
WORKING 30 hrs or more fulltime (ref group)	152.731	.000		41.302	.000		38.397	.000		65.578	.000		93.039	.000	
Working 8–29 hrs a week (p/time)	21.130	.000	.721	3.128	.077	1.237	16.729	.000	1.753	12.849	.000	1.622	.006	.938	1.009
Not working—homemaker	5.737	.017	1.385	17.145	.000	1.990	.005	.941	.980	10.982	.001	.182	17.054	.000	.052
Not working—retired	92.679	.000	7.405	.074	.786	.924	5.477	.019	.404	11.906	.001	.082	39.482	.000	.025
Not working—student	1.012	.314	1.222	3.954	.047	1.555	1.912	.167	.514	3.764	.052	.308	2.263	.132	.335
Not working—sick, disabled, other	18.259	.000	2.377	3.175	.075	1.582	.450	.502	.770	6.986	.008	.069	17.604	.000	.114
Not working—unemployed	.133	.715	1.051	27.835	.000	2.500	10.368	.001	2.054	12.582	.000	.121	20.862	.000	.119
EDUCATION No formal quals (ref group)	.836	.997		28.112	.000		13.812	.055		7.158	.413		24.792	.001	
Doctorate	.001	.973	.992	2.831	.092	2.002	3.992	.046	2.452	.238	.625	.775	2.516	.113	.551
Masters degree	.655	.418	.902	11.466	.001	2.244	7.709	.005	2.136	.098	.754	.922	11.161	.001	.538
Bachelors degree	.174	.677	.955	12.018	.001	2.138	2.614	.106	1.510	.217	.641	.897	9.005	.003	.628
A levels or equivalent	.219	.640	.949	7.628	.006	1.840	.996	.318	1.296	.036	.850	.956	2.865	.091	.770
GCSE or equivalent	.305	.581	.941	1.341	.247	1.294	.958	.328	1.286	.087	.768	1.071	.026	.871	.977
Vocational qualification	.282	.596	.937	1.957	.162	1.411	2.122	.145	1.499	.027	.869	1.043	.684	.408	.872
Other qualification	.131	.718	.939	5.012	.025	1.977	1.336	.248	1.525	4.924	.026	.252	.082	.775	.934
INCOME up to £11,499 (ref group)	31.699	.000		14.942	.011		6.506	.260		22.255	.000		65.558	.000	
£11,500 to £17,499	1.964	.161	1.168	.154	.695	1.064	.189	.664	1.096	7.133	.008	.528	2.143	.143	.742
£17,500 to £29,999	6.806	.009	1.302	1.262	.261	.846	.520	.471	.868	10.682	.001	.509	.579	.447	.873
£30,000 to £49,999	2.362	.124	1.169	.116	.733	.950	1.473	.225	.784	6.175	.013	.605	.028	.867	.970
£50,000 to £99,999	2.034	.154	1.166	5.350	.021	.683	.147	.702	.924	7.116	.008	.569	1.740	.187	1.274

	B	Sig.	Exp(B)	B	Sig.	Exp(B)	B	Sig.	Exp(B)	B	Sig.	Exp(B)	B	Sig.	Exp(B)
£100,000 or more	6.512	.011	.704	5.051	.025	.597	2.636	.104	.638	.023	.881	1.038	21.795	.000	2.684
ETHNICITY White British (ref group)	50.742	.000		50.592	.000		32.542	.003		9.074	.826		7.157	.928	
White Irish	.032	.858	.970	1.066	.302	1.284	.830	.362	.710	.541	.462	1.252	.091	.763	.919
White Other	.472	.492	.918	4.520	.033	1.454	.416	.519	.852	.001	.981	.994	.324	.569	.889
White and Black Caribbean	5.965	.015	.421	6.080	.014	2.920	3.347	.067	2.745	.202	.653	1.398	.430	.512	.508
White and Black African	1.987	.159	.540	6.004	.014	3.120	.121	.728	1.307	.238	.626	.597	.000	.998	.000
White and Asian	1.762	.184	.618	.759	.383	1.538	2.573	.109	2.448	.603	.437	1.637	.793	.373	.396
Mixed Other	4.392	.036	.543	2.602	.107	1.776	.007	.934	1.047	3.169	.075	2.326	.527	.468	.582
Indian	1.996	.158	.769	3.463	.063	1.589	.163	.687	1.150	.310	.578	1.213	.006	.936	1.027
Pakistani	2.466	.116	.672	.293	.588	1.206	3.559	.059	2.100	.181	.670	.769	.381	.537	1.368
Bangladeshi	.874	.350	.657	2.123	.145	2.074	.354	.552	.536	.012	.913	.890	.001	.973	1.037
Chinese	.799	.371	1.564	.005	.941	.955	.000	.997	.000	.061	.805	.774	.210	.646	.619
Asian Other	5.492	.019	.556	13.826	.000	2.886	.075	.785	1.146	.003	.954	1.032	1.078	.299	.518
Black Caribbean	15.084	.000	.442	9.452	.002	2.293	12.658	.000	3.021	2.054	.152	1.760	.550	.458	.700
Black African	21.081	.000	.361	29.081	.000	3.718	6.846	.009	2.356	1.478	.224	.469	3.300	.069	.156
Black Other	2.804	.094	.498	2.245	.134	2.172	3.815	.051	3.052	.052	.820	1.192	.000	.998	.000
have start-up skills	597.060	.000	.220	81.479	.000	2.333	96.318	.000	4.102	129.289	.000	7.100	217.544	.000	5.281
fear of failure prevents start-up	109.139	.000	1.810	5.161	.023	.820	29.483	.000	.511	20.389	.000	.580	36.972	.000	.570
good start-up opportunities	184.608	.000	.503	76.264	.000	2.039	74.053	.000	2.398	21.359	.000	1.597	7.767	.005	1.246
know a new entrepreneur	140.410	.000	.537	59.217	.000	1.902	39.755	.000	1.920	26.915	.000	1.712	8.097	.004	1.265
invested in someone else's new business in past 3 years	12.043	.001	.573	.592	.442	1.199	10.497	.001	2.101	1.388	.239	1.352	2.507	.113	1.415
closed a business in last 12 months	17.339	.000	.570	5.097	.024	1.578	8.667	.003	1.861	4.035	.045	1.562	.250	.617	1.107
Live in Inner London	21.872	.000	.627	6.141	.013	1.401	1.918	.860	.828	12.354	.030	1.086	11.405	.044	.910
2003 (ref group)	23.126	.000		21.601	.001		.977	.323		.188	.664		.392	.531	
2004	.542	.462	.933	4.694	.030	1.362	.316	.574	.905	3.626	.057	1.399	.301	.583	.925
2005	.092	.762	.973	.042	.837	1.030	.357	.550	.903	.314	.576	.903	4.280	.039	.753
2006	7.657	.006	1.279	2.358	.125	.804	.001	.980	.996	.660	.417	.861	2.228	.136	.820
2007	4.543	.033	1.207	.791	.374	.881	.693	.405	.853	.488	.485	1.141	.347	.556	1.084
2008	.031	.861	1.016	2.162	.141	.792	11.534	.001	1.781	.116	.733	1.072	8.490	.004	1.633
Constant	400.569	.000	24.929	349.088	.000	.004	276.517	.000	.003	239.581	.000	.004	172.830	.000	.040

Appendix 5.2. Logistic regression of high-expectation entrepreneurial activity

	Early-stage high-expectation entrepreneur		
	Wald	Sig.	Exp (B)
Male	**16.205**	**.000**	**1.834**
AGE 55–64 YRS (ref group)	11.336	.023	
18–24 YRS	**4.964**	**.026**	**2.247**
25–34 YRS	**9.806**	**.002**	**2.351**
35–44 YRS	**10.229**	**.001**	**2.280**
45–54 YRS	**6.822**	**.009**	**1.989**
MIGRANT life-long residents (ref group)	20.834	.000	
in-migrants	**16.596**	**.000**	**1.947**
Immigrants	**13.794**	**.000**	**2.585**
WORKING 30 hrs or more fulltime (ref group)	5.657	.463	
Working 8–29 hrs a week (p/time)	.000	.998	.999
Not working—homemaker	4.147	.042	.344
Not working—retired	.000	.988	.000
Not working—student	.000	.993	.000
Not working—sick, disabled, other	.219	.640	.794
Not working—unemployed	.894	.345	1.351
EDUCATION No formal quals (ref group)	6.140	.524	
Doctorate	.124	.724	.803
Masters degree	.198	.656	.855
Bachelors degree	.242	.623	.852
A levels or equivalent	.173	.677	1.145
GCSE or equivalent	.053	.818	1.078
Vocational qualification	.205	.651	.845
Other qualification	2.088	.148	.384
INCOME £100,000 or more (ref group)	19.279	.002	
up to £11,499	**3.843**	**.050**	**.534**
£11,500 to £17,499	**10.167**	**.001**	**.372**
£17,500 to £29,999	**15.890**	**.000**	**.364**
£30,000 to £49,999	**13.032**	**.000**	**.435**
£50,000 to £99,999	**7.243**	**.007**	**.547**
ETHNICITY White British (ref group)	14.846	.389	
White Irish	.201	.654	.822
White Other	3.455	.063	.542
White and Black Caribbean	.005	.945	1.073
White and Black African	.025	.876	.847
White and Asian	6.130	.013	4.136
Mixed Other	.510	.475	1.515
Indian	.007	.933	.964
Pakistani	.238	.626	1.323
Bangladeshi	.577	.448	1.830
Chinese	.000	.997	.000

Asian Other	.635	.426	1.514
Black Caribbean	.269	.604	1.291
Black African	.582	.445	1.399
Black Other	.032	.858	.828
have start-up skills	**45.534**	**.000**	**3.905**
fear of failure prevents start-up	**17.872**	**.000**	**.498**
good start-up opportunities	**24.556**	**.000**	**1.941**
know a new entrepreneur	**37.853**	**.000**	**2.347**
invested in someone else's new business in past 3 years	**14.693**	**.000**	**2.638**
closed a business in last 12 months	.726	.394	1.280
Live in Inner London	1.344	.930	
2003 (ref group)	.641	.423	.823
2004	.917	.338	.802
2005	.870	.351	.812
2006	.701	.402	.830
2007	.930	.335	.787
2008	17.924	.000	2.364
Constant	179.685	.000	.001

References

Aldrich, H. and Waldinger, R. (1990), Ethnicity and Entrepreneurship. *Annual Review of Sociology* 16: 111–35.

Altinay, L. and Altinay, E. (2008), Factors influencing business growth: The rise of Turkish entrepreneurship in the UK. *International Journal of Entrepreneurial Behaviour & Research* 14(1): 24–46.

Arenius, P. and Minniti, M. (2005), Perceptual Variables and Nascent Entrepreneurship. *Small Business Economics* 24(3): 233–47.

Athayde, R. (2009), Measuring enterprise potential in young people. *Entrepreneurship Theory & Practice* 33(2): 481–500.

Bachkaniwala, D., Wright, M., and Ram, M. (2001), Succession in South Asian family businesses in the UK. *International Small Business Journal* 19(4): 15–27.

Basu, A. and Altinay, E. (2002), The Interaction between Culture and Entrepreneurship in London's Immigrant Businesses. *International Small Business Journal* 20(4): 371–93.

BERR—Business, Enterprise, and Regulatory Reform Department (2008), Government White Paper on Enterprise. London, United Kingdom.

Blackburn, R. and Ram, M. (2006), Fix or fiction?: The contributions of small firms to social inclusion. *Entrepreneurship and Regional Development* 18: 73–89.

Borooah, V. K. and Hart, M. (1999), Factors affecting self-employment among Indian and Black Caribbean men in Britain. *Small Business Economics* 13(2): 111–29.

Chaudhry, S. and Crick, D. (2004), The business practices of small Chinese restaurants in the UK. *Strategic Change* 13(1): 37–49.

Chaudry, S. and Crick, D. (2005), A case history of a "successful" Asian entrepreneur in the UK: Moni Varma of Veetee Rice Ltd. *Strategic Change* 14(7): 391–400.

Clark, K. and Drinkwater, S. (2006), Changing Patterns of Ethnic Minority Self-Employment in Britain: Evidence from Census Microdata. IZA Discussion paper no. 2495. Bonn: IZA.

Dana, L.-P. and Morris, M. (eds.) (2007), *Handbook of research on ethnic minority research.* Cheltenham, UK: Edward Elgar.

Deakins, D., Ishaq, M., Smallbone, D., Whittam, G., and Wyper, J. (2007), Ethnic Minority Businesses in Scotland and the Role of Social Capital. *International Small Business Journal* 25(3): 307–26.

Ekwulugo, F. (2006), Entrepreneurship and SMEs in London (UK): Evaluating the role of black Africans in this emergent sector. *Journal of Management Development* 25(1): 66–79.

Fairlie, R. W. and Robb, A. M. (2008), *Race and Entrepreneurial Success.* Cambridge, MA: MIT Press.

Hanson, G. H. (2009), The Economic Consequences of the International Migration of Labor. *Annual Review of Economics* 1: 179–208.

House of Lords (2008), *The Economic Impact of Immigration. Volume 1: Report.* London: The Stationery Office Ltd.

Hussain, J. G., Scott, J. M., and Hannon, P. D. (2008), The new generation: characteristics and motivations of BME graduate entrepreneurs. *Education + Training* 50(7): 582–96.

Jones, T., McEvoy, D., and Barrett, G. (1994), Raising Capital for the Ethnic Minority Small Firm. In A. Hughes and D. Storey (eds.), *Finance and the Small Firm,* pp. 145–81. London and New York: Routledge.

Kloosterman, R., Van der Leun, J., and Rath, J. (1999), Mixed embeddedness: (in)formal economic and immigrant business in The Netherlands. *International Journal of Urban and Regional Research* 23(2): 252–66.

Köllinger, P. and Minniti, M. (2006), Not for lack of trying: American entrepreneurship in black and white. *Small Business Economics* 27: 59–79.

Levie, J. (2007), Immigration, in-migration, ethnicity and entrepreneurship in the United Kingdom. *Small Business Economics* 28(2): 143–69.

Levie, J. and Autio, E. (2008), A theoretical grounding and test of the GEM model. *Small Business Economics* 31: 235–63.

Levie, J., Hart, M., Anyadike-Danes, M., and Harding, R. (2007a), Migrant and Non-migrant Entrepreneurship in the United Kingdom: Individual, local and regional effects on quantity and quality. Presented to Babson College Entrepreneurship Research Conference, Madrid, June.

Levie, J., Anyadike-Danes, M., Hart, M., and Harding, R. (2007b), Drivers of Entrepreneurship in the United Kingdom: Do regions matter? Presented at the GEM Regional Workshop, San Sebastian, July.

Levie, J. and Smallbone, D. (2006), Entrepreneurship, ethnicity and migration: current trends and future directions. In M. Minniti (ed.), *Perspectives on Entrepreneurship Volume 1.* New York: Praeger Publishers, pp. 157–80.

Mascarenhas-Keyes, S. (2006), "Ethnic minority small and medium enterprises in England: diversity and challenges," paper presented to the 51st Conference of the

International Council for Small Business, Melbourne, Australia, 18–21 June, available from authors.

Nwankwo, S. (2005), Characterisation of Black African entrepreneurship in the UK: A pilot study. *Journal of Small Business and Enterprise Development* 12(1): 120–36.

Office of National Statistics (2005), Labour Force Survey Quarterly Supplement 29 (April). London: National Statistics Office.

Ormerod, C. (2007), What is known about numbers and "earnings" of the self-employed? *Economic & Labour Market Review* 1(7): 48–56.

Ram, M. and Jones, T. (2008), Ethnic Minority Business: Review of Research and Policy. *Environment and Planning C: Government and Policy,* 26: 352–74.

Reynolds, P., Bosma, N., Autio, E., Hunt, S., De Bono, N., Servais, I., Lopez-Garcia, P., and Chin, N. (2005), Global Entrepreneurship Monitor: Data Collection Design and Implementation 1998–2003. *Small Business Economics* 24(3): 205–31.

Senik, C. and Vernier, T. (2008), Entrepreneurs, social networks and work values of ethnic minorities in France. *International Journal of Manpower* 29(7): 610–29.

Smallbone, D., Bertotti, M., and Ekanem, I. (2005), Diversification in ethnic minority business: The case of Asians in London's creative industries. *Journal of Small Business and Enterprise Development* 12(1): 41–56.

Smallbone, D., Ram, M., Deakins, D., and Baldock, R. (2003), Access to Finance by Ethnic Minority Businesses in the UK. *International Small Business Journal* 21(3): 291–314.

Vertovec, S. (2007), Super-diversity and its implications. *Ethnic and Racial Studies* 30(6): 1024–54.

Volery, T. (2007), Ethnic entrepreneurship: A theoretical framework. In L.-P. Dana and M. Morris (eds.), *Handbook of research on ethnic minority research.* Cheltenham, UK: Edward Elgar.

Walstad, W. B. and Kourilsky, M. L. (1998), Entrepreneurial attitudes and knowledge of black youth. *Entrepreneurship Theory & Practice* 13: 5–18.

Whitehead, E., Purdy, D., and Mascarenhas-Keyes, S. (2006), Ethnic Minority Businesses in England: Report on the Annual Small Business Survey 2003 Ethnic Boost. URN 06/958. London, UK: Small Business Service.

Williams, A. M., Balaz, V., and Ward, C. (2004), International Labour Mobility and Uneven Regional Development in Europe: human capital, knowledge and entrepreneurship. *European Urban and Regional Studies* 11(1): 27–46.

6

Entrepreneurship in World Cities

Zoltan Acs, Niels Bosma, and Rolf Sternberg

6.1 Introduction

Living in an era of increased globalization requires discussing the distinctive role of (large) cities in their countries. The general importance of world cities for economic development is underlined by the fact that, in 2010, 50.6 percent of the global population lives in urban areas according to the UN definitions (United Nations 2007). Furthermore, using the common definition of a city (as opposed to urban areas), by 2030 nearly 5 billion people will live in cities—roughly fifty percent of the world population—whereas only thirteen percent lived in cities in 1900.[1] A recent issue of *Science* (2008) took a broad perspective and emphasized the impacts of urban life on global development. Similarly, in line with Jacobs' seminal work on cities' externalities (Jacobs 1969), Glaeser et al. (1992) stressed the importance of the availability of human capital in cities. Finally, some studies have discussed how a high degree of cultural and economic diversity in metropolitan areas, compared to the rest of the country, may enhance growth (Florida 2004), especially if entrepreneurial activity is abundant (Lee et al. 2004).

Despite the observation that entrepreneurship is a worldwide phenomenon, only in the past two decades has it been identified as a crucial driver of both national and regional economies (Acs et al. 2004). Schumpeter's (1942) creative destruction argument supports the idea that new (and very often small) firms have a significant impact on structural change both from an industrial perspective and from a spatial perspective (national, regional).

---

[1] We refer to the UN definition of a "proper city" (http://esa.un.org/unup): "A locality defined according to legal/political boundaries and an administratively recognized urban status that is usually characterized by some form of local government." That means that cities are not characterized by the same minimum number of inhabitants in all countries but by country-specific limits.

Today there is a general consensus that a distinct theoretical and empirical relationship between entrepreneurial activities and economic performance of nations and subnational regions exist. As a consequence, the link between entrepreneurship and world cities has emerged as a very important and under-studied field of inquiry (Acs 2002).

Writing about entrepreneurship means to define it. Although entrepreneurial activities may occur in large and established firms, in this chapter entrepreneurship is related to young and small firms. We understand entrepreneurship as a combination of some elements of behavioral science with some aspects of occupational choice, making new venture creation the hallmark of entrepreneurship (Cooper 2003). At the national level, cross-countries studies have demonstrated a consistent U-shaped association between a country's level of economic development and its level of entrepreneurial activity (e.g., Bosma et al. 2009). At the regional level, results of empirical studies are not as clear but local influences on regional entrepreneurship activities are predominantly positive (see Sternberg 2009).

Considering the increased attention paid to urban areas and world cities, it is not surprising that the regional dimension of entrepreneurship is a subject of great interest (Acs and Armington 2004; Wagner and Sternberg 2004; van Stel and Storey 2004; Acs and Storey 2004). However, two issues loom rather large on the horizon. First, the interplay between regional entrepreneurship and regional economic development has not been theoretically grounded in either the new growth theory or the new economic geography (Acs and Varga 2005). Second, the empirical studies that focus on this issue have all focused on regional differences within a single country. Therefore, most cross-country comparisons on world cities (Taylor 2004; Beaverstock, Taylor, and Smith 1999; OECD (Organization for Economic Cooperation and Development) 2007) do not have data enabling comparisons on entrepreneurship, and little is known about entrepreneurial activity across world cities.

This chapter provides a first attempt at filling this gap. We set out a framework encompassing the process between entrepreneurial perceptions and entrepreneurial activity at the individual level and demonstrate how the urban environment can have an impact on this process. We use Global Entrepreneurship Monitor (GEM) data to study variations in entrepreneurial perceptions and entrepreneurial behavior across thirty-five world cities. Our work is exploratory and the analytical focus of this chapter is descriptive. We calculate and examine various indicators of entrepreneurial perceptions and activity, and investigate differences between the city-level and country-level for a selection of the indices. These exercises can be seen as initial explorations of the entrepreneurial advantage of world cities.

6.2 Entrepreneurship in world cities:
Relevance and definitions

It is generally accepted that entrepreneurship is primarily a "regional event" as Feldman (2001) put it (for further supporting arguments see Sternberg and Rocha 2007). This means that entrepreneurial decisions by individuals (in favor or against self-employment), as well as the success or failure of a start-up, are influenced, among other factors, by variables related to the region where the individual and the start-up are located. This kind of regional influence—with the region typically being a subnational territory within a radius of no more than 100 km—is often stronger than the impact of the national or continental context. A region, however, is not the same as a world city, metropolitan area, or urban region. In many countries, the majority of regions tend to be rural. Thus, discussing entrepreneurship in world cities calls for a definition of a city or an urban region.

Without adequate quantitative data on qualitative characteristics of urban life, most of the studies on regional entrepreneurship rely on available data covering population size and density. In such studies the latter serve as a proxy "for all kinds of regional influences, such as the availability and cost of needed resources like floor space and qualified labor, the presence of specialized services and venture capital, spatial proximity to customers and to other businesses in the industry, the regional knowledge stock and knowledge spillovers, quality of life etc." (Fritsch and Falck 2007, 159).

There is no doubt that population density and a minimum absolute number of inhabitants are the most popular criteria to distinguish urban from rural areas in empirical studies. Several cross-regional empirical studies in different countries have shown that a positive relationship between population density and size, and new firm formation exist (Fotopoulos and Spence 1999 for Greek regions; Armington and Acs 2002 for US regions; Reynolds et al. 1994 for European regions; Brixy and Grotz 2007 for German regions). However, although necessary, density and absolute population size are not sufficient criteria. According to Friedmann (1986), world cities are defined by their function in the global economy, not by population size. They are the command and control centers of large global companies, and major locations for business services and financial industries. As such, Friedmann argues, they are the controlling network for flows of capital, goods, people, and knowledge and produce a global hierarchy.

An urban climate has a lot to do with cultural richness, economic diversity, international connectivity, and infrastructure excellence (education, transport) that is not available in each city. The Loughborough Globalization and World Cities (GaWC) research network has developed a valuable empirical framework to identify and empirically analyze world cities and metropolitan regions (Taylor 2004). Going beyond Friedmann's hierarchy hypothesis, GaWC investigated empirically how financial and business service firms use cities across the world in their provision of services to global capital, and thereby create a world city network (Derudder et al. 2003). Based on empirical analysis of 234 cities ordered into 22 urban arenas the GaWC network shows an intertwining of hierarchical and regional tendencies in the servicing of global capital with the presence of a trilateral core, the distinctive profiles of US cities, the high degree of trans-regional "hybridity" of European cities, and the marginal position of most African cities. The GaWC classification will be used in the empirical part of this chapter to compare world cities.

6.3 Entrepreneurship in world cities: Theory and measurement

In regionally motivated research we may distinguish three main arguments in favor of a special treatment of large cities/metropolitan areas.

6.3.1 *Jacobs' urban externalities*

In her book on *The Economy of Cities*, Jacobs (1969) focused on a specific type of agglomeration effects. Her basic argument is that the more intensive in traregional competition among firms is, the higher the regional economic growth. The intuition is that an increasing number of firms resulting from more start-ups increase competition and thus regional economic growth. Different from the more static perspective of the Marshall–Arrow–Romer externalities focusing on *intra*-industry agglomeration (or localization economies), Jacobs externalities have a dynamic perspective based upon *inter*-industry agglomeration (urbanization economies). Entry of new firms, exit of incumbent ones, and firm turnover all have a stronger effect on regional innovativeness and productivity than competition among incumbent firms (Falck 2007; Aghion and Howitt 2006). Thus, urbanization economies are positively correlated with the population size of the city because a greater number of new firms, as observable in larger cities, increase the probability of inter-industry connections and spillover effects. Heterogeneity, *not* specialization in sectoral-regional clusters, is seen as the most important determinant of regional economic growth (Feldman et al. 2005).

6.3.2 *Agglomeration and technological change*

Technological change is the most important factor in long-run macroeconomic growth (Solow 1957). In new growth theory, the technological element of the growth process is directly modeled within the economic system as a result of the profit motivated choices of economic agents. Indeed, findings in entrepreneurship, the geography of innovation, and the new economic geography, suggest that the extent to which a country is entrepreneurial, and its economic system is agglomerated, contribute to explaining technological change, via the working of knowledge spillovers.

A large body of literature exists on the spatial extent of knowledge spillovers. At different levels of spatial aggregation (such as states, metropolitan areas, counties) in different countries (e.g., the US, France, Germany, Italy, Austria) and with the application of different econometric methodologies (e.g., various spatial or a-spatial methods) many of these studies conclude that geographical proximity to the knowledge source significantly amplifies spillovers between research and innovating firms. Strong evidence is provided both for the US (Jaffe et al. 1993; Varga 1998) and for Europe (e.g., Autant-Bernard 2001; Fischer and Varga 2003) that knowledge flows are bounded within a relatively narrow geographical range. Although certain industrial differences exist, the hypothesis that spatial proximity is an important factor in innovation is strongly supported in the literature.

The most recent models in the new economic geography incorporate the effects of knowledge spillovers on the formation of spatial economic structure as well as provide an attempt to explicitly integrate new growth theory and new economic geography (Fujita and Thisse 2002; Baldwin et al. 2003). If one takes into account that agglomeration facilitates knowledge spillovers (according to the new economic geography) and knowledge spillovers influence per capita gross domestic product (GDP) growth (according to the new growth theory), then it is not an unrealistic assumption that the spatial economic structure affects macroeconomic growth.[2]

6.3.3 Creativity and the "geography of talent" hypothesis

The idea of creative cities or creative regions is not new (see Andersson 1985). Nonetheless, Florida's (2002, 2004) more recent "geography of talent" hypothesis sheds an empirical light on this concept and is now intensively used by local development agencies in many countries (Florida et al. 2008). While causalities are not always easy to figure out, it seems obvious, and in line with Florida's argument, that a relationship exists between certain

---

[2] Another related strand of recent research deals with "Evolutionary Economic Geography" and focuses on the interaction between firms and the macro environment (regions, sectors) over space and time (Boschma and Frenken 2006; Martin and Sunley 2006). Concepts prominently used in this theoretical framework deal with path dependent processes in the economic landscape, related variety of economic activities in a region (leading to knowledge spillovers) and branching processes (leading to new industries that are technologically related to existing industries in a region).

characteristics of a world city (e.g. cultural and/or ethnic diversity), the number of talented people within that city, and the amount of entrepreneurial activities.

The talented are better equipped to create a self-enforcing intraregional process of economic growth that is knowledge-based and perpetuated by new firms, the founders of which are normally creative persons from within the region. This process also helps to attract highly mobile talented people from other regions as a result of image effects (see, e.g., the argumentation by Glaeser et al. 2001). In her seminal contribution to the role of cultural differences in two prominent US high-tech regions, Saxenian (1994) combined the role of entrepreneurship, culture, and competition to explain why these three *regional* advantages matter—this time in favor of the Silicon Valley and against the Greater Boston area. Both regions are highly urbanized and densely populated but are not home of the biggest cities in the country.

To sum up, agglomeration effects—no matter whether they are Jacobs' externalities in terms of urbanization economies or Marshall-Arrow-Romer externalities in terms of localization economies—are the main argument why cities should have higher start-up rates than non-urban regions. Such effects include, among others, access to higher education, exploitation of local knowledge spillovers, and the presence of highly sophisticated markets which offer a variety of niches that can be exploited by smaller firms. Furthermore, cities offer a great range of infrastructure, which is of interest especially for younger and/or more highly educated people. This is related to the "geography of talent" argument that the creative class is spatially more mobile, prefers urban areas and is more prone to entrepreneurial activities than the rest of labor force (Florida 2004).

Noticeably, the above theories suggest that cities are important for economic development. However, none of them incorporates or integrates the entrepreneur into its core arguments. While some of them hint at it by focusing on people's talent, the connection between agents' entrepreneurial activity and their location in a city is suggested at best. The next section puts forward a way to help us integrate the possible connections.

6.4 The process of entrepreneurial orientation: From perceptions to activity

Urban areas may be distinctive in how agents perceive entrepreneurship. In Figure 6.1 we identify the main components of entrepreneurial perceptions. In this model, Entrepreneurial Framework Conditions (EFCs) affect the extent to which people see *opportunities* to start a business and the extent to which they think they have the required *capabilities* to start a

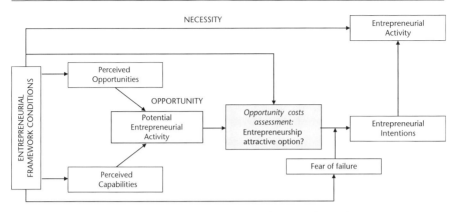

Figure 6.1 National and regional entrepreneurial framework conditions, perceptions about entrepreneurship, and engagement in entrepreneurial activity

Source: Bosma et al. (2008) based on Wennekers (2006).

business.[3] An important issue here is that the model deals with *perceived* opportunities and capabilities rather than "real" opportunities and capabilities. It is people's perception of the environment and themselves that drives them into (or away from) entrepreneurship (Arenius and Minniti 2005). These perceptions are often influenced by other people. The social environments of vibrant world cities lead to more occurrences of contacts between peers sharing similar ideas and entrepreneurial aspirations (Minniti 2005). Thus, world cities, compared with the rest of their respective countries, can be expected to provide more opportunities for networking and role model effects enhancing entrepreneurial perceptions—both in terms of opportunities and capabilities.

While a positive link between entrepreneurial perceptions and entrepreneurial activity seems obvious, it is by no means certain that an individual with positive perceptions about entrepreneurship will actually get involved in entrepreneurial activity. Two important assessments need to be made. First, there is the *assessment of opportunity costs* (Lucas 1978; Shane and Venkataraman 2000), which involves comparing the expected returns of entrepreneurship to the expected returns of an alternative occupation. The most common alternative is "being employed," but "being unemployed" became an increasingly important alternative in several industrialized countries like Germany, where entrepreneurial activities

---

[3] Entrepreneurial Framework Conditions (EFC) "reflect major features of a country's socio-economic milieu that are expected to have a significant impact on the entrepreneurial sector" (Bosma and Levie 2010, p. 32). EFCs include financial support, government programs, government policies, education and training, research and development transfer, cultural and social norms, access to physical infrastructure, internal market openness, and commercial and professional infrastructure. These conditions should be considered both at the national and subnational (regional) level since they may have different characteristics at both spatial levels within the same country (see Sternberg 2009, p. 227, on this distinction).

by unemployed individuals were popular until a Federal government program to support start-ups out of unemployment was stopped (see also Bergmann and Sternberg 2007).

Second, there is a *risk–reward assessment:* even if the expected returns to entrepreneurship are considerably higher than the best alternative, the (perceived) risks involved may be too high for a person who is thinking about starting a business. An individual's risk-avoidance preference may be a significant factor in the transition from potential (or latent) entrepreneurship to entrepreneurial activity (Khilstrom and Laffont 1979). While most empirical studies show that more risk-averse individuals are less likely to become entrepreneurs (Wagner 2008), recent results from experimental studies show that this is only true for previously employed people but not for previously unemployed or inactive individuals for whom risk attitudes did not play a role in the decision whether to start a firm (Caliendo et al. 2009).

There is no general pattern describing the sequence in which assessments are made and steps are taken. From an individual perspective, people decide to start a business when a very specific business opportunity comes into view, albeit at times unexpectedly. Thus, the process described is explored with opportunity-related entrepreneurship in mind. For some people, however, being involved in entrepreneurial activity is a necessity; there are simply no other options to earn a living and there is no comparative assessment to be made.

6.5 Data and methods

We use data from the Global Entrepreneurship Monitor (GEM) project to create indicators of entrepreneurial perceptions and entrepreneurial activity in world cities and the rest of their respective countries (see Reynolds et al. 2005; Kelley et al. 2011). Data are collected through telephone or face-to-face surveys of a representative sample of the adult population. For GEM, entrepreneurial activity starts when individuals commit resources to start a business they expect to own themselves (nascent entrepreneurs). Two consecutive phases are also identified; (i) when individuals currently own and manage a business that has paid salaries for more than three months but less than 42 months (new business owners); and (ii) when individuals own and manage an established business that has been in operation for more than 42 months (established business owners). Combining the phase of nascent entrepreneurship and new business ownership as a percentage of population yields the Total Early-Stage Entrepreneurial Activity (TEA) rate. In this chapter we focus on early-stage entrepreneurial activity.

Previous studies with GEM data have shown that cross-country variation in early-stage entrepreneurial activity is very persistent over years (Bosma et al. 2009). By merging the individual-level GEM data from 2001–6 for thirty-five world cities, we create indicators on entrepreneurial perceptions and entrepreneurial activity. Merging GEM data over six years increases our sample size and, as a result, the accuracy of our estimates. Of course, merging longitudinal data comes at the costs of losing the time dimension. However, the existing evidence points at very limited changes in regional differences in entrepreneurial attitudes over such time period (Beugelsdijk et al. 2006). In this chapter, however, we are interested in the geographical dimensions of entrepreneurship not its time dimensions. In addition, other regional measures of early-stage entrepreneurial activity appear to exhibit a significant amount of path dependence (Minniti 2005; Fritsch and Mueller 2006) and to be largely determined by regional industry structure (Brenner and Fornahl 2008).

The selection of cities is restricted by sample sizes coverage in the GEM project since we require at least 1,000 observations in each urban area. The total sample comprises 78,882 adults between 18–64 years. All city indices were obtained after weighting each respondent according to regional age and gender structures as provided by national census offices. Table 6.1 gives an overview of the world cities included and the boundaries of the urban areas involved. Metropolitan areas are defined by the relevant local labor market area.[4] Of the thirty-five cities included in our study, 30 are ranked in the top 100 (24 in the top 50, 7 in the top 10) of the GaWC dataset on network services connectivity for world cities.[5] This is an indication that our sample consists of a relevant set of world cities—not only based on population but also based on network services connectivity. The distinction between alpha, beta, gamma, and evidence of world cities follows that of the GaWC dataset and indicates each city's ranking among global cities as defined by the GaWC network and described earlier.[6]

---

[4] In some cases, data constraints force us to use wider urban areas than it is optimal. Specifically, the Kanto region is one third larger than what is usually defined as the Tokyo metropolitan area in terms of population size. Also, the identified region of Brussels may be too small with an area of only 161 km[2]. Finally, for Italy, the NUTS 2 level is the most detailed spatial level we could identify. NUTS 2 is a geocode standard developed by the European Union for statistical purposes and it identifies a larger administrative region.

[5] These data are produced by P. J. Taylor and constitute Data Set 12 of the GaWC Study Group and Network (http://www.lboro.ac.uk/gawc/) publication of inter-city data.

[6] The GaWC developed a ranking of world cities based upon their level of advanced producer services. World cities are identified and graded for accountancy, advertising, banking/finance, and law (see Beaverstock et al. 1999, p. 454ff, for details). The ranking is created by aggregating the information from the listings in these four sectors. One hundred-and-twenty-two cities are considered in all. A sum is produced for each city by scoring 3 for a prime center, 2 for a major center, and 1 for a minor center. Given four sectors, the result is a series of estimates of world-cityness ranging from 1 to 12. Any city scoring 10 or above must be a global service center in all four sectors. In addition, it must be prime in at least two sectors, and the other two would have to be major designations. Ten cities qualify as *Alpha world cities*. Any city scoring 7 to 9 must be a global service center for at least three of the four sectors and must be a prime or major center in at least two sectors. Ten such cities qualify as *Beta world cities*. Cities scoring 4 to 6 are called *Gamma world cities*. All these cities must have global service centers for at least two sectors and at least one of those must be a major service provision. Thirty-five cities fall into this group. The remaining 67 cities are designated as having evidence of world city formation processes but the evidence is not strong enough to really call them world cities.

Table 6.1. World cities included in the study

City	Definition of metropolitan area	Population (x 1,000)	Area (km² x 1,000)	Sample Size
Alpha World Cities				
Frankfurt	Raumordnungsregion: Rhine-Main	5,800	13.0	1,552
London	NUTS 1: London	7,600	1.6	4,865
Los Angeles	SMSA: Los Angeles	12,900	12.6	1,034
Milan	NUTS 2: Lombardia	9,300	23.9	1,735
New York	SMSA: New York	18,800	6.7	1,138
Paris	NUTS 1: Ile de France	11,300	12.0	2,168
Tokyo	Kanto Region	41,900	32.4	4,415
Beta World Cities				
Brussels	NUTS 1: Bruxelles	1,000	7.8	1,756
Madrid	NUTS 1: Madrid	5,600	8.0	6,527
Sydney	Metropolitan Area	4,300	12.1	2,937
Toronto	Census Metropolitan Area	5,100	5.9	1,397
Gamma World Cities				
Amsterdam	NUTS 3: Greater Amsterdam	1,200	0.7	1,504
Bangkok	Greater Bangkok	10,700	7.8	1,207
Barcelona	NUTS 3: Barcelona	5,400	4.3	2,463
Berlin	Raumordnungsregion: Berlin (NUTS 1)	3,400	0.9	2,064
Buenos Aires	Census Metropolitan Area	13,000	4.8	2,510
Copenhagen	NUTS 2: Hovedstadsreg	1,900	2.9	4,705
Dusseldorf	Raumordnungsregion: Düsseldorf	5,200	5.3	1,682
Hamburg	Raumordnungsregion: Hamburg (NUTS 1)	1,800	0.8	1,010
Johannesburg	Province Gauteng, urbanized area	3,900	1.6	2,956
Melbourne	Labor market area	3,800	8.8	2,875
Munich	Raumordnungsregion: München	6,000	27.7	1,372
Stockholm	Metropolitan Area	1,900	6.5	2,306
Evidence of World Cities				
Aarhus	NUTS 3: Aarhus	1,200	1.0	2,368
Auckland	Metropolitan Area	1,400	16.1	2,211
Birmingham	NUTS 3: Birmingham	2,600	0.9	1,324
Cape Town	Province Western Cape, urbanized area	3,000	2.5	1,535
Cologne	Raumordnungsregion: Köln	4,400	7.4	1,297
Dublin	NUTS 3: Dublin	1,200	0.9	2,688
Helsinki	Metropolitan Area	1,400	6.4	3,043
Manchester	NUTS 2: Greater Manchester	2,600	1.3	2,757
Rotterdam	NUTS 3: Greater Rotterdam	1,400	1.2	1,643
Stuttgart	Raumordnungsregion: Stuttgart	2,700	3.6	1,514
The Hague	NUTS 3 areas: The Hague, Leiden, Delft	1,400	0.7	1,023
Utrecht	NUTS 3: Utrecht	1,200	1.4	1,301

Table 6.2. GEM measures used in this study

Item	Definition of GEM measure
Perceptions to entrepreneurship	
Perceived opportunities	Percentage of 18–64 population who see good opportunities to start a firm in the area where they live
Perceived capabilities	Percentage of 18–64 population who believe they have the required skills and knowledge to start a business
Perceived opportunities & capabilities	Percentage of 18–64 population who have a positive perception of their own entrepreneurial capabilities and the entrepreneurial opportunities in the area where they live
Early-stage Entrepreneurial Activity	
TEA: Total Early-Stage Entrepreneurial Activity	Percentage of adult population 18–64 years involved in either nascent entrepreneurial activity or owner-managers of new businesses. (A detailed explanation of these terms is provided in section 6.5)
Opportunity TEA	Percentage of adult population 18–64 years involved in TEA (see above) and indicating to be motivated by opportunity (rather than "no better options for work")
Nascent entrepreneurial activity	Percentage of adult population 18–64 years involved in nascent entrepreneurial activity
New business entrepreneurial activity	Percentage of adult population 18–64 years owning-managing a new business (see also Figure 6.2)
Types of Early-stage Entrepreneurial Activity	
TEA job growth expectation	Percentage in TEA who expect at least 10 employees five years from now
TEA in sectors linked to creative class	Percentage in TEA, whose business activities are linked to creative class

Table 6.2 lists the GEM variables included in this chapter. The first set of variables relates to perceptions of entrepreneurship as described in Figure 6.1. The second set identifies various aspects of early-stage entrepreneurial activity (TEA), and the third identifies different features of early-stage entrepreneurship. The third group links entrepreneurial activity to Florida's (2004) creative class as discussed in the theory section. Since the types of entrepreneurial activity are based on a much smaller sample (equal to the number of early-stage entrepreneurs in each city sample) than the other indicators, these results should be interpreted with great care. Nonetheless, they provide some interesting insights on the overall pattern of entrepreneurship in world cities in comparison to the rest of their respective countries.

6.6 Comparing the world cities

Using the data and classifications described earlier, in this section, we capture entrepreneurship in world cities by looking at activities, attitudes, and aspiration respectively.

6.6.1 *Activities: Early-stage entrepreneurship in world cities*

As the first column in Table 6.3 shows, Auckland, Vancouver, Melbourne, Los Angeles, Sydney, and New York rank in the top six of most entrepreneurial cities in developed countries. These are all Anglo-Saxon cities. Early-stage entrepreneurial activity is lowest in Tokyo, Milan, Paris, Brussels, and Rotterdam. In general, European cities exhibit lower rates than other cities in Anglo-Saxon countries like the United States, Canada, and Australia. This suggests that some cultural and institutional effects may be at play. For example, all Anglo-Saxon countries are characterized by a high surplus of in-migration, strong impetus of individualism, and relatively lower government involvement.

Relatively high TEA rates for cities in non-OECD countries mirror results at the country level. The high scores in Buenos Aires and Bangkok, for example, might be explained, to some extent, by lower opportunity costs as outlined in Figure 6.1. Table 6.3 also shows the overall early-stage entrepreneurial activity rates for opportunity motivated TEA.

If we consider the world city categories developed by the GaWC group (see Beaverstock, Taylor, and Smith 1999), some differences in terms of our entrepreneurship indicators occur: Mean un-weighted TEA values are highest for the twelve world cities of category gamma (9.2%), followed by category beta (8.4%), while alpha world cities seem less entrepreneurial (mean TEA value 6.9%). Rankings for the three world city categories do not much differ between the three activity measures: the lower the world city category, the higher the level of entrepreneurial activity is. Also, in Table 6.3, Tokyo pushes the averages of alpha world cities downwards, whereas Bangkok and Buenos Aires push the average of gamma world cities upwards. This may suggest that, independent from world city categories, the national environment is important too and may in fact be the dominating force. Therefore, the regional economic, institutional, and cultural context should be considered for potential future research *explaining* the differences in entrepreneurial activity across world cities.

6.6.2 *Attitudes: Entrepreneurial perceptions in world cities*

The first two columns in Table 6.4 summarize two major perceptions to entrepreneurship as shown in Figure 6.1. Perceived capabilities to start a firm are highest in Auckland, Buenos Aires, and Melbourne. We should note that the general perception of the "average" entrepreneur in, say, Buenos Aires might be different from that of Melbourne. Therefore, this indicator should be seen in the context of the stage of economic development. Also, we cannot rule out that our specific measures of entrepreneurial perceptions reflect some general cultural sentiments. For instance, the city of Tokyo shows by far the

Table 6.3. Early-stage entrepreneurial activity (TEA) in world cities

	TEA	Opportunity TEA	Nascent entrepreneurship	New business entrepreneurship
Alpha world cities				
Frankfurt	7.9	5.7	4.1	4.3
London	7.9	6.6	4.8	3.5
Los Angeles	11.6	9.4	8.9	3.8
Milan	3.3	2.6	1.7	2.0
New York	11.8	9.6	8.5	4.3
Paris	4.2	3.1	3.3	1.0
Tokyo	1.8	1.2	0.9	0.9
– average	*6.9*	*5.5*	*4.6*	*2.8*
Beta world cities				
Brussels	4.4	3.8	3.2	1.3
Madrid	6.8	5.9	3.0	3.9
Sydney	11.1	10.0	6.4	5.2
Toronto	11.3	9.5	6.2	6.4
– average	*8.4*	*7.3*	*4.7*	*4.2*
Gamma world cities				
Amsterdam	6.1	4.7	3.4	2.7
Bangkok	21.5	16.0	11.6	10.8
Barcelona	6.8	5.8	3.4	3.5
Berlin	8.0	5.6	5.5	3.5
Buenos Aires	14.7	9.8	10.6	4.9
Copenhagen	6.1	5.5	3.5	3.0
Dusseldorf	6.5	4.6	4.6	2.2
Hamburg	9.4	8.0	6.9	4.2
Johannesburg	6.7	4.0	4.8	2.3
Melbourne	11.6	9.7	6.6	5.6
Munich	7.7	5.8	4.7	3.5
Stockholm	5.1	4.5	2.2	3.2
– average	*9.2*	*7.0*	*5.7*	*4.1*
Evidence of world cities				
Aarhus	5.6	4.9	3.1	2.6
Auckland	13.1	10.8	8.3	6.2
Birmingham	6.0	4.8	3.3	3.1
Cape Town	8.7	6.5	6.0	3.0
Cologne	7.4	5.4	5.0	2.7
Dublin	8.9	7.9	5.5	3.8
Helsinki	4.8	4.1	2.8	2.3
Manchester	5.7	4.5	2.9	2.8
Rotterdam	4.7	3.7	2.7	2.1
Stuttgart	5.8	4.0	4.2	2.3
The Hague	4.9	4.0	3.6	1.5
Utrecht	6.8	5.6	3.7	3.1
– average	*6.9*	*5.5*	*4.3*	*3.0*

lowest self-confidence when it comes to starting a business. This agglomeration also scores rather low on the perceived opportunities for starting a business. This may partly reflect the importance of modesty within East Asian cultures.

For some cities there is a large gap between the rates in the first two columns of Table 6.4 (attitudes) and involvement in entrepreneurial activity (Table 6.3). This appears to be the case especially for European cities such as Amsterdam, Copenhagen, Stockholm, and Helsinki. In other words, even though there is sufficient potential among inhabitants, the attractiveness of entrepreneurship appears to be low for many Europeans compared to other possible sources of income. This may suggest that in European cities entrepreneurial intentions are lagging behind as compared to, for instance, cities in the United States and Australia. On the other hand, this could also suggest that good job opportunities are available in these European cities (this relates to the opportunity cost assessment in Figure 6.1). For many middle- and low-income countries we observe relatively small differences between entrepreneurial perceptions and entrepreneurial activity.

As for world city categories, results are similar to those for entrepreneurial activities: "Alpha world cities" (un-weighted mean value of perceived opportunity is twenty-five percent, un-weighted mean value of perceived capability is thirty-nine percent) perform worst for both perception indicators reported. Thus, the lower the GaWC world city category, the more optimistic the individual perception of entrepreneurial opportunity and entrepreneurial capability appears to be.

6.6.3 Aspirations: Characteristics of early-stage entrepreneurial activity in world cities

A minority of new entrepreneurs is responsible for the majority of expected job creation (Autio 2007). The third column in Table 6.4 shows differences among world cities in terms of growth orientation by early-stage entrepreneurs. The percentage of high-growth oriented early-stage entrepreneurs during 2001–6 ranged from only four percent in Madrid to as much as thirty-four percent in London. Noticeably, alpha world cities show the highest mean share of entrepreneurs who expect to have at least 10 employees after five years (mean value of 23% for the seven alpha world cities). Since our variable captures *expectations*, this may suggest the presence of entrepreneurial over-optimism (Koellinger et al. 2007).

The last column in Table 6.4 illustrates the connection between early-stage entrepreneurial activity and the existence of the creative class in world cities. Between thirty-four percent (Bangkok) and eighty percent (Amsterdam) of early-stage entrepreneurial activity occurs in a sector that is linked to the creative class. For all cities in developed countries the percentage equals forty-eight or more. This is consistent with research by Lee et al. (2004) who argued that regional social characteristics influenced new firm formation. The

Table 6.4. Entrepreneurial perceptions and aspirations in world cities

	Perceived opportunities for entrepreneurship	Perceived entrepreneurial capabilities	TEA job growth expectation	TEA in sectors linked to creative class
Alpha world cities				
Frankfurt	32.5	41.6	14.6	70.5
London	36.9	51.7	34.1	63.8
Los Angeles	29.6	52.0	28.9	56.0
Milan	30.3	32.7	30.6	68.0
New York	22.5	51.7	23.9	57.9
Paris	16.1	31.2	19.9	67.4
Tokyo	7.4	10.7	10.0	59.8
– average	*25.0*	*38.8*	*23.1*	*63.3*
Beta world cities				
Brussels	31.6	36.1	11.7	59.9
Madrid	37.7	46.0	4.4	54.0
Sydney	48.9	50.8	14.4	55.5
Toronto	32.6	49.9	10.3	63.9
– average	*37.7*	*45.7*	*10.2*	*58.3*
Gamma world cities				
Amsterdam	58.2	39.4	16.8	79.5
Bangkok	20.1	38.2	16.8	34.0
Barcelona	38.9	45.8	6.8	52.7
Berlin	18.3	38.6	21.2	76.4
Buenos Aires	34.7	62.0	22.3	53.9
Copenhagen	60.0	37.8	25.0	70.9
Dusseldorf	24.3	42.4	20.2	65.8
Hamburg	29.3	38.0	23.0	59.2
Johannesburg	26.0	35.3	10.3	46.4
Melbourne	47.5	52.2	12.3	46.6
Munich	38.8	40.7	18.9	66.0
Stockholm	47.0	45.5	16.5	60.5
– average	*36.9*	*43.0*	*17.5*	*59.3*
Evidence of world cities				
Aarhus	65.7	36.1	19.5	58.1
Auckland	48.0	61.7	17.4	60.4
Birmingham	36.6	46.5	30.5	61.8
Cape Town	28.7	50.6	15.9	44.7
Cologne	29.2	42.6	19.3	65.5
Dublin	37.9	47.0	23.8	57.4
Helsinki	60.5	34.7	18.6	60.6
Manchester	33.8	43.6	21.4	55.5
Rotterdam	42.0	37.3	21.4	58.1
Stuttgart	34.6	35.2	16.6	61.6
The Hague	50.7	37.3	24.1	61.1
Utrecht	45.1	39.2	23.6	64.1
– average	*42.7*	*42.7*	*21.0*	*59.1*

share is strongest in Amsterdam, Berlin, Copenhagen, Frankfurt, Milan, Paris, Munich, and London. Thus, from our sample of world cities, early-stage entrepreneurs in European cities appear to be active most in sectors linked to entrepreneurship in creative class industries. Mean values for the creative class variable hardly differ between categories.

Table 6.5. Clustering entrepreneurship measures and the relation with the GaWC classification

Entrepreneurship cluster group and main characteristics	Alpha world cities	Beta world cities	Gamma world cities	Evidence of world cities
Group 1: Medium–high entrepreneurial activity	London Los Angeles New York		Hamburg Munich	Rotterdam Utrecht Birmingham Dublin
Medium high perceived opportunities, capabilities				
High expected job creation				Manchester
Group 2: High entrepreneurial activity		Madrid	Barcelona	Auckland
High perceived capabilities Low expected job creation		Sydney Toronto	Melbourne Stockholm Buenos Aires	Cape Town
Group 3: Low entrepreneurial activity Low entrepreneurial perceptions Low expected job creation	Tokyo			
Group 4: High entrepreneurial activity Low perceived opportunities Low job growth expectations			Bangkok Johannesburg	
Group 5: Medium–low entrepreneurial activity			Amsterdam Copenhagen	Aarhus Helsinki The Hague
High perceived opportunities High creativity related activity				
Group 6: Medium–low entrepreneurial activity	Frankfurt Milan Paris	Brussels	Berlin Düsseldorf	Cologne Stuttgart
Low perceived opportunities High job growth expectations High creativity related activity				

Note: Entrepreneurship groups obtained by means of K-means clustering, based on measures included in Tables 6.3 and 6.4.

As Minniti (2004) argues, entrepreneurship is a complex, multilayer phenomenon, which makes it difficult to capture entrepreneurship in world cities through a single measure. The measures on entrepreneurial activity, perceptions, and aspirations in Tables 6.3 and 6.4 describe only some important components of entrepreneurship. Table 6.5 shows the results of a cluster analysis on these eight measures and how they relate to the word-city categorization proposed by the GaWC group. It appears that entrepreneurship, as we have measured it, does not correspond with the GaWC classification. If we disregard "outlier" Tokyo, the remaining six alpha world cities in our sample are divided in only two of the four GaWC groups. Both groups include several cities from lower categories. Our cluster groups suggest the importance of

global regions and suggest a large impact of cultural and institutional contexts. Groups 5 and 6 consist of European world cities only, and even in these
two groups some distinction can be made between Central-West Europe and
Northern-West Europe. To observe genuine world-city effects it is therefore
useful to examine differences in entrepreneurship between the cities and the
surrounding larger area.

6.7 World cities compared to countries

As suggested earlier, agglomeration effects suggest that cities should have
higher level of entrepreneurship than their respective countries (Stam 2009).
The agglomeration effects include education, knowledge spillovers, the existence of specialized markets, and sophisticated infrastructure.[7]

Figure 6.2 shows the relative percentage difference in early-stage entrepreneurial activity between city and corresponding country. The longer the bar,
the higher the estimated percent difference between the world city and the
country it is situated in.[8] Early-stage entrepreneurial activity rates in cities are
clearly different from rates at the country level. As much as thirty-one (out of
thirty-five) cities have higher early-stage entrepreneurial activity rates than
their countries, and ten differences are statistically significant ($p < 0.05$).
Four German cities stand out with TEA rates that are between sixty percent
(Munich), sixty-five percent (Frankfurt/M.), seventy percent (Berlin), and
eighty percent (Hamburg) higher than the national average over the period
2001–6. Of the thirty-five world cities in our sample only four cities had
lower TEA rates than the national average. They are Milan, Tokyo, Helsinki,
and Auckland, and only the difference for Milan is statistically significant.
London and Paris have TEA rates in excess of the national average as expected, whereas New York and Los Angeles are much closer to the higher US
national average.

If early-stage entrepreneurial activity is higher in cities—as compared to the
rest of the country—one would expect these results to stem from higher levels
of perceived opportunities and capabilities. Both measures are explored in
Figure 6.3 where the percent differences between world cities and their respective countries are shown. Comparing perceived opportunities in Figure 6.3

---

[7] When comparing the world cities to countries, we should stress that TEA rates presented are
overall rates of early-stage entrepreneurial activity and, as such, include small-scaled
entrepreneurial activities that may be relatively more prominent in rural areas. This implies that
the entrepreneurial role of cities may be underestimated.

[8] In these comparisons, by country level we mean the country minus the area(s) included as
world city(ies) in our sample.

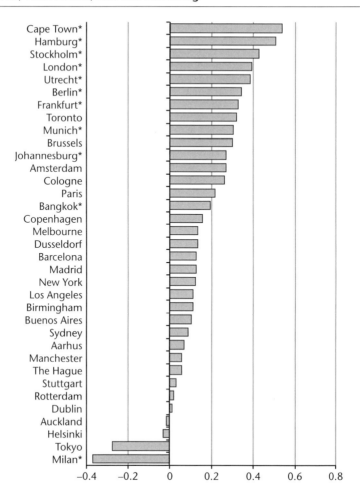

Figure 6.2 Prevalence rates in early-stage entrepreneurial activity: City versus country results (differences in log–log)

Note: differences in log–log

*indicates that the city–country difference is statistically significant ($p < 0.05$)

with early-stage entrepreneurial activity in Figure 6.2, suggests that differences between cities and countries are wider then difference in TEA rates. However, more world cities perceive fewer opportunities than the rest of their country. Looking at the case of Germany, for example, Munich, Stuttgart, Frankfurt, Hamburg, and Cologne occupy five of the top six positions with Berlin well down the list. These results are consistent with the results in Figure 6.2.

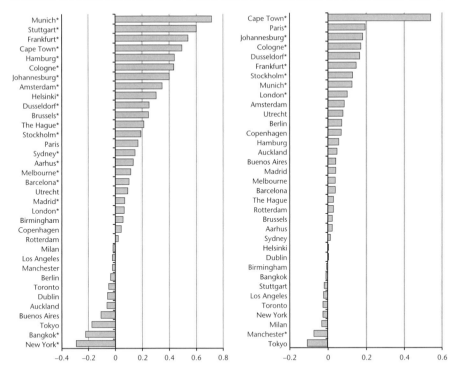

Figure 6.3 Positive perceptions of opportunities and capabilities: City versus country results (differences in log–log)

Note: differences in log–log

*indicates that the city–country difference is statistically significant ($p < 0.05$)

The right hand side of Figure 6.3 shows the results of a similar analysis on perceived capabilities. Perceived skills and knowledge to start businesses are generally higher in cities compared to the rest of the country, but the magnitude of the difference is smaller compared to perceived opportunities.

Surprisingly, New York City and Los Angeles are below the national average for both indicators. In order to probe this result we plot the measure of perceived capabilities (percent difference with country) and *opportunity* early-stage entrepreneurial activity (percent difference with country) in Figure 6.4. The framework described in Figure 6.1 would suggest a positive link.[9] Indeed, Figure 6.5 shows that city–country differences with

[9] Note that, by examining differences between city level and country level on both axes, country effects are ignored.

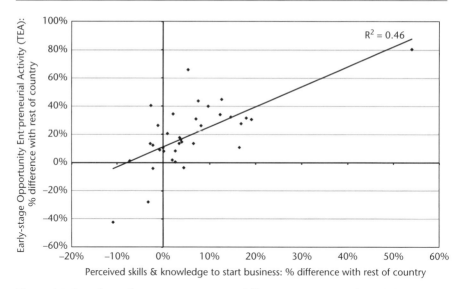

Figure 6.4 Correlation between city–country differences in perceived capabilities (deviation from country-level) and involvement in opportunity-driven TEA (deviation from country-level)

Note: differences in log–log

respect to perception and reality are positively related (correlation coefficient of 0.69). Noteworthy is that all identified German cities, with the exception of Berlin, come up in the upper-right part of the scatter diagram and are, therefore, very different from the rest of the country.

On the left side, Figure 6.5 shows the differences in job growth expectation between cities and countries. Here again most cities have higher expectations than their respective countries. This time, however, the outliers are Tokyo, Toronto, Frankfurt, Johannesburg, Madrid, and Stuttgart. Paris is the clear leader with more than twice the national average, followed by Helsinki, Milan, and Bangkok. Three of the four included Dutch cities score reasonably high, as do Copenhagen and London. On the right side, instead, Figure 6.5 shows that entrepreneurial activity in cities is correlated with the existence of a creative class. In our sample, only Melbourne exhibits relatively few entrepreneurs in sectors linked to the creative class. This particular result is, however, not significant and may be an outlier due to the rather large standard errors. The greatest differences between cities and countries in relation to the creative class industries are observed in cities in lower income countries with Johannesburg and Cape Town ranking at the top. New York, Los Angeles, Paris, and Helsinki are also cities with distinctive (and significant)

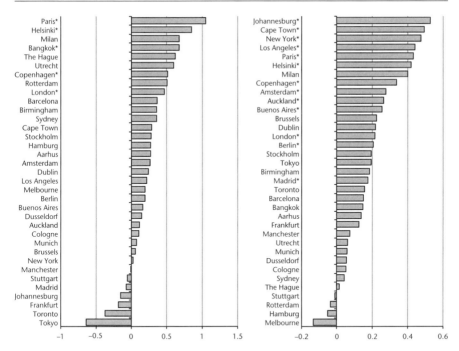

Figure 6.5 Job growth orientation and sectors linked to creative class: City–country differences

Note: differences in log–log

*indicates that the city–country difference is statistically significant ($p < 0.05$)

entrepreneurial activity related to the creative class—as compared to the rest of the country.

It is clear that different measures yield different rankings. This is not surprising given the multifaceted nature of entrepreneurship. If any general pattern can be identified, it suggests that world cities have some advantage in terms of entrepreneurial perceptions and entrepreneurial activity, but a more pronounced one in terms of job growth orientation and business activities linked to the creative class. These specific types of entrepreneurship may be of great importance in stimulating economic performance.

6.8 Discussion

While demographic and economic data on world cities are becoming increasingly available, little is known about entrepreneurial activity across world cities. In this chapter we have set out a framework encompassing the individual process between entrepreneurial perceptions and entrepreneurial activity and highlighted how the urban environment can have an impact on this process. We have provided an exploratory and very preliminary investigation of the differences between the city-level and country-level for a selection of entrepreneurship indices from the GEM database by pooling the 2001–6 data and identifying thirty-five world cities.

The patterns we find are interesting and, to a degree, surprising. First, we used indicators of entrepreneurial activity and of entrepreneurial perception to characterize entrepreneurship for world cities and their related countries.

Second, as predicted by extant theories (Jacobs externalities, agglomeration theory, "geography of talent" hypothesis), we found most world cities to be more entrepreneurial than the rest of the country; probably because of their resilience, creativity, initiative taking, and diversity (Shapero 1984; Malecki 1997). The two most important city–country differences are observed in Germany and Japan. In Japan, one of the most successful economies in the world, Tokyo, one of the largest cities in the world, exhibits one of the lowest entrepreneurship rates, below the Japanese rate. And this holds both for early-stage entrepreneurial activity as well as for entrepreneurial perceptions. In Germany, with an average performance at the country level, we found some of the best performing cities in the world and the largest city–country differences.

Third, our descriptive statistics suggest some interesting differences between the world-city categories both in terms of entrepreneurial activities and entrepreneurial perceptions. We used the nomenclature developed by the Loughborough working group (GaWC) on world cities and their classification in four categories (Taylor 2004). At the top of this hierarchy there are ten "Alpha World Cities" (seven of them included in our sample), ten "Beta World Cities" (four included), thirty-five "Gamma World Cities" (twelve included), and sixty-seven cities with "evidence of world city formation" (twelve included) (Beaverstock et al. 1999, 456). Our results reveal that entrepreneurial activities are highest for gamma world cities and lowest for the alpha world cities. In fact, both levels of entrepreneurial activity and of entrepreneurial perception are higher in lower segments of world-city ranking. Perhaps this may be explained by the fact that talented people in the sense of Florida (2004) do not necessarily prefer to settle in the largest urban agglomerations of a country. Empirical studies for the US (Florida et al. 2008) and for Germany (Fritsch and Stützer 2007), for example, have shown that some of the smaller urban agglomerations show higher shares of talented people than the largest cities. Another explanation for this counterintuitive result is that the opportunity costs to entrepreneurship may be higher in alpha world cities. Cluster analysis confirms that country groupings based on entrepreneurship measures are related to the GaWC classification to a very limited extent. This may suggest that institutional and cultural differences are dominant forces driving differences in entrepreneurship across world cities.

Our results are, of course very preliminary, and more work in this area is needed. Also, our study has several limitations. First, the choice of cities in our sample is data driven and, therefore, suffers from a strong sample selection bias. Second, several of our findings have expected signs but are not statistically significant, probably due to the fact that the sample size, although large in relative terms, is still rather low for a study of this scope. Third, although as a deliberate first step, we chose to explore the *descriptive* characteristics of the data, a more in-depth econometric analysis should be undertaken in the future. Using our data, a multilevel model could be tested to investigate local, regional, and national effects on entrepreneurial activity. Such a study would contribute to our knowledge of the link between city-level characteristics and entrepreneurial activity and account for the importance of (i) individual endowments and (ii) cultural and institutional contexts suggested by our descriptive analysis. In a broader context, this line of research would also help us to bridge the important gap between entrepreneurship research and research on agglomeration economies.

Acknowledgments

The authors are grateful to all national GEM teams for sharing their data. Although GEM data were used in this study, their interpretation and use are the sole responsibility of the authors. The authors would also like to thank Maria Minniti, Sander Wennekers and an anonymous referee for their comments on earlier versions. Financial support for the data preparation was provided by EIM Business and Policy Research. Many thanks go also to an anonymous reviewer for helpful comments. All errors are ours.

References

Acs, Z. (2002), *Innovation and the Growth of Cities*. Cheltenham, Northampton: Edward Elgar.

Acs, Z. and Armington, C. (2004), "Employment Growth and Entrepreneurial Activity in Cities." *Regional Studies* 38 (8): 911–27.

Acs, Z. and Storey, J. D. (2004), "Special Issue: Entrepreneurship and Regional Development: Essays in Honour of David Keeble." *Regional Studies* 38(8): 867–989.

Acs, Z. and Varga, A. (2005), "Entrepreneurship, Agglomeration and Technological Change." *Small Business Economics* 24(3): 323–34.

Acs, Z., Audretsch, D. B., Braunerhjelm, P., and Carlsson, B. (2004), "The Missing Link: The Knowledge Filter and Entrepreneurship in Economic Growth." *CEPR Discussion Paper 4783*.

Aghion, P. and Howitt, P. (2006), "Joseph Schumpeter Lecture–Appropriate Growth Policy: A Unifying Framework." *Journal of the European Economic Association* 4: 269–314.

Andersson, A. (1985), "Creativity and Regional Development." *Papers of the Regional Science Association* 56: 5–20.

Arenius, P. and Minniti, M. (2005), Perceptual Variables and Nascent Entrepreneurship, *Small Business Economics* 24: 233–47.

Armington, C. and Acs, Z. J. (2002), "The Determinants of Regional Variation in New Firm Formation." *Regional Studies* 36: 33–45.

Autant-Bernard, C. (2001), The geography of knowledge spillovers and technological proximity. *Economics of Innovation and New Technology* 10(4): 237–54.

Autio, E. (2007), *Global Entrepreneurship Monitor; 2007 Global Report on High-Growth Entrepreneurship*. Babson College, London Business School, and Global Entrepreneurship Research Association (GERA).

Baldwin, R., Forslid, R., Martin, P., Ottaviano, G., and Robert Nicoud, F. (2003), *Economic Geography and Public Policy*. Princeton, NJ: Princeton University Press.

Beaverstock, J. V., Taylor, P. J., and Smith, R. G. (1999), "A Roster of World Cities." *Cities* 16(6): 445–58.

Bergmann, H. and Sternberg, R. (2007), "The Changing Face of Entrepreneurship in Germany." *Small Business Economics* 28(2–3): 205–21.

Beugelsdijk, S., van Schaik, T., and Arts, W. (2006), "Towards a Unified Europe? Explaining Regional Differences in Value Patterns by Economic Development, Cultural Heritage and Historical Shocks." *Regional Studies* 40(3): 317–27.

Boschma, R. A. and Frenken, K. (2006), "Why Is Economic Geography not an Evolutionary Science? Towards an Evolutionary Economic Geography." *Journal of Economic Geography* 6(3): 273–302.

Bosma, N. S., Acs, Z. J., Autio, E., Coduras, A., and Levie, J. (2009), *Global Entrepreneurship Monitor; 2008 Executive Report*. Babson Park: Babson College, London: London Business School, and Global Entrepreneurship Research Association (GERA).

Bosma, N. S., Jones, K., Autio, E., and Levie, J. (2008), *Global Entrepreneurship Monitor; 2007 Executive Report*. Babson College, London Business School, and Global Entrepreneurship Research Association (GERA).

Bosma, N. S. and Levie, J. (2010), *Global Entrepreneurship Monitor; 2009 Executive Report*. Babson Park: Babson College, Santiago: Universidad del Desarrollo, Reykjavik: Reykjavik University, and Global Entrepreneurship Research Association (GERA).

Brenner, T. and Fornahl, D. (2008), "Regional Path-Dependence in Start-up Activity," Papers in Evolutionary Economic Geography (PEEG) N. 0812, Utrecht University, The Netherlands.

Brixy, U. and Grotz, R. (2007), "Regional Patterns and Determinants of the Success of New Firms in Western Germany." *Entrepreneurship and Regional Development* 19(4): 293–312.

Caliendo, M., Fossen, F. M., and Kritikos, A. S. (2009), "Risk Attitudes of Nascent Entrepreneurs–New Evidence from an Experimentally Validated Survey." *Small Business Economics* 32: 153–62.

Cooper, A. C. (2003), "Entrepreneurship: The Past, the Present, the Future." In Z. J. Acs and D. B. Audretsch (eds.), *Handbook of Entrepreneurship Research,* Kluwer Academic Publishers: Boston and Dordrecht, pp. 21–36.

Derudder, B., Taylor, P. J., Witlox, F., and Catalano, G. (2003), "Beyond Friedmann's World City Hypothesis: Twenty-Two Urban Arenas Across the World." *Mitteilungen der Österreichischen Geographischen Gesellschaft* 145: 35–55. (http://www.lboro.ac.uk/gawc/rb/rb97.html%20-%20ft000).

Falck, O. (2007) *Emergence and Survival of New Businesses*. Heidelberg: Physica.

Feldman, M. P. (2001), "The Entrepreneurial Event Revisited: Firm Formation in a Regional Context." *Industrial and Corporate Change* 10: 861–91.

Feldman, M. P., Francis, J., and Bercovitz, J. (2005), "Creating a Cluster while Building a Firm: Entrepreneurs and the Formation of Industrial Clusters." *Regional Studies* 39: 129–41.

Fischer, M. and Varga, A. (2003), "Spatial Knowledge Spillovers and University Research: Evidence from Austria." *Annals of Regional Science* 37: 303–22.

Florida, R. (2002), "The Economic Geography of Talent." *Annals of the Association of American Geographers* 92: 743–55.

Florida, R. (2004), *The Rise of the Creative Class. And how it's Transforming Work, Leisure Community and Everyday Life*. New York: Basic Books.

Florida, R., Mellander, C., and Stolarick, K. (2008), "Inside the Black Box of Regional Development–Human Capital, the Creative Class and Tolerance." *Journal of Economic Geography* 8: 615–50.

Fotopoulos, G. and Spence, N. (1999), "Spatial Variation in New Manufacturing Plant Openings: some Empirical Evidence from Greece." *Regional Studies* 33: 219–29.

Friedmann, J. (1986), "The World City Hypothesis." *Development and Change* 17(1): 69–84.

Fritsch, M. and Falck, O. (2007), "New Business Formation by Industry over Space and Time: a Multidimensional Analysis." *Regional Studies* 41: 157–72.

Fritsch, M. and Mueller, P. (2006), "The Evolution of Regional Entrepreneurship and Growth Regimes." In M. Fritsch and J. Schmude (eds.), *Entrepreneurship in the Region,* New York: Springer, pp. 225–44.

Fritsch, M. and Stützer, M. (2007), "Die Geographie der kreativen Klasse." *Raumforschung und Raumordnung* 65: 15–29.

Fujita, M. and Thisse, J. (2002) *Economics of Agglomeration. Cities, Industrial Location, and Regional Growth*. Cambridge: Cambridge University Press.

Glaeser, E., Kolko, J., and Saiz, A. (2001), "Consumer City," *Journal of Economic Geography* 1: 27–50.

Glaeser, E., Kallal, H., Scheinkman, J., and Shleifer, A. (1992), "Growth of Cities." *Journal of Political Economy* 100: 1126–52.

Jacobs, J. (1969), *The Economy of Cities*. New York: Random House.

Jaffe, A., Traijtenberg, M., and Henderson, R. (1993), "Geographic Localization of Knowledge Spillovers as Evidenced by Patent Citations." *Quarterly Journal of Economics 63*, 577–98.

Khilstrom, R. E. and Laffont, J.-J. (1979), "A General Equilibrium Entrepreneurship Theory of Firm Formation Based on Risk Aversion." *Journal of Political Economy* 87 (4): 719–48.

Kelley, D., Bosma, N. S., and Amorós, J. E. (2011), *Global Entrepreneurship Monitor 2010 Executive Report*. Babson Park: Babson College, Santiago. Universidat del Desarrollo, and London: Global Entrepreneurship Research Association.

Koellinger, P., Minniti, M., and Schade, C. (2007), "I think I Can, I think I Can"': Overconfidence and Entrepreneurial Behavior, Journal of Economic Psychology 28: 502–27.

Lee, S. Y., Florida, R., and Acs, Z. J. (2004), "Creativity and Entrepreneurship: A Regional Analysis of New Firm Formation." *Regional Studies* 38(8): 879–91.

Lucas Jr., R. E. (1978), "On the Size Distribution of Business Firms." *Bell Journal of Economics* 9(2): 508–23.

Malecki, E. J. (1997), "Entrepreneurs, Networks, and Economic Development: A Review of Recent Research." *Advances in Entrepreneurship, Firm Emergence and Growth* 3: 57–118.

Martin, R. and Sunley, P. (2006), "Path Dependence and Regional Economic Evolution." *Journal of Economic Geography* 6: 395–437.

Minniti, M. (2004), "Entrepreneurial Alertness and Asymmetric Information in a Spin-Glass Model." *Journal of Business Venturing* 19: 637–58.

Minniti, M. (2005), "Entrepreneurship and Network Externalities." *Journal of Economic Behavior and Organization* 57: 1–27.

OECD (2007), *Competitive Cities: A New Entrepreneurial Paradigm in Spatial Development.* Organization for Economic Cooperation and Development (OECD) Paris, France.

Reynolds, P., Bosma, N., Autio, E., Hunt, S., De Bono, N., Servais, I., Lopez-Garcia, P., and Chin, N. (2005), "Global Entrepreneurship Monitor: Data Collection Design and Implementation, 1998–2003." *Small Business Economics* 24(3): 205–31.

Saxenian, A. (1994), *Regional Advantage. Culture and Competition in Silicon Valley and Route 128.* Cambridge, MA: Harvard University Press.

Schumpeter, J. A. (1942), *Capitalism, Socialism and Democracy.* New York: Harper Collins.

Science (2008), Cities, Special Section, Ash, C., Jasny, B. R., Roberts, L., Stone, R., and Sugden, A. M. eds. American Association for the Advancement of Science, 319:739–55.

Shane, S. and Venkataraman, S. (2000), "The promise of Entrepreneurship as a Field of Research." *Academy of Management Review* 25: 217–21.

Shapero, A. (1984), "The Entrepreneurial Event." In C. A. Kent (ed.),*The Environment for Entrepreneurship,* Lexington, MA: Lexington Books, pp. 21–40.

Solow, R. (1957), "Technical Change in an Aggregative Model of Economic Growth." *International Economic Review* 6: 18–31.

Stam, E. (2009), *Entrepreneurship, Evolution and Geography.* Jena: Max Planck Institute of Economics, Evolutionary Economics Group (Papers on Economics and Evolution, 0907).

Sternberg, R. (2009), *Regional Dimensions of Entrepreneurship.* Boston, Delft: Now Publishers (Foundations and Trends in Entrepreneurship 5, Issue 4).

Sternberg, R. and Rocha, H. O. (2007), "Why Entrepreneurship Is a Regional Event: Theoretical Arguments, Empirical Evidence, and Policy Consequences." In M. P. Rice and T. G. Habbershon (eds.), *Entrepreneurship: The Engine of Growth,* Volume 3: Place, Westport/CT, London: Praeger, pp. 215–38.

Taylor, P. J. (2004), *World City Network: a Global Urban Analysis.* London and New York: Routledge.

United Nations, Population Division of the Department of Economic and Social Affairs (2007), *World Population Prospects: The 2006 Revision* and *World Urbanization Prospects: The 2007 Revision,* (http://esa.un.org/unup).

van Stel, A. J. and Storey, D. J. (2004), "The Link between Firm Births and Job Creation: Is there a Upas Tree Effect?." *Regional Studies* 38: 893–909.

Varga, A. (1998), *University Research and Regional Innovation: A Spatial Econometric Analysis of Academic Technology Transfers.* Boston: Kluwer Academic Publishers.

Wagner, J. (2008), "Nascent and Infant Entrepreneurs in Germany. Evidence from the Regional Entrepreneurship Monitor (REM)." In J. Merz and R. Schulte (eds.), *Neue Ansätze der MittelstandsForschung,* pp. 341–95. LIT Verlag, Berlin, Gemany.

Wagner, J. and Sternberg, R. (2004), "Start-up Activities, Individual Characteristics, and the Regional Milieu: Lessons for Entrepreneurship Support Policies from German Micro Data." *The Annals of Regional Science* 38: 219–40.

Wennekers, A. R. M. (2006), *Entrepreneurship at Country Level; Economic and Non-economic Determinants,* ERIM Ph.D. Series Research in Management. Erasmus University Rotterdam.

7

Interregional Disparities, Entrepreneurship, and EU Regional Policy

Rolf Sternberg

7.1 Introduction

Neither policy evaluation research nor research on regional entrepreneurship has so far dealt specifically, either theoretically or empirically, with the relationship between regional economic policies and regional entrepreneurship activities (exceptions include Wagner and Sternberg 2004). This is astonishing, as policy programs and initiatives to support entrepreneurial activities have been launched in many European countries in recent years (see Audretsch et al. 2002 for an overview).

The majority of these policy instruments are based on the assumption of a positive influence of entrepreneurial activities on regional economic growth. Although the relationship between entrepreneurship and regional economic development is very complex and has only just begun to be analyzed, both empirically and theoretically (see Sternberg 2009 for an overview), sufficient arguments exist to support this assumption. Nevertheless, some empirical studies have shown that entrepreneurial activities may have positive as well as negative effects on regional development (Fritsch and Mueller 2004).

This chapter sheds an empirical light on the aforementioned relationship based on three countries and the regions within them. Spain, Great Britain (excluding Northern Ireland), and Germany are suitable case studies for various reasons. The three countries are (in the case of Spain and Germany) or were for a long time (Great Britain) marked by significant and in some cases growing interregional disparities in important economic indicators like rates of unemployment or gross domestic product (GDP) per capita (see Dunford and Smith 2000; Bosker 2009). This is one reason why the European

Commission's regional policy has given massive support to individual regions in these countries in the past to achieve the goals of EU regional policy (convergence, regional, and national competitiveness). Also, these three countries have for many years been participants in the Global Entrepreneurship Monitor (GEM) project, the world's largest research consortium on entrepreneurship research. This implies the existence of extensive empirical data on entrepreneurial activities and entrepreneurial attitudes. Although GEM was originally created to enable a comparison between entire countries, the particularly large sample sizes in these three countries also allow interregional comparisons between subnational regions under certain circumstances and for certain variables. This chapter exploits that potential to illuminate empirically the relationship between entrepreneurship activities, entrepreneurship attitudes/perceptions, and EU regional policies over a period of several years.

The chapter is based on the following assumptions derived from prior empirical and theoretical research on the relationship between entrepreneurship, interregional disparities, and regional policy:

- Economically backward regions are characterized by comparatively low levels of entrepreneurship activities, whereas prosperous regions, particularly those that belong to leading urban areas, have above-average levels of entrepreneurial activities (see Fritsch and Mueller 2008 for the situation in Germany or Malecki 1997).

- Economically backward regions suffer from the fact that entrepreneurial attitudes and entrepreneurial perceptions in those regions are less favorable, which at the same time is associated to their lower entrepreneurship rates (see Bosma 2009 for European GEM countries).

- The lower the national level of entrepreneurship activities, the higher the entrepreneurial disparities between the biggest cities and the rest of the same country (see Acs, Bosma, and Sternberg 2011, in this volume).

Within this context, the main research questions of the chapter are:

- How are entrepreneurial attitudes and entrepreneurial activities distributed across the regions of the three countries? Does this spatial pattern show parallels to the interregional disparities in terms of unemployment and GDP/capita, that is, are the economically strong regions also the regions with high entrepreneurial activity rates?

- Is any statistical relationship observable between entrepreneurial activities and/or entrepreneurial attitudes on the one hand and the status of a region as a "convergence" region supported by EU regional policies on the other?

- Do data show any statistical impact of former EU regional policies (period 2000–6) on recent entrepreneurial activities or entrepreneurial attitudes?

The chapter begins with a brief outline of the complex and interdependent relationships between entrepreneurship and regional development, the emphasis being on the regional impact of entrepreneurship. The relationship between regional policies and interregional disparities is the focal point of section 7.3, which looks in particular at the situation in the EU and the three member states of Spain, Great Britain, and Germany. Following a presentation of the data basis and the research questions, section 7.4 presents the empirical results of the descriptive as well as the bivariate and multivariate analyses. The focus here is on the relationship between regional entrepreneurship activities and regional policies. The chapter closes with concluding remarks concerning recommendations for regional policies in general and regional policies of the EU in particular.

7.2 Entrepreneurship and regional development

7.2.1 *Defining and explaining regional entrepreneurship*

In line with the argumentation of Sternberg and Wennekers (2005), entrepreneurship is understood as a combination of some elements of behavioral entrepreneurship with some aspects of the dynamic perspective of occupational entrepreneurship, making new venture creation the hallmark of entrepreneurship (Gartner 1989; Cooper 2003). In this chapter, the operational definition is based upon an interpretation of entrepreneurship as a process (see Reynolds et al. 2005). Entrepreneurial activity is defined to comprise individuals who commit resources to start a business they expect to own themselves (nascent entrepreneurs) plus individuals who own and manage a new business that has paid salaries for more than three months but less than forty-two months (young entrepreneurs). Combining these two phases of the entrepreneurial process yields total early-stage entrepreneurial activity (TEA for brevity in the rest of the chapter).

Traditional regional growth theories such as the neoclassical regional growth theory or the polarization theory in the tradition of Gunnar Myrdal do not help much in explaining and conceptualizing the regional effects of entrepreneurial activities. The same is true for more recent approaches like the new growth theory according to Romer (1990) or the "new economic geography" approach developed by Krugman (1991). They all suffer from the fact that the role of entrepreneurship, a crucial element in the innovation process, is missing (Acs 2000).

Other theoretical approaches are more helpful. Three of them point to the special role of urban areas for entrepreneurship-led regional economic development (see Acs, Bosma, and Sternberg 2011): urban externalities as put forward by Jane Jacobs (1969), agglomeration theory, and Richard Florida's

(2002) argument in favor of creativity and the "geography of talent." Combined, these approaches show that agglomeration effects are the main argument why cities should have higher start-up rates than non-urban regions. Furthermore, cities offer a great range of infrastructure, which is of interest especially for younger and/or more highly educated people. So, besides the enhancement of demand, cities also have larger proportions of highly educated people, which increase the pool of potential entrepreneurs. Economically backward regions, which very often are characterized by small population sizes and geographical peripherality, have, according to this approach, comparative disadvantages in terms of entrepreneurial activities. At the same time—and partly for the reasons mentioned before—many of these very regions are eligible for funding of regional policy programs of supranational, national, or regional governments.

Finally the concept of sectoral-regional clusters is also a useful one when explaining the regional effects of entrepreneurial activities. As several theoretical and empirical studies have shown (see, e.g., Romanelli and Feldman 2006), the concrete impact of entrepreneurial activities on cluster emergence differs from region to region, from time to time, and from sector to sector, nonetheless, in general, at least from a theoretical perspective, entrepreneurship seems to have a positive impact.

7.2.2 Empirical evidence for the impact of entrepreneurial activities on regional development in Germany, the United Kingdom, and Spain

The local effects of regional entrepreneurship provide one of the most active fields of empirical entrepreneurship research in recent years (see, for example, the theme issues of "Regional Studies" No. 8/2004 and "Small Business Economics" No. 1/2008). Empirical research on the regional variation of entrepreneurial activities clearly shows that the latter differ depending on the definition of entrepreneurial activities, the entrepreneurship indicators used, and the country, and time examined. However, three findings seem to be unambiguous (see Sternberg 2009 for an overview). First, there are clear and statistically significant interregional differences in the scope of entrepreneurial activities (e.g., Brixy and Grotz 2007 for Western Germany and Reynolds 2007 for US Labor Market Areas). Second, in most countries, urban areas clearly have higher start-up rates than the other region types (like rural areas or areas dominated by small cities, see, e.g., Bosma and Schutjens 2007). This may be attributable to regional causes, but also to determinants that have nothing to do with regional attributes. Third, interregional differences in start-up rates are rather stable over time (see, e.g. Armington and Acs 2002).

Interregional differences in entrepreneurial activities, however, do not automatically translate into different interregional impacts, for example in terms of employment effects or GDP effects. The intuition is that the positive nexus between high entrepreneurship rates and economic growth in the same region is often true for opportunity-driven entrepreneurship, but, in most cases, not for necessity-driven entrepreneurship. This is particularly common in developing countries, but is also observable in a country like Germany (see Wong, Ho, and Autio 2005). In other words, a high total rate of entrepreneurship need not necessarily correspond to high economic growth. The following considerations are restricted to Germany, Great Britain, and, to a lesser extent, Spain.

There are numerous empirical studies of the regional effects of entrepreneurship in Germany (e.g., Fritsch and Mueller 2004; Audretsch and Fritsch 2002) showing a distinction between direct and indirect effects. Direct effects encompass those effects that have a direct impact on the newly-founded firm itself such as the new employees, or the revenues. Indirect effects, instead, influence the remainder of the regional economy. In other words, they impact incumbent firms in the form of displacement effects or employment changes for suppliers or customers of the new firm. Compared to direct employment effects (see Fritsch and Weyh 2006), the indirect or supply-side regional employment effects such as crowding out competitors, the improvement of supply conditions and improved competitiveness seem to be more relevant. According to Fritsch and Mueller (2004) they are maximized about eight years after start-up. The lag structure they found suggests that new business formation during a given year has a positive impact on employment change. For years t-1 to t-5, the effect is negative, followed by a positive relationship between entrepreneurship and employment and a decrease afterwards, before the magnitude of the effect becomes slightly negative in the tenth year after start-up. In an alternative, Audretsch and Keilbach (2004) selected a different procedure and calculated a positive relationship between entrepreneurship activities and regional productivity growth and regional GDP growth. The regional effects of entrepreneurship activities in Germany vary significantly from one region to another (see also Sternberg 2006 on fifteen German case-study regions). If the region types (e.g., large agglomerations, rural areas, areas with small cities) are taken as the reference basis, then the employment effects of start-ups in urban agglomerations are considerably greater, at least in western Germany, than in moderately congested regions with lower population density or even in rural areas (cf. Fritsch and Mueller 2004, 2008). This fits with the empirical finding that, at least in the seventy-five western German planning regions, population density is the dominant factor affecting the scale of the regional employment effect of start-ups (Fritsch and Schroeter 2007).

Two recent studies have analyzed the regional effects of entrepreneurship activities in Great Britain. Van Stel and Storey (2004) did not find a significant impact of regional start-up activities and regional employment creation in the 1980s across all sixty British regions. However, they did find a positive impact for the 1990s, and a negative effect of entrepreneurship activities in those regions that had a low start-up rate in either or both decades (Scotland, Wales, North East). Mueller, Van Stel, and Storey (2008) found evidence of a "wave structure" for the regional employment effects of start-up activities. Again, British regions with high start-up rates show more comprehensive positive employment effects (per start-up) than regions with low start-up rates. Given the fact that the regions with low start-up rates are concentrated in Scotland and the North East of England, one consequence is that entrepreneurship activities tend to increase interregional economic disparities in Great Britain.

Finally, for Spain, Coduras, Cruz, and Justo (2009) have shown that interregional differences in entrepreneurship activities, as measured by the TEA rate, follow predictable patterns. Namely, the TEA of Madrid, the leading region, is almost three times higher than the TEA of the region at the bottom of the ranking. Vaillant and Lafuente (2007) show significant differences between entrepreneurial activity levels in rural Catalonia as compared to rural areas in the rest of Spain. This difference is largely explained by the distinct impact of the entrepreneurial role models favoring entrepreneurial activity in rural (Catalonia) areas where a strong industrial tradition exists. These results prompted the authors to plea for territorial specificity in the formulation and application of entrepreneurship support measures, with distinctions made between rural and urban areas.

7.2.3 *Entrepreneurial attitudes and perceptions, gender and role models as determinants of entrepreneurial activities*

Not only entrepreneurial activities but also entrepreneurial attitudes might have an impact on regional development. Entrepreneurial attitudes influence, for example, opportunity recognition or fear of failure as a start-up deterrent. An important aspect of entrepreneurial perception deals with the perception of one's own skills, competences, and experiences necessary for starting a firm (Koellinger, Minniti, and Schade 2007). Empirical studies based upon GEM data clearly reveal that both entrepreneurial attitudes and entrepreneurial perceptions are strongly associated with entrepreneurial activities (Arenius and Minniti 2005). This is true at the individual level as well as for the aggregated level of a subnational region, as empirical studies for some of the countries and regions considered in this paper have shown (Bergmann 2004). Consequently, if entrepreneurial activities are to have a stimulating effect on regional economic growth, it would be helpful if supporting policy instruments would address perceptions and attitudes of the people living in the respective region as well. For these reasons, it seems desirable to include perceptual variables in the empirical analysis in section 7.4.

A wide array of empirical studies has shown that gender is an important determinant of entrepreneurship activities (Bosma et al. 2009). Men launch companies far more frequently than women. Admittedly, there are gradual differences between states and continents in this respect, but the core statement holds true for virtually the whole world. Finally, knowing other entrepreneurs (e.g. parents or close friends) can, by providing role models, reduce individuals' fear of failure and provide information on how knowing other entrepreneurs influences the start-up process (see Mueller 2006). In cases where an entrepreneur known to the individual has failed, however, this acquaintance may have a contrary effect, turning the individual against entrepreneurship.

7.3 Interregional disparities and regional policy in the EU

Interregional economic disparities are a well-known issue for the EU integration process and have been analyzed frequently (see, e.g., Dunford and Smith 2000). Regional economic policies are dedicated to achieve goals that are defined by the central government and that are to be realized in the subnational regions of the overall territory. The goals differ over time and over spatial entities. Traditionally, the reduction of interregional disparities in terms of unemployment or GDP per capita were the most popular goals. In recent years, however, for some territories, the economic and technological competitiveness of the subregions has gained in importance as a way to achieve an increase in the competitiveness of the overall territory. In several countries that conduct their own regional policies, as well as at the supranational level of the European Union, a shift from a purely balance-oriented regional policy (reducing interregional inequalities) to a mix of growth-oriented policies ("strengthen the strength") and policies to reduce interregional disparities has been observed in recent years.

Starting with the Treaties of Rome (1957) there is a long history of regional policies in the EU and preceding institutions. European regional policy always tried to react to the opportunities and threats derived from the vertical and horizontal integration process within Europe. There are now twenty-seven member countries with very different economic and technological situations. The expansion to the east in 2005 and 2007 (increase from fifteen to twenty-five and then twenty-seven countries) brought with it a drastic increase in interregional (and international) economic disparities within the territory of the EU. An increase stronger than the one experienced during the expansion of the then European Community to the South in the 1980s to include Portugal, Spain, and Greece. According to most recent data from EUROSTAT, the relation between the strongest and the weakest NUTS 2 region in terms of GDP/capita measured in Euros was 38.8:1 in 2006 (Inner London with €89,300 vs Severozapaden in Bulgaria with only €2,300) and still 13.7:1, if purchasing power standards (PPS) are used as the measure (Inner London €79,400 vs North East Romania with €5,800).[1] As Figure 7.1 shows, there is a deep west–east divide among the NUTS 2 regions of the EU in terms of per-capita GDP. Most of the new member states in Eastern Europe have GDP/capita that are lower than seventy-five percent of the EU average, which makes them eligible areas for part of the EU regional policies. Within the western member states of the EU, that is, the longer-standing fifteen members, the map shows a clear north–south divide with the relatively weak regions in the southern part of the Iberian Peninsula, Southern Italy, and Greece.

Financial instruments and initiatives to address economic and social imbalances at the European Community level have existed since the beginning of European integration. However, only in 1986 legal foundations introduced by the Single European Act paved the way for an integrated cohesion policy. The European Social Fund (ESF, since 1958), the European Agricultural Guidance and Guarantee Fund (EAGGF, since 1962), and the European Regional Development Fund (ERDF, since 1975) cofinanced projects which had been selected beforehand by member states. In the current EU regional policy period (2007–13), the European Fund for Regional Development (EFRD), the European Social Fund (ESF), and the Cohesion Fund have contributed to the three objectives of Convergence, Regional Competitiveness and Employment, and European Territorial Cooperation (European Commission 2009).

The European Council agreed in December 2005 on the budget for the period 2007–13 and allocated €347 billion to structural and cohesion funds (European Commission 2008). The "Lisbon Strategy," agreed by the European Council in Lisbon in 2000, with its focus on growth, employment, and innovation became more and more the leitmotiv of many EU policies including regional policy. The radical shift in the EU policy priorities was the momentum for a paradigm shift in cohesion policy. This means that a quarter of resources is now earmarked for research and innovation and about thirty

[1] NUTS is the abbreviation for the French "Nomenclature des Unités Territoriales de Statistique" (Nomenclature of Territorial Units for Statistics). This geocode standard has been developed by the European Union and it shows the subdivisions of EU countries for statistical purposes. EUROSTAT, the statistical office of the EU, has established a hierarchy of three NUTS levels for each EU member country (e.g. for Germany NUTS 0 = country, NUTS 1 = federal states or "Bundesländer," NUTS 2 = "Regierungsbezirke" (larger administrative regions), and NUTS 3 = districts or "Kreise"). The NUTS system is instrumental in EU's Regional Policy Fund delivery mechanisms.

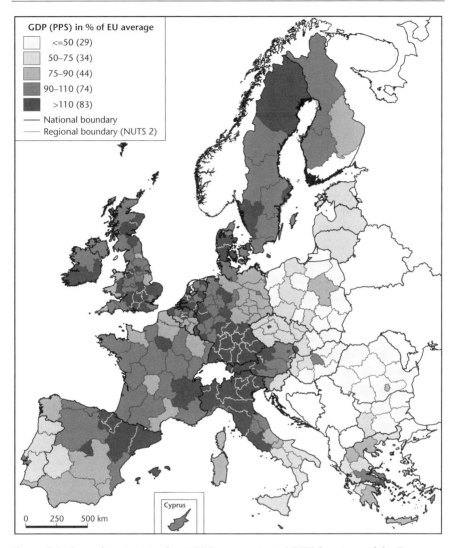

GDP (PPS) in % of EU average

- ☐ <=50 (29)
- ☐ 50–75 (34)
- ☐ 75–90 (44)
- ☐ 90–110 (74)
- ☐ >110 (83)
- — National boundary
- — Regional boundary (NUTS 2)

Cyprus

0   250   500 km

Figure 7.1 Gross domestic product (GDP) per capita in NUTS 2 regions of the European Union (purchasing power standards) in percent of EU average in 2006

percent for environmental infrastructure and measures combating climate change.

The rationale of the convergence objective is to promote growth-enhancing conditions and factors leading to real convergence for the least-developed member states and regions. In EU-27, this objective concerns eighty-four regions with a total population of 154 million, and per-capita GDP at less than seventy-five percent of the European Community average, and—on a phasing-out basis—another sixteen regions with a total of 16.4 million inhabitants and GDP only slightly above the threshold. Figure 7.2 shows the geographical allocation of the "convergence regions." The amount available under the Convergence objective is €282.8 billion, representing eighty-one point five percent of the total (European Commission 2008).

About a decade ago the EU Commission recognized that conditions for start-up companies are not as favorable in the EU as they are in the US and

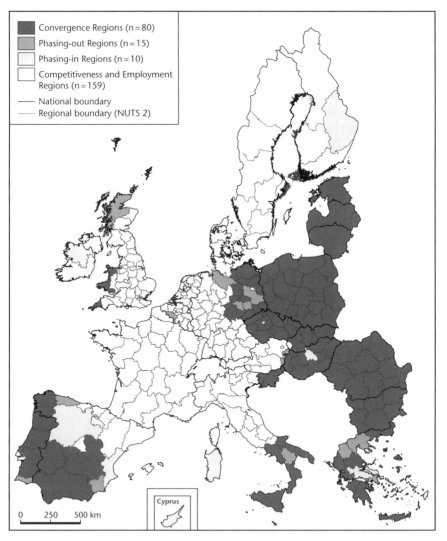

Figure 7.2 EU regional policy 2007–13: Eligible areas under the convergence objective and the European competitiveness and employment objective

that entrepreneurial initiatives are less developed (see also http://www.euractiv.com/en/innovation/entrepreneurship-europe/article-117477 on entrepreneurship as part of the EU Commission policies). Grilo and Thurik (2006) found that EU citizens are less inclined to become entrepreneurs, and are more risk-averse than their American counterparts. Moreover, conditions for start-up companies vary widely across Europe. The EU recognized this problem and made entrepreneurship one of the main objectives of the Lisbon agenda in 2000. The Commission launched a series of initiatives aimed at fostering support for small businesses in the EU. In its "Green Paper on Entrepreneurship in Europe" the EU Commission (2003) intended to stimulate the debate amongst policymakers, businesses, representative organizations, and experts on how to promote entrepreneurship in Europe more effectively. In the Green Paper, the connection between (the reduction of) interregional economic disparities and entrepreneurship is explicitly acknowledged: "Entrepreneurship can also contribute to fostering social and economic cohesion for regions whose development is lagging behind" (ibid., p. 7).

Following the Green Paper consultation process, the EU Commission published an Action Plan designed to provide a strategic framework for boosting entrepreneurship and aimed at encouraging more people to start businesses and to help entrepreneurs thrive (EU Commission 2004). At its Spring Summit meeting in March 2004, the European Council recognized that entrepreneurship is a major driver of innovation, competitiveness, employment, and growth and that encouraging and training more people to become entrepreneurs are key requirements for the achievement of the Lisbon objectives. Later in 2004, the Commission published details of the key actions of the above-mentioned Action Plan, describing the thirty-eight planned sub-actions, objectives, and the impact the activities are expected to have in various regions (see EU Commission 2006).

The Action Plan also identified geographical areas (at the NUTS 2 regional level) as areas that are eligible to receive support from EU regional policies under the convergence objective. This is particularly important for this study since only the convergence objective supports exclusively defined areas on the basis of their economic performance, whereas the programs supporting competitiveness and employment apply to all NUTS 2 regions regardless of their regional economic performance. Moreover, this is by far the program to which the most EU funding has been allocated. The phasing-out regions are also counted among the eligible areas.

Germany, Great Britain, and Spain are all three characterized by marked regional disparities in terms of unemployment (see Figure 7.3) and GDP per capita (see Figure 7.4), although these disparities have decreased slightly in recent years. In Germany there continues to be a gap between the western and eastern (the former German Democratic Republic—GDR) parts of the country since their reunification two decades ago. Smaller (and older) disparities within the former West Germany between the wealthier south (Bavaria, Baden-Württemberg) and the north still exist but are less severe than the east–west divide. In Spain, a similar distinction exists between the relative wealthy north and northeast (e.g., Catalonia) and the capital region of Madrid, versus the more backward south and west of the country. Finally, in Great Britain, a sharp north south divide is found between Greater London and some wealthier parts along the "Western Crescent" and East Anglia and the rest of the country. Noticeably, however, due to structural problems, Wales in the southwest and the old industrialized areas around Manchester, Birmingham, and Sheffield are also target regions for European regional policies as well as for regional policies of the national government.

As Figures 7.3 and 7.4 show, for the NUTS 2 regions in all three countries, interregional disparities for both unemployment and per-capita GDP exhibit systematic and consistent characteristics, that is, most of the low income regions also suffer from high unemployment. Since Spain, Great Britain, and Germany belong to the relatively wealthy countries in the enlarged EU (with 75% of the average EU GDP per capital as a crucial threshold value for EU regional policy support, see also Figure 7.1), they had to accept a reduction in the number of their EU supported regions in the current EU regional policy period (called "statistical effect"). Altogether, the three countries receive about €72 billion during the current EU regional policy period, more than a fifth of total EU regional policy funding between 2007 and 2013. Spain receives €35.2 billion (10.1% of total EU regional policies), while Germany and Great Britain receive significantly less funding (7.6% and 3.1% respectively).

7.4 Empirical results

7.4.1 *Data and selection of the countries*

Data on entrepreneurial activities and entrepreneurial attitudes are from the adult population surveys of the Global Entrepreneurship Monitor (GEM). Forty-three countries were involved in the 2008 GEM study. While the main level of analysis within GEM is the comparison of entire countries, interregional comparisons within (or across) national boundaries are possible for some of the GEM member countries for which sample sizes are sufficiently large. Between 2003 and 2008, 130,339 interviews with 18–64 year old inhabitants were conducted in Spain, 147,867 in Great Britain, and 26,782 in Germany. All GEM data used in this chapter are individual level data aggregated at the NUTS 2 level (nineteen regions in Spain, thirty-six regions in Great Britain, forty-one regions in Germany). Data for the regional economic

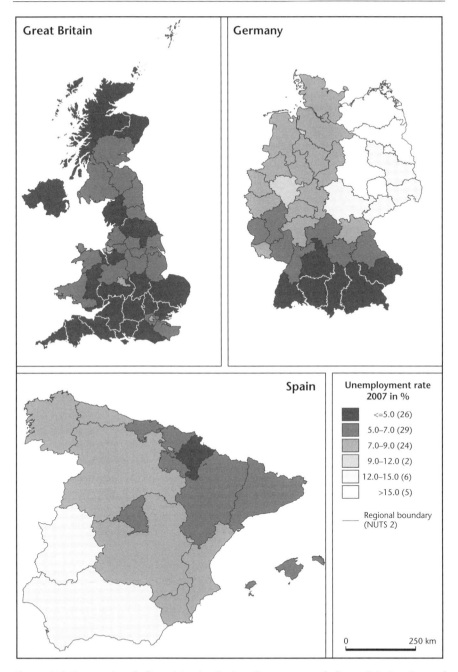

Figure 7.3 Interregional disparities in Spain, Germany, and Great Britain: Rate of unemployment (2007) at NUTS 2 level

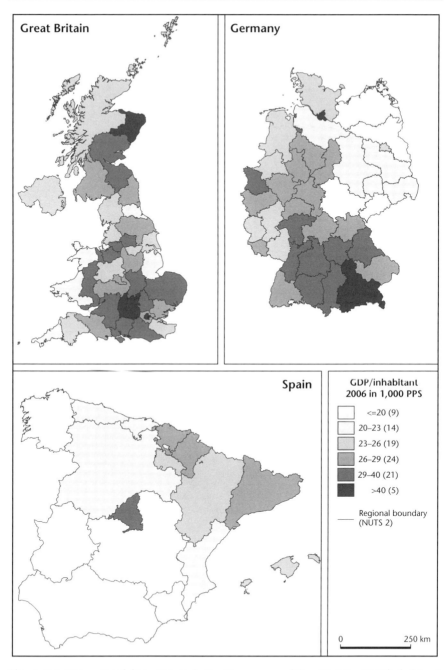

Figure 7.4 Interregional disparities in Spain, Germany, and Great Britain: GDP/inhabitant (2006) at NUTS 2 level

performance of the NUTS 2 regions as well population data are from the publicly available EUROSTAT databases.

In section 7.4.4, separate multivariate and bivariate analyses will be run for each of the three countries as there are slight differences in the reference years and considerable structural differences between them. Spain is traditionally a country that receives a great deal of support from EU regional policy and that lags behind Great Britain and Germany in all significant economic indicators. Until the beginning of the 1990s, Germany was one of the strongest member states of the European Community with relatively small interregional disparities. Since reunification, however, there have been, and continue to be, significant disparities between the former West and East Germany. Finally, Great Britain and most of its regions are among the leading regions in Europe for many of the economic indicators used here—but not for the indicators of entrepreneurial activity and entrepreneurial attitudes. Among the forty-three countries that participated in GEM in 2008 (see Bosma et al. 2009). Germany, Great Britain, and Spain all show relatively low TEA rates ranking with Spain at twenty-nine (TEA 7.0%), Great Britain at thirty-three (TEA 5.9%), and Germany at forty-two (TEA 3.8%).

7.4.2 Descriptive empirical results on spatial distribution of entrepreneurial activities and entrepreneurial attitudes

The regional distribution of early-stage entrepreneurial activity measured by TEA rate for Germany, Great Britain, and Spain is shown in Figure 7.5. The spread between the highest and lowest regional rate within each of the three countries are relatively similar; specifically, between 4.2 and 6.1 percentage points. Thus, interregional TEA differences exist but are not that large. Also, TEA rates are quite similar for the NUTS 2 regions in all three countries (between 3% and 8–9%). Differences between economically backward and prosperous regions across the three countries, however, are very pronounced. Although not perfect, for Germany and Great Britain a certain congruence of economically strong regions and more entrepreneurial regions seems to exist. Most of the NUTS 2 regions with above-average TEA rates have also above-average GDP per capita and below-average rates of unemployment. In Spain no clear relationship between GDP per capita and TEA exists. Some of the more backward regions (Extremadura) have relatively high TEA rates, but so do some of the economically prosperous regions (Aragon and Madrid). One possible explanation may be the higher relevance of necessity entrepreneurship in Spanish regions compared, at least, to British regions. This is consistent with existing research based on GEM data showing that opportunity-driven TEA has a clear and positive correlation with GDP per capita (and GDP

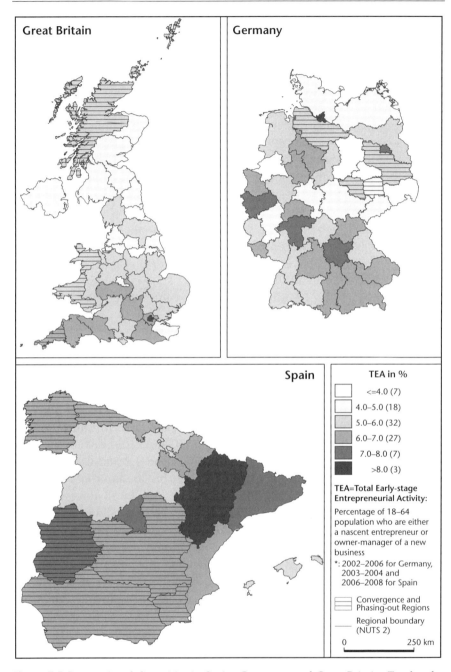

Figure 7.5 Interregional disparities in Spain, Germany, and Great Britain: Total early-stage entrepreneurial activity (TEA) rate at NUTS 2 level (averages 2003–8*) and EU regional policy

growth) but that the same is not true for necessity-driven TEA (see, e.g., Wong, Ho, and Autio 2005 and Bosma 2009).

Interregional disparities for the opportunity recognition variable are much higher than for TEA—and this holds true for all three countries (see Figure 7.6). A visual comparison of Figures 7.5 and 7.6 reveals that the interregional differences for both variables differ in terms of the level but not for the broad spatial pattern: in all three countries those regions that have high TEA rates are also characterized by above-average opportunity perceptions. As shown from Halman et al. (2008), the German population is less optimistic in its perception of entrepreneurial opportunities in the area where they live and during the next six months compared to the people living in Spain and Great Britain. For Germany and Great Britain the spatial pattern of opportunity perception resembles the patterns shown for per capita GDP and unemployment (see Figure 7.5). For Spain, instead, both patterns differ significantly.

7.4.3 Association between regional policies and entrepreneurial activities or entrepreneurial attitudes

The observations above suggest that interregional disparities in entrepreneurial activities and, even more, in entrepreneurial perceptions are a common phenomenon in Spain, Germany, and Great Britain. We now intend to examine whether EU regional policy, which specifically aims at achieving regional targets and has certain promotion regions in its convergence objective, also demonstrates a relationship with entrepreneurship. This will be examined first descriptively and then analytically using a multivariate logit–loglinear model.

Do the data show a relationship between living in an area eligible for support under EU regional policy (in either 2000–6 or 2007–13) and the entrepreneurial activities and entrepreneurial perception of an individual? Table 7.1 differentiates between three types of independent variables that are assumed to cover adequately entrepreneurial activities and entrepreneurial attitudes of the respondents in the GEM adult population surveys. Specifically, the study considers:

- Actual entrepreneurship activity
- Entrepreneurial attitudes and entrepreneurial capabilities of the respondent according to his/her own perception
- Evaluation/perception of the respondent regarding the attitude of the regional population at large towards issues relevant to entrepreneurship, which may also exert an influence on one's own attitudes and activities.

As Table 7.1 shows, most of the eleven independent variables show statistically significant mean differences according to the non-parametric U-Mann-Whitney test. Most of the cited hypotheses on backward regions are confirmed: Spanish

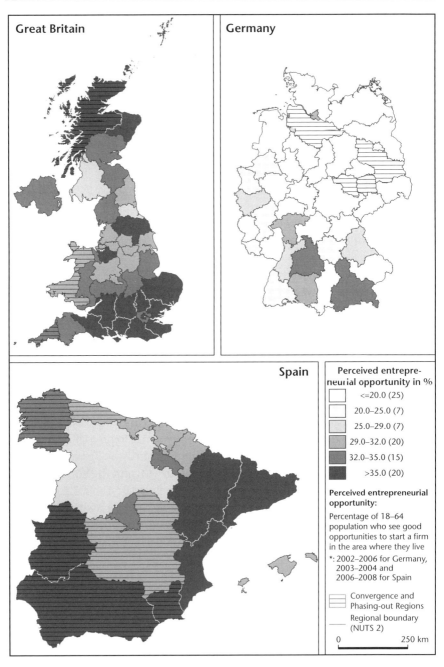

Figure 7.6 Interregional disparities in Spain, Germany, and Great Britain: Perceived entrepreneurial opportunity at NUTS 2 level (averages 2003–8*) and EU regional policy

adults are less likely to launch firms, have weaker entrepreneurial attitudes, and are more likely to have closed down a self-launched company than is the case in non-promoted regions. But there are exceptions: successful entrepreneurs are more often respected in convergence regions than in other regions.

In Germany, only about one fifth of adults interviewed live in convergence regions or phasing-out regions. The eligible German regions are almost exclusively in eastern Germany, in other words the differences between assisted and non-assisted areas in terms of entrepreneurship largely reflect the country's east–west divide. This is also true of other indicators of regional economic disparities: in contrast to Spain and other European countries, the disparities are narrower between urban agglomerations and rural regions and wider between eastern and western Germany in general. The hypotheses are confirmed in Germany, too, with only a few exceptions. The relationship appears to be particularly strong between convergence regions and entrepreneurship activities, while this relationship is weaker in the other two countries. The only exception is, surprisingly enough, the perception of media reports on entrepreneurs.

Of the three countries, Great Britain was home to the smaller number of people living in convergence regions in both policy periods. It is noticeable that the relationships are weakest in this country; in particular, none of the entrepreneurship activity variables shows any statistically significant mean difference. Similarly, the hypotheses are only confirmed in part: for about half the independent variables the eligible areas have better values while for the other half it is the non-eligible areas that score better.

It may be observed across all NUTS 2 regions in the three countries that statistically significant mean differences exist between convergence regions and other regions for over half the independent variables, which makes more in-depth analysis appear appropriate. It is also noticeable that the relationships between regional policy and the independent variables are stronger and more frequent for the past regional policy period (2000–6) than for the current period (2007–13). This may be an indicator of the direction of causality, that is, an EU regional policy in the past has had more time to influence entrepreneurship activities and attitudes than a current one. For this reason, the following multivariate analysis takes past EU regional policy periods as an independent variable to explain more recent entrepreneurship activities.

The differences between the results of the two EU regional policy periods (2000–6 vs 2007–13) shown in Table 7.1 may also be affected by the fact that the number of NUTS 2 regions promoted has decreased to differing extents in the three countries. In Spain, for example, a great many NUTS 2 regions ceased to receive promotion as convergence regions.

Table 7.1. Entrepreneurship activities and entrepreneurship attitudes in and off NUTS 2 regions eligible for EU regional policies

Entrepreneurial activity, entrepreneurial attitude (% of adults 18–64)	Spain — NUTS 2 region eligible for EU regional policy 2000–2006?			Spain — NUTS 2 region eligible for EU regional policy 2007–2013?			Great Britain — NUTS 2 region eligible for EU regional policy 2000–2006?			Great Britain — NUTS 2 region eligible for EU regional policy 2007–2013?			Germany — NUTS 2 region eligible for EU regional policy 2000–2006?			Germany — NUTS 2 region eligible for EU regional policy 2007–2013?		
	Yes	No	Sign.	Yes	No	Sign.	Yes	No	Sign.	Yes	No	Sign.	Yes	No	Sign.	Yes	No	Sign.
Entrepreneurial activity																		
TEA	6.51	6.77	(*)	6.43	6.66		5.14	5.67	*	5.50	5.57		4.57	6.18	***	5.40	6.02	(*)
Nascent	2.89	3.15	(*)	2.92	3.00		2.75	3.04		2.87	3.00		2.88	3.60	**	3.42	3.48	
Baby business	3.77	3.71		3.65	3.80		2.66	2.87		2.84	2.82		2.02	3.12	***	2.47	3.04	*
Start-up closed	12.9	10.5	***	12.8	12.0		1.8	2.0		1.9	1.9		1.8	2.0		1.8	2.1	
Entrepreneurial attitudes and capabilities																		
Eship skills	50.0	51.1	**	50.3	50.3		47.7	49.3	**	48.6	49.0		37.2	44.5	***	39.2	44.2	***
Good opportunities	32.7	34.3	***	33.5	33.0		30.8	34.8	***	30.4	34.7	***	12.1	23.0	***	14.2	22.8	***
Fear of failure (% "yes")	46.4	45.6	*	45.9	46.3		33.7	34.8		33.9	34.7		50.6	43.0	***	48.2	43.3	***
Knowing an entrepreneur	35.1	34.9		35.9	34.6	***	23.9	25.6	**	25.1	25.3		43.2	42.4		43.5	42.2	(*)
Interviewee's perception of the regional populations attitudes																		
Self-employment attractive?	67.6	67.6		66.5	68.2	***	55.2	52.5	***	54.8	52.7	**	51.3	51.3		48.6	52.0	**
Successful entrepreneurs respected?	58.7	57.1	***	58.5	58.2		72.4	72.6		72.4	72.6		73.9	73.3		72.7	73.6	
Many media reports	44.7	43.7	*	43.5	44.8	**	56.6	55.0	**	56.9	55.0	**	55.3	46.7	**	51.0	47.4	***
No of cases	76,731–110,955						35,812–129,602						13,210–33,293					

Sign.: *U-Mann-Whitney Test*; ***: $p < 0.1\%$, **: $p < 1\%$, *: $p < 5\%$, (*): $p < 10\%$

Data source: GEM adult populations surveys for Spain, Germany and Great Britain, various years

7.4.4 *Multivariate analysis of the relationship between EU regional policies and entrepreneurial activities*

A multivariate analysis is performed to examine whether the fact that a NUTS 2 region was eligible for EU regional policy funding (convergence objective) in the past had an influence on early-stage entrepreneurial activity (TEA), and entrepreneurship perceptions. Attitudes and capabilities are in turn very important determinants of entrepreneurship activity (Arenius and Minniti 2005), which is why it is also worthwhile to ascertain the policy impact on these attitudes. Our hypothesis is that such an impact of regional policy on entrepreneurship does exist. Empirical entrepreneurship research has demonstrated that a variety of variables influence an individual's entrepreneurship activities and perceptions (see Sternberg 2009 for an overview), and—aggregating individuals—the activities and perceptions of an entire region. In rough terms, these variables can be assigned to the three categories of personal characteristics of the entrepreneur (gender, age, see, e.g., Chell and Baines 2000), context variables relating to the entrepreneur (networks, knowing other persons including entrepreneurs; see, e.g. Brüderl and Preisendörfer 1998; Davidsson and Honig 2003) and the regional/national environment (economic prosperity, housing prices, see, e.g., Wagner and Sternberg 2004). These variables not only exert a direct influence on the dependent variable, they can also have a combined impact via interaction variables. In order to identify these relationships, a logit–loglinear model is used to conduct an exploratory analysis aimed at explaining three dichotomous dependent variables, namely, involvement in early-stage entrepreneurship activity (i.e., TEA yes/no), entrepreneurship perception (good start-up opportunities, yes/no), and entrepreneurship attitude (entrepreneurship skills yes/no). In each case, three independent variables are used. In line with the principle of parsimonious parameterization, in addition to the regional policy variable (area eligible for EU convergence funding between 2000–6 yes/no), only gender (male = 1), and the variable "knowing an entrepreneur (yes/no)" are integrated in the models, again separately for the three countries. This process makes it possible to estimate the relative significance of the policy variable compared with a small number of other determinants.

The λ coefficients in the logit–loglinear model measure the explanatory relevance of each variable for the model as a whole and also serve to identify interaction effects between the corresponding variables (see, for example, Bühl and Zöfel 2002). In the case of logit–loglinear models, these coefficients make it possible to estimate the ranking of independent variables in terms of their influence on the dependent variable.

Table 7.2 shows a marked correlation for the three countries analyzed and in all nine logit–loglinear models. Gender and knowing other entrepreneurs are

Table 7.2. Effects of EU regional policies on entrepreneurial activity and perception (logit–loglinear models)[1]

	Dependent variables								
	Spain			Great Britain			Germany		
Independent variables	TEA: yes=1 no=0	Good Opportunities: yes=1	Entrepreneurial skills: yes=1	TEA: yes=1; no=0	Good Opportunities: yes=1; no=0	Entrepreneurial skills: yes=1; no=0	TEA: yes=1; no=0	Good Opportunities: yes=1; no=0	Entrepreneurial skills: yes=1; no=0
Single interdependent variables									
EU regional policy 2000–2006: yes=1, no=2	−0.065	−0.093*	−0.015	−0.180	−0.113(*)	−0.070	+0.507*	−0.791***	−0.304***
Gender: 1=male, 2=female	+0.320***	+0.211***	+0.305***	+0.561***	+0.298***	+0.798***	+0.550***	+0.458***	+0.661***
Knowing an entrepreneur: no=0, yes=1	+0.974***	+0.691***	+0.929***	+1.290***	+1.066***	+0.030***	−1.369***	+0.731***	+0.936***
Interaction variables (if statistically significant only)									
EU regional policy & Knowing an entrepreneur						−0.167*			
Gender & Knowing an entrepreneur	−0.155(*)					−0.079(*)			
EU regional policy & gender & Knowing an entrepreneur								−0.358(*)	+0.112(*)
No of cases	109,432	81,903	104,077	68,152	55,708	66,437	24,700	22,076	24,295

[1]Significance of λ coefficients: ***: $p < 0.1\%$, *: $p < 1\%$, *: $p < 5\%$, (*): $p < 10\%$, for definition of variables see annex table

Data source: GEM adult populations surveys for Spain, Germany and Great Britain, various years

both highly significant variables in all models. These results suggest these variables contribute to increasing the probability of an individual becoming an entrepreneur. In fact, knowing other entrepreneurs is the variable with the greatest influence in most models and it always increases the probability of entrepreneurship. The same systematic positive association is found when the respondent is male. With the exception of one model (opportunity recognition in Germany), the regional policy variable is the one variable with the weakest influence on the probability of becoming an entrepreneur. Nonetheless, its influence is statistically significant in over half of the models, including all three models relating to Germany. Apart from a few λ coefficients for the regional policy variable, the algebraic signs are all as expected. Accordingly, this suggests that the positive association between entrepreneurial activity and the perceptions of entrepreneurial opportunities and of one's own skills is most strongly affected by the respondent's acquaintance with other entrepreneurs. With the second strongest influence being that of gender, and the third being whether the respondent lives in an area identified as a convergence region under the EU regional policy in the 2000–6 period.

In relative terms, the strongest influence of EU regional policy (in the sense defined here) seems to be associated to the perception of good start-up opportunities. Only for this variable, statistically significant influences of regional policy can be seen in all three countries. The policy variable has the greatest influence in Germany, suggesting that the regions with weak or low entrepreneurship perceptions and entrepreneurship activities are generally the same regions that lag behind other parts of the country in economic terms, specifically broad areas of eastern Germany.[2]

7.5 Conclusions

This chapter has addressed three main research questions. First, in the three countries investigated regional disparities for economic indicators and for entrepreneurship indicators show roughly the same pattern: the stronger the economic performance of the region, the higher the entrepreneurial activity rate. The same is true for entrepreneurial attitudes. Second, across all NUTS 2 regions in the three countries, statistically significant mean differences exist between convergence regions and other regions for over half the independent variables. The strongest association between entrepreneurial activities and regional policies is in Germany, the weakest in the UK. Third, the relationships

---

[2] Only in a very few cases the several hundred interaction variables (most of them not documented in Table 7.2 due to lack of space and content relevance) exhibit a statistically significant influence. More details are available from the author upon request.

between regional policy and independent variables are stronger and more frequent for the regional policy period (2000–6) than for the current policy period (2007–13).

Individuals living in areas that were eligible for EU convergence funding between 2000 and 2006 have a lower probability of starting/launching a firm than other individuals. They also have a less optimistic perception of the start-up opportunities. However, two other determinants of entrepreneurial behavior show a closer association with entrepreneurial activities than EU regional policy: the gender of the individual and knowing another entrepreneur.

Since the purpose of its regional policy for the period 2007–13 is to support both cohesion and competitiveness, the EU should probably pay more attention to entrepreneurship than has been the case to date. Entrepreneurship activities can contribute to the achievement of both objectives, even if not to the same extent in all countries or at the same time. It would seem desirable for many regions; in particular more backward ones like most regions benefiting from EU convergence policy are, to work to improve their population opportunity recognition. This is particularly relevant with respect to women who have more pessimistic perceptions of start-up opportunities and of their own entrepreneurial skills than men do, a phenomenon that makes them considerably less likely to start a company. Only by considering these issues, regional policy may hope to contribute in the long term to increasing opportunity-driven entrepreneurship activities in economically backward regions. Albeit exploratory, results presented in this chapter suggest that entrepreneurship policy can play an important role in influencing entrepreneurial performance, but the policy should be closely tailored to the specific needs, capabilities, and institutional structures of each country/region. In fact, national and supranational efforts to promote entrepreneurship capital may be inherently doomed to failure since entrepreneurship capital is embedded in regions. Consequently, as Audretsch and Keilbach (2007) put it, local and regional (rather than national or supranational) policies should emerge as relatively more effective and important.

Unfortunately, in countries where numerous regional policy programs aimed at supporting entrepreneurship exist (as in Germany), lack of coordination has reduced effectiveness and significant room for improvement exists. Nonetheless, Shane's (2009) pessimistic view of all entrepreneurship support policies may be excessive. Some systems in which entrepreneurship support is integrated into a nationwide program of multilevel policies (as in Great Britain or in the Netherlands, for example, Brixy et al. 2009), policies have shown signs of effectiveness and should be praised. The empirical results of this chapter suggest that such comprehensive and multilevel approaches that privilege regional and local intervention may be a very good idea.

Acknowledgments

My particular thanks go to Jonathan Levie (University of Strathclyde, team leader GEM UK) and Alicia Coduras (Instituto de Empresa; GEM team Spain) for providing individual level data for the UK and Spain. Nicolas Reum deserves special praise for the laborious processing of the Spanish individual data without which the estimates presented here would not have been possible. Many thanks go also to an anonymous reviewer for helpful comments. Although GEM data were used in this study, their interpretation and use are the sole responsibility of the author. All errors are mine.

References

Acs, Z. J. (ed.) (2000), *Regional Innovation, Knowledge and Global Change*. London: Pinter.

Acs, Z. J., Bosma, N., and Sternberg, R. (2011), "Entrepreneurship in World Cities:" In *The Dynamics of Entrepreneurship*, M. Minniti (ed.), pp. 125–51, Oxford University Press: Oxford, NewYork.

Arenius, P. and Minniti, M. (2005), "Perceptual Variables and Nascent Entrepreneurship." *Small Business Economics* 24: 233–47.

Armington, C. and Acs, Z. J. (2002), "The Determinants of Regional Variation in New Firm Formation." *Regional Studies* 36: 33–45.

Audretsch, D. B. and Fritsch, M. (2002), "Growth Regimes over Time and Space." *Regional Studies* 36(2): 113–24.

Audretsch, D. B. and Keilbach, M. (2004), "Entrepreneurship and Regional Growth–An Evolutionary Intepretation." *Journal of Evolutionary Economics* 14(5): 605–16.

Audretsch, D. B. and Keilbach, M. (2007), "The Localization of Entrepreneurship Capital: Evidence from Germany." *Papers in Regional Science* 86(3): 351–65.

Audretsch, D. B., Thurik, A. R., Verheul, I., and Wennekers, A. R. M. (eds.) (2002), *Entrepreneurship: Determinants and Policy in a European-US Comparison*. Boston, Dordrecht: Kluwer, 11–81.

Bergmann, H. (2004), *"Gründungsaktivitäten im regionalen Kontext, Gründer, Gründungseinstellungen und Rahmenbedingungen in zehn deutschen Regionen" [Start-up Activities in a Regional Context, Founders, Entrepreneurial Attitudes and Framework Conditions in ten German Regions]*. Cologne: Institute of Economic and Social Geography (Kölner Forschungen zur Wirtschafts- und Sozialgeographie, 57).

Bosker, M. (2009), "The spatial evolution of regional GDP disparities in the 'old' and the 'new' Europe." *Papers in Regional Science* 88: 3–27.

Bosma, N. and Schutjens, V. (2007), "Patterns of Promising Entrepreneurial Activity in European Regions." *Tijdschrift voor ecconomische en sociale Geografie* 98(5): 675–86.

Bosma, N. (2009), *The Geography of Entrepreneurial Activity and Regional Economic Development*. Utrecht (PhD dissertation).

Bosma, N., Acs, Z. J., Autio, E., Coduras, A., and Levie, J. (2009), *"Global Entrepreneurship Monitor 2008 Executive Report."* Wellesley, London, Santiago de Chile: Babson

College, London Business School, Universidad del Desarrollo, Global Entrepreneurship Research Consortium (GERA).

Brixy, U. and Grotz, R. (2007), "Regional Patterns and Determinants of the Success of New Firms in Western Germany." *Entrepreneurship and Regional Development* 19(4): 293–312.

Brixy, U.; Hessels, J.; Hundt, C., Sternberg, R., and Stüber, H. (2009), *Global Entrepreneurship Monitor (GEM). Länderbericht Deutschland 2008*. Hannover, Nürnberg: Institut für Wirtschafts- und Kulturgeographie, Universität Hannover; Institut für Arbeitsmarkt- und Berufsforschung der Bundesagentur für Arbeit (IAB).

Brüderl, J. and Preisendörfer, P. (1998), "Network Support and the Success of Newly Founded Businesses." *Small Business Economics* 10: 213–25.

Bühl, A. and Zöfel, P. (2002), *SPSS 11* (8th edn). München: Pearson.

Chell, B. and Baines, S. (2000), "Does Gender Affect Business "Performance"? A Study of Microbusiness in Business Services in the UK." *Entrepreneurship and Regional Development* 10: 117–35.

Coduras, A., Cruz, C., and Justo, R. (2009), *Global Entrepreneurship Monitor. Informe Ejecutivo GEM Espana 2008*. Madrid: Instituto de Empresa.

Cooper, A. C. (2003), "Entrepreneurship: The Past, the Present, the Future." In *Handbook of Entrepreneurship Research*, Z. J. Acs and D. B. Audretsch (eds.), pp. 21–36. Kluwer Academic Publishers: Boston and Dordrecht.

Davidsson, P. and Honig, B. (2003), "The Role of Social and Human Capital among Nascent Entrepreneurs." *Journal of Business Venturing* 18: 301–31.

Dunford, M. and Smith, A. (2000), "Catching up or falling behind? Economic performance and regional trajectories in the 'New Europe.'" *Economic Geography* 76: 169–95.

European Commission (2008), *Cohesion policy 2007–2013: Indicative financial allocations* (http://ec.europa.eu/regional_policy/policy/fonds/pdf/annexe-recto.pdf, download 2009–7–6).

European Commission (2003), *Green Paper: Entrepreneurship in Europe*. Brussels: Enterprise Directorate General.

European Commission (2004), *Action Plan: The European Agenda for Entrepreneurship*. Brussels.

European Commission (2006), *Report on the Implementation of the Entrepreneurship Action Plan*. Brussels (Commission Staff Working Paper, SEC(2006)1132).

European Commission (2009), *Regional Policy–Info Region* (http://ec.europa.eu/regional_policy/policy/htm; download 2009–7–12).

Florida, R. (2002), "The Economic Geography of Talent." *Annals of the Association of American Geographers* 92: 743–55.

Fritsch, M. and Schroeter, A. (2007), "Why Does the Effect of New Business Formation Differ across Regions?." *Jena Economic Research Paper No. 2007–077*.

Fritsch, M. and Weyh, A. (2006), "How Large are the Direct Employment Effects of New Businesses? An Empirical Investigation." *Small Business Economics* 27: 245–60.

Fritsch, M. and Mueller, P. (2004), "Effects of New Business Formation on Regional Development over Time." *Regional Studies* 38: 961–75.

Fritsch, M. and Mueller, P. (2008), "The Effect of New Business Formation on Regional Development over Time: The Case of Germany." *Small Business Economics* 30(1): 15–29.

Gartner, W. B. (1989), "Some Suggestions for Research on Entrepreneurial Traits and Characteristics." *Entrepreneurship: Theory & Practice* 14: 27–37.

Grilo, I. and Thurik, R. (2006), *Latent and Actual Entrepreneurship in Europe and the US: Some Recent Developments*. Zoetermeer: EIM Scales-paper.

Halman, L. C. J. M., Inglehart, R., Diez-Medrano, J., Luijkx, R., Moreno, A., and Basánez, M. (2008), *Changing Values and Beliefs in 85 Countries. Trends form the Values Surveys from 1981 to 2004*. Leiden: Brill.

Jacobs, J. (1969), *The Economy of Cities*. New York: Random House.

Koellinger, P., Minniti, M., and Schade, C. (2007),"I Think I Can. I Think I Can: A Study of Entrepreneurial Behavior." *Journal of Economic Psychology* 28: 502–27.

Krugman, P. (1991), *Geography and Trade*. Cambridge, MA: MIT Press.

Malecki, E. (1997), "Entrepreneurs, Networks, and Economic Development: A Review of Recent Research." In J. A. Katz (eds.), *Advances in Entrepreneurship, Firm Emergence and Growth,* pp. 57–118. JAI Press: Greenwich.

Mueller, P. (2006), "Exploring the Knowledge Filter: How Entrepreneurship and University–Industry Relationships Drive Economic Growth." *Research Policy* 35: 1499–1508.

Mueller, P., Van Stel, A. J., and Storey, D. J. (2008), "The Effects of New Firm Formation on Regional Development over Time: The Case of Great Britain." *Small Business Economics* 30(1): 59–71.

Reynolds, P. D. (2007), *Entrepreneurship in the United States*. New York: Springer.

Reynolds, P. D., Bosma, N., Autio, E., Hunt, S., De Bono, N., Servais, I., Lopez-Garcia, P., and Chin, N. (2005), "Global Entrepreneurship Monitor: Data Collection and Implementation 1998–2003," *Small Business Economics* 24: 205–31.

Romanelli, E., and Feldman, M. (2006), "Anatomy of Cluster Development: Emergence and Convergence in the US Human Biotherapeutics, 1976–2003." In P. Braunerhjelm and M. Feldman (eds.), *Cluster Genesis: Technology-Based Industrial Development,* pp. 87–112. Oxford: OUP.

Romer, P. (1990), "Endogenous Technological Change." *Journal of Political Economy* 98: 71–102.

Shane, S. (2009), "Why Encouraging More People to Become Entrepreneurs Is Bad Public Policy." *Small Business Economics* 33: 141–9.

Sternberg, R. (ed.) (2006), *Deutsche Gründungsregionen (Entrepreneurial Regions in Germany)*. Berlin, Münster: Lit (Wirtschaftsgeographie, 38).

Sternberg, R. (2009), *Regional Dimensions of Entrepreneurship*. Boston, Delft: Now Publishers (Foundations and Trends in Entrepreneurship 5, Issue 4).

Sternberg, R. and Wennekers, S. (2005), "Determinants and Effects of New Business Creation Using Global Entrepreneurship Monitor Data." *Small Business Economics* 24: 193–203.

Vaillant, Y. and Lafuente, E. (2007), "Do Different Institutional Frameworks Condition the Influence of Local Fear of Failure and Entrepreneurial Examples over Entrepreneurial Activity?" *Entrepreneurship and Regional Development* 19(4): 313–37.

Van Stel, A. J. and Storey, D. (2004), "The Link between Firm Births and Job Creation: Is there a Upas Tree Effect?" *Regional Studies* 38(8): 893–909.

Wagner, J. and Sternberg, R. (2004), "Start-up Activities, Individual Characteristics, and the Regional Milieu: Lessons for Entrepreneurship Support Policies from German Micro Data." *Annals of Regional Science* 38: 219–40.

Wong, P. K., Ho, Y. P., and Autio, E. (2005), "Entrepreneurship, Innovation and Economic Growth: Evidence from GEM data." *Small Business Economics* 24: 335–50.

8

Entrepreneurship in Transition Economies: The Role of Institutions and Generational Change

Saul Estrin and Tomasz Mickiewicz

8.1 Introduction

After a period of deteriorating performance, stagnation, and recession in the 1980s, the command economy system finally imploded in 1989–91. Communism had previously dominated a vast geographical area stretching from Berlin, Prague, and Ljubljana in Central Europe to Ulan Bator and Vladivostok in Far East Asia. Now, its collapse leaves North Korea as the only surviving example of a traditional communist system in Euro-Asia (see Svejnar 2002). While the old regime was based on a hierarchical, administrative mode of organizing production coupled with detailed monitoring and surveillance of economic actors, a wave of reforms that followed aimed at establishing a market economy, with a significant role intended to be played by entrepreneurship. Drawing on the ideas of Schumpeter (1934), and Kirzner (1973; 1979), many reformers viewed the creation of numerous new firms as the principal mechanism whereby the heavily industrialized structures of planning would be transformed into a market oriented system for allocating resources (see Kornai 1990; Djankov and Murrell 2002).

The reforms of the early 1990s, however, concentrated on stabilization, liberalization, and the privatization of existing firms (Estrin, Hanousek, Kocenda, and Svejnar 2009). Some countries, such as Poland and Slovenia, did display considerable entrepreneurial activity, but Aidis, Estrin, and Mickiewicz (2008) show that entrepreneurship levels were in fact lower in transition economies as a group than in other developed and developing economies. Moreover, the probability of becoming an entrepreneur was even lower in

Russia than in the other former socialist economies. These findings were consistent with numerous other studies (e.g. McMillan and Woodruff 2002; Estrin, Meyer, and Bytchkova 2006; Aidis and Mickiewicz 2006) and, following the literature, we link them partly with the need to replace the legacy of communist planning with formal market-supporting institutions. Moreover, the aversion to entrepreneurship in many transition economies has deep roots and we use the change in *informal* institutions as our frame of reference. Specifically, we argue that changes of informal institutions have been even slower in the former Soviet Union than in Central and Eastern Europe because communist rule was much longer, leading to a lack of institutional memory.

To explain the low levels of entrepreneurial activity, we first point to the weakness of institutions such as property rights enforcement (McMillan and Woodruff 2002). The European Bank for Reconstruction and Development (EBRD) transition indicators (EBRD Transition Report, 1994–2009) show that implementing many aspects of the reform of formal institutions can be brisk, though arriving at a well-functioning set of new institutions takes much longer, largely because informal institutions are more difficult to change than formal ones (North 1990). Thus the rapid pace of formal institutional change in transition economies during the 1990s was not matched by changes in informal institutions (Meier and Stiglitz 2001). Moreover, the legacy of communism was not conducive to entrepreneurial activity (Estrin et al. 2006), as reflected not just in the remnants of the command economy, but more importantly by the social attitudes shaped during the communist period (Schwartz and Bardi 1997).

We will posit that the level of generalized trust remains low in transition economies. That is probably an important explanation of why entrepreneurial entry has been found to be less common and why we observe the phenomenon of "insider entrepreneurship" in the transition economies: new ventures are more likely to be started by those who have already established themselves in business (Aidis et al. 2008). We also find that the age profiles associated with entrepreneurial entry are distorted. Thus, being a member of the oldest age group has a significantly more negative impact on entrepreneurial entry in the transition economy than elsewhere. These findings have wider implications because they help us to understand the process of change in informal institutions. We suggest that in practice generational change may be required to bring about the shift in values and attitudes necessary for changes in informal institutions, thereby creating conditions more conducive to entrepreneurship.

The main contribution of this chapter is to develop these intuitions and to test them empirically using the Global Entrepreneurship Monitor (GEM) dataset (Reynolds et al. 2005) combined with cross-country data about the quality of institutions, derived from the Heritage Foundation (Aidis, Estrin, and Mickiewicz 2010; Beach and Kane 2007). We first briefly summarize how the legacy that transition economies inherited from their communist past affects entrepreneurship. In Section 8.3, we consider in more detail the implications for institutions, social attitudes, and entrepreneurial entry rates, and illustrate cross-country differences using the GEM dataset combined with a variety of measures on formal and informal institutions. In Section 8.4, we test our hypotheses and present the results of our econometric analysis. Our approach is to explore how the process of transition affects some of the key drivers of entrepreneurial entry, notably indicators of formal and informal institutions as well as the age profile of entrepreneurs. We consider further developments and limitations in the concluding section.

8.2 The Legacy of Communism for entrepreneurship

Though transition opened many opportunities for entrepreneurs, the heritage from the planned era was in many ways not favorable (Estrin et al. 2006) and several aspects of the reform process acted to make the environment even less conducive to entrepreneurship. In this section, we review the evolution of the institutional, social, and cultural environment for entrepreneurs in transition economies. We commence with the financial system and institutional barriers to entrepreneurship, before turning to the supply of human capital and social and cultural factors.

8.2.1 *The supply of finance and institutional obstacles to entrepreneurship*

Entrepreneurs require financial resources in order to establish and run their new firms (Hurst and Lusardi 2004), and they must either provide these resources from their own (or family) saving, or borrow them from financial markets (Stanworth and Gray 1991; Storey 1994; OECD 2006; Beck, Demirgüç-Kunt, and Maksimovic 2005, 2008; Beck et al. 2006). Neither of these sources was widely available in the transition economies initially. Under communism, individuals were not permitted to accumulate financial assets—almost all wealth was owned by the state—and this was probably a major constraint on early entrepreneurial activity (Pissarides 1999). According to the EBRD's transition indicators, progress in reform of the securities market and non-bank financial institutions has typically been modest (EBRD Transition Reports 1994–2009). By 1994 only five countries had attained a ranking of 3 (which may be seen as the threshold level for successful reforms) for the capital market indices and the situation had not improved markedly by 2000.[1]

---

[1] On a scale of 1–4, 1 represents little progress, 2 indicates a rudimentary exchange and legal framework, 3 means making some progress (securities being issued by private firms, some

Moreover, the banking sector was inexperienced in private sector lending, and lacked the organizational capability to finance entrepreneurial businesses (Pissarides 1999). The evidence suggests that state owned banks continued to favor state owned firms and, to some extent also large privatized firms by providing soft loans (Lizal and Svejnar 2002), but rarely lent to the de novo private sector, particularly at the start of the transition process (see Richter and Schaffer 1996; Filatotchev and Mickiewicz 2006).

In addition to financial constraints, the legal and institutional system underlying a market economy was immature in transition economies, having only been introduced in many countries for the first time post-1990 (Svejnar 2002). Institutional obstacles to entrepreneurial activity were first highlighted by Baumol (1990) and have been explored in recent years by a number of economists including McMillan and Woodruff (1999; 2002), De Soto (2000), Djankov, Miguel, Qian, Roland, and Zhuravskaya (2004), and Sobel (2008). Several institutional characteristics are argued to affect entrepreneurial endeavor: the quality of commercial code, the strength of legal enforcement, administrative barriers to entry and to business activities, the prevalence of extra-legal payments and a lack of market-supporting institutions. Empirical work on the importance of legal enforcement is however not conclusive. Johnson, McMillan, and Woodruff (1999) find that the entrepreneur's belief in the courts' inability to enforce contracts efficiently has a negative effect on employment growth, though this effect is not significant with respect to sales growth. Noticeably, Russian entrepreneurs have also been found to have less confidence than non-entrepreneurs in the efficiency of the court system (Djankov et al. 2004).

Within this context, it is useful to draw a distinction between the countries of Central and Eastern Europe (CEE; which includes the three Baltic republics) and those of the former Soviet Union (FSU).[2] As the literature has stressed (e.g. Djankov and Murrell 2002; Estrin et al. 2009), the CEE economies for the most part inherited a stronger legal, institutional, and cultural framework from the perspective of operating a successful market economy, partly because many CEE countries had thriving capitalist economies in the nineteenth century and the inter-war period. Moreover, this initial advantage was amplified by the process of accession to the European Union (EU), during which candidate countries adopted the legal codes and institutions of the EU (Bevan and Estrin

protection of minority shareholders and the beginnings of a regulatory framework), 4 means that countries have relatively liquid and well functioning securities markets and effective regulations, and 4+ implies countries have reached the standard of advanced industrial economies. Only Hungary reached the top ranking of 4 as of 2009.

[2] The Baltic republics of Estonia, Latvia, and Lithuania were annexed by the Soviet Union on the basis of the German-Soviet Non-Aggression Pact of August 1939 and declared Soviet Republics. However, this was not recognized internationally.

2004). Thus, most of the CEE economies did have a commercial code in 1989, though it was typically outmoded; in terms of entrepreneurship for example, the new laws needed to define the concept of a private firm and to create procedures for entry and bankruptcy were usually adopted from the EU.

In contrast, those nations that became part of the Soviet Union when it was established in 1922 and remained so for seventy years had little or no experience of a market economy because communist planning and industrialization were contemporaneous. As a result, laws and market-supporting institutions had to be developed from scratch and without reliance on successful neighbors (there was no realistic prospect of EU accession for these countries). Djankov and Murrell (2002) argue that these differential legacies explain the contrast in enterprise performance post-privatization in the two areas. In CEE, privatization generally led to enhanced performance while little or no impact was discerned in the FSU. The FSU also faced serious difficulties in operating a market economy immediately after the fall of communism. Thus, it was difficult to enforce voluntary contracts such as customers paying for the goods they had purchased or even firms paying workers their contracted wages (see Earle and Sabirianova 1998; Mickiewicz 2009). In many countries, especially but not exclusively in the FSU, the state also continued to be very active and arbitrary in enterprise affairs, putting out its "grabbing hand" (Shleifer and Vishny 1999) to the detriment of new private ventures (Belka, Estrin, Schaffer, and Singh 1995). This is particularly significant for our analysis because entrepreneurs are often more affected by corruption and ineffective regulatory frameworks since, in contrast to large firms, they lack bargaining power vis-à-vis the bureaucracy.

Taxes are a common complaint by entrepreneurs worldwide (see Rosen (2005) for a survey of the effects on entrepreneurship). However, little distinction is made between the level of taxation and the methods of tax collection and enforcement. In transition economies, the costs created by an inefficient, inconsistent, and/or corrupt system of tax collection may substantially add to the costs of running an entrepreneurial business. Some support for this can be found in Aidis and Mickiewicz (2006) who find that perception of high taxes ranks highest amongst the obstacles identified by small firms in Lithuania.[3]

8.2.2 Human capital

Human capital is an important aspect of the supply of entrepreneurship (Davidson and Honig 2003) and this is confirmed for transition economies

---

[3] However, their measure of taxation is correlated with two other variables—"frequent changes to tax policy" and "ambiguity of taxes"—suggesting that all aspects of the system of corporate taxation, rather than the level alone, may inhibit entrepreneurial growth (Korosteleva and Mickiewicz, 2011).

by Barberis, Boycko, Shleifer, and Tsukanova (1996) who show that new human capital was a crucial ingredient for successful new entry by small firms in Russia. In fact, transition countries fare relatively well in terms of formal measures of education. The socialist regimes created extensive education and health services, and CEE economies continue to invest a high proportion of gross domestic product (GDP) in education, even outperforming some West European countries (Barr 2005). As a result, literacy rates are high in transition economies and educational standards are comparable to Western Europe. Also, transition economies typically have a high proportion of students in "hard" subjects such as mathematics and engineering (Estrin et al. 2006). An important aspect of human capital is also the age structure of the population as many entrepreneurs are in the thirty to forty-five age range and young customers are more likely to adopt new products and services.

8.2.3 *Social and cultural factors*

Informal institutions (that is: norms and values) are as important as formal institutions (that is: rules, i.e., norms combined with explicit sanctions) in shaping attitudes and economic behavior, including entrepreneurship (North 1990; Crawford and Ostrom 1995). Research in the sociology of culture documents that communism left a legacy of values and norms that are not conducive to entrepreneurship. Sztompka (1996) describes this legacy as a "bloc culture" which comprised priority of dependence over self reliance; of conformity over individualism; and of rigidity and extremism in beliefs over tolerance and innovation. He also notes that these norms are subject to a generational effect: "the bridge between the influences of the past and the future is provided by generations; congeries of people who—in their formative years—have happened to be exposed to similar, significant social forces" (ibid., p. 126). This implies that changes in informal institutions may be slow.

The same theme is developed and tested by Schwartz and Bardi (1997). They explain that the norms developed in the communist era were adopted mostly, not as an effect of direct indoctrination, but rather as a way of social adaptation to the prevailing economic and social conditions. Indeed their adoption was sometimes in direct contradiction to the official ideology. Thus, while the communist system officially promoted trust and cooperation, the prevailing conditions of surveillance and detailed monitoring of citizens led to distrust, which became deeply rooted in values and resulting social attitudes. Their empirical results confirm that values critical for entrepreneurship, which are clustered around autonomy and mastery, remained much weaker in post-communist societies than in comparator West European societies in the mid-1990s. Schwartz and Bardi (1997) also show that the differences between transition and comparator countries are lower for younger people, both because of the generational effect and the greater capacity of young people to learn and adapt to new conditions and cultural influences.

These findings are confirmed by the World Value Surveys reported by Howard (2000). They show that in the transition economies, lack of generalized trust was partly substituted for by private networks in the communist era. However, these were no longer efficient as ways of dealing with the more sophisticated and larger scale market-based economic activities post-transition; these needed to be based more on impersonal (generalized) trust.

Many aspects of entrepreneurship rely on cooperation in social milieu. This is important not only in the start-up phase, in particular with relation to entrepreneurial finance (see below), but also in the expansion phase, as a larger scale of operation relies on a more extensive network of contacts. Thus, trust is an essential prerequisite for entrepreneurship but transition countries share the negative heritage of a system based on authoritarian hierarchical organization and detailed surveillance of all citizens (Fukuyama 1995).

To conclude, existing research suggests that post-communist societies, and especially members from the older generation, are characterized by a different set of values from that typically pertaining in developed market economies. In particular, autonomy and mastery score lower, and generalized trust is missing; moreover, the difference is more marked in the FSU than CEE. These values affect entrepreneurship directly and may also affect it indirectly via their impact on the way institutions function. In particular, lack of trust affects expectations and may result in a self-fulfilling vicious circle of poor institutional practices and corruption.

8.3 Entrepreneurial entry, attitudes, and institutions

In this section, we use data from the Global Entrepreneurship Monitor (GEM) dataset to compare the levels of entrepreneurial activity amongst the post-communist economies, and between them and the GEM world sample. GEM is an ongoing multinational project created to investigate the incidence and causes of entrepreneurship within and between countries. Data are generated by surveys, which rely on stratified samples of at least 2,000 individuals per country. The advantage of GEM data is that the sample is drawn from the whole working age population in each country and therefore captures both entrepreneurs and non-entrepreneurs. While data on business ownership and individual business financing are included, entrepreneurial activity is primarily viewed as new, nascent start-up activity. Nascent entrepreneurs are defined as those individuals between the ages of eighteen to sixty-four years who have taken some action toward creating a new business in the past year (see definition in Reynolds et al. 2005). To qualify for this category, these individuals must also expect to own a share of the business they are starting and the business must not have paid any wages or salaries for more than three months. Established entrepreneurs are defined as individuals who own or manage a company and have paid wages or salaries for more than forty-two months (ibid.).

We organize our discussion around the theoretical framework proposed by Williamson (2000), starting with a discussion of entrepreneurial actions and moving to attitudes by which those actions are driven. In turn, attitudes are shaped by formal and informal institutions, the latter forming the final link in the analysis. At the end of the section, we consider finance separately, as it reflects the impact of both formal and informal institutions.

8.3.1 *Entrepreneurship in transition economies*

To illustrate the variation in entrepreneurial activity in transition economies, Figure 8.1 below reports the size of the micro, small, and medium-size enterprise sector (MSME) in those transition economies for which comparative data was available. Five years averages are taken to control for cyclical effects.

Starting from the bottom, we have Belarus, one of the countries that consistently scores lowest on the EBRD transition indicators (EBRD 1994–2009). Belarus represents a system where some limited liberalization has been accompanied by a strong element of centralized economic control retained by the government. Next from the bottom is Bosnia, a country which was torn apart by civil war and where basic economic stability is only slowly re-emerging. At the top of the spectrum, we find Slovenia, Poland, and Kyrgyz Republic. The first two Central European countries are advanced in the reform process.[4] The Kyrgyz Republic illustrates a different point. The size of the entrepreneurial sector in Kyrgyz Republic is also larger than in several Central European new EU member states and candidate countries. Kyrgyz Republic is a much poorer country than Slovenia or Poland, with a less sophisticated economic structure of production, and in such conditions even some limited progress with reforms may produce significant results in terms of entrepreneurship.

While the size of the MSME sector can be seen as a proxy for entrepreneurship, new firm entry is at the core of the concept and to measure it we use GEM. Figure 8.2 presents country averages for both prevalence rates of nascent

---

[4] They are also characterized by large residual state sectors: according to the EBRD estimates, 30% of GDP was still originating in the state sector in Slovenia and 25% in Poland in 2008. This may indicate that the size of the entrepreneurial sector is not necessarily related to the pace of privatization. New private firms may emerge regardless of privatization, as long as liberalization creates possibilities for new entry. What is also needed is stability of the political and institutional framework, which makes the long term risk of entry lower (Estrin et al. 2009).

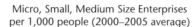

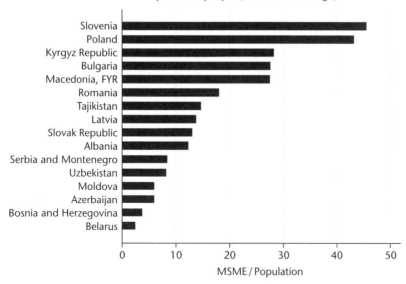

Figure 8.1 Number of micro, small, and medium-size enterprises per 1,000 people (2000–5 average)

Source: Averages computed on the basis of World Bank, World Development Indicators.

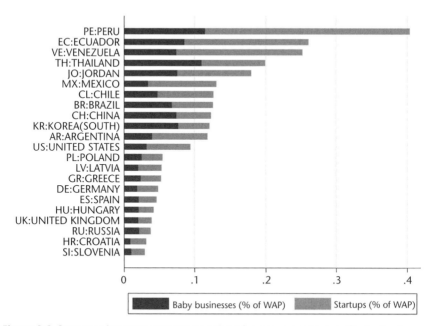

Figure 8.2 Start-ups (nascent entrepreneurs) and owners–managers of baby businesses (ventures not older than 3.5 years) as percentage of working age population (WAP)

Source: Country averages for 1998–5 calculated over individual Global Entrepreneurship Monitor (GEM) data. For more details on GEM methodology see Reynolds et al. (2005).

entrepreneurs (i.e. those currently involved in start-up activities) and owners–managers of young ventures (less than three and a half years old), where those rates are taken over working age population. We use country-level averages calculated over the period of 1998–2005. We focus on differences between the transition economies and other countries at similar level of development (middle income) in Latin America (Argentina, Brazil, Chile, Ecuador, Mexico, Peru, Venezuela), Asia (China, Jordan, Korea, Thailand), as well as two economies from the closer neighborhood of the EU, again relatively similar in terms of GDP per capita (Greece and Spain). Finally, we add two major high income Western EU economies (Germany and UK) and the United States.

Comparing Figure 8.2 with Figure 8.1, we notice that the ranking of countries changes. While Poland retains its position as the most entrepreneurial amongst the transition countries, Slovenia is now relegated to the bottom of the list. Clearly, an extensive MSME sector may not be correlated with high entry rates. More interestingly, we may now see how the transition economies score in comparison to other countries. Entry rates in transition economies as presented on Figure 8.2 are low compared with the comparator countries from other regions of the world except the old EU. Possibly, the most striking comparison relates to China, which shares a command economy past with the transition economies of Central Eastern Europe and Central Asia, yet is characterized by much higher entry rates.

8.3.2 *Attitudes*

What determines entry rates? An individual decision to enter an industry by creating a new firm is directly affected by that individual's attitudes. Entrepreneurial traits conducive to entry relate to confidence in one's own skills and willingness to accept risk of failure (Wadeson 2006). Using 2008 GEM data, Figure 8.3 presents the cross-country heterogeneity (country averages), where transition countries are contrasted with the largest economies outside this group (see Bosma et al. 2008 for more details).

When looking at the percentage of respondents who believe they have the skills and knowledge to start a business, we see no evidence that transition economies are systematically different from comparator countries. There is low confidence in own skills in Russia, but also in Japan. In contrast, respondents in the Balkan nations seem to have a level of confidence in their own skills which is not dissimilar to United States, Mexico, Iran, or India.

However, when looking at the percentage of respondents declaring that fear of failure is not a factor that would prevent them from starting a new venture, the fear-of-failure variable generates a distinctive pattern in which transition countries score lower. A typical respondent in a transition economy seems to

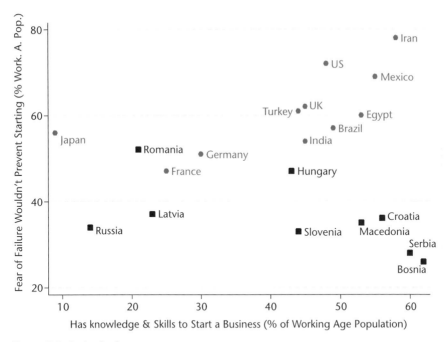

Figure 8.3 Attitudes by country

Source: Country averages, Global Entrepreneurship Monitor data for 2008, based on Bosma et al. (2008).

be less willing to take risks associated with a potential new venture project. We believe this stems from the formal and informal institutional context for entrepreneurship.

8.3.3 *Formal institutions*

Recent theories of entrepreneurship emphasize that the institutional environment affects attitudes and therefore the propensity to start a new business. In particular, Baumol (1990) emphasizes the critical role of institutions in directing entrepreneurship, either to productive or to non-productive or even destructive activity. McMullen et al. (2008) report results of empirical analysis where ten individual dimensions of the Index of Economic Freedom (Heritage Foundation/Wall Street Journal) are used to explain heterogeneity in entrepreneurship rates across nations.

This approach is adopted subsequently by Aidis et al. (2010), who perform factor analysis on the same set of indicators of economic institutions and find that formal institutions have a significant impact on levels of entrepreneurial activity. Moreover, the data reduction techniques permit the large variety of related institutional indices to be reduced to two distinct groupings,

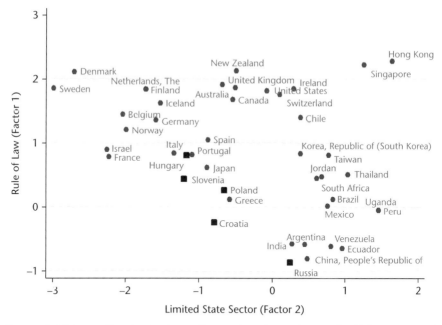

Figure 8.4 Dismantling institutions: Factors based on Heritage/Wall Street Journal Indicators

Source: Factors extracted by authors based on Heritage/Wall Street Journal Indicators. Aidis et al. (2010) provide details on methodology. The graph presents factor scores for GEM countries for 2004 or latest available.

which are denoted the "size of the state sector"[5] and the "rule of law."[6] Figure 8.4 below reproduces the factor scores for the GEM countries with the transition economies highlighted. Given the communist planning legacy, transition economies tend to have relatively larger state sectors and are characterized by weaker rule of law than comparator countries, though the two institutional characteristics are not in general highly correlated.

A larger state sector will typically militate against entrepreneurial activity, both because of high taxation and via state expenditures (Henrekson 2005; Minniti 2008). Taxes and welfare provision may affect entrepreneurial entry via their direct impact on expected returns to entrepreneurial activity and on its opportunity cost. Taken together, we may hypothesize that a larger state sector will crowd out entrepreneurial activity. While transition countries have

---

[5] As measured mainly by both the extent of state expenditures and by taxes; it is measured in reverse order, as "limited state sector."
[6] The key components are (highly correlated) measures of protection of property rights and of freedom from corruption.

generally a large state sector, there are marked differences between CEE and the FSU in this respect. In particular, Russia and other neighboring smaller economies in that region are characterized by smaller state sectors, which can be dated back to collapse of tax revenue in the 1990s and administrative difficulties (Mickiewicz 2005). However, this is not reflected in entrepreneurship rates, as illustrated by Figures 8.1–3 above. Thus, for transition economies, we need to seek for additional explanations, and the institutional component of property rights may be a good point to start.[7]

Harper (2003) emphasizes that "the institution of private property...has an important psychological dimension that enhances our feelings of...internal control and personal agency, and it thereby promotes entrepreneurial alertness" (ibid., p.74). For entrepreneurship, it is also important that property rights not only guarantee the status quo but also include the "find and keep" component, which is essential for the aspects of entrepreneurship related to discovery, innovation, and creation of new resources (Harper 2003). Acemoglu and Johnson (2005) show that property rights institutions have pronounced effects on investment, financial development, and long-run economic growth. Aidis et al. (2010) reveal that among various institutional indicators, the property rights system plays a pivotal role in determining entrepreneurial activity in low income and middle income economies. Johnson, McMillan, and Woodruff (2002) provide evidence that weak property rights discourage entrepreneurs to reinvest their retained profits into business.

Figure 8.5 illustrates how the transition countries score on the property rights (rule of law) dimension. There are a number of international organizations that provide expert-based assessment of property rights. As property rights (and more generally, institutional quality) are highly correlated with GDP per capita, we present residuals from regression of property rights indicators on logarithm of GDP per capita (purchasing power parity). With Estonia as the most notable exception, the overwhelming majority of transition economies are located below the world sample reference line. Once again, the CEE countries score relatively well (though not Bulgaria and Romania). Two countries that have the smallest MSME sector (see Figure 8.1), Bosnia and Belarus, are also characterized by weakest protection of property rights. Russia and Croatia, which come next from the bottom, have also very low entry rates (Figure 8.2; data on MSME sector size was unavailable for those two countries).

---

[7] We will initially proxy property rights directly using the Heritage Foundation measure but in our econometric work we will also alternatively use our "rule of law" factor.

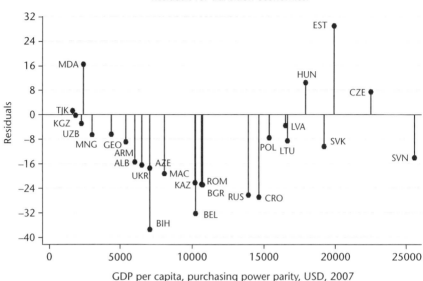

Regression of property rights (2008) on ln (GDP pc ppp) in 2007
Residuals for transition economies:

Figure 8.5 Property rights by country

Source: Authors' calculations. GDP per capita data is from World Bank, World Development Indicators. Property rights indicators come from Heritage Foundation/Wall Street Journal.

8.3.4 *Corruption*

The corruption dimension of institutional quality is interesting because it is located at the intersection of formal and informal institutions, and is likely to have a significant impact on entrepreneurship (McMillan and Woodruff 2002). Aidis and Mickiewicz (2006) provide evidence showing that corruption has been an important obstacle to business expansion in transition economies, and argue that corruption is damaging to entrepreneurial activity and expansion as it increases the level of uncertainty and reduces entrepreneurial gains. Corruption can be seen as a key outcome variable reflecting all institutional weaknesses in the economy, as it results from weak property rights, arbitrariness in state administration, weak judicial system, excessive and non-transparent regulatory frameworks but also prevailing social norms and (self-fulfilling) behavioral expectations (Tanzi 1998; Treisman 2007; Aidt 2009). Therefore, it can be treated as a proxy for overall institutional quality (Tanzi 1998). An additional advantage of empirical measures of corruption is that, unlike property rights, they are not expert-based but gathered via surveys of economic decision-makers.[8]

---

[8] While it can be argued that these perceptions are subjective, the issue is more apparent than real because these perceptions shape attitudes and behavior, including entrepreneurial decisions.

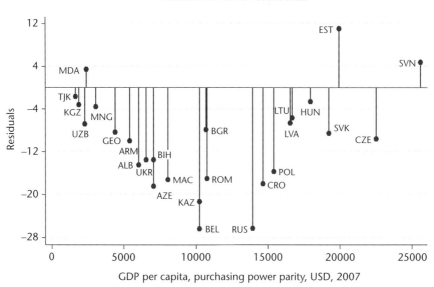

Figure 8.6 Freedom from corruption by country

Source: Authors' calculations. GDP per capita data is from World Bank, World Development Indicators. Freedom from corruption indicators come from Heritage Foundation/Wall Street Journal.

It can be argued that successful entrepreneurs can develop strategies that minimize the detrimental effects of negative informal institutional influences, through for example networking (Minniti and Lévesque 2008), but these adaptations come at a high cost (Aidis et al. 2008). This is probably a reason why we observe very low levels of entrepreneurship combined with greater reliance on informal networks and endemic corruption in Russia (Estrin et al. 2006). In contrast, the levels of entrepreneurship are higher in CEE and reliance on informal networks is lower. Moreover, though corruption still affects a significant percentage of enterprises in these countries, the levels are lower than in the FSU (EBRD Transition Report 1994–2009; Aidis and Mickiewicz 2006; Aidis et al. 2008).

We illustrate this dimension of institutional quality with Figure 8.6, which is analogous to Figure 8.5. We report regressions of freedom from corruption on logarithm of GDP per capita for the world sample and present residuals for the transition economies. Again, the data derive from Heritage Foundation indicators. The results are broadly consistent with those on property rights; as before, the transition economies usually score below the world sample comparator line. Russia and Belarus come at the bottom of the transition economies group. We may note that for those two countries, high corruption is consistent with low scores on actual entrepreneurship (see Figures 8.1–2

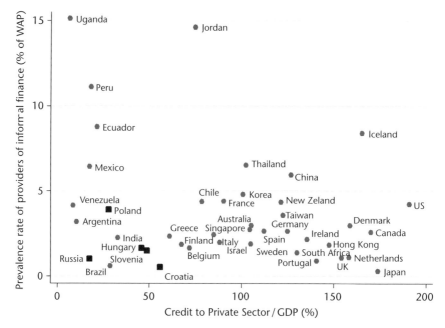

Figure 8.7 The extent of formal and informal finance by country, 1998–2004 averages

Source: Informal finance–prevalence rates of providers of informal finance for start-ups (within 3 year prior to survey) in working age population, authors' calculation based on GEM 1998–2004 consolidated dataset; credit to private sector over GDP 1998–2004 average based on World Bank, World Development indicators.

above) and on lack of confidence towards starting a new business (see Figure 8.3 above). In contrast, Estonia and Slovenia are positive exceptions, apart from Moldova, they are the only two transition economies that score above the horizontal line representing a level of corruption expected at a given level of GDP per capita. While we have no data for Estonia for Figures 8.1–3, Slovenia also scores high both on the confidence measure (Figure 8.3) and on the number of small enterprises (Figure 8.1).

8.3.5 *Finance*

Finally, we now turn to finance, which is another important aspect of institutional quality for entrepreneurship that can be seen as conditional on more basic phenomena rooted in both formal and informal institutions. Figure 8.7 juxtaposes transition economies against GEM-survey countries along two dimensions: the prevalence of informal finance and the extent of formal finance (the latter captured by the ratio of bank credit to GDP).[9]

[9] One would expect some interdependence between formal and informal finance, as the former helps to develop the latter via savings opportunities (Korosteleva and Mickiewicz, 2011).

Transition economies score poorly on both dimensions of the supply of finance, in contrast to some of the developed countries, where formal credit abounds (United States, Japan, United Kingdom) and to some of the developing countries where informal finance is extensive (Uganda, Jordan, Peru, Ecuador, Mexico; note however much lower scores for Venezuela, Argentina, Brazil, and India). Possibly, the most interesting comparison is between the transition economies of the former Soviet bloc with China, which scores much higher both on formal and informal credit dimension and in line with the smaller neighboring Asian economies of Thailand, South Korea, and Taiwan. The high prevalence rates of informal finance fuelling entrepreneurship in China have been noted by other researchers (Smallbone and Jianzhong 2009).

As we discussed above, weak formal institutions in the transition countries may be partly substituted by strong private networks. Therefore, one might expect informal finance to play stronger roles in these countries as, for example in Latin America (see left upper part of Figure 8.7). However, this does not seem to be occurring and a limiting factor here may be the lack of personal wealth, as discussed in Section 8.2.

8.3.6 *Summary*

Building on the theoretical discussion in Section 8.2, we presented descriptive cross-country statistics comparing entrepreneurship and various aspects of institutional development. We established that entrepreneurial entry rates are lower in transition countries as compared with comparator countries at similar level of development in Asia and Latin America. We posit that different attitudes are behind different entrepreneurial outcomes; in particular fear of failure with respect to starting a new business is higher in transition countries than elsewhere. In turn, both attitudes and observed entrepreneurial behavior are conditioned by both formal and informal institutions. Property rights protection remains deficient in transition economies. The level of corruption, a phenomenon observed at the intersection of formal and informal institutions, is high, especially in the FSU. All these dimensions affect access to finance. Supply of formal finance is relatively limited in all transition economies, perhaps because formal finance development is partially conditional on effective property rights protection. In countries outside the transition block (e.g. Latin America or Asia), formal finance for start-ups is to some extent substituted for by informal finance provided by family and friends. However, in transition countries, perhaps because private wealth accumulation is a new phenomenon, the possibilities for informal finance are more limited.

8.4 Estimation results

We now use GEM and Heritage Foundation data (1998–2004) to explore more formally the three main ideas discussed above. First, we investigate whether the level of entrepreneurial activity is lower in transition economies than elsewhere, including emerging markets at comparable levels of development, because of institutional weaknesses as well as social and cultural factors (H1). We build on the descriptive statistics in the previous section but also control for institutional factors when testing for the transition/non-transition economy differences. If differences in the likelihood of entrepreneurial entry in transition as against non-transition economies are driven entirely by differences in formal institutions, the residual difference captured by the transition indicator variable (dummy) should be insignificant. If, as we expect, the transition dummy is significant, one interpretation would be that this is caused by differences in informal institutions that are not captured well in our Heritage Foundation dataset and are difficult to measure directly.

Second, we investigate the impact of informal institutions (H2). Unfortunately, we have no good direct measures of norms and values with sufficient cross-country coverage; the studies we quote in Section 8.2 are all based on a very limited range of countries. We know however that change in informal institutions is embedded in generational change: it takes time to overcome the heritage of communism, which is deeply rooted. Therefore we test whether the likelihood of entrepreneurial entry declines at a faster rate in transition countries than elsewhere at some point on the age distribution. The intuition is that, due to a lack of memory, changes in informal institutions may be delayed until after a full generation change.

Thirdly, as noted above, weak formal institutions in former communist countries were to some extent substituted for by informal social networks, though less so in the provision of finance. Aidis et al. (2008) notice that in Russia this phenomenon results in a higher likelihood that entrepreneurial activity will be associated with other business ownership by the same individual. They argue that this may be because those already in business can build network capital. Here we investigate if similar effects hold for transition economies as a whole as against the comparator countries (H3).

We test these ideas using cross-individual cross-country probit equations in which the dependent variable is the probability of an individual being engaged in a start-up. We follow the literature in controlling for the individual's age, education, gender, previous involvement in business financing, and existing business ownership. In addition, we consider whether differences in the level of entrepreneurial activity between countries can be explained by variation in the quality of formal institutions, utilizing the two variables from the Heritage Foundation data-reduction exercise discussed earlier, namely "rule of law" and "limited government." We include logarithm of GDP per capita (assessed at purchasing power parity) to control for the overall level of development and annual GDP growth rate to check for push and/or pull effects associated with the business cycle as well as country level prevalence rates of informal finance computed as peer effect (see Wooldridge 2002) based on country-years clusters from GEM. Descriptive statistics are provided in Table 8.1.

We test our hypothesis by introducing an indicator variable (dummy) for the transition countries (H1), and next by multiplying it by individual age and age squared (H2) as well as by another indicator variable representing business ownership of a respondent (H3). We cannot reject H1 if the transition country indicator variable retains some explanatory power in addition to the institutional variables; H2 if the interactive effects between the transition dummy and age are significant; and H3 if the interactive effects between determinants of start-up (nascent entrepreneurship) and transition dummy and business ownership are significant.[10] Table 8.2 shows the estimation results.

Our approach is to use probit models to estimate the determinants of entrepreneurial entry (nascent entrepreneurship) using individual level data, a variety of macro controls, and the three sets of dummy and interactive variables. We use two specifications of the formal institutional variables. The first, in models 1 and 3, are the individual Heritage Foundation indicators of property rights. In models 2 and 4, are the two factors extracted from the Heritage Foundation/Wall Street Journal indicators: the "Rule of Law" and "Limited Government." We are unable to include the size of the formal financial sector, because the variable is highly collinear with property rights.

We find a strong impact from formal institutional variables on entrepreneurial activity. In models 2 and 4, "limited government" has a positive and significant coefficient suggesting that the size of the government has a clear-cut negative effect on entrepreneurial entry. Similarly in models 1 and 3 the direct measure, fiscal freedom, also has a positive and significant coefficient (this is also measured on a scale from high to low fiscal freedom). However, the results suggest that entrepreneurial activity is not explained by the quality of formal institutions regarding property rights. In fact, the rule of law and the property rights variables in all four models are insignificant. This finding is consistent with Aidis et al. (2010), who suggest it may be caused by the inclusion in the regression of developed countries, in which variation in institutional quality plays a smaller role on entrepreneurial activity.

---

[10] The design expands on that applied in Aidis et al. (2010).

Table 8.1. Descriptive statistics (GEM data)

	whole sample					transition economies				
	Obs	Mean	Std. Dev.	Min	Max	Obs	Mean	Std. Dev.	Min	Max
Start-up (nascent entr.)	503466	0.033967	0.181143	0	1	29143	0.022578	0.148557	0	1
Age	471037	42.97038	16.98859	1	104	27131	42.43157	15.9094	14	99
Male	503466	0.474405	0.499345	0	1	29143	0.479807	0.499601	0	1
In employment	484814	0.494662	0.499972	0	1	29072	0.511282	0.499881	0	1
Education: secondary or more	460982	0.670254	0.470121	0	1	29114	0.630075	0.482792	0	1
Education: postsec. or more	460982	0.318466	0.465882	0	1	29114	0.187848	0.390597	0	1
Business angel in past 3 years	501983	0.026804	0.16151	0	1	29028	0.016949	0.129083	0	1
Owner/man. of exist. business	503466	0.049543	0.216998	0	1	29143	0.035137	0.184129	0	1
Log GDP pc (ppp)	503466	26350.55	9928.6	802.63	46610.23	29143	14404.38	4028.307	9075.99	22132.83
Annual GDP growth rate	503466	2.950716	2.45264	−10.89	10.06	29143	4.114909	1.294728	1.3	5.58
Informal finance prevalence rate	503466	0.026791	0.020294	0.002712	0.151122	29143	0.01693	0.009075	0.00503	0.038981
Property rights	503466	78.50933	17.70456	30	90	29143	51.83303	16.081	30	70
Fiscal freedom	503466	58.38507	14.78121	29.8	93.8	29143	65.84733	8.844043	51.8	84.9
Rule of law (factor 1)	503466	1.259747	0.751559	−0.86875	2.281132	29143	0.195716	0.566711	−0.8687	0.852315
Limited state sector (factor 2)	503466	−0.87823	1.165031	−3.27673	1.710471	29143	−0.73553	0.438341	−1.2550	0.247147

Table 8.2. Estimation results. Dependent variable: probability of an individual in a country being a nascent entrepreneur

Explanatory variables	(1)		(2)		(3)		(4)	
	dF/dx	Robust Std. Err.	dF/dx	Robust Std. Err.	dF/dx	Robust Std. Err.	dF/dx	Robust Std. Err.
Age	0.0007*	0.0003	0.0006+	0.0003	0.0007*	0.0003	0.0006+	0.0003
Age squared	-.00001***	0.0000	-.00001***	0.0000	-.00001***	0.0000	-.00001***	0.0000
Male	0.0154***	0.0008	0.0153***	0.0008	0.0154***	0.0008	0.0153***	0.0008
In employment	0.0076***	0.0016	0.0081***	0.0016	0.0075***	0.0016	0.0080***	0.0016
Education: secondary or more	0.0050***	0.0015	0.0046**	0.0015	0.0050***	0.0014	0.0045***	0.0015
Education: postsec. or more	0.0080***	0.0012	0.0080***	0.0012	0.0080***	0.0012	0.0080***	0.0012
Business angel in past 3 years	0.0518***	0.0040	0.0517***	0.0040	0.0515***	0.0040	0.0515***	0.0040
Owner/man. of exist. business	0.0024	0.0018	0.0025	0.0018	0.0018	0.0018	0.0019	0.0018
Log GDP pc (ppp)	0.0000	0.0000	0.0000	0.0000	0.0000	0.0000	0.0000	0.0000
Annual GDP growth rate	-0.0011***	0.0003	-0.0010***	0.0003	-0.0011***	0.0003	-0.0010***	0.0003
Informal finan. prevalence rate	0.3264***	0.0735	0.3130***	0.0720	0.3244***	0.0728	0.3112***	0.0714
Property rights	-0.0002	0.0001			-0.0002	0.0001		
Fiscal freedom	0.0004***	0.0001			0.0004***	0.0001		
Rule of law (factor 1)			-0.0024	0.0027			-0.0025	0.0027
Limited state sector (factor 2)			0.0058***	0.0011			0.0058***	0.0011
Transition	-0.0096**	0.0029	-0.0067*	0.0030	-0.0184**	0.0043	-0.0172*	0.0047
Age* Transition					0.0013*	0.0006	0.0013*	0.0006
Age squared* Transition					-.00002**	0.0000	-.00002**	0.0000
Number of observations	434222		434222		434222		434222	
Wald Chi squared	1831.73***		1885.7***		2133.54***		2182.02***	
Log pseudo-likelihood	-57106		-57062		-57087		-57044	
Pseudo R2	0.0932		0.0939		0.0935		0.0942	

Notes to Table 8.2:
a. The table reports marginal mean effects, except that for dummy variables the reported effects are those of switching from zero to one.
b. Robust standard errors clustered on country-years.
c. *** Significant at 0.001,
   ** significant at 0.01,
   * significant at 0.05,
   + significant at 0.10.

Turning to H1, we find that the transition indicator variable has a negative and significant sign in models 1 and 2, providing support for our intuition. Thus, entrepreneurship is found to be significantly lower in transition countries, even when we control for formal institutional differences.[11] We attribute this result to informal institutions and the fact that the communist heritage in norms and values is not consistent with entrepreneurial aspirations.

In models 3 and 4 we estimate entry equations with the additional interactive effects on age and age squared of the owner/manager to test H2 and H3. First, we are interested in testing, albeit indirectly, whether informal institutions and memory of them matter. Thus, we investigate if the impact of age profiles differs for transition and non-transition economies. The intuition is that the prior experience of a command economy may produce a generational effect: for older people, entrepreneurial motivation may be weaker because their generation had no experience of free enterprise for most of its lifetime. Indeed, we find the age square term to have a much larger marginal effect in comparison to non-transition countries. While, for non-transition economies, the highest age point associated with likelihood of entry is about 35 years, it is shifted back to about 33 years in transition economies. Moreover, its rate of increase below this age is steeper in transition economies, which may reflect poorer access to wealth as noted earlier. We also see a steeper decrease with age after the turning point, consistent with the generational effect discussed above. Marginal effects for interactive variables are not calculated well by standard estimations for non-linear models including probit (Ai and Northon 2003). Therefore, to verify our results we ran additional models separating transition and non-transition groups of countries (hence no interactive effects were used) and the results were entirely consistent with those reported in Table 8.2.

Finally, H3 considers the role of informal networks via the possibility of a differential impact of prior business ownership-management on new entry between transition and non-transition economies, a phenomenon identified by Aidis et al. (2008) as "insider entrepreneurship" with reference to Russia. This is tested for the two sets of indicators of institutional quality in models 3 and 4. The coefficient on the interactive dummy is positive and significant, which confirms that in transition economies as a whole, prior business experience increases the probability that an individual will become a nascent entrepreneur more often than in non-transition countries. We interpret this

---

[11] Note however, that the significance of the transition dummy and its marginal effect on entrepreneurship are reduced when we use the institutional factor scores rather than Heritage Foundation direct measures, possibly because the former capture institutional variation better.

result as being the consequence of the weakness of the institutional environment, which grants a stronger position for those who are already in business.

8.5 Conclusions

We have shown that transition economies have lower rates of entrepreneurship than are observed in most developed and developing market economies. The difference is even more marked in the countries of the former Soviet Union than those of Central and Eastern Europe. We link these differences partly with the need to replace the legacy of communist planning with formal market-supporting institutions. However, many of these changes have now taken place, yet entrepreneurial activity remains low in many places. We associate this finding with the slower adaptation of informal institutions, including attitudes and social norms.

In general, our findings are consistent with the perspective of institutional economics, as exemplified in particular by North (1990). While initiating dramatic changes in formal institutions may be difficult, implementation at one level can be relatively quick. It is far more difficult to get those formal institutions working well. The key reason for this is that they rely on the quality of administration and of the system of justice, and these are both conditioned in turn by the prevailing attitudes of those representing the state. Moreover, expectations about the way the state functions may be self-fulfilling. We document that transition countries have low scores on expert-based assessment of protection and stability of property rights and on survey-based indicators of corruption. We also argue that in these economies, generalized trust was severely damaged during the command economy period, and is only recovering slowly. In addition, other values that are conducive to entrepreneurship including mastery, confidence, and autonomy are also weak. Unfortunately, these effects are not captured well either by existing measures of formal institutions or by individual characteristics. We attempt to capture the impact of informal institutions in transition economies indirectly, as a joint transition effect that distinguishes entrepreneurship outcomes in those countries compared with others. In so doing, we discover a clear-cut generational effect: it is the older generation that is far less entrepreneurial than its counterpart in other regions of the world. This is both a cause for concern and a source of optimism since the younger generation carry much less of the burden of the past. We have also shown that in transition economies, outsiders (i.e. those without previous business connections) are less likely than elsewhere to create new ventures; a phenomenon that we label "insider entrepreneurship." This is again consistent with our emphasis on informal institutions: it is likely that prior business ownership comes with better access to key informal networks that facilitate business operation.

A limitation of our research is that we are still missing a comprehensive data set that would capture values and norms in a comparative perspective. This chapter has amassed considerable circumstantial evidence that informal institutions matter for entrepreneurship in transition economies. There are differences in various measures of informal institutions between transition and other economies, for example with respect to corruption, the supply of finance and personal attitudes to entrepreneurial activity such as the fear of failure. However, in the absence of any comprehensive cross-country dataset on informal institutions, we are unable to test the hypothesis directly. One can however partly rely on the World Value Survey, which is informing some of the sociological and political research we quote in Section 8.2, but its coverage is still not extensive and it is not focused on many of the values and norms that are most critical for entrepreneurship.

Overall, our work suggests that levels of entrepreneurial activity may increase in transition economies when a new generation born and educated in a market economy grows to maturity. In particular, although the demographic structure of CEE is now beginning to converge to that of Western Europe with relatively fewer young people, future research might want to concentrate research attention on the potential role of migrants on the next generation of entrepreneurs in transition economies. The younger generation is more mobile and there is a current wave of migrations from Central Eastern to Western Europe, which is already enhancing entrepreneurship in countries like UK and Ireland. The same generation, however, may be also generating positive feedback effects for the home countries via returning migrants with new skills, sources of finance, and trade links.

Acknowledgments

We are grateful to Paul Reynolds for sharing the consolidated 1998–2004 GEM data. Versions of this chapter were presented at University College, London, Birkbeck College, London, University of East London, TIGER Conference in April 2009, the Italian Association for Comparative Economic Systems conference in Perugia, and the University of Tartu. We gratefully acknowledge comments from an anonymous referee, Maria Minniti, Julia Korosteleva, Slavo Radosevic, and conference participants—Michael Keren, Greg Kolodko, Mario Nuti, and Milica Uvalic in particular. Any remaining errors are our own. We also acknowledge the EU support (Seventh Framework Programme, Theme 8, Grant 225134, Project EAGIS). Many thanks go also to an anonymous reviewer for helpful comments. Although GEM data were used in this study, their interpretation and use are the sole responsibility of the authors. All errors are ours.

References

Acemoglu, D. and Johnson, S. (2005), "Unbundling Institutions." *Journal of Political Economy*, 113: 943–95.

Aidis, R. and Mickiewicz, T. (2006), "Entrepreneurs, Expectations and Business Expansion: Lessons from Lithuania." *Europe-Asia Studies*, 58: 855–80.

Aidis, R., Estrin, S., and Mickiewicz, T. (2008), "Institutions and Entrepreneurship Development in Russia: A Comparative Perspective." *Journal of Business Venturing*, 23: 656–72.

Aidis, R., Estrin, S., and Mickiewicz, T. (2010), "Size Matters: Entrepreneurial Entry and Government." *Small Business Economics*, D01 8.01007/s 11187–010–9299–y.

Ai, C. and Norton, C. (2003), "Interaction Terms in Logit and Probit Models." *Economic Letters*, 80: 123–9.

Aidt, T. (2009), "Corruption, institutions, and economic development." *Oxford Review of Economic Policy*, 25(2): 271–91.

Barberis, N., Boycko, M., Shleifer, A., and Tsukanova, N. (1996), "How Does Privatization Work? Evidence from the Russian Shops." *Journal of Political Economy*, 104(4): 764–91.

Barr, N. (2005) (ed.), *Labor Markets and Social Policy in Central and Eastern Europe*. Washington DC: World Bank.

Baumol, W. (1990), "Entrepreneurship: productive, unproductive, and destructive." *Journal of Political Economy*, 98: 893–921.

Beach, W. and Kane, K. (2007), "Methodology: Measuring the 10 Economic Freedoms." Washington: The Heritage Foundation. Retrieved March 5, 2009 http://www.heritagefoudation.org

Beck, T., Demirgüç-Kunt, A., and Maksimovic, V. (2005), "Financial and Legal Constraints to Growth: Does the Firm Size Matter?." *Journal of Finance*, 60(1): 137–77.

Beck, T., Demirgüç-Kunt, A., Laeven, L., and Maksimovic, V. (2006), "The Determinants of Financing Obstacles." *Journal of International Money and Finance*, 25: 932–52.

Beck, T., Demirgüç-Kunt, A., and Maksimovic, V. (2008), "Financial Patterns Around the World: Are Small Firms Different?." *Journal of Financial Economics*, 89(3): 467–87.

Belka, M., Estrin, S., Schaffer, M., and Singh, I. (1995), "Enterprise Adjustment in Poland: Evidence from a Survey of 200 Private, Privatized and State-owned Firms." *Centre of Economic Performance Discussion Paper*, 223. London: CEPR.

Bevan, A. and Estrin, S. (2004), "The determinants of foreign direct investment into European transition economies." *Journal of Comparative Economics*, 32(4): 775–87.

Bosma, N., Acs, Z., Autio, E., Coduras, A., and Levie, J. (2008), *Global Entrepreneurship Monitor. 2008 Executive Report*. Babson Park, MA: Babson College, Universidad del Desarrollo and London Business School.

Crawford, S. and Ostrom, O. (1995), "A Grammar of Institutions." *American Political Science Review*, 89(3): 582–600.

Davidson, P. and Honig, B. (2003), "The Role of Social and Human Capital amongst Nascent Entrepreneurs." *Journal of Business Venturing,* 18: 301–31.

De Soto, H. (2000), *The Mystery of Capital: Why Capitalism Triumphs in the West and Fails Everywhere Else.* New York: Harper & Row.

Djankov, S. and Murrell, P. (2002), "Enterprise Restructuring in Transition: A Quantitative Survey." *Journal of Economic Literature,* 40 (3): 739–93.

Djankov, S., Miguel, E., Qian, Y., Roland, G., and Zhuravskaya, E. (2004), "Who are Russia's Entrepreneurs." Washington. The World Bank. Mimeo.

Earle, J. and Sabirianova, K. (1998), "Understanding Wage Arrears in Russia." *Stockholm Institute of Transition Economics Working Paper* 139.

Estrin, S., Meyer, K., and Bytchkova, M. (2006), "Entrepreneurship in Transition Economies," in A. Basu, M. Casson, B. Yeung, and N. Wadesdon (eds.), *The Oxford Handbook of Entrepreneurship.* Oxford: Oxford University Press: 693–723.

Estrin, S., Hanousek, J., Kočenda, E., and Svejnar, J. (2009), "The Effects of Privatization and Ownership in Transition Economies." *Journal of Economic Literature,* 47(3): 699–728.

EBRD (1994–2009), *Transition Report.* London: European Bank for Reconstruction and Development.

Filatotchev, I. and Mickiewicz, T. (2006),"Private Benefits of Control and Debt Financing," in T. Mickiewicz (ed.), *Corporate Governance and Finance in Poland and Russia.* Houndmills: Palgrave Macmillan: 159–76.

Fukuyama, F. (1995), *Trust.* New York: The Free Press.

Harper, D. (2003), *Foundations of Entrepreneurship and Economic Development.* Abingdon: Routledge.

Henrekson, M. (2005), "Entrepreneurship: A Weak Link in the Welfare State." *Industrial and Corporate Change,* 14(3): 437–67.

Howard, M. (2000), "The Weakness of Post communist Civil Society." *Journal of Democracy,* 13(1): 157–69.

Hurst, E. and Lusardi, A. (2004), "Liquidity Constraints, Household Wealth and Entrepreneurship." *Journal of Political Economy,* 112: 319–47.

Johnson, S., McMillan, J., and Woodruff, C. (2002), "Property Rights and Finance," *American Economic Review,* 95: 1335–56.

Kirzner, I. (1973), *Competition and Entrepreneurship.* Chicago: University of Chicago.

Kirzner, I. (1979), *Perception, Opportunity and Profit.* Chicago: Univerisity of Chicago.

Kornai, J. (1990), *Road to a Free Economy.* New York: Norton.

Korosteleva, J. and Mickiewicz, T. (2011), "Start-up Financing in the Age of Globalisation, Emerging Markets Finance and Trade", 47(3), forthcoming.

Lizal, L. and Svejnar, J. (2002), "Investment, Credit Rationing, and the Soft Budget Constraint: Evidence from Czech Panel Data." *Review of Economics and Statistics,* 84 (2): 353–70.

McMillan, J. and Woodruff, C. (1999), "Inter-firm Relationships and Informal Credit in Vietnam." *Quarterly Journal of Economics,* 114(4): 1285–320.

McMillan, J. and Woodruff, C. (2002), "The Central Role of Entrepreneurs in Transition Economies." *Journal of Economic Perspectives,* 16(3): 153–70.

McMullen, J., Bagby, D., and Palich, L. (2008), "Economic Freedom and the Motivation to Engage in Entrepreneurial Action." *Entrepreneurship Theory and Practice*, 32(5): 875–95.

Meier, M. and Stiglitz, J. (eds.) (2001), *Frontiers of Development Economics: The Future in Perspective*. New York: Oxford University Press and World Bank.

Mickiewicz, T. (2005), *Economic Transition in Central Europe and the Commonwealth of Independent States*. Houndmills: Palgrave Macmillan.

Mickiewicz, T. (2009), "Hierarchy of Governance Institutions and the Pecking Order of Privatisation: Central–Eastern Europe and Central Asia Reconsidered." *Post-Communist Economies*, 21(4): 399–423.

Minniti, M. (2008), "The Role of Government on Entrepreneurial Activity: Productive, Unproductive, or Destructive?." *Entrepreneurship Theory and Practice*, 32(5): 779–90.

Minniti, M. and Lévesque, M. (2008), "Recent Developments in the Economics of Entrepreneurship." *Journal of Business Venturing*, 23(6): 603–12.

North, D. (1990), *Institutions, Institutional Change and Economic Performance*. Cambridge: Cambridge University Press.

OECD (2006), *The SME Financing Gap: Theory and Evidence*. Paris: OECD Publishing.

Pissarides, F. (1999), "Is the Lack of Funds the Main Obstacle to Growth? EBRD's Experience with Small and Medium-sized Businesses in Central and Eastern Europe." *Journal of Business Venturing*, 14: 519–39.

Reynolds, P., Bosma, N., Autio, E., Hunt, S., De Bono, N., Servais, I., Lopez-Garcia, P., and Chin, N. (2005), "Global Entrepreneurship Monitor: Data Collection Design and Implementation 1998–2003." *Small Business Economics*, 24: 205–31.

Richter, A. and Schaffer, M. (1996), "The Performance of De Novo Private Firms in Russian Manufacturing," in S. Commander, Q. Fan, and M. Schaffer (eds.), *Enterprise Restructuring and Economic Policy in Russia*. Washington, DC: EDI/The World Bank.

Rosen, H. (2005), "Entrepreneurship and Taxation," in V. Kanniainen and C. Keusch- nigg, *Venture Capital, Entrepreneurship and Public Policy*. Cambridge, Mass: MIT Press: 251–69.

Schumpeter, J. (1934), *The Theory of Economic Development*. Cambridge, MA: Harvard University Press.

Schwartz, S. and Bardi, A. (1997), "Influences of Adaptation to Communist Rule on Value Priorities in Eastern Europe." *Political Psychology*, 18(2): 385–410.

Shleifer, A. and Vishny, R. (1999), The Grabbing Hand: Government Pathologies and Their Cures. Cambridge, MA: Harvard University Press.

Smallbone, D. and Jianzhong, X. (2009), "Entrepreneurship and SME Development in The People's Republic of China," in L. Dana (ed.), *Handbook of Research and Entre- preneurship in Asia*. Cheltenham: Edward Elgar.

Sobel, R. (2008), "Testing Baumol: Institutional Quality and the Productivity of Entre- preneurship." *Journal of Business Venturing*, 23: 641–55.

Stanworth, M. and Gray, C. (1991), *Bolton 20 Years on–The Small Firm in the 1990s*. London: Paul Chapman Publishing.

Storey, D. (1994), *Understanding the Small Business Sector*. Routledge: New York.

Svejnar, J. (2002), "Transition Economies: Performance and Challenges." *Journal of Economic Perspectives*, 16(1): 3–28.

Sztompka, P. (1996), "Looking Back: The Year 1989 as a Cultural and Civilizational Break." *Communist and Post-Communist Studies,* 29(2): 115–29.

Tanzi, V. (1998), "Corruption around the World: Causes, Consequences, Scope and Cures," *IMF Staff Papers,* 45: 559–694.

Treisman, D. (2007), "What Have We Learned About the Causes of Corruption from Ten Years of Cross-National Empirical Research?," *Annual Review of Political Science,* 10: 211–44.

Wadeson, N. (2006), "Cognitive Aspects of Entrepreneurship; Decision-making and Attitudes to Risk," in A. Basu, M. Casson, B. Yeung, and N. Wadeson (eds.), *The Oxford Handbook of Entrepreneurship.* Oxford: Oxford University Press: 91–113.

Williamson, O. (2000), "The New Institutional Economics: Taking Stock, Looking Ahead." *Journal of Economic Literature* 38(3): 595–613.

Wooldridge, J. (2002), *Econometric Analysis of Cross Section and Panel Data.* Cambridge, MA: MIT Press.

9

Poverty and Entrepreneurship in Developing Countries

José Ernesto Amorós and Oscar Cristi

9.1 Introduction

More than 1.4 billion people live in poverty (World Bank 2008a). And even though the absolute number of poor people has significantly decreased in the last two decades (mainly in South and East Asia), policies and programs for poverty reduction are still the focus of social and economic development discussions.[1] Regions like Latin America and the Caribbean face sluggish economic growth and poverty reduction is proceeding slowly. Similarly, since 1990, poverty reduction in Sub-Saharan Africa has lagged far behind other regions and the trend shows no signs of change (Chen and Ravallion 2008; World Bank 2008b). Of course, poverty is also present in developed economies. The US Census Bureau, for example, reports that the official poverty rate in the United States in 2007 was 12.5 percent. That is, 37.3 million people in the US qualified as poor. Figures are similar for the European Union where approximately 16 percent of the population (79 million people) lives below the poverty threshold (Wolff 2009). Thus, poverty and inequality, albeit to different degrees, characterize all countries. These figures have led to discussions about the necessity of developing efficient mechanisms to combat and reduce poverty, and poverty reduction is considered the first objective among the Millennium Development Goals.[2] Within this context entrepreneurship has emerged

---

[1] In 2009, an estimated fifty-five million to ninety million more people will be living in extreme poverty than anticipated before the crisis (United Nations 2009).

[2] In September 2000, 189 countries signed the Millennium Declaration leading to the adoption of the Millennium Development Goals. These goals call for reducing by half the proportion of people living on less than a dollar a day by 2015. For more information on the Millennium Development Goals see http://www.developmentgoals.org.

increasingly as a possible tool to help in the fight against poverty and income inequality (Kimhi 2009).

Although there is extensive literature on poverty and on entrepreneurial dynamics, only a very small number of works have focused on the relationship between the two phenomena, in spite of increasing empirical evidence showing a connection between poverty and entrepreneurial activity. Banerjee and Duflo (2007: 151), for example, argue that: "All over the world, a substantial fraction of the poor act as entrepreneurs in the sense of raising capital, carrying out investment, and being the full residual claimants for the resulting earnings." In general, the poor have lower labor skills and capital and, as a result, the option to be self-employed is easier than finding a remunerated stable job. Unfortunately, these works have studied primarily developed economies (Naudé 2009), in spite of the fact that, in relative terms, "poor countries" have more entrepreneurs. As Scott Shane puts it " . . . if you want to find countries where there are a lot of entrepreneurs, go to Africa or South America" (Shane 2009: 143).

In this chapter we use data from the Global Entrepreneurship Monitor (GEM) project and poverty indicators from the UNDP, the UNU-WIDER and the World Bank to investigate the relationship between poverty and entrepreneurial activity at the country level. First, we hypothesize that poverty and income inequality are positively associated to the number of people who pursue entrepreneurial activities. That is, we expect higher levels of entrepreneurial activity in less developed countries. Second, we hypothesize that a country's total entrepreneurial activity, as well as its necessity-based entrepreneurial activity are associated to the reduction of poverty over time, and that a more unequal income distribution promotes entrepreneurship. Our goal is to contribute to our understanding of the relationship between entrepreneurial activity and poverty reduction, and to provide some evidence of the importance of entrepreneurship for developing economies.

In the next section we review definitions of poverty, and the relationship between poverty, entrepreneurship, and aggregate economic activity. In Section 9.3 we discuss our data and provide descriptive statistics. In Section 9.4 we present our empirical approach and discuss our results. Finally, in Section 9.5, we conclude by discussing implications for policy and future research.

9.2 Poverty, entrepreneurship, and economic development

Poverty is a complex phenomenon with multiple dimensions encompassing individual, social, and economic issues, as well as political and institutional settings (Shostak 1965; Narayan et al. 2000; Misturelli and Heffernan 2008). Samuel Johnson defined poverty as the "great evil experienced" (Boswell

Table 9.1. Themes and related topics common to most poverty definitions

1	Material factors	housing, clothing, standard of living
2	Physical factors	food, water, health, physical survival
3	Economic factors	poverty lines, low income, unemployment
4	Political factors	rights, lack of political participation (community-level), no voice (individual-level), references to the wider international setting
5	Social factors	lack of social esteem, lack of social life, inability to participate in community life
6	Institutional factors	lack of access to services and institutions such as education and health services
7	Psychological factors	feelings and beliefs associated with poverty

Source: Misturelli and Heffernan 2008: 670

1987). A World Bank statement on understanding poverty remarks: "Poverty is hunger. Poverty is lack of shelter. Poverty is being sick and not being able to see a doctor. Poverty is not having access to school and not knowing how to read. Poverty is not having a job, is fear for the future, living one day at a time. Poverty is losing a child to illness brought about by unclean water. Poverty is powerlessness, lack of representation and freedom" (World Bank 2009). The complex and multidimensional nature of poverty makes its definition and operationalization very difficult.[3] In an extensive review of 578 documents, Misturelli and Heffernan (2008) identified and analyzed 159 different definitions of poverty and, after reviewing them, they categorized seven main topics identified across the definitions and concluded that during the last three and a half decades, material, physical, and economic factors are the predominant themes, but that the presence of other social and psychological components reaffirms the multifaceted nature of poverty. Table 9.1 summarizes the seven common characteristics they identified.

A starting point to understand how entrepreneurial activities interact with poverty and the variables listed in Table 9.1 is to describe the relationship between entrepreneurship, economic activity, and a country's level of development. This

---

[3] The New Oxford American Dictionary (2005) defines poverty as "the state of being extremely poor; the state of being inferior in quality or insufficient in amount." Poor is defined as "lacking sufficient money to live at a standard considered comfortable or normal in a society." Very similar is the definition in the Encyclopaedia Britannica (2009): "the state of one who lacks a usual or socially acceptable amount of money or material possessions." Poverty is said to exist when people lack the means to satisfy their basic needs. In this context, the identification of poor people first requires a determination of what constitutes basic needs. These may be defined as narrowly as "those necessary for survival" or as broadly as "those reflecting the prevailing standard of living in the community." For more examples of definitions of poverty see World Bank's "A Collection of Poems and Personal Accounts of Poverty" http://web.worldbank.org/WBSITE/EXTERNAL/TOPICS/EXTPOVERTY/0,,contentMDK:20158015isCURL:YmenuPK:373757pagePK:148956piPK:216618theSitePK:336992,00.html.

relationship is complex (Spencer and Gómez 2006), and modeling it is not easy because of the many factors affecting simultaneously both entrepreneurial activity and economic growth (Wennekers and Thurik 1999). Moreover, it is particularly difficult to determine the direction of causality between entrepreneurial activities and economic growth at the country level. While some studies emphasize the effect of entrepreneurial activity on national economic growth, others focus on the effect of economic growth on entrepreneurship rates. Carree et al. (2002, 2007) are among the few to have developed a simultaneous equations model for economic growth and entrepreneurship rate able to account for the existence of lags and two-way causality.

In the last ten years, an extended body of research has examined entrepreneurial activities as a factor contributing to economic growth (Wennekers and Thurik 1999; Acs and Storey 2004; Audretch and Keilbach 2004; Karlsson, Friis, and Paulsson 2004; Schramm 2004). Much of this research has provided empirical evidence of a positive effect of entrepreneurial activity on economic growth but only in developed and high-income countries (Tang and Koveos 2004; van Stel, Carree, and Thurik 2005; Wennekers et al. 2005; Acs and Amorós 2008). Some authors, for example, have argued that only a small number of innovative and high-growth entrepreneurs have a positive effect on economic growth (Wong, Ho, and Autio 2005; Autio 2007; Shane 2009). Other scholars, like Carree et al. (2007) and Hessels et al. (2008), instead, have argued that the relationship between business ownership rates and economic growth changes over time and may depend on the level of economic development. Finally, others have argued that the competitive impact, and consequently the contribution of the entrepreneurial efforts to economic growth, differ not only among countries (Grilo and Irigoyen 2006; Carree et al. 2007), but also among regions within countries (Audretsch and Keilbach 2004; Lee, Florida, and Acs 2004; Belso-Martínez 2005).

When causality is reversed and the effect of economic development on entrepreneurial activity is considered, Carree et al. (2002) have found that the relationship between the level of per capita income and the rate of self-employment (or business ownership) across twenty-three Organization for Economic Cooperation and Development (OECD) countries may be approximated by a U-shaped curve. Later, when revisiting this relationship with new data, Carree and his co-authors found evidence of an L-shaped curve (Carree et al. 2007). Wennekers et al. (2005), instead, using GEM data, confirmed Carree's original findings that a U-shaped relationship exists between entrepreneurship rates and level of economic development measured by income per capita, innovation capacity, and diverse associated socio-demographic variables. Acs and Amorós (2008) and Amorós and Cristi (2008) replicated the study by Wennekers et al. (2005) using longitudinal GEM data for Latin American countries and also found evidence of a U-shaped relationship.

Overall, in spite of significant heterogeneity in the literature, general agreement exists among scholars that the percentage of population involved in entrepreneurial activities is higher in developing regions or countries (Acs and Amorós 2008), and that the characteristics of entrepreneurship vary depending on the level of development (Minniti and Lévesque 2010).

But why are there more entrepreneurs in developing countries? And do all entrepreneurs have the same impact on economic performance and, as a consequence, on poverty reduction? Empirical evidence shows that not all entrepreneurial activities contribute to economic growth, and that wealth creation does not necessarily involve substantial poverty reduction (Singer 2006; Naudé 2007). Schumpeter (1912[1934]) describes entrepreneurs as revolutionary innovators motivated by *pull* factors, that is people who desire independence, increased income, status, or recognition. These entrepreneurs are motivated by opportunities. However, there are also many individuals who are *pushed* into entrepreneurship because they do not have better job options. Reynolds et al. (2005: 217), for example, write that these entrepreneurs "cannot find a suitable role in the world of work" and "creating a new business is their best available option." These entrepreneurs are motivated by necessity and they are relatively more prevalent in developing countries.

Although many studies have shown that most entrepreneurial activity results from opportunities (Kolvereid 1996; Feldman and Bolino 2000; Carter et al. 2003; Bosma et al. 2008), we argue that necessity-motivated entrepreneurship is nonetheless significant in many developing countries.[4] The intuition is that entrepreneurs with low levels of education, resources, and social capital, generally are involved in low productivity activities. Consequently, their impact on economic growth is expected to be low. Also, in many developing countries, necessity entrepreneurship results from institutions and policies that cause lower productivity and investment, and higher unemployment rates (Caballero 2006). Many of these entrepreneurs operate in the informal sector and are survival entrepreneurs (Naudé 2007). They are usually self-employed or, in some cases, have a very small number of employees (Banerjee and Duflo 2007).

Baumol (1990) argues that the allocation of entrepreneurship in the economy is influenced by the structure of rewards in a country. Specifically, Baumol (1990: 899) argues that "entrepreneurial behavior changes direction from one economy to another in a manner that corresponds to the variations in the rules of the game." Many poor entrepreneurs operate in environments with institutions that are unreliable, with "rules of the game" that are not clear (or virtually

---

[4] Of course, the distinction between necessity and opportunity motives is somewhat ambiguous since business opportunities depend on their context. The opportunities available to a Sub-Saharan shepherd are different from those available to a Silicon Valley engineer. Both are valid business opportunities but they are both dependent on the context and position of the observer (Naudé 2007). Motivations, as well as innovations, exist only within a specific context (Minniti et al. 2007).

non-existing), and with "destructive uncertainty" (Wood 2003; Berner, Gómez, and Knorringa 2008). These weak institutional environments cause informal, lifestyle, and survivalist entrepreneurs (de Soto 1989). In Baumol's logic, many of these informal survival entrepreneurs could be viewed as unproductive. At the same time, however, as Banerjee and Duflo (2007) and Naudé (2007) point out, they can be crucial in developing and fragile regions.

Overall, we agree with the literature suggesting that higher rates of opportunity-based entrepreneurship are preferable to higher rates of necessity-based entrepreneurship (Acs et al. 2005; Acs and Varga 2005), but argue that necessity entrepreneurs are not necessarily less successful or less important. These entrepreneurs contribute to social and anti-poverty interests even though they may not have a substantial impact on economic growth. In some cases, they may prevent poverty from getting increasingly worse and, under certain circumstances, provide a base for future social mobility (Grosh and Somolekae 1996; Sandy 2004). In general, there is no a priori reason to qualify all necessity-based entrepreneurs as unproductive and, especially, in developing countries they may play the role of building blocks for more productive activities in the future as their businesses provide sufficient resources to improve the human capital of future generations.

In this chapter we also explore the importance of income inequality on entrepreneurial decisions. Kimhi (2009) points out that this relationship is not straightforward to predict. He notes that the "rise in inequality almost always leads to a rise in poverty" (Kimhi 2009: 81). Also, Deininger and Squire (1998) suggest that initial asset inequality hurts the poor via credit-rationing and inability to invest thereby contributing to further poverty. Within this context, some theoretical and empirical research has suggested that factors like start-up costs, access to capital, and some regulations increase income inequality and push some people into starting businesses (although primarily out of necessity) (Lindh and Ohlsson 1998; Mesnard and Ravallion 2006; Fonseca, Michaud, and Soraseuth 2007; Naudé 2008, 2009). This is also consistent with Rapoport (2002), and Naudé (2008) who argue that inequality encourages entrepreneurship in developing countries. To account for this evidence, we hypothesize that total and necessity-based entrepreneurial activity are associated to poverty reduction over time and that a more unequal income distribution promotes entrepreneurial activity.

9.3 Data and descriptive statistics

Given the scope of the concepts under study, the operationalization of the variables is the main challenge in this chapter.

Data on entrepreneurial activity are obtained from the Global Entrepreneurship Monitor (GEM) project. GEM provides harmonized and internationally comparable data that allow us to measure aggregate entrepreneurial activity at the country level. By the end of 2008, sixty-six countries had participated in GEM. Among them, thirty-seven countries could be classified as low and middle-income developing economies. GEM data provide information on early-stage entrepreneurial activity, that is, the percentage of adult population (people between eighteen to sixty-four years old) that is actively involved in starting a new venture. The data also include measures of entrepreneurial activity according to motivation, namely whether individuals are opportunity-based entrepreneurs, or necessity-based entrepreneurs. Opportunity entrepreneurs are people who take actions to create a new venture following a perceived business opportunity; necessity entrepreneurs are people who become involved in entrepreneurial activities because they have no other way to earn a living. More details about GEM data and methodology can be found in Reynolds et al. (2005) and Minniti et al. (2007).

Figure 9.1 shows the percentage of necessity-motivated entrepreneurship against GDP per capita.

Given the multidimensional nature of poverty, measuring and comparing poverty rates across countries is also a complex task. In many countries, primarily developing ones, consumption rates (the minimum expenditure made by people in order to subsist) are the preferred welfare indicators. For example, developed countries define their own poverty thresholds generally based on individual or family income equality (or inequality). However, in many academic studies, a commonly accepted definition uses an income-based approach

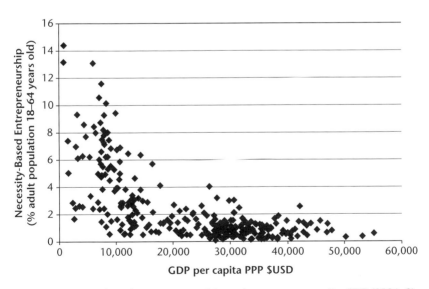

Figure 9.1 Necessity-based entrepreneurship and country per capita GDP (2001–8)
Sources: GEM database and IMF.

according to which poverty is the lack of income or financial resources necessary to satisfy the individuals' basic needs, and/or to achieve a minimum standard of living (Sharp, Register, and Grimes 2003; Singer 2006; Misturelli and Heffernan 2008).

In 1990, following the income-based approach, the World Bank provided a common standard to operationalize poverty empirically by introducing the international poverty line. Poverty lines are calculated from survey sources with several methods (Ravallion, Chen, and Sangraula 2008), and represent an attempt to account for a social perception of relative deprivation that emerges with income (World Bank 2008a: 2).[5] Other indexes take a more comprehensive approach and also include health, education, and estimates of purchasing power parities (PPP), in an attempt to capture the different degrees of development between rich and poor countries. Among such aggregate indexes is the Human Development Index (HDI), calculated by the United Nations Development Programme (UNDP) and published in the Human Development Reports.[6] We use HDI data as our measure of poverty.

HDI is a composite index capturing the average achievement of a country by evaluating three dimensions of human development: life expectancy at birth, adult literacy rate, and gross domestic product (GDP) per capita in purchasing power parities. HDI is among the few measures available over the period 2001–6 for which GEM data are also available. Moreover, it includes most of the major themes and topics related to poverty definitions described by Misturelli and Heffernan (2008) and summarized in Table 9.1. The HDI takes values from 0 to 1, where 1 stands for the highest attainment.

Figures 9.2 and 9.3 depict the relationship between HDI and early-stage and necessity entrepreneurship respectively and show that, in relative terms, poorer countries tend to exhibit higher entrepreneurship rates.

In its Human Development Report 2007–2008, the UNDP also publishes the short-term annual growth rate in HDI (%) calculated over the period 2000–6 with 2000 as base. This indicator captures improvements in human development over that period of time and takes values from −1 to 1, with a negative value representing a worsening trend in the country's poverty as measured by the HDI. We use HDI short-term trends to analyze the lagged effects of entrepreneurial activity on poverty reduction.

Figures 9.4 and 9.5 depict the relationship between HDI short-term trends and the country's average rates of early-stage and necessity entrepreneurship

---

[5] The international poverty line is adjusted and recalculated periodically to reflect changes over time. Recently, it was recalculated in 2008 and it is set at US$1.25 a day measured in 2005 prices. For a detailed explanation of the methodology of the new poverty lines see Word Bank (2008a) and Ravallion, Chen, and Sangraula (2008).

[6] For more information on the methodology of HDI, see Human Development Report 2007–2008, technical notes (UNDP 2007: 355).

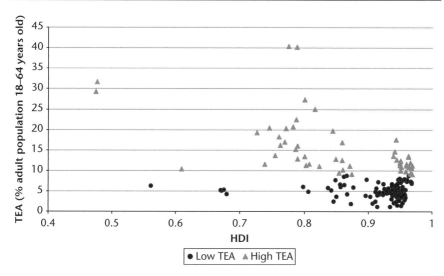

Figure 9.2 Early-stage entrepreneurial activity versus HDI using thresholds (2001–6)
Note: Low TEA are values below TEA sample mean = 8.9

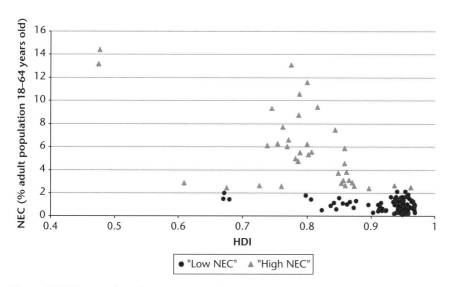

Figure 9.3 Necessity-based entrepreneurial activity versus HDI using thresholds (2001–6)
Note: Low NEC are values below NEC sample mean = 2.3

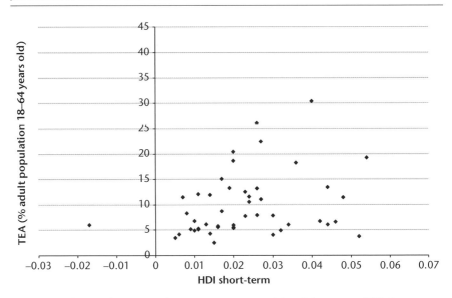

Figure 9.4 Country's mean early-stage entrepreneurial activity versus HDI short-term

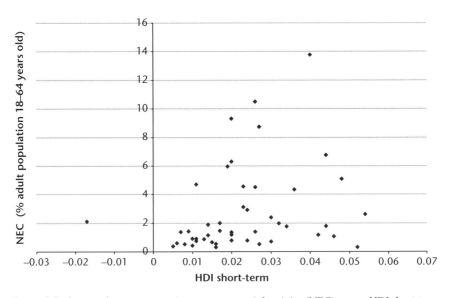

Figure 9.5 Country's mean necessity entrepreneurial activity (NEC) versus HDI short-term

Table 9.2. Variables description

Variable	Description	Source	Mean	Max.	Min.	SD.
TEA	Early-stage entrepreneurship activity; percentage of 18–64 population involved in setting up a business they will own or own and manage up to 3.5 years old.	GEM	8.99	40.34	1.25	6.14
NEC	Percentage of 18–64 population who are involved in TEA (as defined above) and manifest necessity-based motivations to be entrepreneurs (no other ways of earning incomes).	GEM	2.33	14.4	0.09	2.57
HDI	Human Development Index.	UNDP	0.842	0.968	0.45	0.114
HDI short-term	Progress (or decrease) of a specific country's HDI trend over 2000–6.	UNDP	0.025	0.061	−0.017	0.015
GINI	Gini coefficients of countries' income equality (inequality).	World Bank and UN-WIDER	36.56	62.83	22.00	10.08

respectively over time.[7] Our data suggests that higher mean levels of early-stage and necessity entrepreneurship improve human development trends, that are positively related to higher HDI short-term trends.

As a measure of inequality we use the Gini coefficient because it can be used to compare income distributions across different countries. This coefficient takes values from 0 (absolute equality) to 100 (absolute inequality).[8] In this chapter, Gini coefficient data were taken from the World Income Inequality Database published by UNU-WIDER and from the World Development Indicators published by the World Bank.

Descriptive statistics for the variables used in this chapter are presented in Table 9.2.

[7] NEC indicators are 2001–2006 averages.
[8] Specifically, Gini coefficients measure the area between the Lorenz curve and a hypothetical line of absolute equality, expressed as a percentage of the maximum area under the line. The Lorenz curve, in turn, shows the cumulative distribution of total households income going to the lowest percentiles of families (Sharp, Register, and Grimes 2003). About Gini and Lorenz curve calculation see also Gastwirth (1972).

9.4 Empirical Analysis

The goal of this chapter is to conduct an exploratory investigation aimed at establishing whether higher levels of poverty and income inequality are associated to higher levels of entrepreneurial activity, and whether total and necessity-motivated early-stage entrepreneurship are positively associated to poverty reduction trends.

To provide a formal analysis of whether higher levels of poverty and income inequality are associated to higher levels of entrepreneurial activity we test for the effect of the HDI and Gini coefficients on total early-stage entrepreneurial activity (TEA in the rest of the chapter) and on necessity entrepreneurship (NEC in the rest of the chapter). This is consistent with the existing literature discussed in Section 9.2 but, unlike existing works that have only used GDP measures, we use broader indicators of development to better capture aspects of poverty not necessarily reflected in average per capita GDP. The proposed model for TEA or NEC is:

$$EA_{it} = \alpha_0 + \alpha_1 HDI_{it} + \alpha_2 HDI^2 + \alpha_3 GINI_{it} + \epsilon_{it} \qquad (1)$$

With $i=1\ldots,n$ and $t=1\ldots,T$, and where n is the total number of countries, T is the total number of years, EA_{it} represents TEA (or NEC) in country i in year t, HDI_{it} measures poverty, HDI^2_{it} denotes the squared value of HDI_{it}; $GINI_{it}$ is the Gini coefficient in country i in year t; and ε_{it} is a random error term with 0 mean and constant variance. Consistently with existing evidence on the relationship between per capita GDP levels and entrepreneurship rates (Carree et al. 2002; Wennekers et al. 2005; Acs and Amorós 2008), our hypothesis is that while HDI and entrepreneurship move in opposite directions up to a critical threshold level of development, they vary in the same direction once that threshold is reached. In the model, this is captured by introducing both HDI and HDI^2.

We estimate equation (1) by pooling the data in the sample.[9] Consistency of the estimators in this equation requires that HDI and HDI^2 not be endogenous. For this we use a modified Haussmann test proposed by Wooldridge (2002: Chapter 6.2), and the test does not reject the hypothesis of exogeneity of those regressors.[10] We also need to check for the possibility of a spurious

[9] We do not perform panel data estimation because, unfortunately, no sufficient information is available for several countries.
[10] Specifically, we use a residual-based form of the Haussmann test that is asymptotically equivalent to the original form of the Haussmann test. The test involves estimating auxiliary reduced-form regressions for the "regressors" suspected to be endogenous, namely HDI and HDI^2. Those reduced forms include a constant, all the exogenous variables of the model, and regressor-specific instruments. Equation (1) is then estimated including the reduced-form residuals as additional explanatory variables. Next, the joint statistical significance of the coefficients associated with the residuals is evaluated. If those coefficients are jointly not significant then the Haussmann test does not reject the hypothesis of exogeneity of the

relationship between entrepreneurial activity, *HDI*, and Gini coefficients. To do so, we test for the presence of serial autocorrelation since lack of serial autocorrelation among the residuals ensures that no spurious relationship is present (Pindyck and Rubinfeld 1991: section 15.4). We test for serial autocorrelation using the method proposed by Wooldridge (2002: 282–3). The result of the test supports the hypothesis that no spurious relationship among entrepreneurial activity and *HDI* and *GINI* is present.

Table 9.3 shows the parameter estimates for equation (1) using ordinary least squares (OLS).

Results suggest that all parameters are significant at the one percent significance level and support our hypothesis that the relationship between poverty levels and entrepreneurial activity measured as TEA or NEC takes the form of a U-shaped curve. Figures 9.6 and 9.7 illustrate the result using fitted values of TEA and NEC from the estimated models.

As expected, more income inequality is associated to more people starting new businesses. This is consistent with Bosma et al. (2009) and Shane (2009) who have suggested that more entrepreneurs are found in developing countries characterized by greater income inequality. Also, a comparison of

Table 9.3. Regression model for early-stage entrepreneurial activity (TEA) and necessity-based entrepreneurial activity (NEC)

	TEA model	NEC model
HDI	−1174	−347
	(269)	(97)
HDI^2	657	184
	(153)	(55)
Gini	0.27	0.07
	(0.07)	(0.02)
Cons.	521	163
	(118)	(43)
F	24.73	46.60
R^2	0.43	0.63
Adj. R^2	0.41	0.61
n	103	87

Notes: (Standard Errors); all estimates are significant at 1% level.

regressors. As regressor-specific instruments for HDI and HDI^2 we use countries' institutional context (North 1990), proxies by measures of political stability, government effectiveness, rule of law, and control of corruption from the World Bank's Worldwide Governance Indicators (WGI). Baumol (1990), Boettke and Coyne (2007), Minniti (2008), and Amorós (2009) provide theoretical and empirical support for our choice of instrumental variables. Also, for more information on the WGI methodology and descriptions of the variables see Kaufmann, Kraay, and Zoido-Lobatón (1999) and, Kaufmann, Kraay, and Mastruzzi (2008).

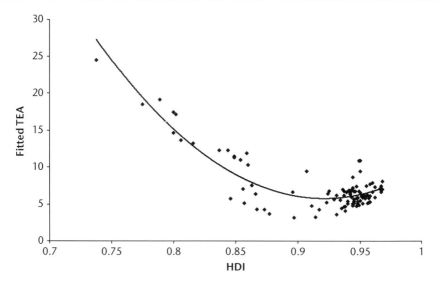

Figure 9.6 Country's conditional expected value for TEA (fitted value) against GDP per capita

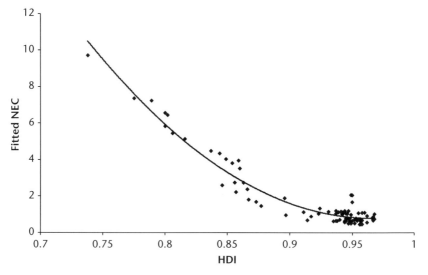

Figure 9.7 Country's conditional expected value for NEC (fitted value) against GDP per capita

the R^2 for the TEA and NEC models shows that poverty and income inequality play a larger role on the explanation of NEC than of TEA.

We now turn to modeling whether total early-stage entrepreneurship (TEA) or, in an alternative, necessity-motivated early-stage entrepreneurship (NEC), are positively associated to poverty reduction trends. In other words, we want to test whether lagged effects of early-stage entrepreneurship (and early-stage necessity entrepreneurship) on HDI are present. HDI trends for the period 2000–6 capture short-term improvements in human development in each country and are a good proxy for the above mentioned lagged effects. In order to formally analyze the effect of mean TEA and mean NEC on HDI short-term trends we propose the following two models for HDI short-term (*HDIS*):

$$HDIS_i = \beta_0 + \beta_1 TEA_i + \beta_2 TEADUMMY_i + \beta_3 NECPARTi + \beta_4 GINI_i + v_i \quad (2)$$

and

$$HDIS_i = \gamma_0 + \gamma_1 NEC_i + \gamma_2 NECDUMMY_i + \gamma_4 GINI_i + v_i \quad (3)$$

In equation (2), *TEADUMMY* is obtained by multiplying TEA by a dummy variable taking a value of 1 for developed countries and 0 otherwise.[11] *NECPART* is the ratio between NEC and TEA, and *v* is a random error with 0 mean and constant variance.

The intuition behind equation (2) is that higher country-average levels of early-stage entrepreneurship result in more pronounced poverty reduction with some lags and that this effect is relatively stronger in developing countries. This effect is captured by *TEADUMMY*. The variable *NECPART*, instead, is included to capture the possible effect resulting from the distribution of early-stage entrepreneurship between necessity and opportunity motives. The intuition is that, due to the strong link between poverty and NEC, the higher a country's value of *NECPART* is, the greater the effect of TEA on poverty reduction will be. Finally, the Gini coefficient (*GINI*) is included because it is expected that countries with lower income inequality perform better on poverty reduction.

Finally, in equation (3), *NECDUMMY* is obtained by multiplying NEC by the above mentioned dummy variable and v_i is a random error with 0 mean and constant variance. In this model, as in equation (2), we hypothesize that higher average levels of NEC are associated to stronger poverty reduction over time.

Importantly, in equation (2) and (3) we postulate that TEA and NEC may affect the level of short-term HDI. However, it is also true that HDI, in turn, can affect TEA and NEC. This suggests an endogeneity problem. Once again, we test for endogeneity by running a modified Haussmann test as proposed by Wooldridge (2002: Chapter 6.2).[12] The test indicates that we must reject the

---

[11] Countries were assigned a value of 0 or 1 following Bosma et al. (2009) and consistently with the World Economic Forum's Global Competitiveness Report 2008–2009 (Porter and Shwab 2008).

[12] For this test we proceed as explained in footnote 10. In this case we estimate auxiliary reduced-form regressions for NEC and TEA. The linear regression for TEA is performed over NECPART, GINI, a constant term, and a variable measuring political stability (PS). Boettke and Coyne (2007), Minniti (2008), and Amorós (2009) provide theoretical and empirical support for the use of political stability as an instrumental variable. The linear regression for NEC is performed over GINI, PS, and a constant term.

Table 9.4. Regression models for HDI using 2SLS. Depended variable: HDI short-term (all the variables correspond to the mean value for each country)

	Model of equation (2)		Model of equation (3)	
TEA	0.0016	***		
	(0.0006)			
TEADUMMY	−0.0017	***		
	(0.0006)			
NECPART	−0.0048			
	(0.0214)			
GINI	−0.0008	***	−0.0009	***
	(0.0003)		(0.0003)	
NEC			0.0046	***
			(0.0015)	
NECDUMMY			−0.0038	
			(0.0038)	
Constant	0.0440	***	0.0447	***
	(0.0096)		(0.0109)	
F	4.29	***	3.95	**
N	45		45	

Notes: (Standard Errors),
*$p < 0.1$;
** $p < 0.05$;
*** $p < 0.01$

hypothesis of exogeneity of TEA and NEC. Thus, we estimate these two models using two-stage least squares (2SLS), where the mean value of TEA and NEC for each country are instrumented using the exogenous variables of the models and a proxy for political stability. Data on political stability are obtained from the World Bank's Worldwide Governance Indicators (WGI).

Table 9.4 shows parameters estimates for equations (2) and (3). Results support the hypothesis that higher mean values of TEA and NEC have a positive effect on countries' poverty reduction trend. Moreover, our results suggest that TEA has a relatively higher effect on poverty reduction in developing countries, whereas the effect of NEC is the same across all countries. With regard to *NECPART*, our results suggest that the composition of TEA has no significant effect on the contribution of TEA to poverty reduction. Finally, and as expected, a reduction in income inequality as measured by the Gini coefficient is associated to poverty reduction over time.

9.5 Conclusion

In this chapter we discuss the relationship between poverty, and entrepreneurial activities. We follow Naudé (2009: 11) who states that "...not only can the entrepreneur be formally modeled to address issues of concern to development economics, such as structural change and growth, inequality and poverty, and market failures, but that such modeling importantly extends not only to our understanding of the development process but also of the accurate role of the entrepreneur in that process."

Unfortunately, we did not have access to data for very poor countries ranking in the bottom quartile of the World Bank's per-capita GDP distribution. Nonetheless, our data include a significant sample of economies with very different degrees of economic and human development, and, to our knowledge, is the largest attempt to date to measure the relationship between different types of early-stage entrepreneurship and poverty across countries. Our results confirm existing evidence showing that, up to a critical threshold level of development, developing countries have more "entrepreneurs" than richer ones (Shane 2009). This is explained, at least in part, by the fact that, as our results show, poverty and income inequalities push a relatively high number of people in developing countries into necessity entrepreneurship. Necessity-based entrepreneurs can be important to a country's development because they represent a form of human resourcefulness (Couyoumdjian and Larroulet 2009). This is confirmed by our results that indicate that entrepreneurship activities, both total and necessity-based, have a positive effect in reducing poverty over time.

Our study is exploratory and more work is needed, nevertheless, this result is important since it suggests that entrepreneurship even in its less glamorous forms is truly relevant, and perhaps necessary, for developing countries. Within this context, our empirical findings complement existing literature that has established that entrepreneurship activities are more relevant or have more relative impact in economic terms in highly developed countries (Tang and Koveos 2004; van Stel, Carree, and Thurik 2005; Wennekers et al. 2005; Acs and Amorós 2008). These works put emphasis on innovative entrepreneurship or high-expectation entrepreneurial activities that contribute to improve countries' competitiveness and economic development.

Our results also help us rethink the effectiveness (or lack thereof) of policy and programs aimed at enhancing entrepreneurial activities in developing countries. Wennekers et al. (2005: 306) point out that "low-income nations should not consider the promotion of new business as a top priority on their policy agenda" and Shane (2009) remarks that entrepreneurship policy is not a good policy. Indeed, promoting entrepreneurship activities does not constitute a panacea for poor nations. However, entrepreneurship does matter for poverty, and developing economies should work to achieve solutions to structural problems like stability, basic infrastructure, and regulatory transparency in order to create an environment in which people may have incentives to be entrepreneurial (Amorós and Cristi 2008; Baumol 1990; Boettke and Coyne 2007).

Finally, we remark on the great power that entrepreneurship could have for the poorest people and as consequence for countries' development goals. The well known case of 2006 Nobel Peace Prize laureate Dr Muhammad Yunus and his micro-credit Grameen Bank is a heartening example of this power. Grameen is a real model of how very poor people from a poor country, Bangladesh, use entrepreneurial activities to eradicate extreme poverty situations (Powell 2008).

Although exploratory, this chapter has provided some new empirical evidence on the entrepreneurial dynamics of developing countries and, we hope, it will motivate others to continue exploring the relationship between entrepreneurship and human development. It is important that more work in this area be conducted so that future research on developing countries may help us to better understand how important entrepreneurship really is for poverty alleviation.

Acknowledgments

The authors would like to extend their gratitude to the GEM Consortium, the GEM Project Coordination team, and especially to Maria Minniti for her support and comments. Many thanks go also to an anonymous reviewer for helpful comments. Although GEM data were used in this study, their interpretation and use are the sole responsibility of the authors. All errors are ours.

References

Acs, Z. J. and Amorós, J. E. (2008), "Entrepreneurship and Competitiveness Dynamics in Latin America," *Small Business Economics*, 31(3): 305–22.

Acs, Z. J., Arenius, J. P., Hay, M., and Minniti, M. (2005), "Global Entrepreneurship Monitor: 2004 Executive Report," Babson Park, MA. and London, UK: Babson College and London Business School.

Acs, Z. J. and Varga, A. (2005), "Entrepreneurship, Agglomeration and Technological Change," *Small Business Economics*, 24(3): 323–34.

Acs, Z. J. and Storey, D. J. (2004), "Introduction: Entrepreneurship and Economic Development," *Regional Studies*, 38(8): 871–7.

Amorós, J. E. (2009), "Entrepreneurship and Quality of Institutions: A Developing-Country Approach," *WIDER Research Paper No. 2007/02*. Helsinki: UNU-WIDER.

Amorós, J. E. and Cristi, O. (2008), "Longitudinal Analysis of Entrepreneurship and Competitiveness Dynamics in Latin America," *International Entrepreneurship and Management Journal*, 4(4): 381–99.

Audretsch, D. and Keilbach, M. (2004), "Entrepreneurship and Regional Growth: an Evolutionary Interpretation," *Journal of Evolutionary Economics*, 14(5): 605–16.

Autio, E. (2007), "GEM 2007," *Global Report on High–Growth Entrepreneurship,* Babson Park, MA and London, UK: Babson College and London Business School.

Banerjee, A. V. and Duflo, E. (2007), "The Economic Lives of the Poor," *Journal of Economic Perspectives,* 21(1): 141–67.

Baumol, W. J. (1990), "Entrepreneurship: Productive, Unproductive and Destructive," *The Journal of Political Economy,* 98(5): 893–921.

Belso-Martínez, J. A. (2005), "Equilibrium Entrepreneurship Rate, Economic Development and Growth. Evidence from Spanish Regions," *Entrepreneurship & Regional Development,* 17(2): 145–61.

Berner, E., Gómez, G. M., and Knorringa, P. (2008), "Helping a Large Number of People Become a Little Less Poor: The Logic of Survival Entrepreneurs," *Paper presented at the conference UNU-WIDER Project Workshop on Entrepreneurship and Economic Development,* 21–23 August 2008. Helsinki: UNU-WIDER.

Boettke, P. and Coyne, C. (2007), "Entrepreneurial behavior and institutions," in M. Minniti (ed.), *Entrepreneurship: The engine of growth,* Vol. 1 perspective series Westport, CT: Praeger Press—Greenwood Publishing Group: 119–34.

Bosma, N., Jones, K., Autio, E., and Levie, J. (2008), "Global Entrepreneurship Monitor, 2007 Executive Report," Wellesley, MA., Babson Park MA. and London, UK: Babson College and London Business School.

Bosma, N., Acs, K. Z., Autio, E., Coduras, A., and Levie, J. (2009), "Global Entrepreneurship Monitor, 2008 Executive Report," Wellesley, MA., Babson Park, MA.: Babson College.

Boswell, J. (1987, first published in 1791), "Life of Samuel Johnson," in. R. W. Chapman (ed.), *Oxford.* Oxford: Oxford University Press: 312.

Caballero, R. (2006), "The Macroeconomics of Specificity and Restructuring," Cambridge, MA: MIT Press.

Carree, M., van Stel, A., Thurik, R., and Wennekers, S. (2002), "Economic Development and Business Ownership: an Analysis Using Data of 23 OECD Countries in the Period 1976–1996," *Small Business Economics,* 19(3): 271–90.

Carree, M., van Stel, A., Thurik, R., and Wennekers, S. (2007), "The Relationship between Economic Development and Business Ownership Revisited," *Entrepreneurship and Regional Development,* 19(3): 281–91.

Carter, N. M., Gartner, W. B., Shaver, K. G., and Gatewood, E. J. (2003), "The Career Reasons of Nascent Entrepreneurs," *Journal of Business Venturing,* 18(1): 13–39.

Chen, S. and Ravallion, M. (2008), "The Developing World Is Poorer Than We Thought, but No Less Successful in the Fight Against Poverty," *Policy Research Working Paper 4703.* Washington, DC: World Bank.

Couyoumdjian, J. P. and Larroulet, C. (2009), "Entrepreneurship and Growth: A Latin American Paradox?," *The Independent Review,* 14(1): 81–100.

Deininger, K. and Squire, L. (1998), "New Ways of Looking at Old Issues: Inequality and Growth." *Journal of Development Economics,* 57(2): 259–87.

De Soto, H. (1989), "The other path: The invisible revolution in the Third World," New York: Harper & Row.

Encyclopædia Britannica (2009), "Poverty." in Encyclopædia Britannica. Retrieved May 30, 2009, from Encyclopædia Britannica Online: http://www.britannica.com/EB-checked/topic/473136/poverty

Feldman, D. C. and Bolino, M. C. (2000), "Career Patterns of the Self-employed: Career Motivations and Career Outcomes," *Journal of Small Business Management*, 38(3): 53–67.

Fonseca, R., Michaud, P.-C., and Sopraseuth, T. (2007), "Entrepreneurship, Wealth, Liquidity Constraints, and Start-Up Costs," *Comparative Labor Law and Policy Journal*, 28: 637–74.

Gastwirth, J. L. (1972), "The Estimation of the Lorenz Curve and Gini Index," *The Review of Economics and Statistics*, 54(3): 306–16.

Grilo, I. and Irigoyen, J. M. (2006), "Entreprencurship in the EU: To wish and not to be," *Small Business Economics*, 26(4): 305–18.

Grosh, B. and Somolekae, G. (1996), "Mighty Oaks from Little Acorns: Can Microenterprises Serve as the Seedbed of Industrialization?," *World Development*, 24(12): 1879–90.

Hessels, J., Van Gelderen, M., and Thurik, R. (2008), "Entrepreneurial Aspirations, Motivations and their Drivers," *Small Business Economics*, 31(3): 323–39.

Karlsson, C., Friis, C., and Paulsson, T. (2004), "Relating Entrepreneurship to Economic Growth," *CESIS Electronic Working Papers Series No. 13*.

Kaufmann, D., Kraay, A., and Zoido-Lobatón, P.(1999), "Governance Matters," *World Bank Policy Research Working Paper 2196*, Washington, DC: World Bank.

Kaufmann, D., Kraay, A., and Mastruzzi, M. (2008), "Governance Matters VII: Aggregate and Individual Governance Indicators, 1996–2007," *World Bank Policy Research Working Paper 4654*, Washington, DC: World Bank.

Kimhi, A. (2009), "Entrepreneurship and income inequality in southern Ethiopia," *Small Business Economics*, 34(1): 81–91

Kolvereid, L. (1996), "Organizational Employment versus Self-Employment: Reasons for Career Choice Intentions," *Entrepreneurship Theory & Practice*, 20(3): 23–31.

Lee, S. Y., Florida, R., and Acs, Z. J. (2004), "Creativity and Entrepreneurship: A Regional Analysis of New Firm Formation," *Regional Studies*, 38(8): 879–91.

Lindh, T. and Ohlsson, H. (1998), "Self-Employment and Wealth Inequality," *Review of Income and Wealth*, 44(1): 25–42.

Mesnard, A. and Ravallion, M. (2006), "The wealth effect on new business startups in a developing economy," *Economica*, 73(291): 367–92.

Minniti, M. (2008), "The Role of Government Policy on Entrepreneurial Activity: Productive, Unproductive, or Destructive?," *Entrepreneurship: Theory & Practice*, 32(5): 779–90.

Minniti, M. and Lévesque, M. (2010), "Entrepreneurial Types and Economic Growth," *Journal of Business Venturing*, 25(3): 305–314.

Minniti, M., Bosma, N., and Quill, M. (2007), *The 2006 Global Entrepreneurship Monitor Technical Assessment*. London, U.K. and Wellesley, MA: London Business School and Babson College.

Misturelli, F. and Heffernan, C. (2008), "What is Poverty? A Diachronic Exploration of the Discourse on Poverty from the 1970s to the 2000s," *European Journal of Development Research*, 20(4): 666–84.

Narayan, D., Patel, R., Schafft, K., Rademacher, A., and Koch-Schulte, S. (2000), "Voices of the Poor: Can anyone hear us?," Oxford: The World Bank and Oxford University Press.

Naudé, W. A. (2007), "Peace, Prosperity, and Pro-Growth Entrepreneurship," *WIDER Research Paper 2007/02*, Helsinki: UNU-WIDER.

Naudé, W. A. (2008), "Entrepreneurship in Economic Development," *WIDER Research Paper 2008/20*, Helsinki: UNU-WIDER.

Naudé, W. A. (2009), "Entrepreneurship, Developing Countries, and Development Economics: New Approaches and Insights," *Small Business Economics*, 34(1): 1–12.

North, D. C. (1990), "Institutions, institutional change and economic performance," Cambridge: Cambridge University Press.

Oxford American Dictionary (2005), "The New Oxford American Dictionary," 2nd. Edition, New York: Oxford University Press.

Pindyck, R. S. and Rubinfeld, D. L. (1991), "Econometric Models and Economic Forecast," New York: McGraw-Hill.

Porter, M. E. and Schwab, K. (2008), "The Global Competitiveness Report 2008–2009," Geneva: World Economic Forum.

Powell, B. (2008), "Making Poor Nations Rich: Entrepreneurship and the Process of Economic Development," Stanford: Stanford University Press.

Rapoport, H. (2002), "Migration, Credit Constraints and Self-Employment: A Simple Model of Occupational Choice, Inequality and Growth," *Economics Bulletin*, 15(7): 1–5.

Ravallion, M., Chen, S., and Sangraula, P. (2008), "Dollar a Day Revisited," *Policy Research Working Paper No. 4620*, Washington, DC: World Bank.

Reynolds, P., Bosma, N., Autio, E., Hunt, S., De Bono, N., Servais, I., Lopez-Garcia, P., and Chin, N. (2005), "Global Entrepreneurship Monitor: Data Collection Design and Implementation 1998–2003," *Small Business Economics*, 24(3): 205–31.

Sandy, D. M. (2004), "Determinants of Successful Entrepreneurship in Sierra Leone," in K. Wohlmuth, A. Gutowski, T. Knedlik, M. Meyn, and S. Pitamber (eds.), *African Development Perspectives Yearbook 2002/2003, African Entrepreneurship and Private Sector Development*. Munster: Lit Verlag.

Schramm, C. J. (2004), "Building Entrepreneurial Economies," *Foreign Affairs, 83*(4): 104–15.

Schumpeter, J. A. (1912, reedit 1934), "The Theory of Economic Development," Cambridge, MA: Harvard University Press.

Shane, S. (2009), "Why Encouraging more People to Become Entrepreneurs is Bad Public Policy," *Small Business Economics*, 33(2): 141–9.

Sharp, A., Register, C., and Grimes, P. (2003), "Economics of Social Issues," 16th Edition. New York: McGraw-Hill/Irwin.

Shostak, A. (1965), "New Perspectives on Poverty," New York: Prentice Hall.

Singer, A. E. (2006), "Business Strategy and Poverty Alleviation," *Journal of Business Ethics*, 66(2): 225–31.

Spencer, J. W. and Gómez, C. (2006), "The Relationship among National Institutional Structures, Economic Factors, and Domestic Entrepreneurial Activity: a Multicountry Study," *Journal of Business Research*, 57(10): 1098–1107.

Tang, L. and Koveos, P. E. (2004), "Venture Entrepreneurship, Innovation Entrepreneurship and Economic Growth," *Journal of Development Entrepreneurship*, 9(2): 161–71.

United Nations (2009), "The Millennium Development Goals Report," New York: Department of Economic and Social Affairs of the United Nations Secretariat.

United Nations Development Programme (2007), "Human Development Report 2007/2008," New York: Palgrave Macmillan.

van Stel, A., Carree, M., and Thurik, R. (2005), "The Effect of Entrepreneurial Activity on National Economic Growth," *Small Business Economics,* 24(3): 311–21.

Wennekers, S. and Thurik, R. (1999), "Linking Entrepreneurship and Economic Growth," *Small Business Economics,* 13(1). 27–55.

Wennekers, S., van Stel, A., Thurik, R., and Reynolds, R. (2005), "Nascent Entrepreneurship and the Level of Economic Development," *Small Business Economics,* 24(3): 293–309.

Wolff, P. (2009), "Population and Social Conditions," *EUROSTAT, Statistics in focus—46/2009,* Luxemburg: Office for Official Publications of the European Communities.

Wong, P. K., Ho, Y. P., and Autio, E. (2005), "Entrepreneurship, Innovation and Economic Growth: Evidence from GEM Data," *Small Business Economics,* 24(3): 335–50.

Wood, G. (2003), "Staying Secure, Staying Poor: The Faustian Bargain," *World Development,* 31(3): 455–71.

Wooldridge, J. M. (2002), "Econometric Analysis of Cross Section and Panel Data," Cambridge MA.: MIT Press.

World Bank (2008a), "Global Monitoring Report 2008," Washington DC: The International Bank for Reconstruction and Development/The World Bank.

World Bank (2008b), "World Development indicators: Poverty data," Washington DC: The International Bank for Reconstruction and Development/The World Bank.

World Bank (2009), "PovertyNet," Washington DC: The International Bank for Reconstruction and Development/The World Bank.

10

Ambitious Entrepreneurship, High-Growth Firms, and Macroeconomic Growth

Erik Stam, Chantal Hartog, André van Stel, and Roy Thurik

10.1 Introduction

Although entrepreneurship has long been considered a crucial mechanism of economic development (Schumpeter 1934; Landes 1998; Baumol 2002; Audretsch et al. 2006), empirical studies on the role of entrepreneurship in economic growth show mixed evidence (Stam 2008; Parker 2009). This is not surprising given the heterogeneity characterizing both the kinds of entrepreneurship and the economic contexts in which economic growth takes place. In addition, issues concerning the measurement of entrepreneurship (Wennekers and Thurik 1999) and reversed causality (Thurik et al. 2008; Parker 2009) also exist. Heterogeneity, both at the micro and macro level has thus far rarely been taken into account. This, in turn, limits our understanding of the specific role of entrepreneurship in economic growth. Important questions in this respect are: "How does the role of entrepreneurship differ between high-income and low-income countries?" and "What kinds of entrepreneurship are most crucial for economic growth?" The objective of this chapter is to provide insight about the relationship between different types of entrepreneurship and economic growth, and into its possible difference between low and high-income countries.

We investigate four research questions. First, we examine whether the relationship between entrepreneurship and macroeconomic growth differs between high and low-income countries. Second, we look at whether ambitious entrepreneurship plays a different role in achieving economic growth compared to entrepreneurship in general. Third, we investigate the relationship between the prevalence of established high-growth firms and macroeconomic growth. Finally, we examine the relationship between the prevalence of ambitious entrepreneurship (consisting of entrepreneurs expecting to grow their firm considerably) and the prevalence of established high-growth firms (firms that have actually realized high growth rates). To investigate these issues, we use data from the Global Entrepreneurship Monitor (GEM) project for ambitious entrepreneurship, and from EIM's International Benchmark Entrepreneurship database for high-growth firms. We take into account the relationship between (ambitious) entrepreneurship and macroeconomic growth in four subsequent data waves. Thus, the analyses presented in this chapter are more comprehensive than previous studies in this field (van Stel et al. 2005; Wong et al. 2005; Stam et al. 2009; Valliere and Peterson 2009). In addition, we take into account realized firm growth measures, in order to perform a robustness check over intended entrepreneurial (growth) activities.

Our evidence shows that once we control for the share of ambitious entrepreneurs, the overall positive effect of entrepreneurship on macroeconomic growth disappears. Growth-oriented entrepreneurship seems to contribute heavily to macroeconomic growth in both low- and high-income countries. In low-income countries, the overall positive effect of entrepreneurship on macroeconomic growth does not disappear after introducing the share of ambitious entrepreneurs into the statistical model. In contrast to ambitious entrepreneurship, established high-growth firms do not seem to contribute to macroeconomic growth. These established high-growth firms seem to flourish in countries with high levels of entrepreneurship in general, while there appears to be no connection between the rate of high-growth firms and the share of ambitious entrepreneurs. In the final section of this chapter, we summarize and discuss our findings.

10.2 Related literature and hypotheses

Entrepreneurship has been identified as one of the four production factors in the aggregate production function (Audretsch and Keilbach 2004; Audretsch et al. 2006). It is the factor that creates wealth by combining other production factors in new ways (Audretsch 2007). Entrepreneurs experiment with new combinations whose outcomes are uncertain, but alternative variations need to be considered to find out which ones will improve (economic) life (Rosenberg and Birdzell 1986). Key elements in this regard are the creation and introduction of new products and processes, and a selection process used to test their value in a way that assures their rapid adoption or rejection. Ambitious entrepreneurs whose aim is to create, introduce and/or diffuse these innovations on a large scale are important players in this game.

Entrepreneurship unlocks economic development only if a proper institutional setting is in place (Baumol 1990; Powell 2008; Boettke and Coyne 2003). The latter, in turn, includes both formal and informal institutions (North 1990;

Boettke and Coyne 2009). Clear property rights are an essential formal institution with regard to welfare-enhancing entrepreneurship. Unclear property rights, for example, are a stronger constraint on investments in transition countries than capital market rigidities (Johnson et al. 2000), and their absence is an even more severe problem in developing countries (De Soto 1989). To give a specific example, private firms with more than seven workers were not even allowed to operate legally in China until 1988 (Dorn 2008: 301). It may be argued that capital, labor, technology, and entrepreneurship are the sources of economic development, while institutions are its fundamental cause (Acemoglu et al. 2004). Without the proper institutions in place, it would be hard for entrepreneurs to invest in promising new combinations. Encouraging entrepreneurs to invest in their domestic economy is one of the best ways to stimulate growth in poor countries (Rodrik 2007: 44–50). In this context, investments refer to innovation (e.g. employing new technology, producing new products, searching for new markets, etc.) and expanding capacity. These investments trigger a combination of capital investment and technological change. Many low-income countries are faced with a situation in which, although local investments by entrepreneurs could be a way out of poverty and into prosperity, due to an insufficiently developed institutional infrastructure, individuals will either not start investing in promising new combinations or, when they start doing so, face too many hurdles. Without promising start-ups, foreign direct investments may be the only way out (Blomstrom and Kokko 1996). In advanced capitalist economies, innovation and structural change take place through the combined efforts of small (independent inventors) and large innovative (organized research and development) firms, which complement each other in changing the economy (Nooteboom 1994; Baumol 2002) and which play different roles throughout the business cycle (Koellinger and Thurik 2009). In developing countries, large firms are very scarce and small firms have to be the prime movers in the process of structural change.

In contrast to high-income countries, entrepreneurship in low-income countries is driven significantly by necessity (Reynolds et al. 2001; Bosma et al. 2008; Naudé 2010). Many entrepreneurs in these economies do not start a firm because they want to be independent or increase their income as compared to being employed; they start out of necessity because they have no better way to make a living. This is somewhat reflected in the finding that in low-income countries self-employed people are less happy than employees, while the opposite is true in high-income countries (Blanchflower and Oswald 1998; Graham 2005). These entrepreneurs are not likely to be involved in a process of opportunity discovery and their actions are not likely to have an effect on the restructuring and diversification of low-income economies (Rodrik 2007: 110). From the theoretical and empirical evidence reviewed so far, we derive a set of testable hypotheses aimed at improving our understanding of the relationship between entrepreneurial activity and growth.

Hypothesis 1: Entrepreneurship in general is a more important determinant of macroeconomic growth in high-income countries than in low-income countries.

We expect that the level of ambitious entrepreneurship in a country is a more relevant driver of economic growth than the most frequently used indicators of entrepreneurship such as self-employment and new firm formation. Entrepreneurs aspiring to produce new products, make their company grow, or engage in export-related activities are expected to contribute more to economic growth than their less ambitious counterparts (Bellu and Sherman 1995; Kolvereid and Bullvag 1996; Wiklund and Shepherd 2003). Thus,

Hypothesis 2: Ambitious entrepreneurship is a more important determinant of macroeconomic growth than entrepreneurship in general.

Looking at nascent entrepreneurship and young businesses may reveal more about *stated* preferences regarding entrepreneurial behavior and employment growth than about surviving in a competitive environment and creating substantial growth, that is a *revealed* preference for growth. In response to this argument, we analyze the effect of realized firm growth on economic growth. Thus,

Hypothesis 3: The prevalence of high-growth firms is positively related to macroeconomic growth.

In addition, we expect established high-growth firms to be related to nascent entrepreneurship and young businesses, with the latter providing a pool of potential high-growth firms and serving as an indicator of competitive pressure, which forces less efficient incumbents to vacate the market and other incumbents to step up their performance (Thurik and Wennekers 2004; Bosma et al. 2011). As a result, the quality of the firm population in the industry improves, which in turn leads to an improved aggregate performance (Fritsch and Mueller 2004). These effects may be stronger when ambitious entrepreneurship is considered compared to entrepreneurship in general. Thus,

Hypothesis 4: Entrepreneurship in general is positively related to the prevalence of established high-growth firms.

Hypothesis 5: Ambitious entrepreneurship has a stronger positive relationship to the prevalence of established high-growth firms than entrepreneurship in general.

10.3 Data and sources

We use data from a sample of countries participating in the Global Entrepreneurship Monitor (GEM) project between 2002–5 complemented by data from the International Monetary Fund (IMF) and EIM as described below.

For growth of gross domestic product (GDP) (ΔGDP) we use a four-year average of real GDP growth. Real GDP growth rates are taken from the IMF

World Economic Outlook database of the International Monetary Fund, version April 2008. The lag structures imply that the estimation sample of GDP growth is 2005–8. This is appropriate since the sample for early-stage entrepreneurship is for 2002–5. To limit the potential impact of reversed causality, we include lagged GDP growth as an additional explanatory variable. The lagged GDP growth variable refers to the four years prior to the measurement period of the dependent variable. When growth expectations for a national economy are good, more entrepreneurs may expect to watch their business grow in years to come. Hence, there may also be a (reversed) effect of economic growth on (ambitious) entrepreneurship.

Total early-stage entrepreneurial activity (*TEA*) is defined as the percentage of adult individuals who are either actively involved in starting a new venture or are the owners/managers of a business that is less than 42 months old. Data on TEA are taken from the GEM adult population survey (see Reynolds et al. (2005) for details).

Ambitious entrepreneurship *(Ambitious)* is defined as a subset of TEA, specifically, the share of entrepreneurs within TEA who expect their firm to grow with at least six employees within five years.[1] These data are also taken from the GEM adult population survey.

Data for established high-growth firms (*High-growth*) are taken from EIM's International Benchmark Entrepreneurship database. EIM has constructed a comprehensive set of harmonized data for the rate of established high-growth firms across several (developed) countries which, however, exclude NACE sectors A, B, and J (agriculture, fishery, and financial and other services).[2] The rate of high-growth firms is defined as the share of incumbent firms realizing sixty percent growth or more over a period of three years (from t-3 to t). We use two variants: growth in terms of turnover and growth in terms of employment. Firms that realize fast turnover growth may not realize fast employment growth and vice versa. Importantly, when we computed the rate of high-growth firms, we only included firms with between 50 and 1,000 employees at the start of the observation period. This implies that small firms growing sixty percent or more while employing just a few employees are not included.

Most studies on GDP growth include the initial level of income in their analysis and find it to be significant (see Abramovitz (1986) on the conditional convergence effect hypothesis). Thus, we use data from the IMF World Economic Outlook database (version April 2008) and include GDP per capita

---

[1] Unfortunately, multicollinearity problems prevent us from dividing ambitious entrepreneurship into entrepreneurs who expect a growth between 6 and 19 people and entrepreneurs who expect a growth of at least 20 people.

[2] For more details see EIM (2008, 2009a, and 2009b). The data can be downloaded at www.entrepreneurship-sme.eu.

expressed in (thousands of) purchasing power parities per international dollar. This is our measure of per capita income (*GDPC*).

Finally, we include a Growth Competitiveness Index (GCI). Data on the GCI are taken from various versions of *The Global Competitiveness Report*. The GCI consists of three main factors assessing a country's potential for economic growth. The three factors are the quality of the macroeconomic environment, the state of the public institutions, and the level of technology. For further details about this index, see McArthur and Sachs (2002).

As an illustration of the data at hand, we report descriptive statistics for our entrepreneurship variables for the most recent year in our sample (2005) in Table 10.1.[3]

10.4 Models

It is generally accepted that the level of entrepreneurial activity differs across countries (Blanchflower et al. 2001; Djankov et al. 2002; Grilo and Thurik 2008; Wennekers 2006). Studies exploring these differences often focus on the incidence of new firm registration or self-employment, which may not be reliable indicators when applied to transition countries and developing countries with significant informal economies. For these reasons we use total early-stage entrepreneurial activity (TEA) which is a more accurate measure of the entrepreneurial propensity of a nation.

As mentioned earlier, in this chapter, we investigate four topics. First, we look at whether the relationship between entrepreneurship and macroeconomic growth is different for high-income and low-income countries. Second, we examine whether ambitious entrepreneurship plays a different role in achieving economic growth compared to entrepreneurship in general. Third, we investigate the relationship between the prevalence of established high-growth firms and macroeconomic growth. Fourth, we examine the relationship between the rate of ambitious entrepreneurship and the rate of established high-growth firms.

The *first* part of our empirical analysis deals with the first two research questions. We build on van Stel et al. (2005), who investigated whether TEA influences GDP growth in a cross-section of thirty-six countries participating in GEM in 2002 and found that, although that is the case, the influence depends on the level of per capita income. In particular, they found the contribution to economic growth to be stronger in high-income countries

---

[3] Due to the unbalanced nature of our panel dataset, Table 10.1 does not contain all countries included in the sample. The additional countries (for which we do not have data for all years) are: Hong Kong, India, Israel, Poland, Korea, Russia, and Taiwan.

Table 10.1. Entrepreneurship rates (TEA) in 2005

Country		TEA	Share ambitious entrepreneurs	Rate of high-growth firms based on	
				Turnover	Employment
High-income	Australia	10.9	0.45	–	–
	Belgium	3.9	0.41	11.7	5.6
	Canada	9.3	0.55	–	–
	Denmark	4.8	0.30	16.9	11.6
	Finland	5.0	0.35	17.3	8.8
	France	5.4	0.32	12.3	6.8
	Germany	5.4	0.50	10.6	7.8
	Hungary	1.9	0.16	–	–
	Iceland	10.7	0.74	–	–
	Ireland	9.8	0.31	24.3	–
	Italy	4.9	0.20	16.3	13.2
	Japan	2.2	0.51	6.8	2.0
	Netherlands	4.4	0.40	11.0	7.5
	New Zealand	17.6	0.43	–	–
	Norway	9.2	0.26	–	–
	Singapore	7.2	0.42	–	–
	Slovenia	4.4	0.56	–	–
	Spain	5.7	0.25	23.5	23.5
	Sweden	4.0	0.31	17.7	17.7
	Switzerland	6.1	0.28	–	–
	United Kingdom	6.2	0.52	19.8	10.9
	United States	12.4	0.49	38.4	20.1
Low-income	Argentina	9.5	0.59	–	–
	Brazil	11.3	0.55	–	–
	Chile	11.1	0.64	–	–
	China	13.7	0.89	–	–
	Croatia	6.1	0.43	–	–
	Mexico	5.9	0.19	–	–
	South Africa	5.1	0.45	–	–
	Thailand	20.7	0.31	–	–
Mean		7.8	0.43	17.4	11.3
Standard deviation		4.4	0.16	8.1	6.3

Note: Data regarding TEA and ambitious entrepreneurial activity refer to 2005, while data regarding the rate of high-growth firms refer to the period 2002–5.

Sources: GEM and EIM.

than in low-income countries, and argued that this may be related to higher human capital levels of entrepreneurs in those countries. In this chapter, we perform a similar regression analysis but, instead of using data on a cross-section of countries for a given year, we use an unbalanced panel data set for thirty-seven countries over the years 2002–5 (see Table 10.1).[4] Also, in

[4] The distinction between high and low-income countries is based on the World Bank 2002 classification: the lower-income category includes "low-income economies," "lower-middle-income economies," and "upper-middle-income economies," while the higher-income category includes "high-income economies."

addition to the general TEA index, we use the share of ambitious entrepreneurs within TEA as an independent variable to test whether the impact of ambitious entrepreneurs is higher than that of non-ambitious entrepreneurs. We also investigate whether these effects are different for high-income as compared to low-income countries.[5] In the *second* part of our empirical analysis, we investigate the relationship between the rate of high-growth firms and subsequent macroeconomic growth (our third research question), which allows us to perform a robustness check over intended entrepreneurial (growth) activities. In the *third* part, we investigate the link between the rate of high-growth firms and the rate of ambitious entrepreneurship. Below, we present the models used in this chapter.

Model 1

In our first model, we investigate whether (ambitious) entrepreneurship may be considered a determinant of economic growth, alongside other well-known determinants that are captured in the *Growth Competitiveness Index* (GCI) published by the World Economic Forum. As both entrepreneurship and the factors underlying the GCI are assumed to be structural characteristics of an economy, we want to explain economic growth in the medium term rather than in the short-term. As a dependent variable, we use average annual growth over a period of four years following the year for which we measure TEA. In line with van Stel et al. (2005), we also use (the log of) initial income level of countries to correct for catch-up effects, and lagged growth of GDP to correct for reversed causality effects, as additional control variables.[6]

We allow for different effects in high-income compared to low-income countries (including transition countries). TEA rates may reflect different types of entrepreneurs in countries with different development levels, implying a different impact on growth. This is tested using separate TEA variables for different groups of countries (high-income versus low-income). Our first model is represented by Equation 1:

---

[5] This first part of our analysis is an update of Stam et al. (2009) who used GEM data for 2002 only. Similar analyses focusing on the importance of entrepreneurs' export orientation and on entrepreneurial diversity (in terms of age, education, and gender) can be found in Hessels and Van Stel (2008) and Verheul and van Stel (2007), respectively.

[6] When growth expectations for the national economy are good, more entrepreneurs may expect to see their business grow in years to come. Hence, there may also be a (reversed) effect of economic growth on (ambitious) entrepreneurship. To limit the potential impact of reversed causality, we include lagged GDP growth as an additional explanatory variable. We also measure TEA rates in the year (t) preceding the period over which the dependent variable is measured (t–(t+3)). Of course, we realize that the possibility of reversed effects cannot be ruled out completely.

$$\Delta GDP_{i(t-(t-3))} = a + b_1\ TEA^{high-income}_{i,(t-3)} + c_1 TEA^{low-income}_{i,(t-3)}$$
$$+ b_2\ Ambitious^{high-income}_{i,(t-3)} + c_2 Ambitious^{low-income}_{i,t-3}$$
$$+ d\log(GDPC_{i,t-3}) + e\ GCI_{i,t-3} + f\Delta GDP_{i,((t-4)-(t-7))} + \varepsilon_{it} \qquad (1)$$

where ΔGDP is the annual real growth rate of GDP (this variable is averaged over a four year period), TEA the total early-stage entrepreneurial activity index, $Ambitious$ the share of ambitious entrepreneurs (those expecting to employ six or more people within five years), $GDPC$ per capita income, and GCI the Growth Competitiveness Index.

Hypothesis 1, which states a more positive effect of entrepreneurship in general for high-income countries, is supported if coefficient b_1 would be larger than coefficient c_1. Furthermore, Hypothesis 2, which states that ambitious entrepreneurs contribute more to national economic growth than entrepreneurs in general, is supported if b_2 and c_2 are greater than zero.

Model 2

In our second model, we test whether the rate of high-growth firms has a positive effect on subsequent macroeconomic growth. The data involved relate only to high-income countries. We use data on two rates of established high-growth firms, one referring to turnover growth and the other to employment growth. We use the same control variables as in Equation 1. Model 2 reads as follows:

$$\Delta GDP_{i,(t-(t-3))} = a + b\ High\text{-}growth_{i,((t-3)-(t-6))} + c\log(GDPC_{i,t-3}) \qquad (2)$$
$$+ d\ GCI_{i,t-3} + e\Delta GDP_{i,((t-4)-(t-7))} + \varepsilon_{it}$$

where $High\text{-}growth$ is the rate of high-growth firms (firms growing by at least sixty percent in a three year period).

Hypothesis 3, which states that the rate of high-growth firms is positively related to macroeconomic growth, is supported if coefficient b is greater than zero.

Model 3

As mentioned above, in our third model we test whether a relationship exists between the number of (ambitious) entrepreneurs and the number of high-growth firms in a given country. Model 3 is:

$$High\text{-}growth_{i,(t-(t-3))} = a + b\ TEA_{i,t} + c\ Ambitious_{i,t} \qquad (3)$$
$$+ d\log(GDPC_{i,t-3}) + e\ GCI_{i,t-3} + \varepsilon_{it}$$

Hypotheses 4 and 5, which state that (ambitious) entrepreneurship is positively related to the rate of high-growth firms, are supported if coefficients b and c are greater than zero, respectively. Note that we measure TEA in period t. Although this is not ideal in terms of establishing a causal relationship, if using t-3 we would lose too many observations to estimate the model. As a result, we are unable to establish a causal relationship, but merely a conditional correlation.

10.5 Results

Results for Model 1 (Equation 1) are presented in Table 10.2. Our estimation sample is 2005–8. This corresponds to an unbalanced panel of 119 observations of countries participating in GEM in the years 2002–5 (note the three year lag in Equation 1). Because the aim of our model is to explain *country* variations in economic growth rates, we do not include country dummies in our model. On the other hand, we do include year dummies to correct for worldwide cyclical variations in economic growth rates.

Model variant 1 in Table 10.2 presents the estimation results when only the control variables are included. Per capita income has an expected negative effect that is consistent with the conditional convergence effect (Abramovitz 1986). Remarkably, the Growth Competitiveness Index (GCI) is not significant. The impact of lagged growth is significantly positive, suggesting a considerable degree of path dependency. In the second model variant, TEA is added and its effect is significantly positive at the ten percent level. Next, we add the share of ambitious entrepreneurship to the model. Here, its effect is strongly positive. In the fourth model variant, the effects of TEA and the share of ambitious entrepreneurs are allowed to be different for high-income and low-income countries. Likelihood ratio tests reveal that, when comparing model variant 4 to either model variant 2 or 3, model variant 4 significantly outperforms models 2 and 3 at the five percent level.[7] Hence, we conclude that the relationship between entrepreneurship and macroeconomic growth is indeed different for high-income and low-income countries. In particular, we see that entrepreneurship in general (TEA) has no significant impact in high-income countries, while it has a significantly positive impact in low-income countries. This is remarkable, since van Stel et al. (2005) and Stam et al. (2009) found an opposite pattern. They use a cross-section of countries for a single year, while we use data regarding four years. One explanation is that the effect was different in the period 2003–5 when compared to 2002. Another explanation is that the estimated effect of TEA on subsequent

---

[7] Comparing model variants 2 and 4 requires using three degrees of freedom for the critical value of the null distribution, while comparing model variants 3 and 4 requires using two degrees of freedom.

Table 10.2. Explaining economic growth from TEA rate and share of ambitious entrepreneurs

	Model 1	Model 2	Model 3	Model 4
Constant	20.3***	17.3***	15.5***	4.8
	(8.6)	(9.8)	(9.2)	(1.1)
TEA		0.073*	0.064	
		(1.7)	(1.6)	
TEA high-income countries				0.01
				(0.1)
TEA low-income countries				0.13**
				(2.3)
Share ambitious entrepreneurs			2.2***	
			(3.3)	
Share ambitious entrepreneurs, high-income countries				2.1***
				(3.3)
Share ambitious entrepreneurs, low-income countries				3.2***
				(2.8)
log (GDPC)	−1.7***	−1.4***	−1.3***	−0.3
	(6.0)	(5.1)	(4.7)	(0.6)
GCI	−0.075	−0.23	−0.28	−0.2
	(0.2)	(0.7)	(0.8)	(0.5)
lagged GDP growth	0.29**	0.30***	0.28**	0.35***
	(2.3)	(2.8)	(2.6)	(3.4)
R^2	0.426	0.445	0.469	0.495
adjusted R^2	0.395	0.410	0.430	0.448
loglikelihood	−218.7	−216.7	−214.1	−211.1
N	119	119	119	119

Absolute heteroskedasticity-consistent t-values are between brackets. Year dummies included but not reported.
* Significant at 0.10 level
** Significant at 0.05 level
*** Significant at 0.01 level

economic growth is robust enough to examine different time periods. Hypothesis 1 is not supported.

With regard to Hypothesis 2, we see that, both for high-income and for low-income countries the share of ambitious entrepreneurship significantly contributes to economic growth, over and beyond the effect of entrepreneurship in general. Hypothesis 2 is supported. To a certain extent, this is at odds with Valliere and Peterson (2009), who identified a positive effect of ambitious entrepreneurship in high-income countries, but no effect in low-income countries. The absence of an effect in the latter group of countries may be explained by the fact that they did not include India and China in their sample, two low-income countries that seem to drive the relationship between ambitious entrepreneurship and economic growth in low-income countries in the study of Stam et al. (2009).

Table 10.3 shows the results of the estimations of Model 2 (Equation 2) about the effect of the growth of established firms on macroeconomic growth. Model variants 1 and 2 refer to *turnover* growth, while variants 3 and 4 refer to *employment* growth. As the data we use refers to high-growth firms in

Erik Stam, Chantal Hartog, André van Stel, and Roy Thurik

Table 10.3. Explaining economic growth from rates of high (realized) growth firms

	Model 1	Model 2	Model 3	Model 4
Constant	17.1***	8.2	19.0***	22.0***
	(4.8)	(0.8)	(5.1)	(2.9)
Rate of high-growth firms, in terms of turnover	−0.003	0.077***		
	(0.2)	(3.1)		
Rate of high-growth firms, in terms of employment			−0.001	0.009
			(0.1)	(0.3)
log (GDPC)	−2.0***	−0.85	−2.2***	−2.5***
	(5.1)	(0.8)	(5.4)	(2.8)
GCI	0.88***	0.36	0.96***	1.2***
	(6.2)	(0.9)	(5.9)	(3.6)
lagged GDP growth	0.66***		0.59***	
	(13.7)		(7.0)	
R^2	0.830	0.273	0.771	0.299
adjusted R^2	0.803	0.176	0.732	0.199
loglikelihood	−33.0	−70.8	−30.8	−58.2
N	52	52	49	49

Absolute heteroskedasticity-consistent *t*-values are between brackets. Year dummies included but not reported.
* Significant at 0.10 level
** Significant at 0.05 level
*** Significant at 0.01 level

high-income countries only, the results presented in Tables 10.3 and 10.4 also relate to high-income countries only.

Although the effect of the rate of high-growth firms (turnover) is not significant in model variant 1, it turns out to correlate strongly with lagged GDP growth. When we remove the latter variable, there is a strong positive relationship between the rate of high-growth firms and subsequent macroeconomic growth. The different outcomes in Model 1 and 2 can be interpreted in at least two ways. On the one hand, although it does not provide evidence of a causal effect (in a Granger sense), there is a strong conditional correlation between the rate of high-growth firms (in terms of turnover) and GDP growth in the subsequent period. This suggests that high-growth firms play an important role in achieving macroeconomic growth. On the other hand, a reverse causality in which GDP growth drives the growth of established firms may be more relevant. Interestingly, we find no effect of high-growth firms in terms of employment, even after removing the lagged growth variable. Perhaps fast growing firms in terms of employment have smaller productivity growth compared to fast growing firms in terms of turnover. This would suggest that their impact on macroeconomic growth is smaller (or even zero, according to Table 10.3). Table 10.3 provides hardly any support for Hypothesis 3.

Finally, Table 10.4 presents the results of Model 3 (Equation 3), where we investigate whether (ambitious) entrepreneurship is related to the share of high-growth firms among incumbents (note again that realized high growth is

Table 10.4. Explaining rates of high (realized) turnover growth firms from TEA

	Model 1	Model 2
Constant	132.2***	135.3***
	(3.2)	(3.1)
TEA	2.5***	2.6***
	(8.1)	(8.0)
Share ambitious entrepreneurs		−5.8
		(0.9)
log (GDPC)	−13.1***	−13.3***
	(3.2)	(3.0)
GCI	1.3	1.5
	(1.1)	(1.3)
R^2	0.714	0.718
adjusted R^2	0.674	0.671
loglikelihood	−139.2	−138.8
N	50	50

Absolute heteroskedasticity-consistent t-values are between brackets. Year dummies included but not reported.
* Significant at 0.10 level
** Significant at 0.05 level
*** Significant at 0.01 level

measured among firms with 50–1,000 employees). Because we only find a positive relationship with GDP growth for the rate of high-growth firms in terms of turnover, Table 10.4 focuses on this group of firms. The main result is that there is a strong statistical association between TEA and the rate of high-growth firms, with a t-value of no less than eight. By contrast, we do not find an additional effect for the share of ambitious entrepreneurs. These results support Hypothesis 4 but not Hypothesis 5.

These results indicate that it is entrepreneurship in general, rather than specifically ambitious entrepreneurship, which is positively associated with the prevalence of established high-growth firms, suggesting that all different types of new firms contribute to a process of variety and selection, from which a number of high-growth firms eventually emerges. The strong positive relationship between TEA and the prevalence of established high-growth firms is illustrated by Figure 10.1, which plots the fifty observations used in Table 10.4.

10.6 Discussion

In general, ambitious entrepreneurship has a stronger impact on economic growth than overall entrepreneurial activity in a given country, as was expected. In contrast to expectations, however, our findings suggest that the relationship between ambitious entrepreneurship and macroeconomic growth is stronger in low-income countries than in high-income countries. Established firms with considerable growth (either in turnover or employment) do not seem to be

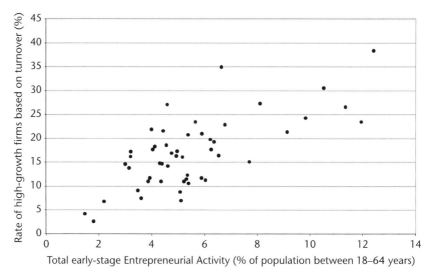

Figure 10.1 Relationship between TEA and rate of high-growth firms (turnover)
Sources: GEM and EIM.

connected to economic growth. These established high-growth firms seem to flourish in countries with high levels of entrepreneurship in general, while there appears to be no relationship between the share of ambitious entrepreneurs and the rate of high-growth firms.

The ambiguous findings on the relationship between entrepreneurship and economic growth in low-income countries may reflect the complexity involved in the underlying institutional dimension, which affects the prevalence (Hessels et al. 2008) as well as the effects of the different types of entrepreneurship in different ways. We expected that, in low-income countries, an insufficiently developed institutional framework would reduce growth intentions and curtail entrepreneurial growth. Possibly, the selection of low-income countries in the GEM dataset only contains relatively well-developed economies, which makes it harder to analyze the effects of insufficiently developed institutional frameworks. This calls for more research that takes into account specific types of institutions and their dynamics over time in order to uncover the role of different types of entrepreneurship in economic growth in low-income countries (Naudé 2010).

Largely confirming prior findings (Wong et al. 2005; Stam et al. 2009; Valliere and Peterson 2009), we also find that ambitious entrepreneurship has a positive effect on subsequent macroeconomic growth. Ambitious entrepreneurship seems to be an important vehicle when it comes to creating new value and it is likely to stimulate the creation of genuinely new jobs. An interesting issue for further research would be to examine in which industries most of these ambitious entrepreneurs can be found. It is often implied that young and small high-growth firms are most likely to be found in young and growing industries (Davidsson and Delmar 2006; Acs et al. 2008), but this needs to be investigated in large-scale empirical research.

The positive effect of established high-growth firms on macroeconomic growth often assumed is not confirmed by our results. At first, this goes against the intuition that these firms are important drivers of employment growth, innovation, productivity growth and, ultimately, economic growth (OECD 2006; EIM 2006). However, when we reflect on the nature of firm growth, this outcome is less surprising. Most studies on firm growth do not draw a distinction between organic and acquired growth. The few studies that have made this distinction indicate that young and small firms predominantly grow organically, while old and large firms most often grow through acquisition (Davidsson and Delmar 2006; Deschryvere 2008). Davidsson and Delmar (2006) argue that this implies that young and small firms create the lion's share of *genuinely* new jobs. Acquired growth involves a reallocation or even an overall decline of employment (when acquired firms and/or the acquiring firm are restructured) and, as a result, is less important in terms of macroeconomic growth than organic growth. Given that established high-growth firms are relatively large and old, most of their growth is probably realized through acquisitions, with hardly any effect on the overall growth of the economy. In addition, mergers and acquisitions are pro-cyclical in nature, that is they are driven by GDP growth (Maksimovic and Philips 2001; Bhattacharjee et al. 2009), and most of them erode the value of the acquiring firm (Haleblian et al. 2009).

Finally, we investigated the relationship between the rate of ambitious entrepreneurs (entrepreneurs expecting to grow their firm) and the rate of high-growth firms (firms that have actually realized high growth rates). We find that it is entrepreneurship in general, rather than specifically ambitious entrepreneurship, which is positively associated with the rate of high-growth firms. More research is needed to identify the mechanism underlying this relationship.

To sum up, the aim of this chapter was to test the relationships between ambitious entrepreneurship, high-growth firms and macroeconomic growth, and to provide insight into the links between the microeconomic phenomena of entrepreneurial activities and firm growth and macroeconomic growth. Our study can be seen in the light of other studies that link the effect of microeconomic dynamics to macroeconomic dynamics (Baumol 2002; Metcalfe 2004; Eliasson et al. 2004).[8] To explain aggregate income growth, we need to understand entry, innovation, and growth at the micro level, and to gain

---

[8] Parker (2009: chapter 11) provides a survey of various theories of venture growth and their link to industry dynamics (the intermediate level between the micro and the macro economy).

insight into how competition and learning provide the link between the micro level and the macro level. It has often been too easily assumed—especially in policy documents and debates—that firm entry and growth are driven by innovation. However, empirical research has shown that only a minority of all entrants introduces new processes or products into the economy (Stam and Wennberg 2009) and that firm growth is often a statistical artifact of merging prior separated legal entities (i.e. acquired growth): most entrants and large growing firms do not create new value in society. Our study suggests that high levels of overall entry and firm growth do not automatically lead to macroeconomic growth.

Acknowledgments

This chapter has been written in collaboration with the research program SCALES which is carried out by EIM and is financed by the Dutch Ministry of Economic Affairs. Many thanks go also to an anonymous reviewer for helpful comments. Although GEM data were used in this study, their interpretation and use are the sole responsibility of the authors. All errors are ours.

References

Abramovitz, M. (1986), "Catching Up, Forging Ahead, and Falling Behind," *Journal of Economic History*, 46 (2): 385–406.

Acemoglu, D., Johnson, S., and Robinson, J. (2004), "Institutions as the Fundamental Cause of Long-run Growth," NBER Working Paper 10481 (http://www.nber.org/papers/w10481).

Acs, Z. J., Parsons, W., and Tracy, S. (2008), "High Impact Firms: Gazelles Revisited," An Office of Advocacy Working Paper, U.S. Small Business Administration.

Audretsch, D. B. (2007), "Entrepreneurship Capital and Economic Growth," *Oxford Review of Economic Policy*, 23 (1): 63–78.

Audretsch, D. B. and Keilbach, M. C. (2004), "Entrepreneurship Capital and Economic Performance," *Regional Studies*, 38 (8): 949–59.

Audretsch, D. B., Keilbach, M. C., and Lehmann, E. E. (2006), *Entrepreneurship and Economic Growth*, New York, NY USA: Oxford University Press.

Baumol, W. J. (1990), "Entrepreneurship: Productive, Unproductive, and Destructive," *Journal of Political Economy*, 98 (5): 893–921.

Baumol, W. J. (2002), *The Free-Market Innovation Machine: Analyzing the Growth Miracle of Capitalism*. Princeton, NJ USA: Princeton University Press.

Bellu, R. R. and Sherman, H. (1995), "Predicting Business Success From Task Motivation and Attributional Style: A Longitudinal Study," *Entrepreneurship and Regional Development*, 7 (4): 349–63.

Bhattacharjee, A., Higson, C., Holly, S., and Kattuman, P. (2009), "Macroeconomic Instability and Business Exit: Determinants of Failures and Acquisitions of UK Firms," *Economica*, 76 (301): 108–31.

Blanchflower, D. G. and Oswald, A. J. (1998), "What Makes an Entrepreneur?", *Journal of Labor Economics*, 16 (1): 26–60.

Blanchflower, D. G., Oswald, A., and Stutzer, A. (2001), "Latent Entrepreneurship Across Nations," *European Economic Review*, 45 (4): 680–91.

Blomstrom, M. and Kokko, A. (1996), The Impact of Foreign Investment on Host Countries: A Review of the Empirical Evidence, World Bank Policy Research Working Paper 1745.

Boettke, P. and Coyne, C. J. (2003), "Entrepreneurship and Development: Cause or Consequence?," *Advances in Austrian Economics*, 6: 67–88.

Boettke, P. J. and Coyne, C. J. (2009), "Context Matters: Institutions and Entrepreneurship," *Foundations and Trends in Entrepreneurship*, 5 (3): 135–209.

Bosma, N., Jones, K., Autio, E., and Levie, J. (2008), *Global Entrepreneurship Monitor 2007 Executive Report*, Babson Park/London: Babson College/London Business School.

Bosma, N., Stam, E., and Schutjens, V. (2011), "Creative Destruction and Regional Productivity Growth; Evidence from the Dutch Manufacturing and Services Industries," *Small Business Economics*, 36 (4) forthcoming DOI: 10.1007/s11187-009-9257-8.

Davidsson, P. and Delmar, F. (2006), "High-growth Firms and their Contribution to Employment: The Case of Sweden 1987–96," in: P. Davidsson, F. Delmar, and J. Wiklund (eds.), *Entrepreneurship and the Growth of Firms*, Cheltenham, UK: Edward Elgar, 156–78.

Deschryvere, M. (2008), High Growth Firms and Job Creation in Finland, Discussion Paper 1144, The Research Institute of the Finnish Economy.

De Soto, H. (1989), *The other path: The invisible solution in the Third World*. London, UK: Tauris.

Djankov, S., La Porta, R., Lopez-de-Silanes, F., and Shleifer, A. (2002), "The Regulation of Entry," *Quarterly Journal of Economics*, 117 (1): 1–37.

Dorn, J. A. (2008), "China's March Toward the Market." in: B. Powell, (ed.), *Making Poor Nations Rich. Entrepreneurship and the Process of Economic Development*. Stanford, CA USA: Stanford University Press, 283–308.

EIM (2006), Entrepreneurship in the Netherlands, High Growth Enterprises: Running Fast but Still Keeping Control. Zoetermeer, NL: EIM.

EIM (2008), Internationale Benchmark Ondernemerschap 2008 (in Dutch). EIM Report A200809, Zoetermeer, NL: EIM.

EIM (2009a), Internationale Benchmark Ondernemerschap 2009 (in Dutch). EIM Report A200913, Zoetermeer, NL: EIM.

EIM (2009b), Internationale Benchmark Ondernemerschap 2009: Extra landen (in Dutch). EIM Report M200907, Zoetermeer, NL: EIM.

Eliasson, G., Johansson, D., and Taymaz, E. (2004) "Simulating the New Economy," *Structural Change and Economic Dynamics*, 15 (3): 289–314.

Fritsch, M. and Mueller, P. (2004), "The Effects of New Business Formation on Regional Development over Time," *Regional Studies*, 38 (8): 961–75.

Graham, C. (2005), "Insights on Development from the Economics of Happiness," *The World Bank Research Observer,* 20 (2): 201–31.

Grilo, I. and Thurik, R. (2008), "Determinants of Entrepreneurial Engagement Levels in Europe and the US," *Industrial and Corporate Change,* 17 (6): 1113–45.

Haleblian, J., Devers, C. E., McNamara, G., Carpenter, M. A., and Davison, R. B. (2009), "Taking Stock of What We Know About Mergers and Acquisitions: A Review and Research Agenda", *Journal of Management,* 35 (3): 469–502.

Hessels, J., van Gelderen, M., and Thurik, A. R. (2008), "Entrepreneurial Aspirations, Motivations and their Drivers", *Small Business Economics,* 31 (3): 323–39.

Hessels, J. and van Stel, A. (2008), Global Entrepreneurship Monitor and Entrepreneurs' Export Orientation, in: E.Congregado (ed.), *Measuring Entrepreneurship: Building a Statistical System (International Studies in Entrepreneurship series, Vol. 16),* New York, NY USA: Springer Science, 265–78.

Johnson, S. H., McMillan, J., and Woodruff, C. M. (2000), "Entrepreneurs and the Ordering of Institutional Reform: Poland, Slovakia, Romania, Russia and Ukraine Compared," *The Economics of Transition,* 8 (1): 1–36.

Koellinger, P. D. and Thurik, A. R. (2009), "Entrepreneurship and the Business Cycle, Tinbergen," Institute Discussion Paper T I09–032/3, Rotterdam, NL: Erasmus University Rotterdam.

Kolvereid, L. and Bullvag, E. (1996), "Growth Intentions and Actual Growth: The Impact of Entrepreneurial Choice," *Journal of Enterprising Culture,* 4 (1): 1–17.

Landes, D. S. (1998), *The Wealth and Poverty of Nations: Why Some Are So Rich and Some So Poor.* New York, NY USA: W.W. Norton.

Maksimovic, V. and Philips, G. (2001), "The Market for Corporate Assets: Who Engages in Mergers and Asset Sales and Are There Efficiency Gains?", *Journal of Finance,* 56 (6): 2019–65.

McArthur, J. W. and Sachs, J. D. (2002), "The Growth Competitiveness Index: Measuring Technological Advancement and the Stages of Development," in: M. E. Porter, J. D. Sachs, P. K. Cornelius, J. W. McArthur, and K. Schwab (eds.), *The Global Competitiveness Report 2001–2002,* New York, NY USA: Oxford University Press, 28–51.

Metcalfe, J. S. (2004), "The Entrepreneur and the Style of Modern Economics," *Journal of Evolutionary Economics,* 14 (2): 157–75.

Naudé, W. (2010), "Entrepreneurship, Developing Countries, and Development Economics: New Approaches and Insights," *Small Business Economics,* 34 (1): 1–12.

Nooteboom, B. (1994), "Innovation and Diffusion in Small Firms: Theory and Evidence," *Small Business Economics,* 6 (5): 327–47.

North, D. C. (1990), *Institutions, Institutional Change and Economic Performance.* Cambridge, UK: Cambridge University Press.

OECD (2006), *Understanding Entrepreneurship: Developing Indicators for International Comparisons and Assessments.* Paris, France: OECD.

Parker, S. C. (2009), *The Economics of Entrepreneurship* (2nd edition). Cambridge, UK: Cambridge University Press.

Powell, B. (2008), *Making Poor Nations Rich. Entrepreneurship and the Process of Economic Development.* Stanford, CA USA: Stanford University Press.

Reynolds, P. D., Camp, S. M., Bygrave, W. D., Autio, E., and Hay, M. (2001), *Global Entrepreneurship Monitor 2001 Executive Report*, Wellesley, MA USA: Babson College.

Reynolds, P., Bosma, N., Autio, E., Hunt, S., De Bono, N., Servais, I., Lopez-Garcia, P., and Chin, N. (2005), "Global Entrepreneurship Monitor: Data Collection Design and Implementation 1998–2003", *Small Business Economics*, 24(3): 205–31.

Rodrik, D. (2007), *One Economics Many Recipes. Globalization, Institutions, and Economic Growth*. Princeton, NJ USA: Princeton University Press.

Rosenberg, N. and Birdzell, L. (1986), *How the West Grew Rich*, New York, NY USA: Basic Books.

Schumpeter, J. A. (1934), *The Theory of Economic Development*, Cambridge, MA USA: Harvard University Press.

Stam, E. (2008), "Entrepreneurship and Innovation Policy," in: B. Nooteboom and E. Stam (eds.), *Micro-Foundations for Innovation Policy*, Amsterdam/Chicago: Amsterdam University Press/Chicago University Press, 135–72.

Stam, E., Suddle, K., Hessels, J., and van Stel, A. (2009), "High-Growth Entrepreneurs, Public Policies, and Economic Growth," in: J. Leitao and R. Baptista (eds.), *Public Policies for Fostering Entrepreneurship: A European Perspective (International Studies in Entrepreneurship series, Vol. 22)*, New York, NY USA: Springer Science, 91–110.

Stam, E. and Wennberg, K. (2009), "The Roles of R&D in New Firm Growth," *Small Business Economics*, 33 (1): 77–89.

Thurik, A. R., Carree, M. A., van Stel, A., and Audretsch, D. B. (2008), "Does Self-employment Reduce Unemployment?", *Journal of Business Venturing* 23 (6): 673–86.

Thurik, A. R. and Wennekers, A. R. M. (2004), "Entrepreneurship, Small Business and Economic Growth," *Journal of Small Business and Enterprise Development*, 11 (1): 140–9.

Valliere, D. and Peterson, R. (2009), "Entrepreneurship and Economic Growth: Evidence from Emerging and Developed Countries," *Entrepreneurship & Regional Development*, 21 (5–6): 459–80.

van Stel, A., Carree, M., and Thurik, A. R. (2005), "The Effect of Entrepreneurial Activity on National Economic Growth", *Small Business Economics*, 24 (3): 311–21.

Verheul, I. and van Stel, A. (2007), *Entrepreneurial Diversity and Economic Growth*, EIM Research Report H200701, Zoetermeer, NL: EIM.

Wennekers, A. R. M. (2006), *Entrepreneurship at country level; Economic and noneconomic determinants*. Rotterdam: ERIM Ph.D. Series Research in Management, Erasmus University Rotterdam.

Wennekers, A. R. M. and Thurik, A. R. (1999), "Linking Entrepreneurship and Economic Growth," *Small Business Economics*, 13 (1): 27–55.

Wiklund, J. and Shepherd, D. (2003), "Aspiring for, and Achieving Growth: The Moderating Role of Resources and Opportunities," *Journal of Management Studies*, 40 (8): 1919–41.

Wong, P., Ho, Y., and Autio, E. (2005), "Entrepreneurship, Innovation and Economic Growth: Evidence from GEM data," *Small Business Economics*, 24 (3): 335–50.

11

High-Aspiration Entrepreneurship

Erkko Autio

11.1 Introduction

The few times economic theorists have considered entrepreneurship explicitly, they have treated all entrepreneurs as a cohesive group (Kirzner 1997; Schumpeter 1996; Von Mises 1949). Typically, these theories have emphasized the role of entrepreneurs as agents of innovation and as facilitators of the market process. In such treatments, entrepreneurs operate as alert and innovating individuals who spot opportunities, pursue them, take risks, and by so doing contribute to economic dynamism. The picture emerging from wide population surveys of entrepreneurs is somewhat different. In the Global Entrepreneurship Monitor (GEM) surveys, for example, the majority of entrepreneurs are not very innovative, risk-taking, or growth-oriented. Some one third of all entrepreneurs in fact do not seek to employ any individuals beyond themselves. In light of such observations, the majority of entrepreneurial activity appears to fit poorly with the profile of entrepreneurs inferred from economic theories. This suggests that the bulk of entrepreneurial activity may actually not be that relevant for economic growth.

While the apparent gap between what entrepreneurs are, at least implicitly, thought to do, and what most entrepreneurs actually do is not a novel insight, it nevertheless suggests that a more nuanced view of the entrepreneurial process might be called for. If only a small proportion of all entrepreneurs appear to be performing in the roles assigned to them by economic theories of entrepreneurship, it may make sense to analyze only this sub-group instead of analyzing all entrepreneurs as one group, regardless of their growth orientation. In other words, there is reason to suspect that certain sub-facets of entrepreneurial activity, such as high-aspiration entrepreneurship, might provide (from a macroeconomic perspective) a more relevant country-level benchmark for analysis than would the overall rate of entrepreneurial activity within nations.

In this chapter, we seek to provide a more nuanced perspective of the entrepreneurial process by focusing specifically on high-aspiration entrepreneurial activity. We define high-aspiration entrepreneurial activity as entrepreneurial start-ups that exhibit an aspiration to rapidly grow their employment size. Previous GEM surveys suggest that while high-aspiration entrepreneurship only represents less than ten percent of the overall entrepreneurial process, they nevertheless account for more than seventy percent of the expected employment generation by all entrepreneurial firms. Furthermore, it is often argued that aspiration is a necessary, and valid, precondition for entrepreneurial growth (Krueger, Reilly, and Carsrud 2000; Rauch et al. 2009; Wiklund and Davidsson 2003). We pursue three specific objectives: First, we analyze and describe the variance across nations in terms of high-aspiration entrepreneurship. Second, we explore influences on high-aspiration entrepreneurship at the country level. Third, we analyze individual- and country-level determinants of individual-level selection into high-aspiration entrepreneurship.

11.2 Economic impacts of entrepreneurial activity

There is widespread agreement that entrepreneurship is an important economic and social phenomenon, although dedicated theories regarding the macro-level effects of entrepreneurship remain elusive. Since late 1970s, new firms have been seen as an important source of new jobs (Acs and Audretsch 1987; Birch 1979; Fölster 2000; Storey 1994). There are also persistent arguments that new firms make a positive contribution toward the economy because of their contribution toward a more efficient resource allocation in the economy (van Praag 2007). Finally, numerous studies suggest that new firms can have an important role to play in innovation in selected sectors (Audretsch and Acs 1991; Michelacci 2003). Thus, the economic contributions of entrepreneurship are widely accepted. Of course, from the perspective of public policy, arguably the most important aspect of new firms concerns their contributions to job creation and job stability.

Perhaps the most influential single finding regarding the potency of new firms in job creation was reported by Birch (1979). Birch reported that new firms accounted for the bulk of new job creation in the USA, while large, established firms were net destroyers of jobs during the period studied. Although Birch's findings have been the subject of significant subsequent debate and refinement, the core finding appears robust across time periods and national contexts (Davidsson, Lindmark, and Olofsson 1998; Delmar, Davidsson, and Gartner 2003; Kirchhoff 1994; Picot and Dupuy 1998). According to these studies, and depending on the phase of the economic cycle, new firms may be responsible for anything from one third up to the totality of net job creation. Although many new firms are created as a result of industrial downsizing and re-organization, thus representing job migration rather than genuine job creation, there also seems to be wide agreement that the genuine job creation potential of new firms is significant (van Praag 2007). Even when accounting for the dynamic character of new firms, particularly their high mortality rates (Aghion and Howitt 1992), the net effect appears to remain positive. Fölster (2000) found that every self-employment decision meant the net creation of 1.3 new jobs in Sweden, after the effects of various intervening mechanisms were controlled. According to the Longitudinal Establishment and Enterprise Microdata (LEEM) database, new establishments created sixty-nine percent of net new jobs in the US from 1990 to 1995, and new firm start-ups which did not exist prior to 1990 created twenty-two percent of new jobs (Audretsch 2002). Combined, these studies can be regarded as evidence that entrepreneurs indeed have an important role to play in job creation.

A closer look reveals a more nuanced picture, however. Although entrepreneurs as a group appear important for job creation, this potential is not evenly distributed within populations of new firms. Numerous studies suggest that only a relatively small proportion of all new firms are responsible for creating the majority of new jobs. Storey (1994) found that only four percent of new firms born in any given year accounted for fifty percent of all the jobs created by the surviving firms within that cohort after ten years. Kirchhoff (1994) found that the ten percent of fastest-growing firms contributed up to three quarters of new jobs during an eight-year observation period within a cohort of firms started in the US in 1978. According to Birch et al. (1997), "gazelles" accounted for more than seventy percent of the employment growth in the US between 1992 and 1996, while representing only about three percent of the firm population. Analyses of the GEM data suggest that some ten percent of all nascent and new entrepreneurs aspire to create some seventy percent of all expected jobs by nascent and new entrepreneurs. Summarizing, various studies suggest that only less than ten percent of all new firms may be responsible for anything between fifty percent and seventy-five percent of all new jobs by new firms. These findings underline the need for a more nuanced approach seeking to uncover the job-generation power of entrepreneurship.

While the empirical evidence on overall job creation potential is quite broad, studies on how this potential is distributed within populations of entrepreneurial firms are quite rare. This is because of the very rarity of the high-growth phenomenon, and because of the lack of datasets suitable for the study of firm-level job-creation contributions. Because only a small fraction of all new companies aim for rapid growth, and because entrepreneurial activity, in general, can be typically observed only in a small subset of adult-age

population, studying this phenomenon empirically can be prohibitively difficult. To date, most studies on the phenomenon are ex post studies, which look
at entrepreneurial activity only after the results of this activity are known: we
already know whether a given venture grew or not. There is very little empirical research on ex ante growth aspirations: who aspires for and expects rapid
growth, and what factors are associated with such expectations.

From a policymaker's perspective, the above dilemma is not without consequence. To design effective measures to support job creation through the
entrepreneurial process, empirical data are required, pertaining to the time
both before and after firm-level growth processes have occurred. The scarcity
of received empirical findings, particularly on growth expectations, thus constitutes a serious constraint to the design of effective job creation policies. The
limitation of individual datasets to individual countries has precluded any
systematic examination of the potential effect of the country environment on
the prevalence of high-expectation entrepreneurship. Given the pertinence of
new high-growth firms to job creation and the high priority of employment
for government economic policies, more empirical research on the high-
expectation entrepreneurial phenomenon is urgently required.

11.3 GEM data

The GEM dataset offers a unique platform to analyze high-aspiration entrepreneurial activity within countries (Reynolds, Bosma, and Autio 2005). To our
knowledge, the GEM dataset is the only available dataset that offers extensive
individual-level data on entrepreneurial behaviors, attitudes and aspirations
in standardized form across a wide range of countries and over an extended
time period. An additional valuable aspect of GEM data is their time series
character, which permits cross-sectional time series analysis in panel form. For
the period from 2000 to 2008, the GEM dataset comprises over 900,000 interviews of adult-age individuals in more than sixty countries.

Even with a large cross-country dataset such as the GEM dataset, the analysis of high-aspiration entrepreneurial activity is tricky. In most GEM countries,
the early-stage entrepreneurial activity (TEA) rate, which represents the combined share of nascent entrepreneurs and new business managers of working-
age population (18–64 years), varies from a low of approximately two percent
to a high of up to thirty percent. High-aspiration entrepreneurial activity
represents only a small subset of the TEA rate—typically, only approximately
ten percent of the total entrepreneurial activity, which translates into less
than one percent of all adult-age individuals surveyed. Because of the rarity
of the high-aspiration entrepreneurial phenomenon, very large datasets per
country or region are required in order to estimate the prevalence of high-

expectation activity with a reasonable degree of accuracy. The standard data collection protocol of GEM requires at least 2,000 interviews annually for each participating country. This is a large enough sample if one is interested in estimating the overall TEA rate. However, because of the large standard errors due to the scarcity of the high-aspiration entrepreneurship phenomenon, assessments of high-expectation entrepreneurial activity require much larger sample sizes. This is achieved by combining several years of data from a given country. In the descriptive analyses below, we use combined GEM data from years 2000 to 2008 to describe the level of high-aspiration entrepreneurial activity across the countries in our sample.

GEM measures three types of entrepreneurial activity according to how mature the start-up attempt is. *Nascent entrepreneurs* are individuals who are still in the process of trying to launch a new start-up company. Nascent entrepreneurs are individuals who have done something tangible over the past twelve months to start the new company, who would manage and own at least part of the company, and who have not paid salaries for more than three months. *New entrepreneurs* are individuals who meet the above criteria, except that their companies have already paid salaries for more than three months and up to forty-two months. *Established entrepreneurs* have paid salaries for longer than forty-two months. Our analyses of both individual- and country-level entrepreneurial activity focus on early-stage entrepreneurs, i.e., individuals who qualify as either nascent or new entrepreneurs. Furthermore, in this chapter, we are interested in high-aspiration entrepreneurs. To qualify as a high-aspiration early-stage entrepreneur, the individual needs to expect to employ more than twenty employees in five years' time.

11.4 Prevalence of high-aspiration entrepreneurship in different countries

Since earlier analyses of GEM data indicate significant variance in the base levels of entrepreneurship across countries according to their level of economic development (Bosma et al. 2009), we divided the countries into two groups: those with per-capita gross domestic product (GDP) in purchasing power parity (PPP) greater than US$20.000 and those with per-capita GDP below this threshold level. We also combined all individual-level data across each country from year 2000 to 2008. Figures 11.1 and 11.2 show the prevalence levels of early-stage entrepreneurs as a percentage of the adult-age population (TEA rates) for high-income countries and for low- and middle-income countries respectively. The vertical bars indicate ninety-five percent confidence intervals, the width of these being primarily a function of the sample size for each country.

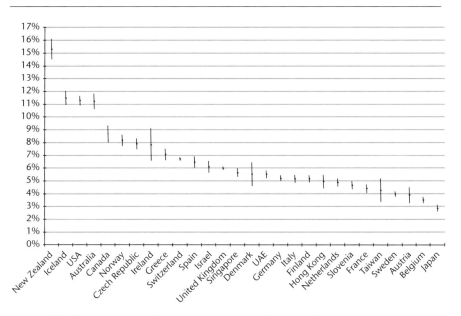

Figure 11.1 Prevalence of early-stage entrepreneurship in high-income economies

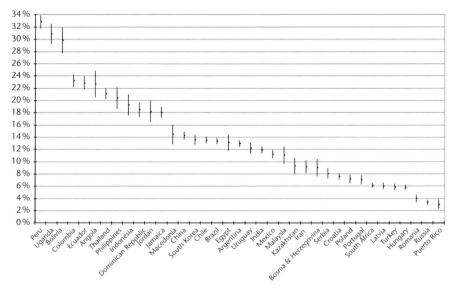

Figure 11.2 Prevalence of early-stage entrepreneurs in low-income economies

Prevalence levels of early-stage entrepreneurship have been widely discussed elsewhere (e.g., Bosma et al. 2009; Minniti, Bygrave, and Autio 2006), thus, only a few summarizing observations are made here: First, the prevalence level of early-stage entrepreneurs tends to be higher in middle- to low-income countries than in high-income countries. Second, in each of the two groups, the variance across countries is very significant. Among the high-income countries, the difference between the most and least active countries is approximately four-fold, and among the low- to middle-income countries, the difference is nearly ten-fold. Third, with the exception of China, former centrally planned economies exhibit relatively low levels of early-stage entrepreneurial activity.

In contrast, Figures 11.3 and 11.4 show the levels of *high-aspiration* early-stage entrepreneurship across the same GEM countries. Overall, the general shape of the distributions is quite similar, with significant variance across countries in both income groups. In the group of high-income countries, the difference between the least and most active country is approximately five-fold. In the group of low- to middle-income countries, the difference between the least and most active country is approximately ten-fold. It is also noteworthy that among high-income countries, high-aspiration entrepreneurs represent approximately twelve percent of all identified early-stage entrepreneurs, whereas in low-income countries, they represent approximately seven percent.

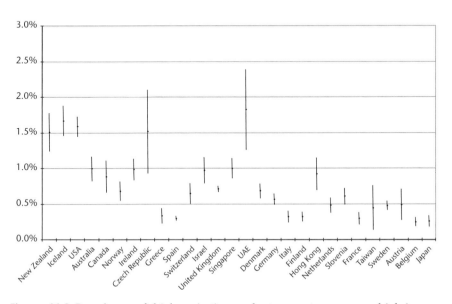

Figure 11.3 Prevalence of high-aspiration early-stage entrepreneurs—high-income economies

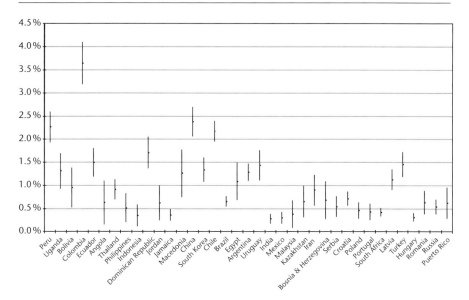

Figure 11.4 Prevalence of high-aspiration early-stage entrepreneurs—low-income economies

The correlations between the prevalence of high-aspiration entrepreneurs (HEA) and all early-stage entrepreneurs (TEA) are quite similar in both country groups. In high-income countries, the correlation between HEA and TEA is 0.67***. In middle- to low-income countries, the correlation is 0.42**. This suggests that the rank ordering of countries remains relatively stable. There exist a few noteworthy exceptions to this general rule, however. In Singapore, the prevalence rate of high-aspiration entrepreneurs is significantly higher relative to its overall prevalence of early-stage entrepreneurs. In Spain and Greece, instead, the prevalence rate of high-aspiration entrepreneurs is significantly lower relative to their overall prevalence of early-stage entrepreneurs.[1]

In summary, while the overall and high-aspiration prevalence rates of early-stage entrepreneurship are correlated at the country level, this correlation is not perfect. Some countries do significantly better in terms of high-aspiration entrepreneurship, relative to their base level of entrepreneurial activity, than do others. Overall, high-income countries exhibit relatively higher levels of

[1] A noteworthy comparison can be carried out between China and India. China's and India's overall rates of early-stage entrepreneurship are quite similar to one another: 14% for China and 11% for India. These rates rank China and India in the middle among the low-income country group. When considering high-aspiration entrepreneurship, however, the situation changes dramatically, with China raising to the second place with some 2.3% prevalence rate, and India falling to the bottom, with a 0.3% prevalence rate. This shift is consistent with anecdotal reports from India lamenting the stifling effect of India's regulatory framework on firm growth aspirations in that country.

high-aspiration activity, as compared to their base level, perhaps signaling the virtual absence of necessity-driven entrepreneurial activity. To understand better the country-level drivers of high-aspiration entrepreneurial activity, we next analyze them using a cross-sectional panel approach.

11.5 Country-level effects on high-aspiration entrepreneurship

In a country-level analysis, we are interested in basic country-level economic and demographic conditions as well as the effect of regulations on the prevalence rate of high-aspiration entrepreneurship.

When considering the effect of regulations, one pertinent question concerns the distinction between selection and behavioral effects: do regulations impact the prevalence rate of high-aspiration entrepreneurship by influencing who self-selects into entrepreneurship, or do regulations operate by influencing the behaviors of existing entrepreneurs? The difference between selection and behavioral effects is important for policy design purposes, as it is directly linked to the broader issue concerning resource allocation trade-offs associated with policy alternatives. If policies operate through their effect on selection rather than behavior, then alternative policies will influence the allocation of human resources to alternative uses in the economy. If, on the other hand, policies operate through their effect on the behavior of already existing entrepreneurs, then policies are less likely to impact the allocation of human resources into alternative uses. While important, the selection–behavior distinction is challenging to address empirically. We seek to address this question both in the country-level analyses as well as in the individual-level analyses. In the country-level analysis that follows, we address this question by separately analyzing influences on high-aspiration nascent entrepreneurship (i.e., individuals who are seeking to start a company but have not yet done so) and on high-aspiration new entrepreneurship (i.e., individuals currently owner-managing a business that is less than forty-two months old).

11.5.1 *Dependent variables*

We perform the same analysis on five different dependent variables. The country-level prevalence rate of early-stage entrepreneurs (TEA) informs us of the adult-population prevalence of either nascent or new entrepreneurs in a given country. The country-level prevalence rate of high-aspiration early-stage entrepreneurs, HEA, represents a subset of people in TEA that expect to employ twenty or more individuals within five years' time. The ratio between HEA and TEA (rHEA) indicates the relative prevalence of high-aspiration entrepreneurs within a given country's population of early-stage entrepreneurs.

Finally, to address the selection issue, we also analyze influences on high-aspiration nascent entrepreneurs and high-aspiration new entrepreneurs.

11.5.2 *Independent variables*

As independent variables, we use GDP per capita (in purchasing power parity [PPP] terms in international dollars). This data was obtained from the International Monetary Fund (IMF) datasets. The squared term of GDP (PPP) per capita is also introduced into the equation to capture any non-linear effects. Because high-aspiration entrepreneurship in particular may react to the prevailing economic climate, we also introduced lagged GDP change, with one year time lag. As demographic variables, we use population size and population growth rate, both variables again sourced from the IMF. Population growth rate provides a proxy of the expansion of domestic markets. To control the effect of industry structure on the prevalence rate of entrepreneurial activity (different industries having different minimum economic scales), we use GEM's adult-population rate of established entrepreneurship in the country. We also included a dummy for transition economies (i.e., former centrally planned economies) to account for the specific conditions in such countries often characterized by an extensive and scale-intensive industrial base and an underdeveloped service sector.

To account for prevailing regulatory conditions within the country, we use two measures both sourced from the World Bank's Ease of Doing Business (EDB) datasets. The EDB Difficulty of Firing index provides a measure of how difficult it is to terminate employment in a given country. Countries with greater difficulty of firing might exhibit lower levels of entrepreneurial growth aspirations, since entrepreneurs recognizing this difficulty might become more conservative in their hiring decisions. The EDB Cost of Starting a Business indicator measures the typical expense, indicated as percentage of the GDP per capita, associated with paperwork, licenses, and other expenditures incurred when starting a new company.

11.5.3 *Method and results*

Our data is cross-sectional country-level panel data, with a relatively short and broad structure, and an often incomplete time series for individual countries. A limitation of the EDB data is that it only spans years from 2004 to 2009, thus limiting our analysis to years from 2004 to 2008. Consequently, we employed panel regression techniques that allow data to be clustered around individual countries. All predictors were introduced as random effects, and numerous checks were carried out to make sure that the patterns reported below are robust. The regressions for TEA, HEA, and rHEA are shown in Table 11.1.

Table 11.1. Effects on country-level early-stage entrepreneurship

	TEA	HEA	rHEA
GDP per capita (ppp)	−3.07E-06***	−8.74E-08	7.28E-07
GDP per capita (squared)	8.88E-11***	6.45E-12	−1.08E-11
GDP change (t-1)	0.001313	0.000853***	0.003253+
Population size, millions	−2.12E-11	2.62E-12	3.18E-12
Population growth, %	0.273523	0.008225	0.005066
Established entrepreneurship prevalence rate	0.514404***	0.009899	−0.184412+
Difficulty of firing (index)	−0.00038	−8.98E-05*	−0.000669**
Cost of starting a business (% GDP per cap)	3.74E-05	−3.81E-06	−5.86E-05
Transition country (1=yes)	−0.029606+	−0.001324	0.023209
_cons	0.122585***	0.007744*	0.081935***
R2 (within)	0.070	0.032	0.001
R2 (between)	0.738	0.353	0.419
R2 (overall)	0.633	0.329	0.231
Number of obs	165	164	165
Obs per group	3.2	3.2	3.2
Prob > chi2	0.0000	0.0000	0.0000

GLS coefficients
*** $p < 0.001$,
** $p < 0.01$,
* $p < 0.05$,
+ $p < 0.10$, 2-tailed significances

Generalized least squares (GLS) regressions are shown with 2-tailed significances. Regarding influences on TEA, we observe a non-linear relationship with GDP (PPP) per capita, with higher levels of early-stage entrepreneurial activity observed for countries with low levels of GDP per capita. Also the prevalence rate of established entrepreneurs, the proxy for industry structure, shows a significant positive association with TEA. Transition economies exhibit lower levels of TEA than other countries.

Looking at high-aspiration early-stage entrepreneurship, as well as the relative prevalence of high-aspiration entrepreneurs in the entrepreneurial population, we observe a positive association with GDP change in the previous year. This suggests that entrepreneurs react to favorable economic conditions by raising their employment expectations. However, no association is observed with the general level of economic wealth in the country. Regarding regulatory conditions, we observe a negative and significant effect of the difficulty of firing: The more difficult it is to terminate employment relationships, the lower the job growth expectations exhibited by early-stage entrepreneurs. This association is particularly significant for rHEA, suggesting a positive behavioral effect. On the other hand, the cost of starting a business does not appear associated with any of the entrepreneurship prevalence indices.

The same effects for high-aspiration nascent and new entrepreneurship prevalence rates are shown in Table 11.2. Again, both indices are associated positively with GDP changes in the previous year. Looking at the effect of the difficulty of firing, a negative, and significant, relationship is found for the prevalence rate of high-aspiration new entrepreneurs. However, no significant association is observed for the prevalence rate of high-aspiration nascent entrepreneurs. This pattern again suggests a possible behavioral effect of this regulatory condition, although it cannot be ruled out that it might result from high-aspiration nascent entrepreneurs being less likely than low-aspiration nascent entrepreneurs to eventually launch their business. It is interesting that the cost of starting a business is not flagged as a significant effect on any of the entrepreneurship indicators. Particularly for TEA, a negative relationship might have been expected. A possible reason for the absence of this effect might be that the TEA index captures all kinds of start-up activity, even self-employment and informal ones, and such an activity would be less sensitive to the stringency of regulatory requirements imposed upon formal incorporations.

Overall, our analysis suggests that the rates of early-stage entrepreneurial activity are associated with prevailing economic and regulatory conditions in expected ways. The strong negative association between TEA and GDP per capita suggests that entrepreneurship is likely to be quite a different phenomenon in high- and low-income countries. This might have implications for if and how entrepreneurship contributes to economic growth. Our analysis also

Table 11.2. Effects on high-aspiration nascent and new entrepreneurship

	Nascent	New
GDP per capita (ppp)	−6.42E-08	−2.33E-08
GDP per capita (squared)	2.98E-12	2.76E-12
GDP change (t-1)	0.000574**	0.000389**
Population size, millions	−4.07E-13	3.15E-12
Population growth, %	0.024874	−0.022363
Established entrepreneurship prevalence rate	0.004679	0.007181
Difficulty of firing (index)	−3.19E-05	−5.75E-05**
Cost of starting a business (% GDP per cap)	−8.59E-06	3.84E-06
Transition country (1=yes)	−0.000289	−0.001571
_cons	0.004077*	0.003486*
R2 (within)	0.015	0.050
R2 (between)	0.307	0.343
R2 (overall)	0.273	0.294
Number of obs	164	164
Obs per group	3.2	3.2
Prob > chi2	0.0000	0.0000

*** $p < 0.001$,
** $p < 0.01$,
* $p < 0.05$,
+ $p < 0.10$, 2-tailed significances

indicates that regulatory conditions matter as well, particularly for high-aspiration entrepreneurship. Although we have studied only two of numerous alternative framework conditions, the association with the difficulty of firing emerges as robust against alternative dependent variables and alternative equation specifications. The patters observed were also more consistent with the notion of a behavioral effect than of a selection effect, although the latter cannot be ruled out. In the following section we pursue a more detailed analysis using individual-level data.

11.6 Individual-level effects on high-aspiration entrepreneurship

From an individual's perspective, the decision to start a new company is a major, strategic decision that involves significant trade-offs (Cassar 2007). Most of these trade-offs arise from the fact that the human and social capital possessed by individuals is non-alienable and non-tradable. Thus, human capital allocated into one use, such as starting a company, cannot be simultaneously allocated to another use, such as pursuing a career in employment. Because of such trade-offs, it is "... improbable that entrepreneurship can be explained solely by reference to a characteristic of certain people independent of the situations in which they find themselves" (Shane and Venkataraman 2000: 218). Thus, to fully understand why some individuals and not others choose to pursue entrepreneurial growth, it is important to consider not only individual-level characteristics, but also, the context within which those characteristics influence entrepreneurial behaviors (Busenitz et al. 2003; Davidsson and Wiklund 2001; Phan 2004).

The pursuit of growth is a fundamental aspect of strategic entrepreneurship (Davidsson, Delmar, and Wiklund 2002; Ireland, Hitt, and Sirmon 2003; Lumpkin and Dess 1996). Although there exists an extensive literature that studies entrepreneurship as an occupational choice (Blanchflower and Oswald 1998; Dunn and Holtz-Eakin 2000; Evans and Jovanovic 1989; Hellmann 2007; Lazear 2005), much less has been said about the choice to aspire for growth, once the entry decision has been made (Cassar 2006; Davidsson 1989; Wiklund and Davidsson 2003; Wiklund and Shepherd 2003). In this chapter, we consider both individual-level and contextual determinants of the decision to pursue a high-aspiration entrepreneurial firm. The determinants of greatest interest at the individual level have to do with an individual's human and financial capital. For nascent and new ventures, the entrepreneur's human capital constitutes arguably the single most important initial resource endowment (Shrader and Siegel 2007; Wright et al. 2007). Education represents a key aspect of human capital (Bosma et al. 2004; Cooper, Gimeno-Gascon, and Woo 1994; Ucbasaran, Westhead, and Wright 2008). Education enhances an individual's cognitive abilities, thereby enabling them to better recognize opportunities, as well as to manage the complexities involved with the start-up process (Shane and Venkataraman 2000). Through the process of obtaining formal education, individuals may acquire valuable social capital and contacts that can be leveraged to mobilize resources for the pursuit of entrepreneurial opportunities (Gerber and Cheung 2008; Stevens, Armstrong, and Arum 2008). All these arguments lead us to expect that education should be positively associated with the likelihood that an individual qualifies as a high-aspiration early-stage entrepreneur.

The skill-enhancing effects of education should influence entrepreneurial growth aspirations through their effect on entrepreneurs' behaviors: highly educated entrepreneurs will recognize more opportunities, will be better equipped to pursue opportunities and manage organizational complexities, and should possess social capital necessary to access resources for entrepreneurial growth. In addition, we also propose that education should operate on the self-selection of individuals into high-aspiration entrepreneurship because of the trade-offs discussed above: Due to their high opportunity costs, highly educated individuals should be more choosy about which opportunities they pursue, and therefore, be more likely to qualify as high-aspiration entrepreneurs.

The financial resources available to an individual constitute another important determinant of their entrepreneurial growth aspirations. Entrepreneurs require financial resources to discover and pursue entrepreneurial opportunities. Empirical surveys suggest that founders' own capital inputs, combined with those obtained from family and friends, constitute by far the most important source of financial resources for new and aspiring ventures (Minniti et al. 2006). In addition to providing for more significant opportunity creation and pursuit, high-income households are also likely to see more entrepreneurial growth opportunities (Dunn and Holtz-Eakin 2000). We therefore expect an individual's household income to be positively associated with the likelihood that they qualify as a high-aspiration early-stage entrepreneur.

Finally, in addition to an individual's human and social capital, the decision to pursue growth ventures should be subject to contextual influences. Because of the significant opportunity costs involved, individuals will carefully consider their likelihood of success. An important consideration concerns the regulatory regime to which the new venture will be subjected. Consistent with our country-level analysis, we expect the cost of starting a new business, as well as the difficulty of terminating employment relationships, to exercise a negative influence on entrepreneurial activity in general and high-aspiration entrepreneurial activity in particular.

11.6.1 *Method*

Analyzing entrepreneurial growth aspirations poses methodological chal-lenges, as entrepreneurial growth aspirations can be observed only for those individuals who first self-select as nascent or new entrepreneurs. This self-selection, if not controlled for, may bias results. To control for the self-selec-tion, we employ the Heckman method and compute an inverse Mill's ratio on an equation that predicts the status of individuals as early-stage entrepreneurs. This ratio is then used to control for any selection effects.

In our analysis, a further complication emerges because we expect growth aspirations to be influenced by both individual-level and country-level factors. As a result, multi-level techniques are required for our analysis. Specifically, since the self-selection of individuals into entrepreneurship is likely to be also affected by contextual factors, we allow for clustered error terms in both the selection and the evaluation equations.

11.6.2 *Dependent variables*

The status of an individual as either nascent or new entrepreneur (being part of TEA) is used as dependent variable in the selection equation. Status as a high-aspiration early-stage entrepreneur (individuals who qualify as early-stage entrepreneurs and expect to employ twenty or more employees in five years' time) is instead used in the evaluation equation.

11.6.3 *Independent variables*

We evaluate two equations, the selection equation and the evaluation equa-tion. In both equations, individual and country-level variables are both used. At the individual level, we control for an individual's age in years, squared term of age, and gender (1 = male). Our predictor variables of interest are education (3 levels) and household income (3 levels). Additionally, in the selection equation, we use three dummy variables from the GEM dataset. First, we control whether the individual personally knows people who have started new firms (1 = yes). Second, we control whether the individual believes to possess sufficient skills to successfully start a new company (1 = yes). Third, we control whether the individual believes that fear of failure would prevent him from starting a new business (1 = yes).

Our country-level variables include the country's GDP (PPP) per capita, the squared term of the same, and GDP change. In the selection equation, we also control for the cost of starting a business, indicated as percentage of GDP per capita. Finally, in the evaluation equation, we additionally use the difficulty of firing index.

11.6.4 *Analysis and results*

In the selection equation, we look at what variables are associated with an individual being an early-stage entrepreneur. Data are grouped by year and country and cover the period 2004–8, since the World Bank Ease of Doing Business data are available only from year 2004 onwards. In total the analysis covers 336,586 (unweighted) individuals in fifty-three countries, and it is grouped into 173 year-country clusters. Because we have individual and country-level predictors, the selection equation was evaluated as mixed-effects logit in which country-level variables were introduced as fixed effects. Results are shown in Table 11.3.

All individual-level predictors exhibit very statistically significant associations with TEA. An individual's age and the squared term of age are negatively associated with TEA, as is gender, indicating that men are significantly more likely to qualify as early-stage entrepreneurs than women. Both education and household income are positively associated with TEA. TEA is also statistically significantly associated with an individual's exposure to other entrepreneurs, the perception of their own skills, and negatively associated to their fear of failure. Finally, TEA status is also significantly and negatively associated with GDP per capita. None of the other country-level variables is associated with TEA.

In the second stage, we look at what variables are associated to high-aspiration TEA within the population of early-stage entrepreneurs. The high-aspiration TEA dummy was used to indicate whether a given early-stage entrepreneur exhibited high-growth aspirations (1 = yes). In the evaluation equation, the same predictors were used as in the selection equation, with the exception that the GEM instruments were removed from the equation (i.e., knowing other entrepreneurs, perception of one's own skills and fear of failure). In addition, the inverse Mill's ratio, computed from the selection equation, was added into the evaluation equation, as well as the World Bank Difficulty of Firing index (a country-level variable). As in the case of the selection equation, the evaluation equation was analyzed using mixed-effects logistic regression, with all country-level predictors introduced as fixed effects. The results are shown in Table 11.4.

In the evaluation equation, once selection is controlled for, age is no longer shown as a significant direct influence on high-aspiration TEA. The squared term of age remains significant, indicating that both younger and older individuals are more likely to qualify as high-aspiration early-stage entrepreneurs. A significant association is observed for gender, with men remaining more likely than women to qualify as high-aspiration early-stage entrepreneurs.

Table 11.3. Mixed-effects logit on individual-level TEA

Mixed-effects logistic regression		Number of obs			336586
Group variable: year_country		Number of groups			173
		Obs per group: min			275
		avg			1945.6
		max			22249
Integration points = 1					
Log likelihood = −94901.631		Prob > chi2			0.0000

TEA (1=early-stage entrepreneur)	Coef.	Std. Err.	z	[95% Conf. Interval]	
Age	−0.01509	0.00056	−27.17***	−0.01618	−0.01400
Age (squared)	−0.00126	0.00004	−28.75***	−0.00134	−0.00117
Gender (0 = female)	−0.21492	0.01241	−17.31***	−0.23925	−0.19059
Education (3 levels)	0.01980	0.00593	3.34***	0.00817	0.03143
Household income (3 levels)	0.07091	0.00839	8.45***	0.05446	0.08735
Know entrepreneurs? (1=yes)	0.61807	0.01284	48.12***	0.59289	0.64324
Perception of skills (1=yes)	1.59536	0.01703	93.67***	1.56198	1.62874
Fear of failure (1=yes)	−0.41707	0.01384	−30.14***	−0.44420	−0.38995
GDP per capita (ppp)	−1.3E-05	3.6E-06	−3.54***	−1.97E-05	−5.67E-06
GDP per capita (squared)	1.2E-10	7.8E-11	1.47	−3.77E-11	2.67E-10
GDP change	0.02032	0.01813	1.12	−0.01522	0.05587
Cost of starting a business	0.00035	0.00140	0.25	−0.00240	0.00310
_cons	−2.35151	0.15933	−14.76***	−2.66378	−2.03923

Random-effects parameters year_country: identity				Estimate	Std. Err.
	sd (_cons)			0.4962145	0.0281023

| LR test vs. logistic regression: | chibar2(01) = 5324.36 | | | Prob>chibar2 = 0.0000 | |

Table 11.4. Variables influencing high-aspiration TEA

Mixed-effects logistic regression			
Group variable: year_country	Number of obs	35308	
	Number of groups	173	
	Obs per group: min	16	
	avg	204.1	
	max	1724	
Integration points = 1			
Log likelihood = −9955.2269	Prob > chi2	0.0000	

High-aspiration TEA (1=yes)	Coef.	Std. Err.	z	[95% Conf. Interval]	
Age	−0.0022719	0.001881	−1.21	−0.005958	0.0014142
Age (squared)	0.0004721	0.000152	3.11**	0.0001747	0.0007696
Gender (0 = female)	−0.4756849	0.043961	−10.82***	−0.561846	−0.3895236
Education (3 levels)	0.1719001	0.018635	9.22***	0.1353772	0.208423
Household income (3 levels)	0.4224151	0.028185	14.99***	0.3671742	0.477656
GDP per capita (ppp)	0.0000223	4.73E-06	4.71***	0.000013	0.0000316
GDP per capita (squared)	−4.28E-11	1.03E-10	−0.42	−2.44E-10	1.59E-10
GDP change	0.1187268	0.023537	5.04***	0.0725951	0.1648584
Difficulty of firing	−0.0068488	0.002497	−2.74**	−0.011743	−0.0019548
Cost of starting a business	0.0008401	0.001993	0.42	−0.003C66	0.0047458
Inverse Mill's ratio	−0.2936159	0.036775	−7.98***	−0.365693	−0.2215392
_cons	−3.329698	0.253174	−13.15***	−3.825911	−2.833486

Random-effects parameters year–country: identity					
sd(_cons)				Estimate	Std. Err.
				0.5702069	0.0420858

LR test vs logistic regression: chibar2(01) = 547.52 Prob>chibar2 = 0.0000

Among individual-level variables, both education and household income continue to exhibit significant, positive influences on high-aspiration TEA, even after the selection is controlled for. Among country-level variables, instead, GDP per capita exhibits a statistically significant positive association with high-aspiration TEA, as does GDP change. The squared term of GDP per capita does not exhibit significant influences. Also, the inverse Mill's ratio exhibits a significant, negative influence on high-aspiration TEA. This suggests that unobserved variables influence individuals' selection into entrepreneurship, and that those influences are also negatively associated with high-aspiration TEA.

Finally, the Difficulty of Firing index exhibits a significant, negative association with high-aspiration TEA, whereas no association is observed for the Cost of Starting a Business variable. The significant influence of the Difficulty of Firing index suggests that Difficulty of Firing exercises a significant, negative influence on high-aspiration TEA above and beyond its effect on the self-selection of individuals into entrepreneurship. Combined with the country-level analysis, this result suggests that difficulty of hiring dampens entrepreneurial growth aspirations because of its effect on the growth aspirations of entrepreneurs, rather than its effect on the self-selection of individuals into entrepreneurship.

11.7 Discussion

This chapter is based on the assumption that entrepreneurship is important for economic development, and that this is particularly true for high-aspiration entrepreneurship. In our analysis, we have sought to contribute to test whether this is true, as well as examine the effect of country-level institutional conditions (notably, regulations that constrain and facilitate entrepreneurial behaviors) on high-aspiration entrepreneurial behaviors.

Thus far, most tests of the relationship between high-aspiration entrepreneurship and economic development have remained descriptive and based on cross-sectional correlation tests. These limitations have been mainly due to the scarcity of longitudinal data, both at the individual and country levels (Levie and Autio 2008; Levie and Autio, In Press). To our knowledge, GEM data are the only ones that provide an explicit, internationally comparable measure of individual-level growth aspirations, both before and after the creation of the start-up. This makes GEM data unique among indicators of economic activity. Unfortunately, up to date, even tests using GEM data have been limited to cross-section designs because of the relatively short history of the GEM project (Bowen and De Clercq 2008; Wong, Ho, and Autio 2005). In this chapter, we have sought to move beyond cross-sectional correlation type studies with the goal to provide a more robust examination of the relationship between country-level institutional conditions and high-aspiration entrepreneurial behaviors. In our design, we were able to combine five years of country-level GEM data with data obtained from the World Bank's Ease of Doing Business project and analyze the influence of the regulatory environment on the adult-population prevalence rate of high-aspiration entrepreneurs. Even with this relatively short panel design, several findings of interest emerged.

First, and relevant to our analysis, the World Bank's Difficulty of Firing index was found to be negatively associated with the prevalence rate (both absolute and relative) of high-aspiration entrepreneurs, but not with the overall rate of nascent and new entrepreneurs in the population. This finding suggests that the regulatory framework in a given country exercises a non-trivial influence on entrepreneurial activity, as well as on entrepreneurs' growth aspirations. Although the finding is purely exploratory given the short time span of the panel, it is nevertheless noteworthy given the disproportional impact that high-aspiration entrepreneurs have on economic development. Interestingly, we did not observe a relationship between the Cost of Starting a Business and any of the different forms of entrepreneurial activity. This finding, if confirmed in subsequent studies, could imply that different types of regulation matter differently for different types of entrepreneurs. However, it could also mean that entry regulations, if rigid, could push a greater proportion of entrepreneurs into the "grey" economy, as they might avoid registering their ventures in order to reduce the cost of compliance (Levie and Autio, In Press). Unfortunately, GEM data do not permit us to examine this possibility, as they do not record the legal status of individual entrepreneurs.

Our results in Table 11.1 also suggest that high-aspiration entrepreneurship may be a lagging indicator of economic development. In this dataset, it appears that many high-aspiration entrepreneurs choose entrepreneurship as a response to perceived favorable conditions. Note, however, that the closer examination of temporal relationships was outside the scope of this analysis, and a closer examination might have revealed alternative types of temporal relationships. Our analysis in Table 11.1 also suggests that structural conditions matter for both the prevalence rate of entrepreneurial activity, as well as its structure. These interesting associations merit further examination in future inquiries.

In light of these findings, are high-aspiration entrepreneurs selected or are they made? In Table 11.2, we tested the effect of the Difficulty of Firing index separately on the prevalence rates of high-aspiration nascent and high-aspiration new entrepreneurs, respectively. The results showed that the index is negatively associated to the prevalence rate of high-aspiration new entrepreneurs, but not that of nascent entrepreneurs. This finding provides anecdotal evidence that difficulty of firing may influence the behaviors of individuals who have already selected into entrepreneurship, rather than influencing the entry of individuals into entrepreneurship.

Whereas one would not expect the difficulty of firing to significantly influence entrepreneurs' entry decisions, a link between this index and the growth aspirations of existing entrepreneurs seems entirely plausible. Nascent entrepreneurs would be naturally more concerned with problems associated with entrepreneurial entry, as well as problems associated with initial resource mobilization, rather than problems associated with shedding excess resources. However, the difficulty of terminating a new employment relationship rapidly becomes a concern when entrepreneurs actually start hiring people. This is when the resource commitment is made, and it would be natural for entrepreneurs, at that stage, to consider also the potential opportunity costs associated with employment decisions.

Again, no relationship was observed for the cost of starting a business and the prevalence rate of nascent high-aspiration entrepreneurship. Following the above reasoning, a negative association would have been expected. Although the relationship is indeed indicated as negative, it is not shown as statistically significant. However, here too, the overall pattern makes sense. For nascent entrepreneurs, the cost of starting a business is shown as negatively, although not statistically significantly, associated with nascent high-aspiration activity. For new high-aspiration activity, the relationship is shown as positive and non-significant. Given that high barriers to entry accord protection against competition amongst those who already have entered, this pattern appears reasonable, and it is left for further studies to examine whether longer time series will reveal a statistically significant association. Overall, the country-level analysis has highlighted interesting country-level institutional influences on the prevalence rate of high-growth entrepreneurship, suggesting that this is a worthwhile and important avenue to pursue in further research.

In addition to country-level data, we also sought to understand individual-level determinants of high-growth aspirations and took advantage of the clustered nature of GEM data to apply multi-level analysis techniques that allow the study of both individual- and country-level influences on individuals' growth aspirations. Although there have been numerous recent calls in the literature for the application of more robust, multilevel techniques to analyze entrepreneurial phenomena, the vast majority of empirical studies on entrepreneurial behaviors are limited to a single level of analysis (Davidsson, Delmar, and Wiklund 2002; Phan 2004). This is a serious shortcoming, as entrepreneurship clearly represents a type of economic behavior that is not only influenced by individual-centric factors (such as education, age, and employment status, for example), but also, by the institutional, social, and cultural settings in which the individual is embedded.

Within this context, Table 11.3 reports the results of the selection equation—a mixed-effects logit analysis that predicted the self-selection of individuals into entrepreneurship. As expected, we found age, gender, education, income, knowing other entrepreneurs, and perception of one's own skills to have a significant association with the probability that a given individual was identified as a new entrepreneur in the GEM dataset. Interestingly, the cost of starting a business—a country-level variable—was not found to be significantly associated with this probability, again suggesting that this country-level condition does not significantly influence the prevalence of entrepreneurial activity within a given country, although it may still influence significantly the choice between registered and informal entrepreneurial activity.

From the second equation, predicting an individual's high-growth aspirations while controlling for the self-selection of individuals into entrepreneurship (Heckman 1979), several interesting observations also emerged. First, age has a U-shaped curvilinear influence, suggesting that both younger and older individuals are more likely to seek to grow their ventures rapidly. Gender exercises a strong negative influence on growth aspirations, but both education and household income have strong, positive influences, even after controlling for the self-selection effect. Interestingly, GDP per capita is significantly and positively associated to entrepreneurial growth aspirations, but significantly and negatively associated to the probability of entrepreneurial entry. Whereas individuals in high-wealth countries are less likely to start new firms, they are more likely to seek to grow their firms, suggesting a possible influence of the average level of human capital in a country. In addition, GDP change was also strongly and positively associated with individual-level growth aspirations, consistent with the country-level analysis. Our country-level conjecture, that the difficulty of firing influences the behaviors of individuals already selected into entrepreneurship, receives support in the analysis shown in Table 11.4 where this country-level influence is shown to exercise a significant, negative influence on individual growth aspirations among early-stage entrepreneurs. Conversely, the cost of starting a business did not influence individual-level behaviors.

Combined with the country-level analysis, the individual-level analysis confirms the importance of distinguishing between different types of entrepreneurship, and between selection and behavioral effects when analyzing how the institutional and regulatory context influences entrepreneurship in a given country. Also, the numerous statistically significant influences observed here demonstrate the salience of both longitudinal panel regression techniques, as well as multilevel regression techniques. After more than three decades of studying individuals only, it is high time for entrepreneurship research to take a step forward and start considering if, and how, the individual's context influences the entrepreneurial choices that they make. This type of analysis is important for the development of entrepreneurship theory, and also, it is important for the development of evidence-based entrepreneurship policies. Only when taking variance in institutional and other country-level conditions into account can entrepreneurship researchers claim some confidence about the implications of their research for entrepreneurship policy.

Acknowledgments

This research was supported by the QinetiQ-EPSRC Chair in Technology Transfer and Entrepreneurship as well as the EPSRC Innovation Studies Centre Grant. Many thanks go to an anonymous reviewer for helpful comments. Although GEM data were used in this study, their interpretation and use are the sole responsibility of the author. All errors are mine.

References

Acs, Z. J. and Audretsch, D. B. (1987), "Innovation in Large and Small Firms." *Economics Letters,* 23(1): 109–12.

Aghion, P. and Howitt, P. (1992), "A Model of Growth Through Creative Destruction." *Econometrica,* 60(2): 323–51.

Audretsch, D. B. and Acs, Z. J. (1991), "Innovation and Size At the Firm Level." *Southern Economic Journal,* 57(3): 739–44.

Audretsch, D. B. (2002), "The Dynamic Role of Small Firms: Evidence from the U.S." *Small Business Economics,* 18(1–3): 13–40.

Birch, D. (1979), *The Job Generation Process.* Unpublished M S Thesis. Cambridge, Boston: MIT.

Birch, D., Haggerty, A., and Parsons, W. (1997), Who's Creating Jobs? Cambridge, MA: Cognetics.

Blanchflower, D. G. and Oswald, A. J. (1998), "What Makes an Entrepreneur?" *Journal of Labor Economics,* 16(1): 26–60.

Bosma, N., van Praag, M., Thurik, R., and de Wit, G. (2004), "The Value of Human and Social Capital Investments for the Business Performance of Startups." *Small Business Economics,* 23(3): 227–36.

Bosma, N., Acs, Z., Autio, E., Coduras, A., and Levie, J. (2009), Global Entrepreneurship Monitor 2008 Executive Report: 65. London: GERA.

Bowen, H. P. and De Clercq, D. (2008), "Institutional Context and the Allocation of Entrepreneurial Effort." *Journal of International Business Studies,* 39(1): 1–21.

Busenitz, L. W., West III, G. P., Shepherd, D., Nelson, T., Chandler, G. N., and Zacharakis, A. (2003), "Entrepreneurship Research in Emergence: Past Trends and Future Directions." *Journal of Management,* 29(3): 285–308.

Cassar, G. (2006), "Entrepreneur Opportunity Costs and Intended Venture Growth." *Journal of Business Venturing,* 21 (610–32).

Cassar, G. (2007), "Money, Money, Money? A Longitudinal Investigation of Entrepreneur Career Reasons, Growth Preferences and Achieved Growth." *Entrepreneurship & Regional Development*, 19(1): 89–107.

Cooper, A. C., Gimeno-Gascon, F. J., and Woo, C. Y. (1994), "Initial Human Capital as Predictor of New Venture Performance." *Journal of Business Venturing*, 9(5): 371–95.

Davidsson, P. (1989), "Entrepreneurship–and After? A Study of Growth Willingness in Small Firms." *Journal of Business Venturing*, 4(3): 211–26.

Davidsson, P., Lindmark, L., and Olofsson, C. (1998), "The Extent of Overestimation of Small Firm Job Creation–An Empirical Examination of the Regression Bias." *Small Business Economics*, 11(1): 87–100.

Davidsson, P. and Wiklund, J. (2001), "Levels of Analysis in Entrepreneurship Research: Current Research Practice and Suggestions for the Future." *Entrepreneurship: Theory & Practice*, 25(4): 81.

Davidsson, P., Delmar, F., and Wiklund, J. (2002), "Entrepreneurship as Growth: Growth as Entrepreneurship." In M. A. Hitt, R. D. Ireland, S. M. Camp, and D. L. Sexton (eds.), *Strategic Entrepreneurship, Creating a New Mindset:* 26–44. Oxford: Blackwell Publishers.

Delmar, F., Davidsson, P., and Gartner, W. B. (2003), "Arriving at the High-Growth Firm." *Journal of Business Venturing*, 18(2): 189–216.

Dunn, T. and Holtz-Eakin, D. (2000), "Financial Capital, Human Capital, and the Transition to Self-Employment: Evidence from Intergenerational Links." *Journal of Labor Economics*, 18(2): 282–305.

Evans, D. and Jovanovic, B. (1989), "An Estimated Model of Entrepreneurial Choice under Liquidity Constraints." *Journal of Political Economy*, 97(4): 808–27.

Fölster, S. (2000), "Do Entrepreneurs Create Jobs?" *Small Business Economics*, 14(2): 137–48.

Gerber, T. P. and Cheung, S. Y. (2008), "Horizontal Stratification in Postsecondary Education: Forms, Explanations, and Implications." *Annual Review of Sociology*, 34: 299–318.

Heckman, J. J. (1979), "Sample Selection Bias as a Specification Error." *Econometrica*, 47(1): 153–61.

Hellmann, T. (2007), "Entrepreneurs and the Process of Obtaining Resources." *Journal of Economics & Management Strategy*, 16(1): 81–109.

Ireland, R. D., Hitt, M. A., and Sirmon, D. G. (2003), "A Model of Strategic Entrepreneurship: The Construct and Its Dimensions." *Journal of Management*, 29(6): 963–89.

Kirchhoff, B. (1994), *Entrepreneurship and Dynamic Capitalism*. Westport, CT: Praeger.

Kirzner, L. (1997), "Entrepreneurial Discovery and the Competitive Market Process: An Austrian Approach." *Journal of Economic Literature*, 35: 60–85.

Krueger, N. F., Reilly, M. D., and Carsrud, A. L. (2000), "Competing Models of Entrepreneurial Intentions." *Journal of Business Venturing*, 15(5–6): 411–32.

Lazear, E. (2005), "Entrepreneurship." *Journal of Labor Economics*, 23(4): 649–80.

Levie, J. and Autio, E. (2008), "A Theoretical Grounding and Test of the GEM Model." *Small Business Economics*, 31(3): 235–63.

Levie, J. and Autio, E. (In Press), "Institutions and Strategic Entrepreneurship." *Journal of Management Studies*. Forthcoming in the Special Issue "Revitalizing Entrepreneurship".

Lumpkin, G. T. and Dess, G. G. (1996), "Clarifying the Entrepreneurial Orientation Construct and Linking it to Performance." *Academy of Management Review*, 21(1): 135–72.

Michelacci, C. (2003), "Low Returns in R&D Due to the Lack of Entrepreneurial Skills." *The Economic Journal*, 113(484): 207–25.

Minniti, M., Bygrave, W. D., and Autio, E. (2006), Global Entrepreneurship Monitor GEM 2005 Executive Report. in M. Minniti (ed.). London: Global Entrepreneurship Research Association GERA.

Phan, P. H. (2004), "Entrepreneurship Theory: Possibilities and Future Directions." *Journal of Business Venturing*, 19(5): 617–20.

Picot, G. and Dupuy, R. (1998), "Job Creation by Company Size Class: The Magnitude, Concentration and Persistence of Job Gains and Losses in Canada." *Small Business Economics*, 10(2): 117–39.

Rauch, A., Wiklund, J., Lumpkin, G., and Frese, M. (2009), "Entrepreneurial Orientation and Business Performance: An Assessment of Past Research and Suggestions for the Future." *Entrepreneurship Theory and Practice*, 33(3): 761–87.

Reynolds, P. P., Bosma, N., and Autio, E. (2005), "Global Entrepreneurship Monitor: Data Collection Design and Implementation 1998–2003." *Small Business Economics*, 24(3): 205–31.

Schumpeter, J. A. (1996), *The Theory of Economic Development*. London, UK: Transaction Publishers.

Shane, S. and Venkataraman, S. (2000), "The Promise of Entrepreneurship as a Field of Research." *Academy of Management Review*, 25(1): 217–26.

Shrader, R. and Siegel, D. S. (2007), "Assessing the Relationship between Human Capital and Firm Performance: Evidence from Technology-Based New Ventures." *Entrepreneurship Theory and Practice*, 31(6): 893–908.

Stevens, M. L., Armstrong, E. A., and Arum, R. (2008), "Sieve, Incubator, Temple, Hub: Empirical and Theoretical Advances in the Sociology of Higher Education." *Annual Review of Sociology*, 34: 127–51.

Storey, D. J. (1994), *Understanding the Small Business Sector*. London, UK: Routledge.

Ucbasaran, D., Westhead, P., and Wright, M. (2008), "Opportunity Identification and Pursuit: Does an Entrepreneur's Human Capital Matter?" *Small Business Economics*, 30 (2): 153–73.

van Praag, M. C. (2007), "What is the Value of Entrepreneurship? A Review of Recent Research." *Small Business Economics*, 29(4): 351–82.

Von Mises, L. (1949), *Human action*. New Haven, CT: Yale University Press.

Wiklund, J. and Davidsson, P. (2003), "What Do They Think and Feel About Growth? An Expectancy-Value Approach to Small Business Managers' Attitudes Towards Growth." *Entrepreneurship Theory & Practice*, 27(3): 247–69.

Wiklund, J. and Shepherd, D. (2003), "Aspiring for, and Achieving Growth: the Moderating Role of Resources and Opportunities." *Journal of Management Studies*, 40(8): 1911–41.

Wong, P. K., Ho, Y. P., and Autio, E. (2005), "Entrepreneurship, Innovation and Economic Growth: Evidence from GEM data." *Small Business Economics*, 24(3): 335–50.

Wright, M., Hmieleski, K. M., Siegel, D. S., and Ensley, M. D. (2007), "The Role of Human Capital in Technological Entrepreneurship." *Entrepreneurship Theory and Practice*, 31(6): 791–806.

12

Entrepreneurship and the Decision to Export

Kent Jones and Megan McDonald Way

12.1 Introduction

What motivates entrepreneurs, particularly early-stage entrepreneurs, to export? Are there particular characteristics of entrepreneurs, their products, or their technologies that make them more likely to export? Small and medium-size enterprises (SMEs) have been increasing their role in international trade (OECD 2006). Export market strategy is of increasing importance to entrepreneurs and the study of exports by entrepreneurial firms has moved beyond the traditional theories of comparative advantage to consider firm-specific export strategies.[1]

This chapter uses data from the 2005 wave of the Global Entrepreneurship Monitor (GEM 2005), which surveyed around 16,000 entrepreneurs in thirty-five countries, to identify how specific characteristics of entrepreneurs and their products are related to export participation. It exploits unique questions regarding the innovativeness of the product, the stage of development of the firm, and the newness of the technology required. The cross-country nature of the survey provides a view of how entrepreneurship and innovativeness correlate with export activity on a global level. This cross-country analysis adds to the current literature, which is strongly dominated by studies that examine export participation by firms in a single industry within a single country (Coviello and Jones 2004; Coviello and McAuley 1999; Dana, Hamilton, and Wick 2009). While the firm-level details are not extensive, an

---

[1] See, for example, Lloyd-Reason and Sear, eds. (2007) and Dickson's (2007) survey, plus citations therein.

examination of the data extends our understanding of "born global" companies across many countries.

The analysis begins with a look at various conceptual frameworks for understanding exports by SMEs. The discussion then turns to the data, examining the characteristics of entrepreneurial businesses as they relate to export participation, and offering possible explanations for the patterns revealed by the data. Finally, we provide some suggestions to help future research to broaden our understanding of export activity among entrepreneurial firms.

12.2 Conceptual frameworks for entrepreneurial exports

12.2.1 *The cost factor*

Exporting is a costly endeavor, particularly for smaller, resource-strapped firms. The decision to enter export markets involves a variety of sunk, fixed, and variable costs, allowing in many cases only the most productive firms to take that step. Anderson and van Wincoop (2004), in their comprehensive survey of trade costs, estimate a 170 percent total trade barrier as a representative rich country ad valorem tax equivalent of the costs to export. This includes transport costs, tariff and non-tariff-barrier costs, border-related costs, and local distribution costs. Various forms of risk, intellectual property rights protection, contract enforcement, and exchange rate fluctuations also must be taken into account, not to mention language and cultural differences that must be factored into product development, packaging, and marketing.

At the same time, certain costs have been decreasing rapidly in the recent years. Advances in telecommunications, the advent of the internet, and the efficiencies of container ship transport have lowered the transaction costs of trade (Hummels 2007; Vemuri and Siddiqi 2009). Advances in production technology have lowered the costs of small-scale output, and the international standardization of technology, as well as the trend toward global networks have exerted downward pressure on the overall costs of trade, particularly in knowledge-intensive industries (Knight and Cavusgil 1996). Yet even with these advances, participating in trade remains costly, evidenced by the small percentage of firms that participate. In the year 2000, only four percent of the 5.5 million firms in the United States reported export participation (Bernard et al. 2009). Countries that have closer geographic ties to potential trade partners, such as those in the European Union, have higher export participation rates, but the rates are still low compared to overall economic activity. In Belgium, for example, around seven percent of all firms exported in 2004 (Muûls and Pisu 2009). Eaton et al. (2004) found that French manufacturing firms participate in exports at a rate of about seventeen percent while US manufacturers participate at a rate of about fourteen percent. These studies also indicate a very high concentration of export volume coming from the largest sized firms. In view of the high costs of exporting, especially for small firms, and of the high risks of exporting for start-up firms, there must be particularly strong and compelling reasons and incentives for entrepreneurs to enter export markets.

12.2.2 *The entrepreneurship component of factor endowment models*

Can economic theory help to explain the motives for exports? Neo-classical economic theory has in fact paid little attention to entrepreneurship in explaining international trade and investment.[2] Comparative advantage theories, for example, set out to explain patterns of trade, usually at the national level, and typically do not take into account "entrepreneurial" decisions at the firm level. Heckscher-Ohlin trade theory is based on the pattern of relative factor endowments among countries in determining the pattern of imports and exports.[3] Firms are defined as disembodied combinations of labor and capital in perfectly competitive markets, producing homogeneous commodity goods. There is no distinctive role for entrepreneurial activity in this model, as outcomes follow deterministically from impersonal market forces. As Baumol has put it, "the theoretical firm is entrepreneurless—the Prince of Denmark has been expunged from the discussion of Hamlet" (Baumol 1968: 66).

However, to the extent that entrepreneurs are part of a larger national economy subject to market-driven allocations of resources, it is important to consider how the underlying factor endowments and market forces in an economy may contribute to the export *capabilities* of entrepreneurs. One avenue for this influence comes from a consideration of entrepreneurial financing. Wynn (2005) identifies entrepreneurial ventures as small businesses that have limited access to traditional financing. A country with greater accumulated wealth among entrepreneurs will allow the small firms to overcome financing constraints, and thereby induce greater output (and exports) from them. Therefore, the larger a country's relative endowment of wealth, the more it will tend to export the output of its small, entrepreneurial firms. Another entrepreneurship-related factor of production is *human capital,* the value of education, training, and experience, in a country's workforce.[4] Higher levels of education among the population, for example, particularly in science and engineering, may contribute to increased capabilities to develop new technologies and produce innovative products for export. In addition,

---

[2] See Glancey and McQuaid (2000), Chapter 3, for a general discussion of neo-classical economic theory and its view towards entrepreneurship.

[3] Chipman (1965) provides a comprehensive summary of the Heckscher-Ohlin model.

[4] See Schultz (1971) and Becker (1993). The value of human capital can be estimated as the accumulated value of investments in education and training among workers over time.

entrepreneurial education itself represents a specialized type of human capital. Enrollments in entrepreneurship programs, or statistical measures of entrepreneurial activity, such as the number of new start-ups, or trends in new patent filings and patent commercialization, could perhaps measure a country's "endowment" of entrepreneurship. This extension of trade theory predicts that a country's relative "endowment" of human capital linked to entrepreneurship, compared to other countries, will help to determine its export performance in "entrepreneurship-intensive" goods such as new products. On the other hand, the underlying factor endowments in an economy may lead an SME to export in an attempt to seek access to financial capital that may not exist in the country of origin.[5]

12.2.3 *Market structure and the sources of innovation*

Other trade theories have tended to imply the presence of entrepreneurship without ascribing a systematic role to it.[6] In monopolistic competition, for example, firms compete by varying the characteristics of a basic product type. Thus entrepreneurial strategies to create innovative designs, quality enhancements, and other differentiating features play a prominent role in this form of market structure. Market advantages—perhaps extending to international markets—often emerge as the result of introducing new and different products for which there is little direct competition. Barriers to market entry typically come from specific firm assets, such as patents, capital-intensive or research-and-development activity, and exclusive access to inputs that result from entrepreneurial innovation and effort. Entrepreneurial value may also derive from strategies to develop distinctive capabilities and to maintain networks of supplier and customer relationships that are difficult for rivals to imitate. Capturing and retaining market power may in fact be instrumental in establishing export capabilities for the start-up firm, since the correspondingly higher price-cost margins may allow it to overcome the higher cost and risk factors associated with exports, as opposed to domestic sales.

Global trade patterns tend to support the predictions of the Linder (1961) model that tastes converge globally among consumers of similar income levels, as world trade in consumer products occurs predominantly among high-income countries. Progressive globalization in consumer markets has been marked by a convergence in tastes in some (not all) products (De Mooij 2004), which implies that entrepreneurs in high-income countries will have

---

[5] Hessels (2008) provides a broad survey of the literature relating internationalization of SMEs to the host country's deficits in factor endowments.

[6] Helpman and Krugman (1986) develop an extended model of the firm incorporating imperfect competition, technology, product differentiation, transport costs, and trade.

increasing export opportunities in other high-income countries' markets. Vernon's (1966) product life cycle model of trade also includes innovation as a central part of the story: the entrepreneur introduces a new product in the home market, acquiring a monopolistic advantage on world markets and leading to exports from the country of innovation.[7] As the product cycle progresses, rival entrepreneurs from other countries may develop similar technologies or products and begin to compete with the innovating firm, undermining its monopoly and reducing its exports. In the mature stage, the product becomes standardized, and the innovating firm may need to establish production in the lowest cost locations in order to harvest profits from the product, so that any exports now come from low-cost countries. Across the product life cycle, the innovating firm thus faces a series of decisions on which current and future profits for the firm from this product will depend.

12.2.4 *The business environment*

The business environment may also affect incentives to export. Porter's (1990) model of "competitive" advantage develops a broader and more eclectic paradigm of global trade markets, in which entrepreneurship plays a central role:

> Invention and entrepreneurship are at the very heart of national advantage. Some believe these acts are largely random...Our research shows that neither entrepreneurship nor invention is random...determinants [of national advantage] play a major role in locating where invention and entrepreneurship are most likely to occur in a particular industry (ibid., pp. 125–126).

Porter's paradigm of national competitive advantage reflects the influences of traditional trade theories, such as the imperfect competition, Linder's model, and Heckscher–Ohlin theory. Competition provides the ultimate test of world-class performance. At the same time, national industries grow from the soil of their own traditions and culture and markets, enhanced by incentives emanating from government policies. Globalization provides the incentives for national competitive advantages to grow, but it can also be disruptive, as increased competition and technological change cause the decline of some firms and the rise of others.

Government policies and programs that benefit or support new and growing businesses, along with embedded entrepreneurship education in schools and colleges, contribute to a country's "endowment" of entrepreneurship, which tends to make the economy more competitive in world markets. In addition, government policies that support openness to foreign markets also

---

[7] See Vernon (1966). For a more general treatment of technology and trade, see Grossman and Helpman (1995).

provide incentives for entrepreneurs to take advantage of global market opportunities (see Jones 2006). An additional link between government economic policies and trade exists between *internal* market openness and efficiency. Policies of open trade require countries to adjust their *internal* economies in order to gain from trade, through a re-allocation of domestic resources (Jones and Levie 2008). As a result, less efficient activities can give way to more productive activities. Yet this is exactly the same requirement that a growing domestic economy has in promoting entrepreneurship and exports. Start-up and growing firms, with their new products and innovative production processes need room to grow, which requires an economic system that allows for change, and does not protect existing firms with special-interest regulations and provisions.

12.2.5 *Trade and firm characteristics*

While traditional economic and business environment models focus on national exports, decisions to enter export markets are ultimately made at the level of individual firms. Surveys of the literature on firms of all sizes in a variety of countries and industries find that exporters are a self-selected group of firms with higher-than-average productivity (Wagner 2007; Bernard et al. 2007; Greenaway and Kneller 2007). Exporters tend to be larger firms and it is generally accepted that the sunk costs of exporting and the barriers to foreign market entry discourage many SMEs from exporting. Nonetheless, the Organization for Economic Cooperation and Development (OECD) estimates that SMEs account for about thirty percent of exports worldwide (OECD 2006), and a great deal of attention is being paid to how barriers to SME export activity can be lowered.

Studies of the microeconomics of trade and firm characteristics, questioning the heterogeneity of export activity among firms in the same industry, began with Bernard et al. (1995). This study focused on US manufacturing, asking how important exports are to the firms that participate, if these firms' productivity, wages, and employment levels are higher than industry averages, and how they respond to events such as exchange rate shocks. The findings of higher productivity, firm size, and wages among exporters, have been verified by other studies looking at other countries and industries, and much attention has been paid to the direction of causality in the productivity–export relationship. Wagner (2007) and Greenaway and Kneller (2007) provide extensive summaries of these empirical studies, and conclude that while the best firms are exporters, ex ante, exporting does not serve to improve firm productivity, ex post. The high sunk costs of exporting mean that particularly productive firms self-select to be exporters. These studies have focused mainly on the range of firms within a particular country and industry, and not specifically on SMEs or early-stage firms.

12.2.6 *Behavioral models of entrepreneurship and exports*

Entrepreneurship is about individuals acting upon their perceived opportunities: each individual enterprise has a story to tell with regard to its decision to enter international markets. This aspect of international business activity has given rise to a growing literature on the management of the global entrepreneurial venture.[8] While for some firms, international opportunities appear only after their formation, as an extension or supplement of their domestic market, other firms are "born global." The form that the international enterprise takes depends largely on the type and incidence of transaction costs, network structures across borders, the resources of the firm, and how knowledge and technology regarding the business opportunity spread (Oviatt and McDougall 1994). The international aspect of entrepreneurial ventures therefore combines national characteristics and firm- and industry-specific elements.

Entrepreneurial studies have set out to fill the "Prince of Denmark" gap suggested by Baumol; that is, to explain strategic decision-making by SMEs based on characteristics and attributes of the firm and its managers. The traditional strategic analysis of firms entering export markets had assumed a gradualist, incremental approach to foreign market entry, in which it was necessary to accumulate domestic market experience and foreign market knowledge before venturing into export markets (see Pedersen and Petersen 1997). Oviatt and McDougall (1994), however, proposed an alternative model of the more rapidly globalizing firm based on its ability to internalize critical transactions, establish foreign location advantages, and control unique resources. Thus in addition to "gradual" globalizers there can be "born global" firms. Kuivalainen, Sundqvist, and Servais (2007) provide evidence that globalization represents a continuum, bounded at the low end by minimal export activity in (usually) near-by foreign markets, and on the high end by export intensive operations in multiple and distant markets.

With technological advances and increased globalization, research has focused increasingly on the "born global" type of company. Knowledge-intensive industries in particular have been prone to internationalizing from their inception (Oviatt and McDougall 1994; Bell et al. 1998). Knight and Cavusgil (1996) identify a number of trends that lower the costs of trade for new firms, increasing the speed with which firms can respond to global market

---

[8] See, for example, the collections of essays in Etemad and Wright (2003) and Jones and Dimitratos (2004), and the many references they provide.

opportunities. Empirical studies, such as Bell et al. (1998) which examines small firms in the UK, point to knowledge-intensive companies being most likely to start export activity at an early stage. Acs et al. (1997) point to the "creative destruction" benefits of innovative new firms operating internationally, and how the particular issues of property rights and barriers to market entry affect their entry into global markets.

More recently, Hessels and Terjesen (2008) perform a cross-country examination of the role of entrepreneurial human capital and entrepreneurial social capital, along with firm innovativeness, on the early export activity of a new venture. Using GEM data from 2002 and 2003, they find that entrepreneurs who perceive they have entrepreneurial skills, who have prior experience as entrepreneurs and/or investors and who know other entrepreneurs are more likely to participate in export activity. They also find that firm innovativeness, represented by a firm's product being perceived by the entrepreneur as new to the market, is also correlated with a new venture's propensity to export. They do not find that the newness of the technology employed by the firm is significantly correlated with exports.

In the following section, we also use GEM data (from 2005) to take a cross-country look at the characteristics of entrepreneurs, their firms and their participation in export activity, controlling for country characteristics. Instead of focusing on entrepreneurial human and social capital, we focus on the stage of the firm and control for the business environment of the host country using various measures of ease of doing business and entrepreneurial activity.

12.3 Data analysis

12.3.1 *Data overview and descriptive statistics*

Data for our study are from the Global Entrepreneurship Monitor (GEM) project. Started in 1999, GEM is a large cross-country study of entrepreneurial dynamics aiming at collecting data on entrepreneurial activity that are comparable across countries and over time. In 2005 the GEM data included thirty-four countries, surveying over 118,000 people. Survey questions used in this chapter focused on the scale of the entrepreneurs' participation in the firm's operations, the type of product or technology, current and anticipated firm size, and some limited personal demographic data including education, gender, and income level. Firms are grouped according to the elapsed time since paying their first employee. *Nascent* firms are start-ups with three months or fewer of payroll activity, *early-stage* firms include those with an active payroll of between three months and three and a half years, and *established* firms are those that have paid employees for more than three and a half years. There are 16,050 entrepreneurial ventures from thirty-four countries represented in the survey: 4,489 in the *nascent* category, 3,817 in the *early-stage* category, and 7,744 in the *established* category. The basic survey question linking entrepreneurship and exports asks each respondent what proportion of their customers normally reside outside the entrepreneur's country. The potential responses are 0, 1 to 25 percent, 26 to 50 percent, 51 to 75 percent, 76 to 90 percent, and 91 to 100 percent.

Figure 12.1 shows the overall responses, grouped in each category by nascent, early-stage, and established entrepreneurs. It is interesting to note that within this unique sample, almost twenty percent of firms report some level of export activity. Figure 12.2 shows the overall country-by-country export participation rates, based on this survey question.

The GEM data includes information about the firm's product and technology that could be related to exports. Table 12.1 shows how GEM participants categorized the newness of their firm's product or the newness of their technology (represented by "years of availability" of the technology) by stage of the firm. These characteristics could be important in explaining imports for two reasons. The first is that a firm with a product that is new or unfamiliar to customers may have to look to export markets to find customers if their domestic customer base is not big enough. The second is that potential export customers themselves seek out particularly new or innovative products they cannot obtain in their own countries and instigate a relationship with the exporting firm.

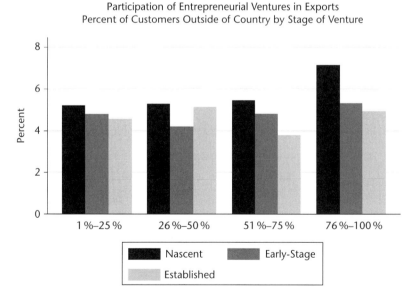

Figure 12.1 Participation of entrepreneurial ventures in exports

Source: GEM Survey 2005

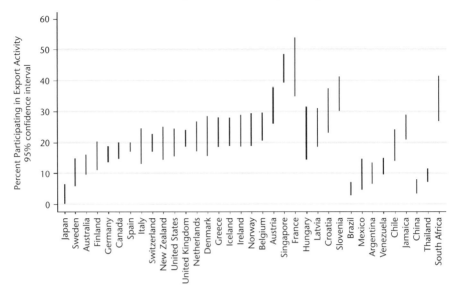

Figure 12.2 Export participation rates by country

Source: GEM Survey 2005

Table 12.1. Cross tabulation of newness of product and newness of technology by firm stage

Newness of product to customers*	Nascent		Early-stage		Established		Total
	Freq.	%	Freq.	%	Freq.	%	
All	646	14.4	445	11.7	676	8.9	1,767
Some	1,314	29.3	975	25.6	1,496	19.6	3,785
None	2,525	56.3	2,395	62.8	5,459	71.5	10,379
Total	4,485	100	3,815	100	7,631	100	15,931

Years of availability of technology**	Nascent		Early-stage		Established		Total
	Freq.	%	Freq.	%	Freq.	%	
Less than 1 year	959	21.4	602	15.8	964	12.6	2,525
1 to 5 years	830	18.5	694	18.2	623	8.2	2,147
More than 5 years	2,694	60.1	2,517	66.0	6,043	79.2	11,254
Total	4,483	100	3,813	100	7,630	100	15,926

Source: GEM Survey 2005

* Question asked is "Will all, some, or none of your potential customers consider this product or service new or unfamiliar?"

** Question asked is "Were the technologies or procedures required for this product or service generally available for less than a year, between one to five years, or longer than five years?"

Country characteristics are also important in explaining export activity and in exploring possible links to entrepreneurship and innovation. Index rankings from the World Bank, such as the Ease of Doing Business Ranking (EDB), the World Bank Red Tape Index (WB RT) and the GEM-based Red Tape Index[9] (GEM RT) give a sense of how supportive the business environment is for

Table 12.2. Country-level characteristics—2005

Country	EDB	WB RT	GEM RT	Patents/$bill	GDP ($bill)
Argentina	102	0.61	4.43	3.28	183.4
Australia	10	0.04	3.37	15.41	712.8
Austria	23	0.52	2.98	6.11	301.8
Belgium	16	0.46	3.94	1.64	373.0
Brazil	126	0.61	4.67	1.65	883.6
Canada	8	0.03	3.34	18.13	1,131.2
Chile	36	0.36	3.22	2.40	118.2
China	90	0.82	3.08	9.36	2,237.1
Croatia	107	0.73	4.24	2.92	44.4
Denmark	5	0.23	3.05	1.27	257.5
Finland	13	0.29	2.68	7.00	193.9
France	32	0.10	3.79	6.97	2,131.0
Germany	20	0.50	3.84	7.51	2,769.4
Greece	106	0.83	3.95	18.76	244.0
Hungary	50	0.65	4.53	4.27	110.2
Iceland	11	0.24	2.26	14.73	16.3
Ireland	7	0.19	3.03	2.48	200.2
Italy	59	0.51	4.10	4.04	1,764.8
Jamaica	62	0.24	3.90	3.86	11.2
Japan	12	0.65	4.17	44.05	4,552.1
Latvia	26	0.35	3.54	4.52	16.2
Mexico	42	0.63	3.83	9.90	844.0
Netherlands	27	0.50	3.67	4.82	633.8
New Zealand	2	0.07	3.78	38.83	110.8
Norway	9	0.28	3.20	9.69	302.1
Singapore	1	0.10	1.97	61.85	121.3
Slovenia	64	0.62	4.34	5.79	35.7
South Africa	35	0.39	4.00	***	242.3
Spain	46	0.66	3.57	2.84	1,122.0
Sweden	14	0.28	4.00	5.04	366.2
Switzerland	15	0.40	3.12	2.93	370.5
Thailand	19	0.34	3.74	0.44	176.6
UK	6	0.14	3.05	3.56	2,277.3
United States	3	0.10	2.71	13.39	12,421.9
Venezuela	175	0.70	4.21	***	145.5

Sources: Ease of Doing Business 2005 (EDB) and Red Tape Index 2005 (WB RT) from World Bank (available at www. doingbusiness.org). GEM Red Tape Index (GEM RT) from *Global Entrepreneurship Monitor: 2007 Executive Report,* using 2005 index or next closest year if 2005 not available. Patents/Billion from authors' calculation using new patent information for 2005 from WTO Trade Profiles Database. GDP 2005 from International Monetary Fund (IMF) Financial Statistics.

[9] The GEM Red Tape Index is based on the regulatory environment and the difficulties presented for entrepreneurs in starting a business, described in the Global Entrepreneurship Monitor: 2007 Executive Report.

Table 12.3. Correlation of country export participation rate with 2005 country characteristics

Correlation of export participation rate with	Corr.
WB EDB	−.2112
WB Red Tape	−.2894
GEM Red Tape	−.2572
Patent Index	.1098
GDP (US $)	.1517

firms. The GEM RT measures the business and regulatory environment particularly as it relates to entrepreneurs. Another measure of innovativeness at a country level is a Patent Index, created by the authors using new patent information for 2005 from the World Trade Organization (WTO) Trade Profiles Database. This index reflects the degree of intellectual property protection in the country, measured as patents issued per billions of US dollars of gross domestic product (GDP) in 2005. These indices are reported in Table 12.2

Taking the mean export participation for all entrepreneurial ventures, by country, and testing correlations with the countries' rankings and indices above, yields the expected results, although the small number of observations results in the correlations not being statistically significant (see Table 12.3). Country-level export participation rates are positively correlated with the ease of doing business in that country (shown as a negative correlation because a ranking of "1" corresponds with the easiest environment for doing business). The greater the degree of red tape, both on the World Bank and entrepreneurial-focused GEM indices, the lower the observed participation in exports. A higher Patent Index is correlated with greater export participation. The size of a country's GDP is negatively correlated with export participation, which for the newer firms examined in this study is to be expected. The larger the domestic economy, the less need a small firm has to look to foreign markets.

12.3.2 Conditional correlations—probit analysis

In order to examine those factors that may be linked to export activity, we combine GEM data with the various ease of doing business, patent, and GDP data to present a probit model of conditional correlations between export participation (at any intensity) and these factors, as well as some of the demographic variables of the responding entrepreneur. It could be that nascent ventures or ventures with highly innovative products are correlated with exports for underlying reasons that are specific to the country in which the firm operates. For example, if countries with policies that encourage entrepreneurship and innovation are also countries with favorable policies toward trade, controlling for the country might eliminate any relationship observed between exports and the stage of the firm or the newness of products or technologies. Additionally, controlling for the specific business conditions, using the ease of doing business or red tape rankings, might provide more insight into how relevant innovativeness at a firm level is to trade.

Ideally, we would include a variety of country-specific variables to see how those factors relate to exports, but due to the lack of within-country variation, we cannot examine more than one of these variables at a time. There are also other types of unobserved heterogeneity between the countries, which can be controlled for using fixed effects or a dummy variable representing each country. The probit analysis in Table 12.4 shows the conditional correlations between export participation and all these factors.[10] In addition to the firm-level variables discussed earlier, the probit analysis also includes a dummy for Eurozone membership to test the impact of monetary integration and dummies for designation as an "easy" or a "difficult" country in the World Bank EDB. Other dummy variables indicate the number of competitors and demographic variables for the entrepreneur: gender, age, education level, and income level. The different specifications use different country variables to control for country effects, including (1) country specific dummy variables, (2) the country's 2005 log GDP, (3) the national patent index described above, and (4) the WB RT and (5) the GEM RT. The reported coefficients indicate the incremental impact of the variable on the probability of exporting.[11]

Results for variables indicating an innovative product and recent technology are significantly positive across all specifications. Having a product that is "new to all" is correlated with an increase in the likelihood of export participation ranging from about eleven percent to fourteen percent depending on the specification, while offering a product that is "new to some" increases export likelihood by about six percent to seven percent. The coefficients on employing technology available less than one or from one to five years are not as large, but range from three percent to five percent and are statistically significant. Even when controlling specifically for countries' overall innovativeness or support of intellectual property rights, using the patent index, or controlling for ease of doing business, these coefficients remain relatively large and highly significant. The implication is that innovativeness of the product and newness of the technology are key components of the entrepreneur's

[10] These regressions were also run using an ordered probit, with results similar to those reported here.
[11] Multiple dummy variables around a single characteristic typically imply an omitted variable. For Ease of Doing Business the omitted variable is "moderate." Regarding the number of competitors, the category "no competitors" is omitted. For education level the variable "less than high school" is omitted. Regarding income level the "low" category is omitted, so that the reported results are for the top and middle terciles of household income in that country. Regarding the country dummies, Spain was the omitted variable, having the largest number of observations.

Table 12.4. Probit analysis

	(1) dF/dx	(1) z-value	(2) dF/dx	(2) z-value	(3) dF/dx	(3) z-value	(4) dF/dx	(4) z-value	(5) dF/dx	(5) z-value
Nascent	0.018	2.17	0.025	2.97	0.018	2.07	0.021	2.57	0.025	3.02
Early-stage	-0.006	-0.74	-0.007	-0.85	-0.008	-0.87	-0.010	-1.14	-0.010	-1.24
Prod new all	0.136	10.42	0.114	9.04	0.119	9.07	0.122	9.56	0.118	9.27
Prod new some	0.070	7.67	0.058	6.35	0.057	6.11	0.061	6.68	0.059	6.45
Many compet.	-0.056	-4.10	-0.069	-5.09	-0.075	-5.31	-0.063	-4.61	-0.069	-5.02
Few compet.	-0.029	-2.22	-0.035	-2.63	-0.036	-2.61	-0.034	-2.54	-0.035	-2.61
Tech <1yr	0.051	4.15	0.030	2.83	0.040	3.49	0.039	3.67	0.043	3.98
Tech 1–5 yrs	0.050	4.41	0.044	3.97	0.048	4.15	0.044	3.93	0.046	4.09
Male	0.043	5.76	0.050	6.73	0.048	6.19	0.049	6.55	0.048	6.41
Age	0.000	-0.76	0.000	-0.60	0.000	-0.88	0.000	-1.27	0.000	-0.89
HS educ.	0.016	1.40	0.039	3.62	0.030	2.65	0.028	2.65	0.037	3.43
College educ.	0.013	1.02	0.037	3.15	0.020	1.63	0.026	2.18	0.036	3.01
Grad educ.	0.056	5.43	0.066	6.52	0.054	5.28	0.053	5.27	0.059	5.85
Middle Inc.	-0.002	-0.22	0.002	0.17	0.000	0.04	0.001	0.10	0.003	0.28
High Inc.	0.034	3.50	0.038	3.87	0.031	3.07	0.037	3.72	0.036	3.66
Eurozone	0.000	0.00	0.037	4.29	0.029	3.51	0.063	5.70	0.033	3.75
EDB–easy	0.074	2.84	0.034	3.06	-0.009	-0.82	-0.048	-3.61	-0.031	-2.53
EDB–difficult	-0.076	-1.44	-0.059	-3.47	-0.116	-4.84	-0.067	-4.06	-0.064	-3.80
Country	Not reported									
Log GDP USD			-0.023	-8.35						
Patent index					0.002	5.42				
WB RT 05							-0.157	-6.41		
GEM RT 05									-0.045	-5.69
Obs	11,312		11,312		10,617		11,312		11,312	
Chi-squared	899.45		544.64		567.20		514.93		506.13	
Prob >Chi-sq	0.000		0.000		0.000		0.000		0.000	
Pseudo R2	0.0822		0.0498		0.0453		0.0471		0.0462	

decision to enter export markets. These results also give at least indirect support to the idea that technology- and entrepreneurship-oriented human capital is an important determinant of exporting activity. In addition, a business environment favorable to entrepreneurship (see results below for the GEM Red Tape and World Bank indexes) is also favorable to exporting.

Firm stage does correlate with exports. Being a *nascent* company is correlated with about a two percent *increase* in the probability of exporting when compared with established firms, while firms at the next level of maturity (*early-stage*) show a negative but statistically insignificant decline in exporting likelihood. Having competitors is negatively correlated with exports, which may indicate a relationship between the size of the domestic market and the costs and risks of exporting. If a domestic market supports many firms in a given product or service area, firms have less incentive to export. Alternatively, more competitors may indicate that the firm offers a less differentiated product that is thereby also less competitive globally. The link between less competitive market structure and increased exports supports the idea discussed earlier that international competitive advantage comes with offering a highly differentiated product with few substitutes, presumably generating the higher profit margins needed to overcome the significant costs and risks of exporting.

The demographic variables show that male entrepreneurs are about four to five percent more likely to export,[12] but that age is uncorrelated with exports. If unobserved country characteristics are controlled for, the only education level correlated with exports is a graduate school education, which increases the probability of exporting by five to seven percent, another possible indication that exporting among entrepreneurs tends to depend on the level of human capital. When unobserved country characteristics are not controlled for, any education level above grade school is positively correlated with exports. Across all the specifications, the entrepreneur having a high income level (the top third in one's country) is correlated with a three to four percent increase in the likelihood of exporting. The income level of the entrepreneur thus appears to play a small, but significant, role in exporting. As suggested in the earlier discussion of wealth endowments, it may be that higher individual income, or perhaps the

---

[12] The positive relationship between entrepreneurial export activity and the entrepreneur/manager being male is found in other GEM Reports (see "GEM 2007 Report on Women and Entrepreneurship" by Allen et al. 2008). Westhead et al. (2001) uses survey data from Britain to find a similar significant relationship between male entrepreneurs and export activity. Welch et al. (2008) provides a brief survey of entrepreneurial scholarship related to gender and exports, and uses interview data to examine some of the factors underlying female entrepreneurs' lower propensity to export.

higher wealth that may be associated with it, provides additional financial resources that are necessary for the exporting venture.

The Eurozone indicator is insignificant when country indicators are used, but in other specifications is correlated with about a three to six percent increase in export participation. The coefficient for the *easy-to-do-business* dummy does not always have the expected positive sign, although the *difficult-to-do-business* dummy is consistently negative and significant in all but one variant.[13] The red tape indices are significant and negative, as expected. The World Bank Red Tape Index for these countries ranges from 0.03 to 0.83, and deteriorating from 0.03 to 0.13 is correlated with a 1.5 percent drop in the likelihood of exporting. The GEM Red Tape Index ranges from 1.97 to 4.67, and its coefficient implies that an increase of one leads to a 4.5 percent drop. The Patent Index ranges from 0.44 to 61.85 patents per US$billion GDP, and its coefficient is also significant and implies that an increase of ten patents per US$billion GDP is correlated with a two percent increase in export participation. An increase in a country's GDP significantly decreases the likelihood of exports, suggesting that, ceteris paribus, greater domestic market size tilts SME strategies away from exports. Country dummies themselves generally reflect the GEM country patterns of Figure 12.2, with varying levels of significance.[14]

12.3.3 *The pattern of exports across firms of differing maturity*

The GEM data show that the decision to export also has a temporal dimension, based on the age of the firm. One surprising result of the GEM survey was that exports tended to be more intensive in earlier rather than later stages of the firm's maturity. Table 12.5 reveals that *nascent* firms are the most likely to report export participation, with 21.26 percent reporting at least some foreign customers, compared with 17.66 percent for early-stage firms and 17.19 percent for established firms. These differences between *nascent* firms and the other categories are statistically significant. How can these results be explained? It is difficult to draw conclusions from the data, due to the lack of contextual information. There is, for example, no information on the changing export intensity of individual firms as they pass from nascent to early-stage to established, and the entrepreneurs are not asked to comment on

---

[13] There is some correlation between these variables. An "easy" country is more likely to have a lower red tape ranking, numerically with lower indicating less red tape.

[14] The country dummy results (not reported in the table) show that a firm residing in France, Austria, Singapore, Croatia, Slovenia, Venezuela, or Jamaica is more likely to export (with coefficients ranging from 0.11 for Venezuela to around 0.20 for France and Singapore and 0.28 for Slovenia), and that a firm in Germany, Mexico, Australia, Japan, Thailand, or Finland is less likely to export (with coefficients ranging from −0.03 for Germany to a low of −0.14 for Japan). All other country coefficients are insignificant.

Table 12.5. Cross tabulation of export intensity by firm stage

% customers international*	Nascent		Early-stage		Established	
	Freq.	%	Freq.	%	Freq.	%
None	3,117	69.44	2,946	77.18	6,103	78.81
1–25%	205	4.57	171	4.48	336	4.34
26–50%	218	4.86	148	3.88	374	4.83
51–75%	227	5.06	165	4.32	263	3.4
76–90%	110	2.45	80	2.1	127	1.64
91–100%	194	4.32	110	2.88	231	2.98
Missing	418	9.32	197	5.16	310	4.01
Total	4,489	100	3,817	100	7,744	100

Source: GEM Survey 2005
* Question asked is "What proportion of your customers will normally live outside your country?"

the reasons their exporting activity has changed, or whether early exporters have exited the market. There are in fact many studies of SMEs that have focused in detail on the exporting activities of smaller subsets of firms (see Dickson (2007) for an overview and summaries), but the pattern of declining export intensity in the much larger GEM study remains a puzzle.

Based on the importance of market structure and the product life cycle discussed earlier, one possibility is that nascent *exporting* firms tend to exit the market before reaching later stages of entrepreneurial development. Given the higher cost of exports, as opposed to domestic sales, this explanation suggests that the harsh discipline of international markets, which may have turned out to be more competitive than the entrepreneur initially thought, filters out the weaker firms, in part because they began as exporters. However, this is not the only possibility. For example, nascent entrepreneurs may begin with higher exports, only to retreat from export markets in favor of domestic markets as they reach early-stage and established firm status. This pattern, if true, would contradict the prediction of most models of SME globalization. Perhaps again the pitfalls and harsh international market discipline cause the retreat, while the firms continue under a more successful domestic market strategy. Many scenarios are possible for foreign market failure: the product does not "catch on"; foreign competitors enter subsequently and undermine the exporter's market (as in the product life cycle model); foreign legal or regulatory issues arise to discourage or increase the cost of exports (Julien and Ramangalahy 2003).

In any event, the pattern of a declining intensity of exports as the firm matures suggests that there is a decision by entrepreneurs to enter export markets, but also a decision by many to exit export markets, a behavioral aspect of exporting activity that is not captured in economic models of comparative advantage. The entrepreneur chooses an export strategy, based on motivations linked with perceived market opportunities, managerial characteristics, knowledge of the market, and supporting networks and technology. Yet the entrepreneur at this point is typically still in a discovery phase of the firm's foreign market development, and adjustments may be necessary as the market response becomes evident. The foray into export markets, in other words, may in some cases turn out to have been a mistake, requiring retreat from the export market, or even the closing of the firm. Other firms, in contrast, may receive positive market signals and proceed to expand their export activities. Recent efforts in the literature to develop models of "effectuation" to explain entrepreneurial decisions in the face of uncertainty and unknown and unordered utility functions may provide some insight into such strategic failures and/or reversals (Sarasvathy 2008). The entrepreneur, acting on his or her personality, knowledge, and networks sets out to design a product and alliance strategy for exports that will ideally increase the firm's control over the future course of the market. Yet export markets are difficult and the strategy may fail, despite the entrepreneur's human and social capital. The high potential payoff of a successful export strategy nonetheless provides a strong motive to try.

12.4 Conclusion

Exporting by entrepreneurs is the result of a multidimensional and interactive set of factors, including the economic and business environment, market structure, market opportunity and strategic decision-making. Exporting tends to be significantly more expensive and riskier than selling in one's own domestic market, and so exporting entrepreneurs must be particularly skillful, and sell products that are particularly profitable, in order to overcome this cost barrier. GEM data, combined with business environment, patent, and other economic data, suggest that technology and innovation are important drivers of export activity among entrepreneurs. These factors, in turn, imply the importance of a regulatory and business environment conducive to new business development and open access to foreign markets in creating export opportunities. In addition, the education level of the entrepreneur appears to have a significant impact on exporting activity, which may relate in part to the "human capital" component of the technology content of exports and also to the knowledge and skill required to recognize and develop the export market opportunity. It appears in this regard to be important for the entrepreneur to be creative in the application and commercialization of new technologies, knowledgeable about foreign markets and the foreign business environment, and savvy in positioning the product to be truly distinctive, reducing the ability of rivals to enter the market. The data also indicate that *earliest*-stage enterprises are most likely to report export participation, with subsequently declining export intensity. The GEM survey does not contain questions that would indicate why this might be, but adverse developments in the competitive environment in the export market are the likely reason.

These results apply to exporting activity among all entrepreneurs in the GEM survey. At the same time, export participation rates vary widely from country to country as a result of business environment, technological capabilities, geography, and perhaps even national and cultural patterns. In the probit analysis, GEM RT and WB RT and EDB show a strong correlation between export activity and a business-friendly regulatory environment. Higher rates of patent creation also imply more export activity, while the size of the country (in GDP terms) is inversely related to export activity, probably as a result of the relative attractiveness of domestic, as compared to export, market opportunities in large countries, especially if export markets are distant. Many other unobserved characteristics are associated with country dummy variables, which also contribute to each country's degree of export participation.

SME export activity is therefore the result of a multiplicity of factors, some of which lend themselves to economic and business analysis, while others are rooted in the specific characteristics and decisions of the firm. In the end, the entrepreneurial decision to export is shaped by the qualities of the entrepreneur but is contingent on the business and economic environment. In view of the broad and extensive cross-country basis of the survey data as it stands now, more detailed survey questions would be a valuable addition to the study of the SME decision to export. For example, new GEM survey questions might inquire if the entrepreneur was born abroad, traveled abroad, spoke foreign languages, or was previously linked to foreign business or social networks. More specific information on the destination of exports (near or far, single country or multiple countries), on possible links with imports, global supply chains and foreign investment, and on the channels used for exports would add to our understanding of export decision variables. Information on the source of financing for firms that export could be revealing. The survey might also ask if the firm's exports increased or decreased over the past year and why (failure to meet profit targets, new competition, new foreign regulation, sales did not catch on, etc.). A better understanding of the small start-up firm's decision and strategies used to export will require, in other words, a more in-depth understanding of the individual entrepreneurs themselves.

Acknowledgments

Many thanks go also to an anonymous reviewer for helpful comments. Although GEM data were used in this study, their interpretation and use are the sole responsibility of the authors. All errors are ours.

References

Acs, Z. J. et al. (1997), "The Internationalization of Small and Medium-Sized Enterprises: A Policy Perspective." *Small Business Economics* 9(1): 7–20.

Allen, I. E., Elam, A., Langowitz, N., and Dean, M. (2008), "Global Entrepreneurship Monitor: 2007 Report on Women and Entrepreneurship." Babson College and the Babson Center for Women's Leadership.

Anderson, J. E. and van Wincoop, E. (2004), "Trade Costs." *Journal of Economic Literature* 42(3): 691–751.

Baumol, W. (1968), "Entrepreneurship in Economic Theory." *American Economic Review* 58(2): 64–71.

Becker, G. (1993), *Human Capital: A Theoretical and Empirical Analysis, with Special Reference to Education*. Chicago: University of Chicago Press.

Bell, J., Young, S., and Crick, D. (1998), "A Holistic Perspective on Small Firm Internationalisation and Growth." in C. C. Millar and C. J. Choi (eds.) *International business and emerging markets, proceedings of the 25th UK AIB Conference*. London, City Business School, London. 1: 9–29.

Bernard, A. B. and Jensen, J. B. (1995), "Exporters, Jobs, and Wages in U.S. Manufacturing: 1976–1987." *Brookings Papers on Economic Activity, Microeconomics* 1995: 67–119.

Bernard, A. B. et al. (2007), "Firms in International Trade." *Journal of Economic Perspectives* 21(3): 105–30.

Bernard, A. B. et al. (2009), "Importers, Exporters, and Multinationals: A Portrait of Firms in the U.S. that Trade Goods," in T. Dunne, J. B. Jensen, and M. J. Roberts (eds.) *Producer Dynamics: New Evidence from Micro Data*, Chicago: University of Chicago Press.

Chipman, J. S. (1965), "A Survey of the Theory of International Trade." *Econometrica*, 33(3): 477–519 and 685–760.

Coviello, N. E. and Jones, M. V. (2004), "Methodological Issues in International Entrepreneurship Research." *Journal of Business Venturing* 19(4): 485–508.

Coviello, N. E. and McAuley, A. (1999), "Internationalisation and the Smaller Firm: a Review of Contemporary Empirical Research." *Management International Review* 39(3): 223–57.

Dana, L. P., Hamilton, R. T., and Wick, K. (2009), "Deciding to Export: An Exploratory Study of Singaporean Entrepreneurs." *Journal of International Entrepreneurship* 7: 79–87.

De Mooij, M. (2004), *Consumer Behavior and Culture*. Thousand Oaks, CA and London: Sage.

Dickson, P. H. (2007), "Going Global," in A. Zacharakis and S. Spinelli, Jr. (eds.) *Entrepreneurship: the Engine of Growth, Vol. 2: Process*. Westport, Connecticut and London: Praeger.

Eaton, J., Kortum, S., and Kramarz, F. (2004), "Dissecting Trade: Firms, Industries, and Export Destinations." *The American Economic Review* 94(2): 150–4.

Etemad, H. and Wright, R. (eds.) (2003), *Globalization and Entrepreneurship: Policy and Strategy Perspectives*. Cheltenham, UK and Northampton, Massachusetts: Edward Elgar.

Glancey, K. S. and McQuaid, R. W. (2000), *Entrepreneurial Economics*. Houndsmill and New York: Palgrave.

Greenaway, D. and Kneller, R. (2007), "Firm Heterogeneity, Exporting and Foreign Direct Investment." *Economic Journal* 117(517): F134–61.

Grossman, G. and Helpman, E. (1995), "Technology and Trade," in G. M. Grossman and K. Rogoff (eds.) *Handbook of International Economics, Vol. 3:* 1279–1337. Amsterdam: Elsevier.

Helpman, E. and Krugman, P. (1986), *Market Structure and Foreign Trade*. Cambridge, MA and London: MIT Press.

Hessels, J. (2008), "Overcoming Resource Constraints Through Internationalization? An Empirical Analysis of European SMEs," in J. Hessels (ed.) *International Entrepreneurship, Value Creation Across Borders*, Erasmus Research Institute of Management, Erasmus University, Rotterdam.

Hessels, J. and Terjesen, S. (2008), "Entrepreneurial Career Capital, Innovation and New Venture Export Orientation," in J. Hessels (ed.) *International Entrepreneurship, Value Creation Across Borders*, Erasmus Research Institute of Management, Erasmus University, Rotterdam.

Hummels, D. (2007), "Transportation Costs and International Trade in the Second Era of Globalization." *Journal of Economic Perspectives* 21(3): 131–54.

Jones, K. (2006), "Globalization and Entrepreneurship," in M. Minniti (ed.), *Entrepreneurship and Entrepreneurial Behavior, vol. I* (Prager Perspectives Series). New York: Praeger.

Jones, K. and Levie, J. (2008), "Global Institutions, National Regulations, and Entrepreneurship." Global *Entrepreneurship Monitor, Executive Report*. Babson College, London Business School, and the Global Entrepreneurship Research Consortium.

Jones, M. V. and Dimitratos, P. (eds.) (2004), *Emerging Paradigms in International Entrepreneurship*. Cheltenham, UK and Northampton, Massachusetts: Edward Elgar.

Julien, P.-A. and Ramangalahy, C. (2003), "Competitive Strategy and Performance of Exporting SMEs: An Empirical Investigation of their Export Information Search and Competencies." *Entrepreneurship: Theory and Practice* 27(3): 227–45.

Knight, G. and Cavusgil, S. T. (1996), The Born Global Firm: A Challenge to Traditional Internationalization Theory. *Advances in International Marketing*, New York: Jai Press: 11–26.

Kuivalainen, O., Sundqvist, S., and Servais, P. (2007), "The Knowledge Spillover Theory of Entrepreneurship." *Journal of World Business,* 42(3): 253–67.

Linder, S. B. (1961), *An Essay on Trade and Transformation*. New York: John Wiley.

Lloyd-Reason, L. and Sear, L. (eds.) (2007), *Trading places—SMEs in the Global Economy: A Critical Research Handbook*. Cheltenham, UK: Edward Elgar.

Muûls, M. and Pisu, M. (2009), "Imports and Exports at the Level of the Firm: Evidence from Belgium." *World Economy* 32(5): 692–734.

Organization for Economic Cooperation and Development (2006), "Removing Barriers to SME Access to International Markets." Conference proceedings, Athens: OECD.

Oviatt, B. M. and McDougall, P. P. (1994), "Toward a Theory of International New Ventures." *Journal of International Business Studies* 25(1): 45–64.

Pedersen, T. and Petersen, B. (1998), "Explaining Gradually Increasing Resource Commitment to a Foreign Market." *International Business Review* 7(5): 483–501.

Porter, M. E. (1990), *The Competitive Advantage of Nations.* New York: Free Press.

Sarasvathy, S. D. (2008), *Effectuation: Elements of Entrepreneurial Expertise.* Edward Elgar, New Horizons in Entrepreneurship Series.

Shultz, T. W. (1971), *Investment in Human Capital: The Role of Education and of Research.* New York: Free Press.

Vemuri, V. K. and Siddiqi, S. (2009), "Impact of Commercialization of the Internet on International Trade: A Panel Study Using the Extended Gravity Model." *International Trade Journal,* 23(4): 458–84.

Vernon, R. (1966),"International Investment and International Trade in the Product Cycle." *Quarterly Journal of Economics* 80(2): 190–207.

Wagner, J. (2007), "Exports and Productivity: A Survey of the Evidence from Firm-Level Data." *World Economy* 30(1): 60–82.

Welch, C. L., Welch, D. E., and Hewerdine, L. (2008), "Gender and Export Behaviour: Evidence from Women-Owned Enterprises." *Journal of Business Ethics* 83: 113–26.

Westhead, P., Wright, M., and Ucbasaran, D. (2001), "The Internationalization of New and Small Firms: A Resource-Based View." *Journal of Business Venturing* 16(4): 333–58.

Wynn, J. (2005), "Wealth as a Determinant of Comparative Advantage." *American Economic Review* 95(1): 226–54.

Conclusion

David B. Audretsch

After more than a decade of economic stagnation, rising unemployment, and chronically low rates of growth, perhaps the unveiling of a new and bold policy priority for reigniting European economic growth should not have been unexpected. Nonetheless, when in 2000 the Lisbon Council of Europe suggested that Europe needed to become the global leader in not just knowledge but also entrepreneurship, many scholars and policy makers were surprised.

Historically, one of the policy foundations for the formation of the European Union had been to attain unprecedented productivity and efficiency gains by facilitating large scale production made possible by the creation of a large internal (European) market (Cecchini 1988). A leading visionary for the formation of the internal European market, Jean-Jacques Servan-Schreiber, urged Europeans to meet the "American challenge," in the form of the "dynamism, organization, innovation, and boldness that characterize the giant (American) corporations" (Servan-Schreiber 1968: 153). And argued that rising to this challenge would involve the "creation of large industrial units which are able, both in size and management, to compete with the (American) giants" (Servan-Schreiber 1968: 159).[1]

Along similar lines, writing in the *Harvard Business Review,* Ferguson (1988: 61) argued that entrepreneurship would actually reduce rather than increase economic performance. He condemned entrepreneurship in the context of Silicon Valley for its deleterious impact on economic performance, "because the fragmentation, instability, and entrepreneurialism are not

---

[1] According to Servan-Schreiber (1968: 159), "The first problem of an industrial policy for Europe consists in choosing 50 to 100 firms which, once they are large enough, would be the most likely to become world leaders of modern technology in their fields. At the moment we are simply letting industry be gradually destroyed by the superior power of American corporations."

signs of well-being. In fact, they are symptoms of the larger structural problems that afflict U.S. industry. In semiconductors, a combination of personnel mobility, ineffective intellectual property protection, risk aversion in large companies, and tax subsidies for the formation of new companies contribute to a fragmented 'chronically entrepreneurial' industry. U.S. semiconductor companies are unable to sustain the large, long-term investments required for continued U.S. competitiveness."

There had not been a strong tradition of looking towards entrepreneurship as an engine of economic development and growth in either economic policy or economic thinking.[2] For a very long time, the general view of small business and entrepreneurship had been that they were the weak link in modern business (Chandler 1977 and 1990). This reflected a public policy approach that was essentially preservationist in nature, with the goal of trying to preserve and protect small businesses that were inherently inefficient and would otherwise be driven out of the market. The United States Small Business Administration, for example, was created when the US Congress enacted the Small Business Act of July 10, 1953, with the explicit mandate to "aid, counsel, assist and protect . . . the interests of small business concerns."[3]

By the turn of the century, this thinking, both among academics as well as in public policy, had clearly shifted. As Romano Prodi (2002: 1), serving as President of the European Commission, proclaimed, "Our lacunae in the field of entrepreneurship need to be taken seriously because there is mounting evidence that the key to economic growth and productivity improvements lies in the entrepreneurial capacity of an economy."

Europe is not unique in its exuberance about entrepreneurship as the driving engine of economic growth and development. Mowery (2005: 1) points out that, "During the 1990s, the era of the 'New Economy,' numerous observers (including some who less than 10 years earlier had written off the U.S. economy as doomed to economic decline in the face of competition from such economic powerhouses as Japan) hailed the resurgent economy in the United States as an illustration of the power of high-technology entrepreneurship. The new firms that a decade earlier had been criticized by such authorities as the MIT Commission on Industrial Productivity (Dertouzos et al. 1989) for their failure to sustain competition against large non-U.S. firms were now seen as important sources of economic dynamism and employment growth. Indeed the transformation in U.S. economic performance between the 1980s and 1990s is only slightly less remarkable than the failure of most experts in academia, government, and industry to predict it."

[2] One notable exception is Schumpeter (1911).
[3] http://www.sba.gov/about-sba-services/our-history

How could public policy infer a link between entrepreneurship and economic performance, and in particular growth and development? While such a link had conceptually been suggested already by Schumpeter in 1911, the Schumpeterian tradition offered little in the way of hard statistical evidence supporting this claim. Rather, the fundamental claims upon which key public policy decisions were being made lacked both a systematic theoretical underpinning as well as empirical evidence supporting such linkages.

Both theory and empirical evidence had been limited, to a large extent, because of measurement and data constraints. Because it had not been considered to be particularly important, no systematic attempt had been made to collect data on entrepreneurship. It is typically not easy to justify a costly investment measuring a phenomenon with no apparent significant impact on society. Similarly, without the prospect of subjecting theoretical constructs to the rigors of empirical scrutiny, conceptual development also remains limited.

The development of macroeconomic theory by Keynes is typically attributed to providing public policy with a viable framework for addressing the Great Depression. However, it must not be forgotten, that it also took a revolution in measurement, more specifically the method of national accounts developed by Simon Kuznets, for the theory to be developed and operationalized by a subsequent generation of scholars, as well as applied to public policy instruments in the form of fiscal and monetary policy. The measurement contribution by Kuznets to both scholarship as well as public policy was so compelling that he was ultimately awarded the Nobel Prize.

It is in the context of this renewed interest on entrepreneurship as an engine of growth that data sets of GEM's breath and scope, and systematic studies such as the one provided by this Volume are particularly useful. With the development, application, and diffusion of the Global Entrepreneurship Monitor (GEM) project, consistent measurements of the entrepreneurial process across a broad spectrum of national contexts are finally provided. Being able to systematically measure entrepreneurial propensity and activity across a number of countries is enabling scholars to flesh out empirical linkages between entrepreneurship and economic performance, as well as assess a variety of individual and contextual features of entrepreneurial behavior and of the entrepreneurial process (Levie and Autio 2008; Reynolds et al. 2005).

To identify the relationship between entrepreneurship and economic growth, earlier studies had used various indicators of entrepreneurship, such as business ownership, self employment, or start-up rates for regions within a single country (Audretsch, Keilbach, and Lehmann 2006; Acs and Armington 2006; Audretsch, Boente, and Keilbach 2008; Thurik, Audretsch, Carree, and Van Stel 2008). GEM data provide a more complete and compelling measure of the overall entrepreneurial process. Studies using GEM data confirm that entrepreneurship matters for society, and in particular for generating economic growth. Those places, either cities, regions, or countries, exhibiting a more vigorous degree of entrepreneurship also exhibit a better performance, measured in terms of economic growth (van Stel, Carree, and Thurik 2005; Wennekers, van Stel, Thurik, and Reynolds 2005; Wong, Ho, and Autio 2005). These results certainly support the public policy focus on entrepreneurship as a vehicle for igniting economic growth, employment creation, and competitiveness.

The collection of contributions in this Volume provides a significant and important addition to our knowledge base. A scholarly tradition has been established focusing on the heterogeneity of entrepreneurial activity across individuals (McClelland 1961), that is why some individuals engage in entrepreneurial activities while others do not. While this topic has always attracted some academic attention, as it has become clear that entrepreneurship matters for economic performance, interest in understanding and explaining entrepreneurial heterogeneity has blossomed (Verhuel, van Stel, and Thurik 2006). The first four chapters of this Volume contribute directly to the debate on entrepreneurial heterogeneity at the individual level. By examining the extent to which the decisions of entrepreneurs tend to be characterized by overconfidence, the extent to which gender influences entrepreneurial behavior, how social and family contacts can influence both entrepreneurial opportunities and behavior, and the role played by friends and relatives in supporting nascent entrepreneurs financially, these chapters contribute to our understanding of entrepreneurial heterogeneity.

But entrepreneurial heterogeneity is the result of differences not just across individual-specific characteristics, such as gender, age, or family status, it also depends on the context within which individuals find themselves. Context has many dimensions. The location, or region, where the individual works has been identified as influencing entrepreneurial heterogeneity. Some of the geographic influences result from the spatial structure of economic activity in the relevant region. For example, research has consistently identified a higher propensity for individuals to become entrepreneurs in regions with characterized by a high population density, the existence of firm and industry clusters (Rocha 2004; Rocha and Sternberg 2005) with high rates of growth, the presence of early stage finance, and with higher levels of knowledge investments (Audretsch and Keilbach 2007, 2008).

A complementary insight from the literature is that entrepreneurial heterogeneity is influenced by heterogeneity in regional specific culture and institutions influencing entrepreneurial behavior (van Stel, Storey, and Thurik 2007). While heterogeneity at the individual level influences the perception of entrepreneurial opportunities, heterogeneity of context influences entrepreneurial behavior and the existence of opportunities.

The second group of chapters in the Volume contributes to our knowledge base on the role played by context in entrepreneurial decisions. Immigration and ethnic status, and differences between highly concentrated urban settings and less populated areas are shown to account for some of the entrepreneurial heterogeneity across population groups. The role played by formal and informal institutions is also discussed in a comparative setting by looking at different groups of countries. Compelling empirical evidence is provided that EU regional policies have had some success in facilitating entrepreneurial activity and that a major factor inhibiting entrepreneurial activity in the transitional context found in Central and Eastern Europe is the inability to develop strong informal institutions.

As public policy has become more cognizant of the positive and compelling links between entrepreneurship and economic performance, the mandate for policies to develop and promote what has been referred to as entrepreneurship capital has blossomed. Entrepreneurship capital refers to the capacity of an economy, at the national, regional, or local level, to generate entrepreneurial behavior. One interpretation for an economy exhibiting greater entrepreneurial activity is that it has a higher underlying degree of entrepreneurship capital. The last four chapters in the Volume contribute to our empirical knowledge of entrepreneurship capital by analyzing the role played by ambitious and growth oriented entrepreneurs on poverty reduction, employment, the export capacity of a country and, most important, economic growth. Stam, Hartog, van Stel, and Thurik (Chapter 10) for example, use the GEM data to link more nuanced measures of entrepreneurship, including entrepreneurship with high growth expectations, and high-growth firms, to actual macroeconomic growth, and find that the impact of what they term as ambitious entrepreneurship on economic growth is actually greater than is the impact of high-growth established firms.

Entrepreneurship matters for growth in both poor and rich countries. Thus entrepreneurship capital matters too. Entrepreneurship capital combines all of the different factors mentioned in the chapters of this Volume generating entrepreneurial heterogeneity (Audretsch, Boente, and Keilbach 2008; Audretsch, Keilbach, and Lehmann 2006). Some of these factors are more conducive to policy influence, such as knowledge investments, than are others, such as inherent personality characteristics. Noticeably, while it is a related concept, entrepreneurship capital differs significantly from social capital. Coleman (1988) and Putnam (1993) argued for a link between relationships among people and economic performance. As Putnam (2000: 19) suggests, "Whereas physical capital refers to physical objects and human capital refers to the properties of individuals, social capital refers to connections among individuals—social networks and the norms of reciprocity and trustworthiness that arise from them. In that sense social capital is closely related to what some have called 'civic virtue.' The difference is that 'social capital' calls attention to the fact that civic virtue is most powerful when embedded in a sense of network of reciprocal social relations. A society of many virtues but isolated individuals is not necessarily rich in social capital."

Futhermore, Putnam (2000: 19) points out that, "By analogy with notions of physical capital and human capital—tools and training that enhance individual productivity—social capital refers to features of social organization, such as networks, norms, and trust, that facilitate coordination and cooperation for mutual benefits." Putnam does suggest a link between social capital and economic performance, but there is no explicit role for entrepreneurship. Rather, factors such as associational membership and public trust are the foundations of social capital but do not necessarily suggest entrepreneurial activity.

Entrepreneurship capital is therefore a concept distinct from social capital, and includes the various contexts generating entrepreneurial heterogeneity discussed above, so that it spans a broad spectrum of institutional, legal, and social factors. Public policy is increasingly focused with influencing various aspects of these factors to enhance the degree of entrepreneurship capital, in an effort to increase entrepreneurial activity and ultimately improve economic performance.

Throughout most of the previous century, scholarship on entrepreneurship, at both the conceptual and empirical levels, has been severely limited due to the lack of comparable data measuring the entrepreneurial process. As a result, public policy, even as it turns to scholars for a compelling framework through which to understand the causes and impacts of entrepreneurship, has found confusion and ambiguity. However, the research contained in the chapters of this book suggests more than a promise for the development of a systematic framework to understand entrepreneurship and to guide policy. If future research continues to build upon the solid theoretical basis and meticulous empirical scrutiny exhibited in the chapters contained in this book, entrepreneurship will continue to capture the attention and imagination of the next generation in both realms of scholarship and public policy.

References

Acs, Z. and Armington, C. (2006), *Entrepreneurship, Agglomeration and US Regional Growth.* Cambridge: Cambridge University Press.

Audretsch, D. B. and Keilbach, M. (2008), "Resolving the Knowledge Paradox: Knowledge-Spillover Entrepreneurship and Economic Growth," *Research Policy*, 37(10), 1697–705.

Audretsch, D. B., Boente, W., and Keilbach, M. (2008), "Entrepreneurship Capital and its Impact on Knowledge Diffusion and Economic Performance," *Journal of Business Venturing,* 23(6), November 2008, 687–98.

Audretsch, D. B. and Keilbach, M. (2007), "The Theory of Knowledge Spillover Entrepreneurship," *Journal of Management Studies,* 44(7), November 2007, 1242–54.

Audretsch, D. B., Keilbach, M., and Lehmann, E. (2006), *Entrepreneurship and Economic Growth.* New York: Oxford University Press.

Cecchini, P. (1988), *The European Challenge.* London: Grower.

Chandler, A. (1977), *The Visible Hand: The Managerial Revolution in American Business.* Cambridge MA: Belknap Press.

Chandler, A. (1990), *Scale and Scope: The Dynamics of Industrial Capitalism.* Cambridge, MA: Harvard University Press.

Coleman, J. (1988), "Social Capital in the Creation of Human Capital," *American Journal of Sociology,* 94, 95–121.

Dertouzos, M., Lester, R. and Solow, R. (1989), *Made in America: Regaining the Productive Edge.* Cambridge MA: MIT Press.

Ferguson, C. H. (1988), "From the People who Brought you Voodoo Economics," *Harvard Business Review,* 66, 55–62.

Levie, J. and Autio, E. (2008), "A Theoretical Grounding and Test of the GEM Model," *Small Business Economics,* 31, 235–63.

McClelland, D. (1961), *The Achieving Society.* Princeton: Van Nostrand.

Mowery, D. (2005), "The Bayh-Dole Act and High Technology Entrepreneurship in US Universities: Chicken, Egg, or Something Else? Paper presented at the Eller Centre Conference on "Entrepreneurship Education and Technology Transfer," University of Arizona, 21–22 January.

Prodi, R. (2002), "For a New European Entrepreneurship," public speech, Madrid, Instituto de Empresa.

Putnam, R. (1993), *Making Democracy Work: Civic Traditions in Modern Italy.* Princeton, NJ: Princeton University Press.

Putnam, R. (2000) *Bowling Alone: The Collapse and Revival of American Community.* New York: Simon & Schuster.

Reynolds, P.N., Bosma, E., Autio, E., Hunt, S., De Bono, N., Servais, I., Lopez-Garcia, P., and Chin, N. (2005), "Global Entrepreneurship Monitor: Data Collection Design and Implementation, 1998–2003," *Small Business Economics,* 24(3), 205–31.

Rocha, H. and Sternberg, R. (2005), "Entrepreneurship: The Role of Clusters," *Small Business Economics,* 24(3), 267–92.

Rocha, H. (2004), "Entrepreneurship and Development: The Role of Clusters," *Small Business Economics,* 23(5), 363–400.

Schumpeter, J. (1911), *Theorie der wirtschaftlichen Entwicklung. Eine Untersuchung ueber Unternehmergewinn, Kapital, Kredit, Zins und den Konjunkturzyklus.* Berlin: Duncker & Humblot.

Servan-Schreiber, J.-J. (1968), *The American Challenge.* London: Hamish Hamilton.

Thurik, A. R., Audretsch, D. B., Carree, M., and van Stel, A. J. (2008), "Does Self-Employment Reduce Unemployment?," *Journal of Business Venturing,* 23(6) November 2008, 673–86.

van Stel, A. J., Carree, M. A., and Thurik, A. R. (2005), "The Effect of Entrepreneurial Activity on National Economic Growth," *Small Business Economics,* 24(3), 311–21.

van Stel, A. J., Storey, D. J., and Thurik, A. R. (2007), "The Effect of Business Regulations on Nascent and Young Business Entrepreneurship," *Small Business Economics,* 28(2–3), 171–86.

Verheul, I., van Stel, A. J., and Thurik, A. R. (2006), "Explaining Female and Male Entrepreneurship at the Country Level," *Entrepreneurship and Regional Development,* 18(2), 151–83.

Wennekers, S., van Stel, A., Thurik, R., and Reynolds, P. (2005), "Nascent Entrepreneurship and the Level of Economic Development," *Small Business Economics,* 24(3), 293–309.

Wong, P.K., Ho, Y. P., and Autio, E. (2005), "Entrepreneurship, Innovation, and Economic Growth: Evidence from GEM Data," *Small Business Economics,* 24(3), 335–50.

DATA APPENDIX[1]

Maria Minniti

All Global Entrepreneurship Monitor (GEM) data used in this Volume are survey data collected through annual adult population surveys (APS). This brief Appendix provides some background information on the collection process and statistical properties of the GEM data used in this Volume. This Appendix, however, is not meant to provide a comprehensive statistical description of the data and their properties. For more details and to download the publicly available GEM data, readers should visit the Global Entrepreneurship Monitor website at www.gemconsortium.org.

Since its inception in 1999, the GEM project has collected data annually in more than eighty countries.[2] The principle inspiring the collection of GEM data is that newer and smaller firms are important contributors to national economic growth and to the aggregate level of economic activity in a country. Small and new firms generate innovations, fill market niches, and increase competition, thereby promoting economic efficiency. This perspective gives a clearer understanding of why entrepreneurship is vital to the whole economy and justifies why GEM data focus primarily on providing measures of entrepreneurial activity (within and across countries) and factors determining the entrepreneurial behavior of individuals.

The GEM adult population surveys (APS)

People start firms, and people determine the entrepreneurial attitude of established firms, regardless of size. Thus, people matter for entrepreneurship. GEM data are

---

[1] The material presented in this data appendix relies significantly on Quill, Bosma, and Minniti (2007).

[2] As of 2010, countries involved in the GEM projects are Algeria, Angola, Argentina, Australia, Austria, Bangladesh, Belgium, Bolivia, Bosnia and Herzegovina, Brazil, Chile, China, Colombia, Costa Rica, Croatia, Czech Republic, Denmark, Dominican Republic, Ecuador, Egypt, Finland, France, Germany, Ghana, Greece, Guatemala, Hong Kong, Hungary, Iceland, India, Indonesia, Iran, Ireland, Israel, Italy, Jamaica, Japan, Jordan, Kazakhstan, Korea, Latvia, Lebanon, Macedonia, Malaysia, Mexico, Montenegro, Morocco, Netherlands, New Zealand, Nigeria, Norway, Pakistan, Palestine, Panama, Peru, Philippines, Poland, Portugal, Puerto Rico, Romania, Russia, Saudi Arabia, Serbia, Singapore, Slovenia, South Africa, Spain, Sweden, Switzerland, Syria, Taiwan, Thailand, Tonga, Trinidad and Tobago, Tunisia, Turkey, United Arab Emirates, Uganda, United Kingdom, Uruguay, Unites States, Vanuatu, Venezuela, Yemen, and Zambia. Unfortunately, not all countries participate every year and new countries are added to the project on an annual base. As a result, data are not available for every year for every country.

collected by surveying representative samples of population in each participating country. Within these samples, a minority of individuals is involved in starting, owning, and managing a business. This subset of individuals provides data about entrepreneurship, while the remaining individuals provide a control group. As described in the Introduction to this Volume, the GEM collection process covers the life-cycle of the entrepreneurial process and looks at individuals over the life span of the business from inception to maturity. As a result, GEM data allow researchers to distinguish between nascent, new, and established entrepreneurs, and also between opportunity and necessity driven entrepreneurs. Information about product novelty, competitor differentiation, use of technology, growth aspirations, and export orientation are also provided. Finally, GEM data include information about the socioeconomic characteristics of the individuals surveyed, as well as their subjective perceptions and expectations about the entrepreneurial environment.[3]

It is important to stress that, unlike most data sets on entrepreneurship, the GEM Adult Population Surveys are social surveys of individuals rather than surveys of registered businesses. Therefore, GEM's data do not necessarily compare to business registration data. Since the intuition behind GEM's data collection is that people create businesses, not only officially registered business activities are relevant, people attempting to set up a business, as well as their attitudes toward entrepreneurship, matter also in explaining the overall entrepreneurial propensity of a country.

The data collection process

The GEM APS data are obtained from representative samples of randomly selected adults, ranging in size from a minimum of 2,000 to about 45,000 individuals, who are surveyed each year in each participating country.[4] Samples are random thus the individuals interviewed vary over the years. This implies that GEM data do not provide panel data at the individual level.

The annual surveys generally take place between May and August and are based on three main elements: the sample of respondents, the interview schedule used to collect the data, and the creation of measures estimating entrepreneurship at the national level. The survey questionnaire consists of a set of core questions used to derive entrepreneurial activity rates and additional questions concerning the attributes and characteristics of the respondents.

The GEM surveys are conducted in each country by survey firms. Survey firms are research firms selected with care by the national teams, and their proposed sampling methodologies are reviewed and approved for quality and consistency across countries and over time by GEM's coordination team. Survey firms have the primary responsibility for translating the original interview into one or more languages appropriate for

---

[3] See Reynolds et al. (2005) and Levie and Autio (2008) for more details on GEM's conceptual model.
[4] Each GEM national team conducts also a series of face-to-face interviews with experts in their respective countries chosen to represent a number of entrepreneurial framework conditions. The national experts also complete a detailed standardized questionnaire. These data, however, are not used in any of the chapters and this Volume is entirely based on GEM's APS data.

each country. These translations are then reviewed and approved by the respective GEM national teams before data collection is initiated by the survey firm. So far, there has been no evidence suggesting that variations between countries reflect differences attributable to translation issues.

All survey firms are provided with detailed discussions of the rational and focus of each question to facilitate interview training and, in turn, interviewers' confidence in eliciting useful answers from the respondents. The proportion of don't know and refusal responses on the critical items in the survey are usually quite low and below 0.5 percent. The complete survey questionnaire is available on the GEM website.

All countries use regional stratification, except for very small countries like Iceland. Most countries conduct telephone surveys. In some developing countries where phone penetration rates are low, interviews are conducted face to face using random door-to-door procedures that also result in a representative national sample. There is great variation in reported response rates (defined as the number of completed interviews relative to the number of eligible respondents). For face-to-face interviews, the response rate is typically high. For telephone interviews, the number of maximum callbacks per sample unit heavily determines the response rate; if the person in the household who is selected to answer the questions (randomly determined by next-birthday method) is not at home, call-backs are performed until the person is reached, up to a maximum number of call-backs (usually five to seven).

The sampling frame determines the survey method (phone, face-to-face, or combination of both) and the source for the population sample (random direct dialing, random dial from lists such as a phone book, purchased database of mobile phones owners, census data from government bodies, voters lists, etc.). Phone penetration rates identify how many people have phones and, in some countries, people who have more than one phone number. This information is very important in determining whether a representative sample of population can be obtained using a telephone outreach method. In recent years, the issue of representativeness of telephone surveys has been complicated by mobile phones which are included in the sampling universe only in some countries. Given their widespread use, especially among younger generations, the exclusion of mobile phones may be the cause of significant biases.

The quality of the sampling frame (e.g., coverage, updating, and access) is likely to differ from country to country. Therefore, frames are evaluated carefully on an annual basis. Since sampling resources differ greatly between countries, a strategy of flexible sample designs is appropriate and indeed desirable when building a multinational data set such as GEM. Specifically, the choice of specific design depends on the structure and characteristics of the country, available collection infrastructure, and, of course, the costs in each country. If adequate estimators are chosen the resulting values can be reliably compared.

An important step in planning a survey is, of course, the definition of the population under study. The more completely the frame covers the people belonging to the target population, the higher the quality of the resulting sample. Potential under-coverage of certain groups, for example because of language problems or sampling frame deficiencies, is usually assessed before deciding on the final sampling method, so that the problem can, if at all possible, be avoided or reduced.

Once contact is established with an individual, the person with whom contact is first made does not usually turn out to be the respondent because of GEM's attempts to reduce selection biases. Methods employed to reduce self-selection biases include asking to speak to the person in the household who is having the next birthday, or listing all members of the household and randomly selecting an individual from this list. Selection of respondents using methods such as these adds a further element of randomness to the survey. An example of how bias in a survey may be reduced by employing one of these methods might be where more females tend to answer the phone, or more males tend to answer the door. If using the next birthday technique, for instance, there is likelihood that this person will be a male (in the telephone case) or female (in the face-to-face case).

The harmonization process

Once the individual county level data is received at the GEM coordination center, it is coded, weighed, and cleaned to create a harmonized data set which ensures representativeness and consistency across all countries in the study.

Coding

After completing the data collection, each survey firm submits the data in the predefined data input template provided by the GEM coordination team. A small number of questions have open-ended answer categories. These questions are translated by the survey firm and/or national team and submitted separately from the fixed data input. This applies also to some fixed response items if the respondent indicates an answer that differs from the listed categories. In this case, the interviewer ticks the category "other" and asks for the full, open-ended answer. The most important open-ended categories refer to the business activities of potential entrepreneurs. In preparing the data, the survey firms are responsible for providing the descriptions of the business activity reported for the start-ups, new, or established firms, as well as firms receiving funding from informal investors. The GEM coordination team implements a coding protocol to ensure that a single procedure is used to classify business activities across all countries. The International Standard Industry Classification (ISIC) provided by the United Nations (1990) is used for all sector coding.

Weighting

Data are available both as raw observations or weighed so as to be representative of the population in each country. Both weighed and un-weighed data were used in the volume at the discretion of the authors as specified in each chapter. Chapter 1, for example, uses unweighed data. Chapter 3, instead, is based on weighed data. The choice of what data to use is based in part on what question the researcher plans to answer and in part by the method of analysis.

National vendors conducting the surveys supply sample case weights for all observations, developed such that proportions of different subgroups match the most recent official data providing descriptions of the entire population of the country. The basis for weighting varies somewhat among countries. Gender and age are always involved, but other additional features might also be used—e.g., geographic distribution, ethnic background, educational attainment, and household income.

To increase confidence in the extent to which the weighted samples represent the national populations, the GEM coordination team adjusts all case weights for all countries using a standardized estimate of the age and gender structure of each country provided by the US Census International Population Data.[5] These estimates are provided on an annual basis and updated each year. The final weights are adjusted to ensure that the average value of the case weights for each country is exactly one. For most countries the weights range between 0.3 and 5.

Cleaning

While the survey firms used in each country are among the best available, almost every data set requires some adjustments or corrections by the GEM coordination team. Normally, errors consist of variables not being coded properly or omitted from the data set. Such errors are relatively easy to detect and are corrected as soon as they are identified. However, in the very rare case when the GEM coordination team determines the data in a particular country to be of low quality, for example because of an incorrect execution of the survey, the data are rejected and a new survey is requested.

Once the data sets for each and all countries are checked and harmonized, and all individuals have been assigned the appropriate final weights, the files are consolidated into one single master file. In creating the consolidated master file, all respondents are provided with a unique identification number. For convenience in tracking different countries, the first digits consist of the appropriate international phone codes.

The GEM coordination team processes the consolidated and harmonized data set to identify respondents that can be considered entrepreneurially active. Other measures are also computed to characterize additional aspects of the national entrepreneurial context. Once all relevant variables are computed and checked in the individual-level consolidated file, national level measures are computed by aggregating data across all respondents from each country. The use of the individual case weights, developed for each country, ensures that the final aggregate indicators are representative of the adult population in each country.

Data documentation

Of course no data set is perfect. The important thing is that the characteristics of the data be properly documented so that scholars using the data may determine what the data can realistically say versus what the data cannot do. In order to document the statistical properties of the GEM data, for each country, a statistical summary modeled on the European Social Science Survey is created. For every year (beginning with the 2006 collection cycle), each country statistical summary provides information on the

---

[5] The Census Population Estimates are published on http://www.census.gov/ipc/www/idbsprd. html. Age has been categorized in five groups between 18–64 years. The age range of respondents varies substantially across national surveys, from as young as 14 to over 90 years in age. A set of weights has been developed from the adjustments based on standardized national population structure estimates for those who, being 18 to 64 years of age, qualify to be active in the labor force.

survey firm that conducted the GEM adult population survey in that country, a description of the population qualifying for the survey (e.g., all individuals between 18–64 years of age) and of the unit of analysis (e.g., a definition of the household), the sampling frame and design, the respondents' selection method, the number of proposed call-backs, the total number of different numbers called and that of answered calls, the total number of eligible households contacted, the number of interviews agreed to, the number of refusal and of incomplete interviews, the number of completed interviews, and the response rate.

References

Levie, J. and Autio, E. (2008), "A Theoretical Grounding and Test of the GEM Model," *Small Business Economics*, 31, 235–63.

Quill, M., Bosma, N., and Minniti, M. (2007), *2006 Global Entrepreneurship Monitor Technical Assessment*. London, UK, and Babson Park, MA: London Business School and Babson College.

Reynolds, P. N., Bosma, E., Autio, E., Hunt, S., De Bono, N., Servais, I., Lopez-Garcia, P., and Chin, N. (2005), "Global Entrepreneurship Monitor: Data Collection Design and Implementation, 1998–2003," *Small Business Economics*, 24(3), 205–31.

Index